The
ABERDEEN LINE

THE
ABERDEEN LINE

GEORGE THOMPSON JNR'S INCOMPARABLE SHIPPING ENTERPRISE

PETER H. KING

FOREWORD BY SIR ANDREW LEGGATT,
GREAT GRANDSON OF GEORGE THOMPSON

The
History
Press

To my late beloved wife, Pat, without whose hard work and constant support this book would never have 'weighed anchor'.

George Thompson Jnr., from the portrait painted by Sir George Reid.

First published 2017

The History Press
The Mill, Brimscombe Port
Stroud, Gloucestershire, GL5 2QG
www.thehistorypress.co.uk

British Library Cataloguing in Publication Data.
A catalogue record for this book is available from the British Library.

ISBN 978 0 7509 7851 4

Typesetting and origination by The History Press
Printed in India

CONTENTS

FOREWORD

BY SIR ANDREW LEGGATT,
GEORGE THOMPSON JNR'S GREAT-GREAT-GRANDSON

My great-great grandfather styled himself George Thompson Junior (hereafter 'GTJ') to distinguish himself from his grandfather. He lived during most of the reign of Queen Victoria, and for much of that time he worked to create what became the legendary Aberdeen Line. He was to become one of the most successful shipowners of Victorian Britain. Success did not come to him overnight: this book describes vicissitudes that he had to overcome; courageous decisions that he had to make; and the patience that helped him to endure adversity. His story shows how with perseverance and integrity ambitious goals can be achieved. It makes those who follow his fortunes ask themselves whether they would have achieved as much and what by following his example they can achieve or help others to achieve now.

GTJ founded his company at the age of 21 and retired from active management when he was 62. However, he continued to keep a watchful and benevolent eye on the affairs of the company until he died aged 94.

GTJ was born in 1804. His father, Andrew, died in 1807. GTJ was educated at the Old Grammar School in Aberdeen before being apprenticed with the London Shipping Company. At the outset in 1825 he advertised his availability as a commission agent, ship and insurance broker. It was a modest start to what the author describes as 'one of the best-respected shipping lines in the history of British shipping'. This is a judgement of which the author is eminently

well qualified to make, since he was for eight years Director of Operations for the Corporation of Trinity House and since 2000 has been Executive Chairman of the independent marine surveyors, Seden Clarke Ltd.

By 1829 GTJ had become a subscribing owner of five ships, and, despite one total loss, was already established in the UK coastal trade, the transatlantic, emigrant and timber trades and the Baltic. He started to acquire an interest in many more vessels.

In 1839 Walter Hood came on to the shipbuilding scene and over the next forty-two years he was to launch 100 ships from his yard in Aberdeen, of which forty-four were for GTJ, who was a partner. In 1842 GTJ was elected to the Aberdeen City Council for a three-year term. He was not re-elected until 1847 when he became Lord Provost. No sooner had he been elected than the Queen arrived in Aberdeen in the course of her first visit to Balmoral. It was the first time a queen had visited Aberdeen since Mary Queen of Scots in 1562.

GTJ's shipping interests continued to develop by taking delivery of more Aberdeen Line ships – always distinguished by their admirable appearance. As Basil Lubbock said in *The Colonial Clippers* (p.152):

No ships that ever sailed the seas presented a finer appearance than these little flyers. They were always beautifully kept and were easily noticeable amongst other ships for their smartness; indeed, when lying in Sydney Harbour or Hobson's Bay with their yards squared to a nicety, their green sides with gilt streak and scroll work at bow and stern glistening in the sun, their figure-heads, masts, spars and blocks all painted white and every rope's end flemish-coiled on snow-white decks, they were the admiration of all who saw them.

The clipper **George Thompson** was commissioned in 1865 for GTJ's close associate, Alex Nicol, reflecting his respect for GTJ, and **Christiana Thompson**, named after my great-great grandmother, in 1866. However, the Aberdeen Line and Walter Hood's shipyard will be remembered in maritime history for the famous clipper **Thermopylæ**, launched in 1868. She was (as the author asserts) one of the finest tea clippers ever built 'a reflection on her owners' ambitions, her design, and her construction'. So I am pleased that my great-grandfather, Cornelius Thompson (always 'Corny' in the family), had a hand in her design.

On her record-breaking maiden voyage after discharge at Melbourne she ballasted to Newcastle, and in so doing overhauled HMS **Charybdis**, whereupon the naval officer made the memorable signal: 'Goodbye. You are too much for us. You are the finest model of a ship I ever saw. It does my heart good to look at you.'

She arrived at the Pagoda Anchorage to take on tea, displaying a gilded cockerel. This evidently had a 'cock of the walk' connotation. So during a party on board a seaman from a rival vessel swam over, climbed aboard and disappeared with the cockerel. It was later returned.

The author has analysed the factors that forged **Thermopylæ**'s success as consisting of:

1. Her initial design and construction;
2. Her maintenance, for which no expense was spared;
3. The quality of her officers; and
4. Luck – that elusive, but indispensable, component.

It was, as the author points out, by rival commanders that she was called that 'Damned Scotsman'.

In 1872 an MP named Samuel Plimsoll began his crusade to cope with 'coffin' ships. In honour of his pioneer work, GTJ named one of his new clippers **Samuel Plimsoll**. An article in the RNLI's *The Lifeboat* brought him to prominence and resulted in 1875 in the Royal Commission of Enquiry into Unseaworthy Ships. But the determination of enforceable load lines was not established until the Merchant Shipping (Load Line) Act of 1890. His memory is perpetuated by the famous Plimsoll line cut into the side of every merchant cargo ship in order to define the depth to which she may be loaded.

GTJ died in 1895. His obituary said 'the Aberdeen Line continues indisputably to hold its own as one of the fastest and most efficient services afloat, and in shipping circles it bears the honourable reputation of having suffered less from accident or loss than probably any of the other great trading companies of the country.' He is famous for not insuring his vessels against loss and spending the premiums saved on the repair and renewal of his fleet.

Increases in insurance premiums expedited the sale of liner sailing ships; and sales in 1898 reduced the sailing ship fleet to six ships on the Australia outwards berth from London, tramping homewards with grain and nitrates. Then **Thermopylæ II** ran aground off Cape Town and became a total loss. Some 20,000 gold sovereigns worth £100,000 and £50,000 in other currency were taken off.

Instead of moving with the times to London, the Aberdeen Line remained firmly rooted in Aberdeen. However, the company was ailing, so the limited partnership was converted into a limited liability company. The new company bought the nine ships of the partnership and immediately mortgaged them. It was still a family affair, and the list of shareholders included GTJ's granddaughter, my great-aunt Muriel Thompson, who in 1908 won the first ever Ladies Race at Brooklands.

A new ship, **Pericles**, was ordered from Harland and Wolff. She could accommodate 100 first-class and 400 third-class passengers. She was also a great cargo carrier, with six holds and hatches. However, in 1910 disaster struck when she was lost. Although in 1914 **Euripides** was launched, she was soon taken up from trade by the Australian government to proceed as a troop transport supporting the Australian contribution to the First World War. She had been made ready to carry 136 officers, 2,204 other ranks and 20 horses. Although Thompson did not suffer any casualties in the war, with all of its five ships on government charter, the Line did not have a profitable war, and afterwards was in sad decline.

The last chapter of the book is an epilogue devoted to the financial management of the Royal Mail Group, of which George Thompson and Co Ltd and Aberdeen and Commonwealth Line were wholly owned subsidiaries, and the Group's subsequent financial disentanglement by the so-called Royal Mail Voting Trustees. It also recounts the fall of the chairman of the Royal Mail Group, Lord Kylsant, who in 1931 was convicted of issuing a false prospectus to support a debenture issue and sentenced to twelve months' imprisonment. His appeal was dismissed. When I was a boy my family regarded him with dubiety but the author is more generous, asserting that 'the verdict was considered by many to be flawed and politically driven'. It was not a view shared by the Court of Criminal Appeal.

My own farewell to the Line came in 1939 when I went with my mother to see my father, then a commander in HMS *Ramillies* in Malta. We sailed in the Aberdeen Line's *Jervis Bay*. Not long afterwards, as HMS *Jervis Bay* under Captain Fegen, she was protecting a convoy when it was attacked by the German pocket battleship *Admiral Scheer*. Although overwhelmingly outgunned, he at once steamed straight at the enemy warship so as to draw its fire. In the ultimate observance of the Thompson motto *Per Periculum Vivo* he lived through the danger, but only for long enough to enable his convoy to scatter before he was killed. His ship later sank, but most of his convoy was saved. He was awarded a posthumous Victoria Cross. It was a fitting end to the Line.

As a boy, I was brought up to admire my great-great-grandfather and to feel that if I have inherited some of his qualities or could emulate some of his achievements, I too should be able to earn a living in my chosen field. To anyone with an adventurous spirit who relishes a challenge and the satisfaction of overcoming adversity to achieve success, this book is custom made to secure a following. In doing so it affords an important contribution to maritime history.

Sir Andrew P. Leggatt
November 2016

AUTHOR'S PREFACE

My interest in George Thompson Jnr and the Aberdeen Line began in the early 1980s, when working in the offshore industry in Aberdeen. I frequently visited the exquisite Aberdeen Maritime Museum and in the course of these visits, purchased two biographical monographs about Aberdeen Line commanders. Here was an extraordinary shipping enterprise, of which I knew very little; I sought further information, and happened upon the only book hitherto written on the Aberdeen Line, *The Sea Carriers*, produced to commemorate the line's centenary in 1925. A book in which one has to travel to Chapter 7 before a mention is made of the line or its founding father could only be regarded as an inspiration to do something about the deficit!

My late wife, Pat, without whose unstinting support this project would never have got off the ground, spent nearly six months in the basement of the Aberdeen Custom House, combing through the Register of British Ships, identifying and recording any ship which bore the name "Thom[p]son" as a participating shareholder. This mammoth task resulted in a skeleton upon which to build further ongoing research. In the ensuing thirty-plus years of research undertaken outwith busy day jobs, I have visited many parts of the world, including Canada, Australia, Hong Kong, Cuba and South Africa, in the course of which I have made many friends who have provided vital advice and information on research lines.

I especially appreciate the friendship and help of descendants of the Thompson and Henderson families, who have taken me into their confidence and supplied vital information: George Thompson Jnr's great grandson, Sir Andrew Leggatt, a retired Lord Justice of Appeal, who painstakingly read the text, dotted the i's and crossed the t's, introduced me to the mysteries of split infinitives and contributed hugely on family matters, as well as furnishing the Foreword to this work and providing often much needed encouragement and friendship over the years; Sir Wm Henderson's great-grandson, the late George Thompson Wordie, farmer of Huntley, who unleashed a wealth of family information from 'a black metal box under the bed'; and Bruce and Malcolm Thompson in Australia, Malcolm, the last Thompson to carry on business in the name of George Thompson.

The numbers of people who I should thank for input over thirty-five years are too numerous to list. However, I do single out for special mention the people of Australia, who through the medium of their National Library, with its extraordinary research tool "Trove", and the State Libraries of New South Wales, Victoria, South Australia and Western Australia, and their respective maritime museums, have not only provided so much research material but have responded to my enquiries with prompt courtesy and good humour – a model to others in this world!; Ian Tulloch in Australia, who provided much early research material; Barbara Jones and her colleagues in the

Lloyds Register Foundation, who provided me with much archive material; the artist, Tim Thomson, who generously gave access to his wonderful painting of *Thermopylæ and Cutty Sark* for the cover artwork; Dr Hazel Carnegie of Aberdeen, whose book *Harnessing the Wind* was one of the monographs which prompted my original researches and who has been a constant source of encouragement and friendship; my old Trinity House colleague, Peter Snadden and his late wife Gina, in Swansea; the late Capt. 'Sam' Wheller in Aberdeen; John Edwards, former Keeper of Maritime History and his staff at the Aberdeen Maritime Museum; Captain John Turner and his colleagues at the Aberdeen Harbour Board; the staff at the Aberdeen City Library; the staff of the School of Oriental and African Studies in London; the staff of the Guildhall Library in London; David Savill, co-author of the Merchant Fleets publication on the Aberdeen Line, who generously entered into dialogue on the ownership of certain early Geo. Thompson Jnr. ships (we did not always agree but the exercise was hugely useful!); Chrissie MacLeod and Andrew Choong and their colleagues at the document and plans departments of the National Maritime Museum; Prof. Rex Hartwell of Oxford University, who gave me unfettered access to his unpublished manuscript on Dalgety; and Douglas Atfield, fellow Deben sailor and photographer, who helped enormously with reprograhic work.

The process of researching, documenting and writing a book of this nature inevitably impacts upon fellow travellers, my work colleagues, especially Pamela Welham, clients, and everyone I have had contact with and who I must have bored to tears, not to mention dominating the office photocopier. Particularly my relatively new wife, Kay, a chartered librarian, who has uncomplainingly taken me on board, proofread the scripts, developed the index, given advice and patiently put up with being shared with George Thompson during the run up to publication, while casting a jaundiced professional eye at the order of my maritime library. To the many of whom I have not made specific mention, I extend my sincere appreciation and apologies for the omission.

The first half of this book inter alia recalls the lives of George Thompson Jnr., the founder of the shipping enterprise which bore his name; and his clerk, later to become his son-in-law, partner, and upon Thompson's retirement, senior partner, (Sir) William Henderson. Both officers served not only the shipping enterprise in which they were engaged, but also the wider Aberdeen community. Through their involvement in the fields of ship owning, shipbuilding, marine insurance, banking and railway promotions, they brought wealth and international renown to the city, and gave employment to hundreds of its inhabitants. Publicly and socially, they were prominent in such developments as the City Library, hospital extensions, the botanical gardens, Aberdeen Harbour, the poorhouse, local charities and the Free Church. George Thompson made very large personal donations in the form of medical bursaries to the Aberdeen University. Both men served with great distinction as Provost (GTJ) and Lord Provost (Wm H.) of Aberdeen. These men were elected to high office against a background of distinguished service to the people of Aberdeen, not petty political rhetoric. To honour their services to the city, their portraits were painted by the eminent portrait painter, Sir George Reid, and these portraits were presented to the City Council by an appreciative community. In this book, I have endeavored to orchestrate the achievements of these two great men and their subsequent families, in terms of their enormous contributions to the City of Aberdeen and British shipping.

When I embarked upon this maiden authorship venture, I little appreciated the role of the publisher and the frustrations of landing one! After a number of false starts, I happened by The History Press, whose interest, quiet enthusiasm and patience have been a bedrock. To my colleagues at The History Press, particularly Amy Rigg, Lauren Newby and Chrissy McMorris, I extend my heartfelt thanks.

P.H.K.
6 June, 2017

1

BIRTH OF A SHIPPING ENTERPRISE

I beg leave to acquaint you that I have commenced business as a Commission Agent, Ship and Insurance Broker, and having been bred in the mercantile line with a general acquaintance of people in business, I flatter myself I shall be able to afford satisfaction to those who may employ me.

I respectfully solicit your patronage with the assurance that my utmost endeavours shall always be used to execute what I may be entrusted with to best advantage.

I am with respect,

Your obedient Servant,

GEORGE THOMPSON.

38, Marischal Street, Aberdeen,

1st November 1825.[1]

Thus the 21-year-old George Thompson launched his business career, whether by way of a newspaper advertisement or personalised mail shots to potential customers is not clear, but from this humble but nonetheless confident beginning was to grow over the next 107 years one of the best-respected shipping lines in the history of British shipping. It was an enterprise that, in its formative years, was a microcosm of British mercantile marine development, and in maturity was the longest-serving line in the Australian trade.

The story of George Thompson Junior (for so he almost always referred to himself in business, with the notable exception of the foregoing announcement) and the shipping enterprise he founded is in fact the story of two Aberdeen families interrelated by marriage, the Thompsons and later the Hendersons. It is also the story of the port city of Aberdeen in the heady days of the Victorian era; and in later years, the rise and fall of Kylsant's Royal Mail Group. However, it is to George Thompson Junior that credit for the foundation of the enterprise and for leadership to initial greatness must fall. Who was George Thompson Junior (GTJ); what were his origins; what was the Aberdeen commercial climate into which he launched his enterprise; and what were his initial moves to establish the business that was to bear his name for the next 107 years (and beyond)?

George Thompson's father, Andrew Thomson, hailed from a crofting background at Hucksterstone, Newhills, in the parish of Old Machar, 4 miles west of Aberdeen. Andrew Thomson was the son of George Thomson and Elizabeth Deuchars, who had been married in Arbroath in 1764.[2] The family croft, now known as East Huxterstone, still stands, having been beautifully refurbished in 1994. Andrew was brought up on the land, and at some time prior to joining the Army, was horseman in the employment of George Stephen, the relatively wealthy farmer of Rubislaw Farm, a couple of miles to the east of Hucksterstone.

On 23 November 1787, Andrew Thomson enlisted in the Royal Regiment of Artillery as a matross (assistant to the gunner) at Aberdeen, and was posted to Captain Hooke's company at

Fort Leith, Edinburgh. From the regimental records we know that Andrew Thomson, upon enlistment at the age of 20, was 6ft tall, of dark complexion, and (unusually for a crofter of that time) he could read and write.[3] From Leith, Andrew Thomson was posted to the regimental depot at Woolwich in early 1788 as a gunner in Captain Robert Lawson's company, 4th Battery, Royal Artillery. In a letter to his parents at Hucksterstone from Woolwich in April 1788 he gave a delightful insight into life in the Royal Regiment of Artillery:

> I love verrey will to be in the Armey for I live cline and gentil as ever I did in my lifes for we have two cline shirts evrey week and all new clothing from top to toes and we have the finest barrek rooms that aney one could desire and fine bedden and clin sheets every month and we have lofe of breed and milk for breakfast and broth and flesh for dener and cold beef for supper. So there is no man could happer than we do for we have only 4 hours douty to do all the day and so I could not think of Bing beter.
>
> And we go to the kirk evry Sabath day. But when I was as Rubeslaw I had many excuses to hold me from the kirk but there is no excuse hear [sic].[4]

In the letter, the original phonetic spelling of which has been retained, Andrew extended his best wishes to John and George Stephen at Rubislaw, so we may surmise that relations with the Stephen family were of the warmest.

In 1794, Andrew Thomson was promoted bombardier and transferred to Captain Dickenson's company. There is some suggestion that this posting might have been back to Aberdeen, and that thereby started the romance with George Stephen's daughter, Ann. About this stage also, the Army bureaucratic machine anglicised the spelling of Andrew's 'Thomson' surname to 'Thompson' (something subsequent biographers of GTJ mistakenly took to indicate an English paternal background). Promotion to corporal followed on 1 October 1799.

Andrew Thomson (the kirk records claimed the spelling of his name back for their own!) married Ann Stephen, daughter of George Stephen of Rubislaw, at Old Machar, Aberdeenshire, on 13 June 1801,[5] and on 4 February 1802, their first child, a daughter Elizabeth, was born in Woolwich.[6] Andrew Thompson was promoted to sergeant in November 1802, sixteen years almost to the day after his enlistment in the Royal Artillery.

George Thompson was born to Ann and Andrew Thompson at Woolwich on 23 June 1804, and was baptised at the High Street Scots Presbyterian Chapel on the eighth day of the following month.[7]

Andrew Thompson's career thus far from Aberdeenshire farm lad to sergeant in the Royal Artillery had been a steady progression, with promotions demonstrating an above-average soldier; he had married well, and now had a young family living within the protective comfort of the sergeants' married quarters at the regiment's Woolwich Depot. This situation was to change dramatically when, on 30 November 1805, after eighteen years' service in the Royal Regiment of Artillery, Andrew Thompson took his discharge[8] from the colours in favour of an appointment as Conductor of Stores in the military service of the Honourable East India Company in India.

A conductor in the HEIC was a warrant officer serving within the Ordnance, Commissariat and Public Works Department; such posts were usually filled by former NCOs from the HEIC's European regiments, but were sometimes, as in the case of Andrew Thompson, recruited from British regiments. In taking the post, Thompson was probably seeking to better himself in a way that he could not have achieved as a non-commissioned officer in the RA; it also demonstrated an adventurous streak, which sadly was to prove fatal in short order. He died of fever at Fort St George, Madras, on 18 April 1807, and was buried the next day,[9] just seventeen months after joining the HEIC.

There is no record to establish whether Ann and her two children had accompanied Andrew out to India, but the family belief is that she did not; rather, after his departure she had returned with her children to her parents' farm at Rubislaw. Certainly, it was here that young George Thompson was brought up, under the care of his maternal grandfather, George Stephen.

While the Thompsons derived from relatively humble, sturdy crofting stock, the Stephens have been described as 'exuberant and colourful'. Tracing back to the late seventeenth century, the early Stephens were noted as 'receivers of contraband' in Aberdeen. Of the two branches of the family, George Stephen's had farmed at the Mansion House of Rubislaw, built in 1688; while the other had variously engaged in the military, law, politics (with especial fervour for the anti-slavery movement), and the civil service, with varying levels of success, but almost invariably with a reputation for strong character. The family tree (p.13) gives a taste of that character.[10]

Given that the young George Thompson (GTJ henceforward) was effectively brought up a Stephen, one can surmise that his early character derived both from a rugged shrewdness inherent to his father, but perhaps more especially, the 'peculiar and volatile'[11] nature of the Stephens.

The Mansion House of Rubislaw has long since been destroyed (and indeed, its stones were used for the construction of the residence in nearby Queen's Road of the renowned Aberdeen lawyer Lachlan MacKinnon, later to become GTJ's grandson-in-law).[12] The farm was ½ mile east of the great Rubislaw granite quarry, a huge hole in the ground from whence, under the proprietorship of the Gibb family, granite was worked and shipped to many parts of the world. Much of the stone used for kerbs and buildings in London, including Waterloo Bridge and the terrace of the Houses of Parliament, was quarried at Rubislaw and shipped south in coastal brigs from Aberdeen.

We know very little of the early years of GTJ at Rubislaw. By general account, he was educated at Aberdeen Grammar School, but there are no records of his having attended the current school of that name, and it is more likely that he attended the Old Grammar School. We have his recollection of youthful fishing for 'bandies' in the Den Burn, which ran past the Mansion House of Rubislaw[13] on its way to discharge into the upper end of Aberdeen Harbour, but precious little else.

After leaving school, GTJ served his apprenticeship with the Aberdeen and London Shipping Company (then commonly known as the London Shipping Company), which in November 1835 was to merge with the Aberdeen and London Steam Navigation Company

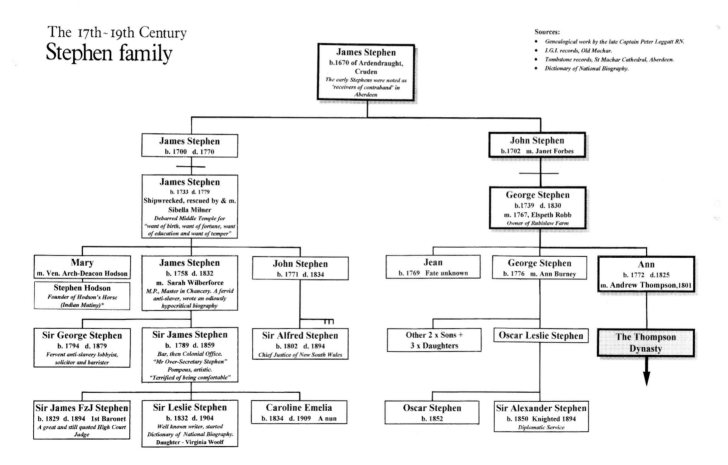

The 17th-19th Century
Stephen family

Sources:
- Genealogical work by the late Captain Peter Leggatt RN.
- I.G.I. records, Old Machar.
- Tombstone records, St Machar Cathedral, Aberdeen.
- Dictionary of National Biography.

James Stephen
b.1670 of Ardendraught, Cruden
The early Stephens were noted as 'receivers of contraband' in Aberdeen

James Stephen
b. 1700 d. 1770

John Stephen
b.1702 m. Janet Forbes

James Stephen
b. 1733 d. 1779
Shipwrecked, rescued by & m. Sibella Milner
Debarred Middle Temple for "want of birth, want of fortune, want of education and want of temper"

George Stephen
b.1739 d. 1830
m. 1767, Elspeth Robb
Owner of Rubislaw Farm

Mary
m. Ven. Arch-Deacon Hodson

Stephen Hodson
Founder of Hodson's Horse (Indian Mutiny) *

James Stephen
b. 1758 d. 1832
m. Sarah Wilberforce
M.P., Master in Chancery. A fervid anti-slaver, wrote an odiously hypocritical biography

John Stephen
b. 1771 d. 1834

Jean
b. 1769 Fate unknown

George Stephen
b. 1776 m. Ann Burney

Ann
b. 1772 d.1825
m. Andrew Thompson, 1801

Sir George Stephen
b. 1794 d. 1879
Fervent anti-slavery lobbyist, solicitor and barrister

Sir James Stephen
b. 1789 d. 1859
Bar, then Colonial Office. "Mr Over-Secretary Stephen" Pompous, artistic. "Terrified of being comfortable"

Sir Alfred Stephen
b. 1802 d. 1894
Chief Justice of New South Wales

Other 2 x Sons + 3 x Daughters

Oscar Leslie Stephen

The Thompson Dynasty

Sir James FzJ Stephen
b. 1829 d. 1894 1st Baronet
A great and still quoted High Court Judge

Sir Leslie Stephen
b. 1832 d. 1904
Well known writer, started Dictionary of National Biography. Daughter - Virginia Woolf

Caroline Emelia
b. 1834 d. 1909 A nun

Oscar Stephen
b. 1852

Sir Alexander Stephen
b. 1850 Knighted 1894
Diplomatic Service

to form the Aberdeen Steam Navigation Company. This business became part of the Coast Lines Group, which in turn became a constituent of Kylsant's Royal Mail Group and finally part of the P&O Group. The London Shipping Company operated fast packet smacks (similar to the famous Leith smacks) and schooners in the Aberdeen to London trade before paddle steamers progressively took over on the route from the second quarter of the century. In this company, trading as it did between Aberdeen and London with passengers and freights of granite, textiles, beefstock, salmon and whisky southbound; and passengers, trans-shipped imports[14] and manufactured goods northbound, GTJ received his basic grounding in shipping.

As we have seen, at the age of 21, he branched out on his own as a commission agent, ship and insurance broker, with offices at No. 38 Marischal Street, a street echoing the former glory of London's Leadenhall Street as a shipowners' centre. This office no longer stands, having been destroyed to facilitate the widening of the road running under a reconstructed Bannerman's Bridge viaduct in the 1980s. We can assume that No. 38 was part of a three-storeyed terraced tenement, stepped to the steep gradient of the hill. Marischal Street, named in honour of Earl Marischal Keith, earned a certain notoriety through the Aberdonian expression 'Aye! He'll finish up lookin' doon Marischal Street', a reference to the fact that the view down Marischal Street from the gallows erected outside the Castlegate Talbooth was the last a condemned man had of the living world before meeting his redeemer![15]

Before following GTJ's early business life, it is appropriate to reflect upon the commercial status of the city of Aberdeen into which he launched. Aberdeen in 1825 was a wealthy city (albeit, the council had only just emerged from effective receivership arising from excessive spending on certain capital projects, notably harbour developments and the construction of King and Union Streets), but it was isolated by virtue of its location. The railway from the south was yet more than twenty years away, and road communications were poor; seaborne trade was the order of the day. Nearly 200 ships, aggregating 30,771 tons, were registered in the port,[16] the small average size reflecting the draught restrictions of the harbour. The coastal trade was largely conducted by packet smacks and brigs, but the first steamer had arrived in 1821, and the progression to steam on the coastal packet trade was inexorable.

Aberdeen's harbour, which in 1825 operated as a municipal function, had received its first Royal Charter in 1136. The harbour was sited on the north bank of the River Dee, in a location where the river divided into three ill-defined channels between sandbanks on its final reaches to the sea. Numerous plans to improve the harbour had been considered, mostly involving a locked basin, but this was still twenty-one years away. The quays or piers serving the harbour stretched over a length of about a mile along the north side, from the confluence of the Den Burn with the River Dee in the west, to the fishing village of Footdee at the mouth of the Dee in the east. Of those quays, only the part of Waterloo Quay, which had been completed by 1825, remains today. The Den Burn discharged raw sewage into the harbour, the stench from which was a source of constant concern and adverse comment. Ships in the harbour took the bottom at low water, with an ever-present risk of strain damage. The Aberdeenshire Canal, built in 1807, ran 18¼ miles from a basin adjacent to Waterloo Quay to Port Elphinstone, near Inverurie to the north-west of Aberdeen. The canal, which principally carried coal, lime and fertilisers, was never a commercial success; it nonetheless played an important part in the development of trade through Aberdeen.[17]

Imports to Aberdeen included wheat, barley, flax and timber, mostly from the Baltic, though the North American timber trade was growing; lime and coal from the Wear and Tyne; salt for fish curing from Spain; slates from Wales; and tea, cotton, wools, dyestuffs, fruit, wine, china and glass. A large proportion of Aberdeen's imports, including all products from the HEIC's monopoly zone, were trans-shipped from the south.

Exports reflected the manufacturing base of Aberdeen – woollen goods, stockings, linen thread, whale oil, ale and spirits. The large Rubislaw granite quarry had started operations in 1775, and fifty years on more than 35,000 tons of granite a year were passing through the dockside stone yards en route to London and elsewhere. Before the days of refrigerated transport, cattle moved on the hoof aboard coastal ships to the south.

The textile industry is worthy of specific consideration for it impacted strongly upon imports and exports; it was a major influence upon commercial and social life in mid-nineteenth-century Aberdeen and its partial collapse in the depressed times of the late 1840s was to adversely affect GTJ at that time. For many years, the spinning of flax and hemp thread had formed a major cottage industry in the countryside surrounding Aberdeen, employing thousands of persons on a piecework basis; the spinning of wool and the knitting of fine stockings and gloves was also 'put out' to the same source. The business was organised and supported by merchant entrepreneurs in Aberdeen. These merchants employed agents, who arranged for the delivery of raw materials to the cottage workers and organised the collection, packaging, marketing and shipping of the finished products. Then, in 1779, the first steps were taken towards the industrialisation of the textile business with the building of the largest and technologically most advanced cotton mill in Scotland on the banks of the River Don at Woodside. There had earlier been established on the opposite bank of the Don what was to become one of the largest flax spinning mills in Britain. Early industrial development was dependent upon water power, and hence co-location with the river bank. Power-driven spinning was broadly introduced in the 1790s, followed by weaving in the early 1820s, spelling the death knell of the cottage industry, though knitting was to continue to be undertaken on a large scale by the so-called cottar women until well into the 1840s. In the early 1800s, steam was successfully introduced as a motive power, releasing the industry from its dependence upon water, and enabling the location of the mills closer to the centre of the city; the introduction of steam power increased the volume of Aberdeen's coal imports. As a measure of the importance of the textile industry to Aberdeen, at its peak in 1830, some 13,000 men, women and children were engaged in the preparation, production and exports of woollen goods, linen and linen thread, a quarter of the population.[18]

Fishing was an industry of increasing importance. A fish market had operated in Aberdeen for many years, initially located in Castle Street but later relocated to a position in way of Ship Row where the boats landed. The nature of the Aberdeen-based fisheries carried out in the early nineteenth century was largely river and foreshore netting for salmon. Salmon from the Rivers Dee and the Don was salted and exported in barrels to London, where in those days it was widely enjoyed as a poor man's sustenance. Offshore, the Dutch dominated fishing operations, with seasonal intervention by the French in mid-summer. Fishing was not the only offshore Aberdeen activity in which the Dutch and Frenchmen engaged; probably far more lucrative was the sourcing of contraband run ashore by local luggers, the processing of which gained the port a significant notoriety. Perhaps this was a portent of offshore service industry

excellence that 150 years later would place Aberdeen on the world oil map?

Greenland whaling, which was regarded as part of the fishing industry, had peaked in Aberdeen in 1817, when five whale fishing companies operating fourteen ships worked out of the port.[19] Immediately behind the foreshore at Footdee were located the five whale fishing company boil yards (Dee, Greenland, Bon Accord, Union and Aberdeen); whalebone arches formed a decorative feature of the gardens of houses with harbour frontage at Footdee. After 1817, the whale fishing industry declined in Aberdeen in favour of Peterhead and Dundee, but the port continued to have an interest in whaling, both in terms of mounting expeditions, processing the catch and building whaling ships for many years to come. GTJ was later to become involved on the periphery of whaling, both as a shipbuilder and shipowner.

By 1825, the port was already a significant shipbuilding centre, with six major and a number of lesser builders crowding the foreshores at Footdee, and the south side of the harbour's upper pool. Of the ship builders, Alexander Hall, John Vernon and J. Duthie Sons & Co. were the most important, with Hall later building a number of GTJ's early ships. In support of the shipbuilding industry, ropewalks were established on the links behind Footdee; the textile industry produced sail cloth; and William Simpson's ironworks provided early engines, boilers and metal fittings for the ships building on the foreshore. The shipbuilding industry with its associated supply infrastructure accounted for a significant level of Aberdeen's imports – timber, masts, flax, hemp, tar, turpentine, pitch and iron.

Such then was the Aberdeen commercial environment into which GTJ launched his new business. He clearly established a multi-faceted trading base in a remarkably short period of time, for advertisements in the Aberdeen Journal showed him buying shares in ships; acting as a passage agent for vessels engaged in the transatlantic emigrant trade; importing North American timber to his own account; and acting as sales broker for shares in ships. He was also undoubtedly engaged in insurance broking from the outset.

It is a matter of conjecture how GTJ raised the capital necessary to launch into business on his own account at that young age. Perhaps at 21 he was the recipient of a legacy, but it is difficult to conceive that his father's estate would have yielded sufficient funds, prudent man though Andrew undoubtedly was. Perhaps the hands of grandfathers Thomson and/or Stephen were involved; we will probably never know, for it would appear that all the forenamed died intestate.[20] Various accounts of GTJ's early business life name a group of local well-established citizens – Alex Jopp (advocate), Thomas Blaikie (plumber), Robert Shand (advocate) and Alexander Anderson (advocate) – as his partners, but in fact the evidence of early shipowning shareholdings demonstrates that this relationship was not to develop until 1841.

From the outset of setting up in business, George Thompson referred to himself as 'Junior'. It is interesting to reflect upon the reason for this; two possibilities suggest themselves. Firstly, he may have wished to show deference to his paternal grandfather of the same name. More likely, it was to differentiate GTJ from two other George Thomsons, one a merchant (hereafter denominated [I]), and the other a ship master/owner (hereafter denominated [II]), who contemporaneously owned ships on the Aberdeen Register with GTJ, and both of whom died within a month of each other in 1853. There appears to have been confusion in respect to some such ownerships in earlier accounts of GTJ, which are alluded to in the next chapter.

GTJ's first shipowning investment was made in late 1825, when he purchased a 2/64 share in the 135-ton brigantine *Douglas*,[21] built in Aberdeen in 1816. The little *Douglas*, which had earlier undertaken voyages to North America, was engaged in the British coastal and seasonal Baltic trades when GTJ took an initial shareholding, and he was to build up a 16/64 interest in her over the next four years before her total loss in 1829.

The ownership of a British ship had, since 1823, been divided into sixty-four equal parts upon the binary principle of halving the ship, and proportions under each, down to a sixty-fourth part.[22] In theory, there could be up to sixty-four owning interests in a ship, but in practice each owning interest usually comprised a block of shares, typically four or eight, with the subscribing owner(s) (the managing owner(s) who initiated the registration) holding eight or more shares. In the nineteenth century, shareholdings in ships were a form of individual investment, and the same philosophy may be seen in the Norwegian KS partnerships to this ▶

day (though, in the latter case, arguably more for tax avoidance than investment purposes). In the UK today, the sixty-four parts in a ship's ownership are usually held by a corporate entity, or each ship may be owned by an individual company within a corporate umbrella holding. The shareholdings and changes of shareholdings in a ship, its official number, tonnage, dimensions and masters are recorded in the register book maintained at the port in which the ship is registered; the register also records mortgages associated with a ship. A Certificate of British Registry, a vessel's prima facie document of ownership, is drawn up from the registry book for each ship. Until recently, the function of a port's Registrar of British Ships was undertaken by the local customs officer.

In June 1826, GTJ took his first step into effective shipowning by becoming the subscribing owner with a 16/64 share in the newly built 78-ton Alexander Hall topsail schooner *Marmion*. Alexander Hall, established in 1790, was one of the principal shipyards in Aberdeen, a yard that over the coming years was to build a succession of innovative, world-class ships. *Marmion* was the yard's forty-seventh keel; Hall's yard book[23] describes her as a square-sterned schooner, with an extreme length aloft of 56ft 8in. Her rig comprised a fore-and-aft sail on each of two masts, crossing square top and topgallant sails on the foremast. *Marmion* was built for a fixed price of £9 per ton, giving a total price of £705 14s 8d against a cost to the builders of £746 9s 11d, a loss of £40 15s 3d.

Marmion, was engaged along with the *Douglas* on the coastal and seasonal Baltic trades. GTJ immediately reduced his initial shareholding in *Marmion* to 8/64, but he was subsequently to build back a 24/64 interest in her before she was sold to Stonehaven owners in 1835.

GTJ's next shipowning interest was a 16/64 share purchased in August 1827 in the former Banff 66-ton sloop *Brothers*, built at Fraserburgh in 1808; this shareholding reduced to 8/64 after only three months, and GTJ disposed of his residual interest in the vessel in December 1828. In November 1827, GTJ acquired 8/64 of the new 294-ton snow *Lady of the Lake* as a subscribing owner. Built in St Johns, New Brunswick, four months earlier, the new ship marked

GTJ's entry into the North Atlantic emigrant and timber trades; GTJ served as her passenger agent.[24] **Lady of the Lake** was one of many such vessels speculatively built of softwood in British North America to satisfy the demand at that time for ready tonnage in the home country; she was to be GTJ's first exposure to a ship built in the North American colonies. GTJ's interest in the ship was to increase to 16/64 before she was lost in ice in 1833 (Chapter 2).

The UK coastal trade to which GTJ committed **Douglas** and **Marmion** must have been extremely hard both on ship and crew. Typically, a vessel working the tramping coastal trade out of Aberdeen loaded granite, wheat and, on occasions, cattle for London. She would thereafter ballast up to either Sunderland or Newcastle, where she would load coal or in summer, lime for Aberdeen or neighbouring ports. Such a round voyage would occupy five to six weeks. Alternatively, the vessel might make a round trip to the Tyne or Wear, omitting London, and such a voyage would occupy two to three weeks. From the outset of engaging in the coastal trade GTJ was a coal merchant,[25] importing cargoes of coal and selling them directly over the ship's rail.

In those days, before the introduction of riverside rail-fed coal shoots at Sunderland and Newcastle, the coal was delivered alongside in shallow draughted 'keels' (double-ended, bluff-bowed barges) from upriver. Sunderland coal stowed at approximately 1½ times the vessel's register tonnage and Newcastle slightly more,[26] so we can assume that the **Douglas** loaded just over 200 tons per voyage, and **Marmion** some 120 tons. In Aberdeen, before the days of organised shore labour and steam dockside cranes, it fell to the crew to discharge the coal cargo by a process known as 'whipping'. A single rope fall passed up from the basket or tub into which the coal had been shovelled in the hold, through a block suspended between the masts or from a cocked yard, and down to a ring on the hauling end, from which three or four manropes hung. The crew members engaged in whipping the cargo mounted a high stage erected beside the hatch, from which they grasped a manrope each and, launching themselves forth, used their combined suspended weight to sweat the loaded basket out of the hold, from whence the coal was shot overside by the 'gangway man' to waiting carts or barges. The Aberdeen coal berths in those days extended from Waterloo Quay in way of the Canal Basin westwards to within two berths of the top of the harbour. Much of the coal was trans-shipped to the Aberdeenshire Canal, but until a locked cut was established

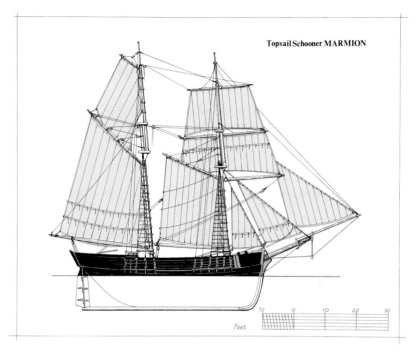

Topsail Schooner MARMION

Feet

Reconstruction of topsail schooner **Marmion**; George Thompson's first commissioned new-build. (P.H.K.)

under Waterloo Quay in 1834 permitting barge access to the tidal harbour, such trans-shipment involved double-handling across the quay by cart.

The Baltic trade was undertaken during the ice-free season, the principal export being herring in barrels. It is interesting to note that the wealth of the Hanseatic League had been founded upon king herring, caught in the great Scania fishery at the mouth of the Baltic. The fishing was carried out by Danes and Swedes, with the Germans acting as middle men, arranging the purchase, curing and distribution of the catch. Then in 1425, by a twist of nature, herring deserted the Baltic[27] and Dutch, Scottish and English fisheries developed, exporting their processed catch to the Hanseatic towns in the Baltic. The Moray Firth herring fishery was undertaken up to the mid-nineteenth century in open double-ended boats similar to the Viking-style boats of the Northern Isles.

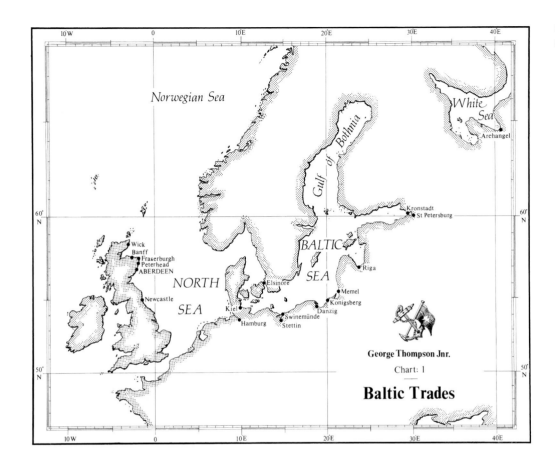

The trade to the German Baltic states was large, encouraged by the more favourable import tariffs levied in the Zoll-Verein semi-free trade states than in the other Continental states. Historically the Dutch were the leading fishers and exporters of North Sea herring to the Baltic, a position based to some measure upon superior curing techniques, but the creation of the British Herring Board in 1807 brought with it quality assurance; 'Crown'-marked barrels of British herring forged ahead in the market. British effort in the trade was further stimulated by Fisheries Acts in 1808 and 1815, which offered a bounty of £3 per ton on herring busses (the traditional British deep water fishing vessel of the North Sea) and a grant of 2s per barrel, increasing to 4s in 1815 with the proviso that the herring should be gutted before curing. These stimuli had the effect of kick-starting the trade, such that in the period from 1827 when

Marmion entered it, to 1843, the annual export of British herring to Stettin increased from 15,082 to 143,659 barrels *per annum.*[28] Another significant factor in the improvement of the British product was the use of Spanish curing salt following the removal of import restrictions in 1825, rather than the native Scots' seaweed-derived salt hitherto used.

Ships loaded barrels of herring at the Moray Firth ports of Banff, Rosehearty or Fraserburgh; and at Peterhead and Wick for the (then) Prussian ports of Stettin or Swinemunde (now Szczecin and Swinoujscie, Poland) in August and September. Two brands of herring were carried – 'white' being pickled in brine, while 'red' were cured by smoking. As a regular annual participant, *Marmion* typically ballasted from Aberdeen[29] in 1829, leaving for Banff on 26 August, where she loaded barrels of British white herring to the value of £700 on 31 August.[30] She then sailed for Stettin, arriving there three weeks later on 21 September. A measure of the overall trade may be gained from the Banff Collector's Quarter Book for the period July to October 1829, which recorded a total of thirty export sailings of herring cargoes to the old Hanseatic ports, mostly Stettin, with an overall value of £15,302;[31] *Marmion*'s cargo was one of the largest in that period. She discharged at Stettin and probably loaded wool at nearby Swinemunde for Kings Lynn, arriving there on 5 November. She then went in ballast up to Sunderland to load coal for Aberdeen, arriving back at her home port on 6 December, after a fifteen-week round voyage.

While **Marmion** appeared as a regular seasonal herring trader from the Moray Firth to Prussia, **Douglas** concentrated on the trade from the Russian Baltic provinces. Voyages in ballast to Memel (now Klaipeda, Lithuania) and St Petersburg were undertaken following the thaw in May, or at the latest in November before the freeze-up. Flax was a typical back-load from St Petersburg; flax, hemp, grain, masts, spars and timber were imported from Memel.

One of the dangers of the Baltic trade was winter ice. Ships caught in the ice risked severe damage or loss; their crews on occasions used ice saws to cut them free and to clear a channel ahead. Such was the scale of the Baltic trade that the shipping and insurance newspaper *Lloyd's List* maintained a regular Sound List of vessels reporting to the Elsinore signal station as they entered or left the sound. Reports in *Lloyd's List* contain graphic records of the extent and pressures of the trade. Captain Jaffrey, master of GTJ's **Douglas**, reported in May 1826:

At the time of the vessel's departure, 200 sail at Memel, 80 British, nearly all destined for Britain or Ireland. A greater number of vessels had arrived than the general depression of the trade had anticipated. Bar very good with 16 or 17 feet of water.'

A year later, **Douglas** and eighteen other British ships were delayed departing Memel for twelve days by bad weather. The ice was setting in very fast and sudden storms were another hazard of the Baltic. The *Aberdeen Journal* reported:

The DOUGLAS, Jaffrey, from Aberdeen to Memel passed the Sound 20th April 1828. During a heavy gale at E.S.E. the following morning, her anchor started and the vessel began to drive so quick, that, before

ABERDEEN LINE — Vessel Voyage Analysis

Sailed	Port	Arrived	Port	Master	Way Ports, Cargo, Comments, Etc.	Ref.
					Initial interest in vessel acquired 5:3:34	RS
10:5:34	Aberdeen	30:5:34	Archangel	Raeburn		AJ
	Archangel	19:7:34	Grangemouth	"		AJ
	Inverkeithing / Aberdeen	7:8:34	Aberdeen / Inverkeithing	Phillips		AJ
28:8:34	Inverkeithing / Aberdeen	21:8:34	Aberdeen / Sunderland	"		AJ
	Seaham	6:9:34	Aberdeen	"		AJ
17:9:34	Aberdeen		London	"		AJ
30:10:34	Sunderland / Aberdeen	12:10:34	Aberdeen / London	"		AJ
	Sunderland	4:12:34	Aberdeen	"		AJ
23:11:35	Aberdeen		St. Davids	"		AJ
	Cardiff	3:6:35	Aberdeen	"		AJ
13:6:35	Aberdeen		Sunderland	"		AJ
	Liverpool	30:8:35	Aberdeen	"		AJ
13:1:35	Aberdeen		Wick	"		AJ
	Liverpool	11:11:35	Aberdeen	"		AJ
29:11:35	Aberdeen		Sunderland	"		AJ
	Sunderland	21:1:36	Aberdeen	"		AJ
7:8:12:36	Aberdeen / Sunderland		Sunderland / Aberdeen	"		AJ
22:3:36	Aberdeen / Inverkeithing	2:4:36	Inverkeithing / Aberdeen	"		AJ
13:4:36	Aberdeen / Sunderland		Sunderland / Aberdeen	"	3:5:36. Put into Harwich.	AJ
28:5:36	Aberdeen		Newcastle	"		AJ
17:6:36	Newcastle / Aberdeen	10:6:36	Aberdeen / Sunderland	"		AJ
9:7:36	Sunderland / Aberdeen	1:7:36	Aberdeen / Charlestown	"		AJ
8:8:36	Charlestown / Aberdeen	1:8:36	Aberdeen / MacDuff	"		AJ
12:8:36	MacDuff	20:8:36	Fraserburgh / Stettin	"	19:8:36. Sound.	AJ
	Stettin / Sunderland	26:9:36 / 19:10:36	Arbroath / Aberdeen	"	15:9:36. Sound.	AJ
30:10:36	Aberdeen / Sunderland	4:11:36	Sunderland / Aberdeen	"		AJ
9:5:37	Sunderland / Aberdeen	22:4:37	Aberdeen / Sunderland	"		AJ
	Sunderland / Aberdeen	23:5:37	Aberdeen / Hartlepool	"		AJ
15:6:37	Hartlepool / Aberdeen	8:6:37	Aberdeen / Newcastle	"		AJ
	Hartlepool / Aberdeen	28:6:37	Aberdeen / MacDuff / F'burgh	"		AJ
	Fraserburgh / Stettin	13:8:37 / 15:9:37	Stettin / London	"	8:8:37. Elsinore / 3:8:37. Sound.	AJ
25:10:37	Aberdeen		Hartlepool	"		AJ
18:11:37	Sunderland / Aberdeen	8:11:37	Aberdeen / Hartlepool	"		AJ
10:12:37	Sunderland / Aberdeen	30:11:37	Aberdeen / Sunderland	"		AJ
	Sunderland	15:12:37	Aberdeen	"		AJ
2:2:38	Aberdeen		Sunderland	"		AJ
7:3:38	Sunderland / Aberdeen	11:2:38	Aberdeen / Grangemouth	"		AJ

Period: 1830's **Vessel:** MANSFIELD /1

The intensity of the Coastal and Baltic trades may be judged by this manuscript copy of the author's research material for the **Mansfield** over a four-year period.

CHILDE HAROLD,
1828.

A painting of brig *Childe Harold*. (From Brig. 'Childe Harold', *The Sea Carriers* (1925))

the other anchor could hold, the vessel was close by the shore, where she rode very heavily till the evening, when her cable parted, when she was driven on shore on Elsinore Beach, near the Harbour. Captain Jaffrey expects to get the vessel off without material damage and to proceed on his voyage in a few days. There are about 12 sail in Elsinore Roads on the 22nd with loss of anchors and cables.

GTJ was not long in returning to Alexander Hall in 1828 for a further new vessel, this time the 116-ton brigantine *Childe Harold*. The new vessel was built for £8 15s 0d per register ton, making her price to GTJ and his co-owners, £1,013 8s 4d. GTJ's initial shareholding was 14/64, but he almost immediately sold 8/64 to London insurance brokers Alexander Howden. GTJ steadily thereafter rebuilt his interest in the ship until by 1835, when he sold his shareholding, he held 32/64. *Childe Harold* has been generally regarded as GTJ's first ship; in fact, as we have seen, she was not. A painting of the ship that appears in *The Sea Carriers* depicts her as a brig, so whether she was subsequently rerigged is unclear; the whereabouts of the painting is unknown. *Childe Harold* took GTJ into further new trades, including the Mediterranean (Trieste) and the West Indies (Port au Prince) in her early years, before settling down to the UK coastal/seasonal Baltic trades in the 1830s. She was finally lost in the Baltic in June 1848 under other owners.

GTJ moved further into shipowning in March 1829 when he took an 8/64 interest as a subscribing owner, along with the Aberdeen timber merchant Wm. Knowles, in the Miramichi, New Brunswick-built 134-ton brigantine *Mary*. She was to be employed in the Baltic herring and timber trades. GTJ was to increase his interest in this ship to 24/64 in 1834, before buying her outright as part of a shipbroking deal to sell the ship in March 1838.

Thus after four years trading, GTJ reached the end of the decade as a subscribing owner of five ships, and was established on the UK coastal trade, the transatlantic emigrant and timber trades, and the Baltic, with a toehold in the Mediterranean. He still referred to his occupation in the Register of Ships as 'insurance broker', but his direction for the future was defined. He had clearly made a most satisfactory start, marred only by the loss of *Douglas* just south of Aberdeen on 25 October 1829:

The DOUGLAS, Jaffray, of and for Aberdeen, from Sunderland, coal laden, was totally lost off Portlethen, on Friday evening [25 October]. The vessel struck rocks, and immediately sank in eight fathoms water; where she now lies with topmasts visible, but little hopes are entertained that any of the materials will be saved. The crew only had time to get into the boat, without saving any of their apparel.[32]

2
GATHERING MOMENTUM – 1830 TO 1839

On 12 July 1830, George Thompson Junior married Christiana Little Kidd, the daughter of the Rev. Prof. James Kidd, who officiated at the wedding.

James Kidd, 1761–1834, was an Ulsterman, the son of poor Presbyterian parents. His father died shortly after his birth, but he was fortunate to be sponsored for a good classical education by a farmer in Co. Antrim. In his early career, Kidd set up a number of schools in the Belfast area, marrying a farmer's daughter, Jane Boyd, before emigrating to America in 1784.

In America, Kidd teamed up with a fellow Ulsterman, Little, to run a school at Philadelphia, before going on to become usher to Pennsylvania College. Here, through a friendship with a Portuguese Jew and by attending the synagogue, he became fluent in Hebrew; oriental languages were to be his favourite studies in the future. Returning to Edinburgh, he read chemistry and anatomy at the university, and joined theological classes, supporting himself by extra-collegiate teaching of oriental languages. In 1793, Kidd was appointed professor of oriental languages in Marischal College, Aberdeen, where in addition to teaching, he completed his theological studies. He became a licensed preacher in February 1796 and an evening lecturer in the Trinity Chapel in the Shiprow.[1] In 1801, he was appointed minister of the Gilcomston Chapel of Ease in Aberdeen, where for the next quarter of a century he established his reputation as a powerful preacher, constantly seeking variety and freshness in his subject.

Such were Kidd's powers of presentation, vigorous character, courage, benevolence and eccentricity, that he invariably attracted controversy. Typical of his character, he not only preached vaccination from the pulpit, but employed his own medical man to undertake such programmes, eventually effecting vaccinations himself in his own home. A strong supporter of the Anti-patronage Movement Society, he favoured the popular election of ministers. His popularity as a preacher remained to the end, his church attracting large congregations. He habitually rose at 3 a.m.

Inevitably, a man of the strength of character and prominence of Kidd attracted a number of anecdotes. One of these told by Alex Keith in *Eminent Aberdonians* is indicative of the public perception of the man:

> Kidd one day encountered the popular Roman Catholic priest Gordon, who was a close friend, a friendship based upon argument. Kidd queried of Gordon, 'Can you tell me the difference between the Virgin Mary and my mother?' Gordon replied. 'No, but there is a mighty difference between their sons.'[2]

On 4 June 1831, GTJ and Christiana Little Thompson's first child was born, a daughter whom they named Jane Boyd in honour of her maternal grandmother.[3] In later life, Jane would play an unobtrusive but nonetheless key role in the development of the company, and one of the earlier prime ships of the Line was to be named after her.

The year 1831 was also to see two further ships added to GTJ's shipowning interests. In March, he acquired an initial 12/64 interest in the 1828-built 116-ton hermaphrodite brig **James Lumsden**. The ship was initially engaged in the Jamaica trade, but in 1833 switched to the coastal trade with occasional voyages in 1834 and 1835 to Lisbon. In those days, an extensive import trade from Spain brought in salt for pickling herring and salmon, and thus we find an advertisement in the *Aberdeen Journal*:[4]

JUST LANDED

ex-JAMES LUMSDEN

A cargo of fine Lisbon salt, well adapted for provision curing;

to be sold per Boll or per Bushell.'

Apply to James Williams, 7 Virginia St.

Then, in October 1831, GTJ acquired a half share in the galleas schooner **Struggler** of 106 tons, engaged in the Iberian and coastal trades. The **Struggler** is of interest insofar that the entry in the Register of Ships recording the purchase of thirty-two shares by GTJ refers to him as 'shipowner', the first time he appears as such, indicating his business inclination towards shipowning as a core activity. GTJ immediately sold 8/64 to Alexander Harvey, farmer of Drums, one of many shareholdings which Harvey and his family were to enjoy with GTJ, starting with an initial 8/64 interest in **Childe Harold** purchased from GTJ in November 1830. By spring 1832, GTJ had moved office from 38 Marischal Street to 13 Quay.

Hermaphrodite-brig and galleas schooner rigs are not commonly referred to these days, and it is appropriate to describe them in passing. The hermaphrodite brig was what today we would regard as a brigantine, i.e. a small two-masted craft, square-rigged on the foremast, and fore-and-aft rigged on the main. A galleas schooner was more a description of a vessel's hull form than her rig; a galleas was a small schooner with a square stern (as opposed to the Continental galliot, which had a rounded stern). It is perhaps relevant to point out the looseness of terminology attaching to the schooner rig at that time. Aberdeen vessels described as schooners were almost invariably topsail schooners, and may indeed have been hermaphrodite brigs.

An indication of the harshness of seafaring (and shipowning) in those days may be gained from the *Aberdeen Journal*[5] reporting the arrival of **Childe Harold** at Cowes on 20 April 1832 from Porto Rico:

> During her passage to Cowes, the vessel had a very adverse passage. A sea, on the 31st March, struck her, and hove her on her beam ends, carried away her bulwarks, galley, round house, top of the companion, water casks, spencer, main top-sail, stay sail, and the man at the helm, who by great exertions was saved.

Perhaps significantly, this episode marked the end of her deep-sea voyaging, for after a fish run from Fraserburgh to the Baltic, **Childe Harold** spent the rest of her GTJ days engaged in intensive trading on the east coast.

Early in 1833, GTJ became subscribing owner with 24/64 of William Duthie's newly built 165-ton brigantine **Dunnator Castle**. The vessel was initially employed on Duthie's berth on the transatlantic trade to New York, but later she went on to worldwide tramping, including a voyage to Otaheite (Tahiti) in 1836, finishing her GTJ days on the Baltic trade.

The Lemon Tree Tavern in Huxter's Row, on whose site the Town House now stands. The Lemon Tree was a meeting place for city businessmen.

Trading in ship shares in Aberdeen was either executed by private treaty, often with the likes of GTJ intervening as broker, or at public roups [auctions], usually held at the old Lemon Tree Tavern in Huxter Row (a narrow street that ran between Broad Street and the Castlegate, destroyed in 1867 to make way for the present Town House). The Lemon Tree served as the local equivalent of the Baltic Exchange, and was a general meeting place for Aberdeen businessmen. It was also the venue for student gatherings and ecclesiastical suppers, and the magistrates were known to gather there for breakfast following public executions. The proprietor of the Lemon Tree for many years was a Mrs George Ronald, a lady noted for her hospitality and fine food. '... there was never seen, one might swear, such creamy Finnan haddocks, such magnificent partan claws as Mrs Ronald was wont to place on the table.'[6]

Advertisements in the Aberdeen press gave details of the ship(s) and the shares to be auctioned. Thus:[7]

PUBLIC ROUP AT THE LEMON TREE TAVERN,
1st February [1833], at 2.00 p.m.

1/16 MARMION Schooner	1/8 PATRIOT Brig
1/16 ARDENT Schooner	1/16 LADY OF THE LAKE Brig
1/8 DAUNTLESS Schooner	1/16 ABBOTSFORD Brig
1/16 GARLAND Schooner	1/16 DIADEM Brig
1/8 JEAN Sloop	1/8 WELLINGTON Sloop

For particulars, apply to George Thompson Jnr,
Insurance Broker, Quay.

The roup in this case arose from the winding up of the estate of the late John Williamson, flescher (i.e. butcher); GTJ bought the shares under offer in **Marmion** to return his shareholding in his first-built ship to 16/64; GTJ subsequently built up his shareholding in **Marmion** to 28/64 before the vessel was sold to Stonehaven owners in February 1835.

GTJ's 16/64 interest in the snow **Lady of the Lake** came to an end when the vessel was lost in tragic circumstances in ice off Newfoundland on 11 May 1833. The report of the master,[8] Captain John Grant, dated 1 June from Quebec, describes the horrific circumstances of the loss:

On the 11th May [1833] in lat. 47.0. N. and long. 47.10. W. at 5, A.M., we were steering W.S.W. with a strong wind at north, when we fell in with several pieces of ice. At 8 o'clock, the ice getting thicker, I judged it prudent to haul the ship out to eastward again, under easy sail to avoid it. About an hour after, in endeavouring to pass between two pieces, a tongue under water, in the lee ice, struck our starboard bow, and stove it entirely in. We immediately wore the ship round, expecting to get the leak out of the water, but did not succeed. The ship now filling fast, the mate, with seven of the crew, and a Mr Wright, a cabin passenger, got into the stern boat, after getting beef, bread, compass, &c. and left us to our fate. The awful scene that then took place is beyond my powers of description. After getting the long-boat out, the passengers crowded into her with such mad desperation that she was twice upset alongside, drowning about eighty of them. I now attempted to save my own life, and succeeded in getting the boat, with thirty-five in her, clear of the ship, without oars, sails, compass, or a mouthful of provisions of any kind. The last time I saw the brig (the ice coming between her and us), she was sunk up to the tops, and about forty persons in the main-topmast rigging. We then tried to pull after the other boat with the batten-boards and thafts, but got beset with ice. We now lay down in her bottom, expecting a worse fate than those who had drowned, viz. to perish with hunger and cold. Next morning, the wind changing to the west, we got clear of most of the ice; and I then steered to the eastward, in the faint hope of some vessel picking us up. At noon, we saw a brig lying to; at 4, P.M. got on board her, and found the crew just leaving her, she being in the same state as our own - sinking. We, however, got some provisions out of her; and there being a boat lying on her deck, I got half of the passengers out of our boat into it. On the 14th, we were picked up by the Stepney of Glasgow, a small brig, bound to St. John's, Newfoundland, after having been for 75 hours exposed to the open sea, naked, wet and frost-bitten. Next morning I left the brig with two boys and passengers, and went on board the Amazon of Hull, bound to Quebec, just as we stood, having lost everything; but we have great reason to be thankful that we are in the land of the living.

In all, at least 120 persons must have perished in this incident. In Chart 2, the dead-reckoned position of the casualty has been recreated. Significantly, Captain Grant did not feature in GTJ's service thereafter. The loss of **Lady of the Lake** seems to have cooled GTJ's enthusiasm for the North Atlantic trade, for it was to be three years before he committed further tonnage to the service.

The iceberg the **Lady of the Lake** hit would almost certainly have been calved from a glacier on the west coast of Greenland the previous summer. From their parent glaciers, icebergs are carried northwards up the west coast of Greenland, and freeze into the sea ice in the Hudson Strait as winter approaches. The current takes the entrapped bergs around the top of Baffin Bay, whence they begin a southerly journey down the Labrador coast until they reach the tail of the Grand Banks to the north-east of Newfoundland around the beginning of April the following year. On arrival on the Grand Banks, the icebergs meet the warm Gulf Stream setting up from the south-west, and generally disintegrate. However, occasional bergs have apparently been reported as far to the east as the Azores. The period of maximum iceberg infestation on the Grand Banks is May each year; an estimated 380 bergs reach south of the 48th parallel per annum.[9]

On a happier note, GTJ's first son, Stephen Thompson was born on 29 June 1833.[10] In time, Stephen was to play a leading role in GTJ's shipping enterprise, eventually becoming the resident London partner.

One of the fascinating conundrums surrounding GTJ's early shipowning career remains confirmation of which ships he actually held a shareholding interest in, a situation compounded by the fleet list contained in *The Sea Carriers*,[11] which is almost certainly inaccurate, though presumably based upon primary corporate material available at the time the book was written for the company's centenary. (According to Sanderson,[12] the company was effectively bankrupt at the time of Cornford's writing *The Sea Carriers*, which may explain the somewhat unsatisfactory nature of his portrayal of the company, out of character for an experienced writer of shipping line histories). Earlier reference has been made to the three shipowners contemporaneously operating in Aberdeen in the period 1825 to 1853 under the name of George Thom(p)son. In the Aberdeen Register of Ships, differentiation can usually be established by virtue of their stated occupation, their shareholder groupings, and the addition of 'Jnr' after George Thompson; in the register, GTJ is not always spelt with a 'p', however. Thus: GTJ is usually referred to as 'George Thompson Jnr, shipowner (or insurance broker)'; George Thomson [I] as 'George Thomson, merchant', based from an office at 22 Regent Quay, with shareholding grouped with the Catto family, Wm. Simpson, John Duncan, Wm. Pirie and certain selected shipmasters; while, George Thomson [II] is simply referred to as 'George Thomson, shipmaster'.

The Thomson [I]/Catto/Pirie association is sometimes collectively referred to in the register as 'Catto, Thomson & Co., Rope and Sail Manufacturers'. The company, which had taken over the earlier ropewalk of George Tower & Co.,[13] had its ropewalk and sail loft on the Fittie Links to the North of Footdee, and was one of the two principal firms operating in this essential shipbuilding support activity in Aberdeen.

In the light of the foregoing, great care is needed in interpreting the register entries; this is particularly the case in the acquisition by GTJ in March 1834 of 4/64 of the 125-ton schooner **Mansfield**. She had been built in Aberdeen in 1825 for the George Thomson [I]/Catto family syndicate, and GTJ only came on the scene ten years later with a small shareholding contemporaneously with George Thomson [I]. **Mansfield** was engaged on the coastal and seasonal herring trade to the Baltic, and GTJ eventually increased his shareholding in the vessel to 12/64 before selling out in 1857. The vessel was finally lost off Peterhead on 20 October 1863,[14] a good age for a ship engaged in such a demanding and rugged trade for all her working life.

In the summer of 1834, **Struggler** (Caie or Kay) made two voyages from Aberdeen to Greenland. The nature of these journeys is unclear; the short duration of the voyages may suggest that the vessel had been carrying stores to the whaling grounds. A reference is made to a back cargo of 'black lead', otherwise known as plumbago or graphite, used amongst other things for blacking stoves. Thereafter, the vessel returned to intensive coastal trading on the east coast.

At a subsequent roup at the Lemon Tree, we see:[15]

SALE BY PUBLIC ROUP
within the LEMON TREE TAVERN,
on Tuesday 10th March 1835, at 6 o'clock of
Hermaphrodite Schooner BRAEMAR
William Donald Jnr.[16]

GTJ in fact bought all the shares in the **Braemar** at this roup, selling them back to Wm. Donald in June the same year; it would appear that in this case, GTJ was acting as a broker or financial intermediary. The scope and extent of GTJ's business in the mid-1830s in addition to shipowning, insurance broking and importing coal, may be gauged, in the absence of any primary material, from his trade advertisements in the *Aberdeen Journal*. Thus we find him acting as passenger agent for Quebec sailings from Aberdeen, Dundee and Liverpool; intervening in the sale of ships by private treaty and through public roups; acting as sub-agent for the recruitment of artisans to work on estates in Jamaica; and importing small cargoes of Ballachulish slates for sale to his own account. He was also clearly actively involved in the insurance market. He was not at this stage importing timber to his own account; timber brought in by GTJ's ships appears to have been to the account of Wm. Knowles (with whom GTJ jointly owned the brigantine *Mary*). Thusfar, these were relatively low capital-based service activities, but activities that established his reputation and made the business contacts vital for subsequent expansion.

In 1835, the Aberdeen Steam Navigation Company was formed through the amalgamation of the Aberdeen and London Shipping Company (the London Shipping Company in which GTJ had served his time) and the Aberdeen and London Steam Navigation Company, which hitherto had been rivals in the trade. Under the merger arrangements, the capital in the new company included 4,000 shares allocated to the former company, and 2,400 shares to the latter; the values of their respective ships were nearly identical at £20,300. The London Shipping Company paid a balancing fee of £5,025 to the Steam Navigation Company to complete the deal. GTJ clearly played a key role in bringing the two companies together, for the directors awarded him a gift of plate in recognition of his services. From the outset of the new company, GTJ was a director and a member of the committee of management, engaging in a number of influential committees and sub-committees, including the freight committee, and the sub-committees on wages, repairs to vessels and repairs to machinery. In 1836, he was one of three directors appointed to examine the master of the *Duke of Wellington* following that vessel being run foul by another in the Thames.[17] His name frequently appeared in the Register of Ships, along with Thomas Blaikie, William Reed, Robert Catto, William Duthie and Alexander Brown, as joint trustees for the ownership of the company's ships. Clearly, GTJ had rapidly established his mark as a prominent Aberdeen man of shipping.

GTJ's second son, George Thompson Youngest, was born on 29 August 1836. While he was to become a shareholder and possibly a partner, he was never apparently a mainstream force in the shipping enterprise.

The year 1836 was to prove a watershed in GTJ's business life. On the shipowning side, he became subscribing owner with a half interest in the William Duthie new-build 132-ton brigantine *Falcon*. This was the first of two successive ships that he would jointly own with William Falconer, an Aberdeen shipmaster, and the first of a number of ships for which, over the course of time, he would provide financial backing on a private basis, where his partner was a local shipmaster. Following a maiden voyage to Rio de Janeiro, the *Falcon* was consigned to the coastal trade, and after a relatively short period in GTJ's stewardship, was sold in 1837 to the Aberdeen Commercial Company, a company in which GTJ was a shareholder. The Aberdeen Commercial Company was primarily engaged in the coastal coal trade to Aberdeen, and GTJ was to move a number of his coastal ships into this company as he progressively withdrew over the next few years from the Aberdeen coastal trade. At the same time as GTJ had invested in the *Falcon*, he disposed of his 48/64 interest in *Struggler* to Wm. Donald.

GTJ then invested in four further ships; a half share in the 321-ton brigantine *Sir William Wallace*, built at St Stephens, New Brunswick, in 1824; all the shares in the 181-ton snow *Shakespeare*, built by Nichol Reed, Aberdeen, in 1825; 12/64 in the brigantine *Brothers* (2), of 93 tons, built in Leith in 1814; and 8/64 in the 197-ton barquentine *Amity*, built in New Brunswick in 1825. Significantly, three of these new ships were deployed back on the North American emigrant and timber trade and consolidated GTJ's position in that trade in his own right, a trade to which he was to commit ships continuously until 1874.

The trade comprised two voyages per ship per annum, the first voyage departing Aberdeen in early April to coincide with the opening of the St Lawrence from ice. From the Aberdeen press, one can conclude that there was strong competition for mounting 'the first ship of the year for Canada'. Westbound, the ships carried passengers and emigrants to the New World. Eastbound, the ships loaded timber, principally from Quebec, but also from Eastern Seaboard ports such as Gaspe, Restigouchi (Dalhousie), Miramichi, Richibucto, and St John, N.B. Typically, *Sir William Wallace* in 1837:

Sailed		Arrived	
Aberdeen	17 April	Restigouchi	date unknown
Dalhousie	7 July	Aberdeen	6 August
Aberdeen	28 August	Quebec	6 September
Quebec	4 November	Hull	14 December

And thence to Aberdeen, sailing for Quebec on 14 April the following year.

Emigration to the New World had taken off in 1815, the product of frustrated ambition in the old country, poverty, famine, displacement of labourers by mechanisation, and in the particular case of Scotland, the infamous highland clearances. The clearances, which occurred over two main periods of time, 1782–1820 and 1840–54,[18] arose essentially from the greed of the local landowners who, capitalising upon the need for sheep to feed the growing population in England, and in particular the standing army in the Napoleonic Wars, leased out the glens and braes for enclosure to support the introduction of high-quality sheep farming, thereby displacing the crofters. Some of the displaced highlanders eked out a miserable living on the west coast curing kelp for salt and iodine, but the abolition of excise duty on salt in 1825 killed this local industry, and the people so employed were further displaced and had to seek solace in emigration. Aberdeen was not a main entrepôt for emigration arising out of the highland clearances, but Aberdeen ships frequently touched by at Cromarty and/or Scrabster in Caithness to pick up such emigrants while on passage to Canada.

An analysis of position reports in the *Aberdeen Journal* and *Lloyd's List* shows that in the main, vessels engaged on the Quebec trade pursued a rhumb-line course from a departure off Cape Wrath in the north-western corner of Scotland to a landfall off Cape Race at the south-east corner of Newfoundland, entering the Gulf of St Lawrence by way of the Cabot Strait; homeward bound, they returned on the same track. Outward-bound, a few vessels took the southern route, striking down from Cape Wrath to catch the north-east trade winds to the south-west of Madeira, before crossing the Atlantic in latitude 28° North, and thereafter heading north to the Cabot Strait, passing to the east of Bermuda. This route almost doubled the ocean passage distance, but optimised prevailing winds and currents. Occasionally on the second voyage of the year, when ice conditions allowed, vessels took the northern route to enter the Gulf of St Lawrence through the Belle Isle Straits to the north of Newfoundland. That the majority of ships ploughed the same track westbound and eastbound throughout the year is evidenced by the number of westbound ship reports arising from eastbound ships. In part this may be due to mutual security; in part it may be due to a lack of understanding of the principles of ocean navigation, which were to be propounded in the published works of Mathew Fontaine

Maury USN; and to have adopted a great circle sailing eastbound (the shortest distance) would have tracked high up into ice infested waters. Chart 2 shows the above tracks.

A voyage analysis of 105 passages on the Aberdeen–Quebec service over the whole period in which GTJ was engaged in that trade and for which records are available, shows the following:

	1st Voyage		2nd Voyage	
	Westbound	Eastbound	Westbound	Eastbound
Average passage time (days)	43.9	32.0	42.2	39.7
Shortest individual passage	33	27	18	27
Longest individual passage	61	40	57	70

These statistics are reasonably predictable; the shortest voyages occurring during the mid-year favourable weather window, with eastbound laden voyages helped by generally fair winds and currents. Within these averages, individual voyage times vary significantly; there is little evidence of trends reflecting evolving ship technology, the performance of individual commanders, or advances in navigation practice over the period.

The second voyage of the year from Canada would arrive in November or December, and then according to evidence given by GTJ to the House of Commons Committee looking into the Aberdeen Harbour Bill in 1839, he generally laid the vessels up for the winter months, unlike Mr Duthie, whose 'Vessels go all year round; in the coasting Trade in the Winter time'. GTJ professed himself to the committee as 'not so fond of making Coasting voyages in the winter', but he certainly made the odd positioning voyage back to Aberdeen in winter, loading coal on the Tyne or Wear en route.

The most notorious emigrant ships sailed out of Liverpool, carrying mainly Irish emigrants, the victims of famine and displacement; horrific conditions of overcrowding, poor ventilation, lack of provisions and pre-embarkation deprivation led to outbreaks of cholera and dysentery on board such ships, often with substantial loss of life. The Aberdeen trade seems to have been carried out on a far superior basis, but certainly there were few comforts on the little

Chart 2 Atlantic Trades.

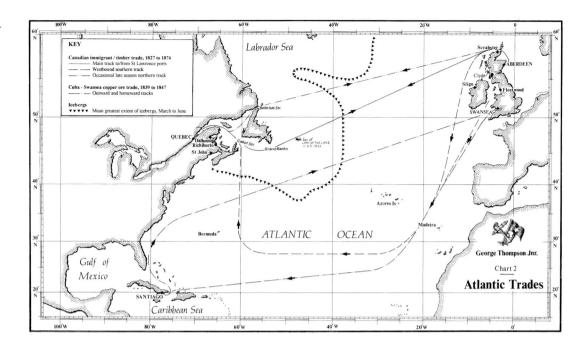

ships plugging out across the North Atlantic.[19] The emigrants were accommodated in makeshift quarters erected in the holds; cooking and ablutions were carried out on the exposed deck; and in times of bad weather, the accommodation had to be battened down, with consequent sealing off of ventilation. As we have seen, ice was a major hazard, and the Gulf of St Lawrence proved a dangerous access route to Canada, with many tragic losses of immigrant ships on its shores. Before entering Canada, each emigrant ship had to be cleared at the quarantine station established on Grosse Isle, 22 miles downstream from Quebec, on pain of the master being heavily fined. Grosse Isle was to prove the last resting place of some 11,000 emigrants,[20] victims of cholera and dysentery.

The trade in timber from North America had its origins in the demand for building and shipbuilding materials against an increasingly short supply of native timber, especially hardwoods, in Britain, a situation exacerbated by the denial of access to Baltic timber following the Treaty of Tilsit between Russia and Napoleon in 1807. In later years, the financial institutions, anxious to bolster the growing trade with North America, successfully secured preferential import tariffs on Canadian timber, 10/- per ton as opposed to 55/-

per ton from the Baltic, which served to protect the trade for the next fifty years.

Canadian timber was cut and skidded by teams of oxen to lake and riverside during the winter months, and formed into huge rafts, fitted with accommodation huts and sails. With the spring thaw, these rafts were floated down to Quebec or the other loading ports, propelled either by long sweeps or latterly by steam tugs. The scene was vividly described by a North-east man, James Thomson, in 1844 in a letter to his father, Alexander Thomson of Aboyne:[21]

We had not gone far up the river from Quebec City when we saw some more wonders ... an immense field of floating timber, the logs squared and built upon one another – I don't know how deep – there were a dozen masts upon it with a sail on each, a great many men with wooden houses and fires and the whole pulled along by a steamer. The first was scarcely passed when we saw another.

On arrival, if the timber had not already been squared, it was fed into the large mills at Quebec, and stored in floating pounds in the riverside coves awaiting shipment. In those days before the advent

The river above Quebec with log rafts and ships loading.

The logs were extracted through ports in the vessel's bows by hand winches fixed on the quay, and, as the vessel rose when lightened, the logs plunged down end first at an angle of 45 degrees with a mighty splash, and on rising to the surface were captured by boat-hooks, secured to those already afloat, and raised to the quay by hand crane for dispatch to the wood yards.

The timber, if not to the private account of timber merchants, was sold by public roup on the Links to the north of the harbour. GTJ later brought such cargoes in to his own account, but at this stage sold them 'afloat' upon arrival in Aberdeen.[23] The subsequent sale of the cargo was typically advertised in the Aberdeen Journal:[24]

of telegraphs, the masters of the timber ships working with local agents had specific responsibilities for the selection of timber on behalf of their principals back home. Timber from the pounds was drawn alongside the waiting vessels, sometimes numbering more than 150 head of sail, and loaded by means of block and tackle taken to the ship's windlass, through ports cut in the bow and stern. In the holds, the baulks were man-handled by gangers of enormous strength, usually of Irish origin, to secure a tight stow.

Many of the ships used on the trade were built of softwood at Miramichi or St John. These colonial-built ships were a phenomenon of the time. Cheaply built from local materials, often by shipwrights from the north-east of Scotland, they were laid down on a speculative basis, and filled a particular need for suitable tonnage at a time when the home market, based on dwindling supplies of hardwood, was not competitive. The colonial-built ships were usually sold to their new principals upon arrival in Britain, having profited by a paying cargo on their delivery voyage. Their softwood hulls leaked and their planking became waterlogged after a few years, but for the carriage of timber in that regulation-free age, this was not a serious consideration. The square ports cut out on either bow, on larger ships at two different levels, presented a potential structural weakness, and specific care had to be paid to their effective securing and caulking upon completion of loading.

In Aberdeen, the timber was discharged into the dock; MacKinnon described the process:[22]

PUBLIC SALE OF RESTIGOUCHI TIMBER

There will be sold by Public Roup on
Saturday 19th Inst.
on the ground of the Old Lime Basin,
Waterloo Quay

The entire cargo of TIMBER,
now landing ex the Brig
QUEEN VICTORIA
Capt. Wm. Rosie, from Restigouchi,
Chaleur Bay, consisting of:

15,000 feet White Pine
1,600 feet Black Birch
7 1/2 cords Cedar Lathwood

The above cargo has been most carefully
selected by Capt. Rosie
and from his long experience in the trade, purchasers may rely
on the Timber being of very superior quality.

Sale to begin at 11 o'clock forenoon
Credit as usual

Aberdeen 18th July 1843   *George Thompson Jnr.*
                                             Wm. Ross, Auctioneer

The critical importance of the master, in this case Wm. Rosie who had joined GTJ with the purchase of the snow **Shakespeare**, in his role as the principal's purchasing agent in Canada is demonstrated in the advertisement. A cord of timber measured 128 cu.ft, and weighed ¾ ton; such timber was typically of a poor quality and indifferent length, used to fill corners and between the beams, and sold for fuel.

In addition to a ship or ships kept constantly on the Aberdeen–Quebec/Gulf of St Lawrence trade bringing in timber to GTJ's own account to Aberdeen, GTJ also operated from the late 1830s a ship or ships from British and Irish ports to Canada. Sligo, Dublin, Lancaster, Liverpool, Fleetwood, Montrose, Leith and the Clyde all featured in this outport trade, with the ships so engaged each making two round voyages a year, sometimes wintering in the outport, sometimes returning to Aberdeen. This pattern of Aberdeen-dedicated and outport ships was to continue until GTJ withdrew from the Canadian timber trade in 1874. Whether the outport sailings were also bringing in timber to GTJ's account for local sale, or whether they operated on voyage charters or contracts of affreightment is not clear.

The year 1836 also saw GTJ enter the higher realms of local business as a founding partner of the North of Scotland Banking Company. The bank, as its name implied, was established to serve the interests of the burgeoning economy of the north-eastern counties; it was at the same time a reflection of the wealth in the area and the inherent parochialism of Aberdeen. In its flotation announcement,[25] the bank set out its pitch:

> It is impossible to take into view the growing intelligence and enterprise of the North of Scotland – the wealth of its Agricultural, Manufacturing and Shipping interest – with the vast accumulations of unemployed Capital, amply sufficient to supply a circulating medium of its own; and, at the same time, the fact that the whole Banking business in the North is conducted through Branches of Edinburgh Banks (with the exception of the two native establishments in Aberdeen), without being fully satisfied that a New Bank, *upon an extended basis and liberal principles* [author's emphasis], is called for.
>
> There are already four Branch Banks, without a local Proprietary, in Aberdeen alone (two of them established within the last three years), and one or more in almost every town and village throughout the country. These Establishments not only draw to a distance large sums of profit, arising from the business of our Merchants and Agriculturists, but are objectionable in times of temporary embarrassment, when, from various causes, the same steady and consistent relief cannot be secured through their operation, as the superior means of information of a local Banking company enables them to extend to the public, and more particularly to their own Partners, who, although under immediate pressure, may still be in a situation to give sufficient security for the accommodation required.
>
> The object of the Projectors of the proposed native Banking company is, to supply the daily increasing demand for Banking accommodation, on a system more suited to the spirit of the times; affording to the landed proprietors – to the resident capitalists labouring under the prevailing difficulty of obtaining safe and profitable investments – and more particularly to the industrious middle classes, actively engaged in agriculture, commerce, and manufactures in the north of Scotland, the means of participating in the prosperity, and securing a voice in the direction of a Bank, to the success of which they may, at the same time, largely contribute; and thus, by the union of all classes in the Northern counties, to render the establishment in reality, as its name indicates, *'The North of Scotland Banking Company'*

The prospectus went on to pour scorn on the capitalisation of the two existing Aberdeen native banks, and to give further details of the proposed new bank's constitution. It was to be formed on the joint-stock principle, with initial capital of £1 million made up of 50,000 shares of £20 each, with the directors' option to increase the share capital to £3 million. The initial shares would carry a premium of one shilling per share to defray start-up costs. The management of the company was to be vested in a governor, deputy governor, twenty-one extraordinary and fifteen ordinary directors, to be elected annually by shareholders. Everyday management powers were to be vested in the ordinary directors, who had the responsibility for the appointment of a cashier and other officers. A key element of the new bank was the establishment of branches throughout the north-eastern counties, each controlled by local committees of management. The bank would issue its own bank notes. The new bank was intended to work on a co-operative basis, with shareholders transacting their business through it, and investing free capital therein.[58]

The proposed new bank was promoted by Aberdeen solicitors, Adam and Anderson. Alexander Anderson, later knighted for his services, was one of the most controversial and most outstanding entrepreneurs of those times. He was to the forefront in promoting large-scale enterprises, especially railways. His name will long be associated with the development of the city of Aberdeen in Victorian times; indeed, the *Aberdeen Journal* at the time of his death in April 1887 said of him that he was 'the man to whom Aberdeen is indebted, above all others, for what of the amenities of public life it now enjoys'. The scope of Anderson's achievements, ruthless methods and controversial involvements is not the function of this book, but it is significant to note that he was clearly a business friend and confidant of GTJ at that time, and was a shareholder in a number of his later ships.

A provisional committee was established at the first general meeting held in July 1836, of which GTJ was made a member. The second general meeting, held on 19 August of the same year, elected the board, and it is interesting in the light of subsequent GTJ developments, to record its constitution:

| Marquis of Huntly | Governor |
| Henry Leith Lumsden | Deputy Governor |

Ordinary Directors

Robert Duthie of Ruthrieston	Lewis Crombie of Union Place
Robert Johnston, merchant	Alexander Jopp, advocate*
John Smith Jnr, advocate	William Adam, advocate
Baillie John Milne, merchant	Alexander Anderson, advocate*
George Thompson Jnr, merchant*	John M. Gerard of Midstrath
James Edmond, advocate*	

Manager

Henry Paterson*

The officers above marked with an asterisk, together with Thomas Blaikie, plumber, who succeeded as governor in 1841, were all shareholders in ships acquired by GTJ in the latter 1840s. Henry Paterson's appointment as manager carried an annual salary of £500.

From the fact that eleven years after the initial foundation of his own business, GTJ was an initial shareholder and director of the bank, it must be assumed that he had achieved relative wealth and a significant stature in the Aberdeen business community. The foundation nature of the bank's business style – 'extended basis and liberal principles' – was also a reflection of GTJ's own business style, later to be enshrined in his armorial motto *Per Periculum Vivo* (through danger I live). The bank's development was to have a significant impact upon GTJ's own business career a decade hence.

An otherwise exciting year was to end in tragedy, however, on 10 December, with the loss of the **James Lumsden** with all hands:

> The schooner JAMES LUMSDEN, Keir, left Sunderland for Aberdeen on 9th December last [1836] and we regret to say has not since been heard of. Her crew consists of six individuals, five of whom have left wives and families.[26]

GTJ held a half share in the vessel at the time of its loss.

With the maturing of GTJ as a shipowner, it is appropriate to comment upon his shareholding strategy. In his earlier ships, he seldom held more than an initial half share, and usually quickly reduced his exposure to 18/64 or 24/64 by selling shares to one or more of a select group of shareholders – Alexander Harvey, farmer of Drums, has already been noted as one such co-venturer. GTJ usually involved the current master of the vessel with a shareholding, and when command was changed, the master's shareholding might be sold on via GTJ to the incoming master; or the outgoing master might retain it as an investment, in which case GTJ would accommodate the incoming master by divesting some of his own shares, or arranging the sale of shares from another shareholder. Lachlan MacKinnon recalls GTJ telling him that he gifted a 2/64 shareholding in the ship to each master on the condition that he did not insure the gift, thereby ensuring an interest in the ship by the master over and above his salary.[27] In fact, the evidence of the Register of Ships would seem to suggest that the master's shareholding could take one of two forms – up to a half share where the ship was a joint venture between GTJ and the master, or between 4/64 and 8/64 if the master was a hired hand. This suggests that the balance over the 2/64 gift had to be purchased by the master, probably on easy terms. In Table 1, the shareholdings in **Lady of the Lake** are analysed as a typical early GTJ ship. In those days of ownership by partnerships, before the advent of the limited liability company as an owning medium, each ship was a trading entity, individually accounted for on a voyage-by-voyage basis. The owner and master paid voyage costs as they arose from freight monies, and the manager took a management fee based on a percentage of the vessel's voyage revenue; any surplus, after agreed retentions, was paid as a dividend to shareholders in proportion to their shareholding. If the vessel made a loss, then the shareholders reimbursed the loss in proportion to their shareholdings. Thus the shareholder master had a two-fold interest in the safety and profitability of his command. In more recent years, the great Blue Funnel Line of Alfred Holt sustained a similar system.

Following the sale of *Falcon* to the Aberdeen Commercial Company in 1837, GTJ and Falconer continued their association with a half share each in the newly built 185-ton William Duthie

Table 1: Lady of the Lake – Shareholding Structure

Ship built St John, New Brunswick, 9 July 1827; Ship lost 11 May 1833

Shareholders	Occupation	Date of Transactions												
		19.11.27	11.12.27	15.03.28	28.05.28	17.03.29	26.02.30	15.11.30	07.04.31	02.11.31	04.02.32	23.02.32	13.04.32	23.02.33
George Thompson Jnr	Insurance Broker	8	8	8	8	8	12	12	12	16	16	16	16	16
Alexander Simpson	Merchant	8	8	8										
William Knowles	Timber Merchant	4	4	4	4	4	4	4	4	4	4	4	4	4
George Watson Black	Merchant	8	8											
Alexander Harvey	Farmer	16	16	20	28	28	28	28	24	20	20	18	20	20
J. Williamson	Flescher	4	4	4	4	4	4	4	4	4				
David Talbot	Ship Master	8	8	8	8	4	4	4	4	4	4	4	4	4
William Fiddie	Merchants in Miramichi NB	8												
William Smith														
Alexander Smith														
Hugh Ferguson	New Brunswick		8	8	8	8	8	8	8	8	8	8	8	
John Dickie	Merchant			4	4	4								
Pat Robertson	Ship Master					4	4	2	2	2	2	2		
J. Mathew	Baker							2	2	2	2	2	2	2
J. Grant	Ship Master								4	4	4	6	6	6
William ?	Merchant													
Alexander Innes	Merchant										4	4	4	4
William Leslie	Builder													
William Donald	Ship Owner													8

brigantine *Flamingo*. Like her predecessor, she was initially placed on the Mediterranean and Rio de Janeiro trades. In March 1838, GTJ sold his 64/64 interest in the snow *Shakespeare* in favour of the much larger new 262-ton Nova Scotian brigantine *Queen Victoria*, which was put on to the Quebec trade, undertaking several round voyages in the late 1830s and early 1840s uplifting Irish emigrants from Sligo. Rounding off a busy 1838, GTJ became a subscribing owner with an 8/64 interest in the new 156-ton Alexander Hall brigantine *Wanderer*, put to work in the coasting and seasonal Baltic trades; and subscribing owner with a half share in the Alexander Duthie (whose name had changed from William Duthie that same year) new-build 249-ton barque *Mungo Park*, to be initially engaged in the Mediterranean and Baltic trades. In August 1838, he disposed of his 32/64 interests in *Childe Harold* and *Dunnotar Castle*. Finally, early in 1839 GTJ became subscribing owner with an 8/64 interest in the newly built 156-ton Alexander

Duthie brigantine *Isabella*, which was put to work initially on the Mediterranean trade, but later in life was to be engaged principally on the Baltic trade to Riga and UK coasting. *Isabella* was significant insofar as, except for the odd vessel purchased in, she was the last GTJ ship to be built outside the 'family' until the coming of steam in 1881.

This completed the initial phase of GTJ's shipping and business careers. He was strongly engaged in the North Atlantic, coasting and Baltic trades, with occasional voyages to the Mediterranean, South America and beyond. His ships were becoming progressively larger, with an increasing emphasis on newly built units. He was a banker, with a respected circle of influential business associates, an insurance and shipbroker, a director of the London Company in which just fourteen years previously he had been an apprentice, and a general trader.

3

Broadening Horizons, Diverse Trades – 1839 to 1848

The year 1839 was to see GTJ engage in a number of high-profile business activities that further confirmed his position in Aberdeen society, in particular his involvement in the progression of the Aberdeen Harbour Bill, his involvement in the formation and management of the Aberdeen Sea Insurance Company, and his entry into shipbuilding.

In May 1839, the Parliamentary Committee scrutinising the Aberdeen Harbour Bill published its findings. The Bill, which finally made the statute books as the seventh Aberdeen Harbour Act in 1843, had as its prime objective the establishment of the long-sought-after locked inner harbour along the lines proposed by the board's appointed engineer, James Walker (who in turn developed upon earlier proposals by Thomas Telford), and the construction of a number of quays complementary to the new wet dock – Waterloo East, Upper, Blaikies and Mathews. It also vested the ownership of harbour property in a reconstituted board of commissioners comprising the magistrates and councillors, nine Burgesses of Guild, and three members of the Incorporated Trades. The report of the Parliamentary Committee,[1] is of particular interest insofar that GTJ was examined as a shipowner and merchant. He was also examined in his capacity as an elective trustee of the Harbour Board; as a member of the Board's Steam Navigation Committee; and as a member of the special committee established by the board to make necessary revisions to harbour dues to realise the capital investment associated with the proposed wet dock. From his evidence, we can gain a pen picture of his operations, confirmation of the ships he owned, and an indication of his general standing in Aberdeen.

The special committee had been convened following objections raised in the second reading of the Bill by its original sponsor, Alderman Thomas Bannerman MP. The objections were generated by the two steamship companies, which had extracted preferential, specially dredged berthing arrangements from the board under the existing dock system, and foresaw themselves being financially disadvantaged by the dues attaching to the proposed wet dock. GTJ's arguments to the committee in favour of the wet dock centred on the relief from hull strain and impact damage afforded to vessels lying afloat in a wet dock, as opposed to the prevailing situation of lying aground on a bad bottom and leaning against each other, sometimes four of five abeam, at low water. He cited the case of his brigantine **Queen Victoria**, which had been neaped in mid-channel in the harbour two months before, and had lain unable to get alongside for some days until the tidal levels rose, with a draft forward at low water of 12ft and aft of 6ft; had she not been a new vessel and very strongly built, she would have broken her back. The proposed wet dock would obviate delays to granite-laden vessels awaiting favourable tides to sail, and the problems that arose from mud banks building up outboard of loading vessels, whereby on

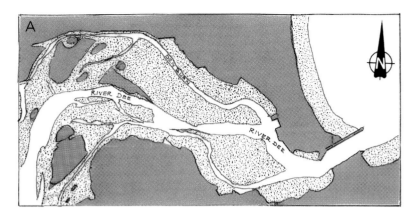

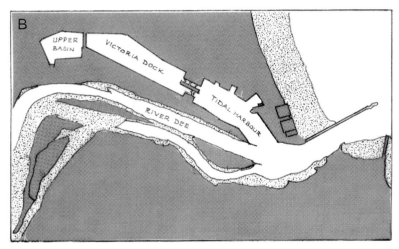

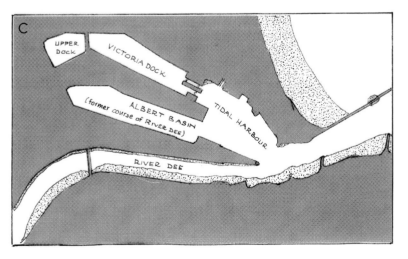

occasions they had to discharge cargo in order to secure release over the banks. He also felt the money expended on the proposed wet dock, the plans for which incorporated the laying of a proper sewer to seaward, would be well spent if for nothing else, 'to get rid of the stench'. He professed himself willing to pay an extra £100 a year for this alone – it must have been powerful!

GTJ was critically and repeatedly examined on how, as a shipowner, he would absorb the additional harbour dues attaching to the proposed wet dock, particularly in respect to coal imports, for which a tariff of a ha'penny per boll would apply. (7.5 bolls were equivalent to a cubic yard of coal; in Scotland, 36 cubic yards of coal were equivalent to 32 tons;[2] accordingly, the increase would amount to less than a farthing per hundredweight). Would not coal ships continue to use the remaining drying berths in the harbour to avoid paying the dues, and would not the imposition of the increased dues drive shipping away from Aberdeen? GTJ vigorously countered the line of questioning by arguing that proximity to the market, which the proposed wet dock would monopolise, would outweigh the additional costs of cartage – some 2 pence a boll – from more distant berths. He would inevitably pass on the additional costs to the consumers in the case of coal; as for timber, he sold his cargoes afloat, so the purchasers would have to pick up the additional costs (this was the first reference to GTJ importing timber cargoes to his own account). He refused to be drawn on the hypothesis that savings arising from freedom from ship damage would offset the additional dues. He believed that the advantages offered by the proposed wet dock heavily outweighed the disadvantages, and that Aberdeen would not be adversely impacted.

In an interesting aside to the examination, GTJ declared the size of his own shipowning activities at that time as being only about one half those of either the Duthies or the Cattos. However, the committee clearly regarded GTJ as one of the most significant and credible operators in Aberdeen.

Chart 3   Progressive development of Aberdeen Harbour 1810 to 1880, based on plans provided by the Harbour Board.
Chartlet A The situation prevailing in 1810; the tidal confluence of the River Dee and the Den Burn.
Chartlet B 1867. Construction of the locked Victoria and Upper Docks.
Chartlet C Development by 1880. The River Dee has been redirected and the tidal Albert Basin created.

From the outset of his business career, GTJ had been involved in insurance broking. Now in May 1839 we find him a director and member of the committee of management of the newly founded Aberdeen Sea Insurance Company; the other directors numbered other contemporary Aberdeen shipowners, including George Thomson (I). The company was almost certainly conducted on a mutual insurance basis, a form still popular with fishing and small vessel owners to this day. In setting out its stall:

> Insurances will be effected on liberal terms; the seaworthiness of Vessels admitted on taking the risk; the usual deduction of one-third on repairs will not be made on British-built Vessels till they are 18 months old; and on Voyage Insurances, the risk of the ship to continue for 10 days after arrival, unless the cargo has been previously discharged.[3]

The new company conducted its business from offices at 47 Marischal Street.

The historical importance of nineteenth-century Aberdeen as a shipbuilding port has never been adequately recognised or understood. Certainly in the first third of the century, Aberdeen was Scotland's prime shipbuilding port, and in the period 1840 to 1870 many of the world's finest clippers took to the water there. While at least half a dozen shipbuilders worked on sites concentrated in areas on the south bank at the upper end of the harbour, and on the north bank immediately to the westward of the fishing village of Footdee, the shipbuilding scene in 1839 was dominated by two firms, Alexander Hall & Co. and J. Duthie Sons & Co. Both of these companies as we have seen, built early ships for GTJ.

Alexander Hall, a shipyard carpenter, had been taken into partnership by his former employer Alexander Gibbon in 1790, along with a draughtsman, James Cochar; by 1811, when he emerged in his own right following the deaths of Cochar and Gibbon, Hall had established a powerful reputation as a shipbuilder. According to research undertaken by the acknowledged local authority on Aberdeen shipbuilding, James Henderson,[4] Alexander Hall built 287 ships in the period 1811 to 1875, including such world-class clippers as *Chrysolite, Schomburg* and *Sobraon*. Halls, in one form or another, continued shipbuilding until 1991, when the yard went into liquidation following the completion of its last ship, RMS *St Helena*, and Aberdeen ceased to be a shipbuilding port.

Hall brought renown to the Aberdeen shipbuilding industry in 1839 when he launched the clipper schooner *Scottish Maid* for a consortium headed by Alexander Nicol. Designed to compete with steam on the Aberdeen to London packet service, *Scottish Maid* was the first vessel to be fitted with what became known as the 'Aberdeen bow'. New tonnage regulations introduced in 1836 sought to place the measurement of tonnage (on which light and port dues were levied) on a more scientific basis than hitherto. The New Measurement was the outcome of these regulations and, like successions of naval architects and shipbuilders over the years, Hall set out to establish means of maximising carrying capacity within minimum tonnage measurement (a measurement ton at that time being a volumetric measure of 92.4 cu.ft). Under the New Measurement, depth became a taxable dimension, thus effectively ringing the death knell of the deep, cumbersome ships designed to the previous tonnage rules. This opened the prospect of shallower, longer and faster ships. The internal volume of the ship was to be obtained by means of a formula that as one of its constituents took three cross-sectional areas of the hull, one amidships and the other two at stations located at one-sixth deck length measured from bow and stern respectively; clearly, by reducing the cross-sectional areas of the two extreme stations, the tonnage measurement for a given length of ship would be minimised. The New Measurement calculation also utilised a length constituent measured at half depth; this also gave potential for minimising the measurement calculation by raking the bow and stern, thus introducing 'free' length/volume above half-depth. Hall capitalised on both these loopholes by raking the stern post more than was normal, but more particularly by introducing an extreme rake to the bow that effectively located the forward cross sectional area measurement station over the forefoot. The resulting hull form was streamlined, with a very fine entry, but was nonetheless a good hull form for head sea conditions and a fast ship to boot. Hall's customers were not initially convinced and he had to build a mock-up of the new bow form before they agreed to its incorporation in their new vessels.

The *Scottish Maid* was followed by many other vessels incorporating the Aberdeen bow, both from Hall's yard, other builders in Aberdeen, and throughout the country; for Hall, while he advertised the bow's potential, does not appear to have patented the concept. A number of GTJ's subsequent ships incorporated Aberdeen bows.

The rationale for the Aberdeen bow ceased with the introduction of the 1854 Tonnage Regulations, which closed the measurement loophole (and which incidentally introduced 100 cu.ft as the measurement ton, a measure that was to remain in force until displaced by the 1969 International Tonnage Convention, which in turn introduced a dimensionless tonnage based upon metric internal volume).

The Duthie enterprise sprang from three brothers, sons of a Stonehaven shipmaster, who were apprenticed by Alexander Hall. Reputation has it that they built their first ship in 1815 out of working hours on a vacant slip afforded by Hall;[5] trading as William Duthie, the brothers started in business with their own Footdee yard the following year. The Duthie family was inexorably linked with the sea, either through shipbuilding, shipowning, rope and sail making, trading, or as shipmasters. They were long established on the North American timber trade, and they operated one of the first regular lines to Australia. The yard, which was to build in addition to coastal trading vessels and fishing vessels, a range of fine clippers, many for the home line, finally merged with Alexander Hall in 1907.

On to the Aberdeen shipbuilding scene in 1839 came Walter Hood. From his yard adjacent to what is now Pocra Quay, the Walter Hood shipyard was to launch 100 ships over the next forty-two years, including such jewels as *Thermopylæ* and *Cimba*, yet he remains something of an enigma. Apart from Lloyd's Register survey reports,[6] few shipbuilding records or yard notebooks are known to have survived as testimony to Hood's professional and commercial endeavours. As the *Aberdeen Weekly Journal* in a series of articles on local shipbuilding bewailed in December 1877: 'It is to be regretted that book-keeping had been so much at a discount amongst the eminently practical men [shipbuilders] to whose indefatigable labour Aberdeen owes so much.'

We are left with little more than press reports of launchings (invariably couched in the glowing journalistic terms tinged with local pride characteristic of the era), a couple of outline plans, a few cross sections in Lloyd's survey reports, a couple of builder's half-models and the achievements of his ships as Walter Hood's legacy.

We know that Hood was born in Brechin, Co. Angus, of John Hood and Jean Crighton on 2 August 1802;[7] he was one of nine children. He served his time in the shipyard of J. & T. Adamson in Aberdeen, on part of the site that his own yard would eventually occupy. Hood married his first wife, Elizabeth Bell, in Aberdeen in October 1828. They had one child, a daughter, Anne Davidson Hood, who was christened in July 1830; her mother appears to have died in childbirth.[8] Hood went into partnership with a Mr Greig to form a new Aberdeen shipbuilding firm, Greig & Co., but the company dissolved upon Greig's death, and Hood went to Dundee for a spell, possibly working for Alexander Stephen. Upon his return to Aberdeen in 1839, Hood established his shipyard on the north side of the harbour, immediately to the west of Footdee. It eventually occupied two adjacent sites earlier leased to J. & T. Adamson and Alexander Stephen,[9] although the lessee immediately prior to Hood's occupancy was John Vernon,[10] shipbuilder. On these sites, Hood eventually erected two covered building slips and a patent slip for ship repair work. Hood's first ship, the 163-ton brig **Milton**, was launched on 13 August 1839.

It is likely that George Thompson Jnr was a partner of Walter Hood from the outset; he had certainly become the principal partner of the Walter Hood shipyard by 1842. Of the 100 ships (all sailing) built by Hood over the next forty-two years, forty-four were built for GTJ; eleven for Alexander Nicol, whose ships were to sail on GTJ's Aberdeen Line berth to Australia; and two for Thompson/Henderson private family interests. The former Keeper of Maritime History in Aberdeen, Dr Jake Duthie, researched a build list for Hood's yard from the Register of Ships and the local press, and this list with some augmentation of detail, is incorporated at Appendix 3.

With a shipyard capable of building the class of ships needed to expand his trades, GTJ now embarked upon a new significant element of his shipping business. As early as mid-1835, Aberdeen brigs had been engaging in the copper ore trade from Cuba to Swansea. Copper had initially been mined by the Spaniards at El Cobre in the Sierra Maestra of south-eastern Cuba from 1546, but the working had been exhausted around 1730. Copper was 're-discovered' at El Cobre around 1830 by a landed proprietor, Mr John Hardy Jnr, the British Consul at Santa Jago de Cuba (Santiago), who had been sent to the area by his father in pursuit of a debt on a neighbouring property. Hardy analysed slag from the earlier workings near the village of El Cobre, 9 miles (15km) inland from Santiago, abandoned 100 years previously, and found it to be sufficiently rich in copper to warrant its development.[11] For the workings to be competitive with Cornwall, the ore content had to exceed 16 per cent to 18 per cent. In fact, the pure metal content of the El Cobre ore averaged 27 per cent, some samples containing up to 53 per cent. A company

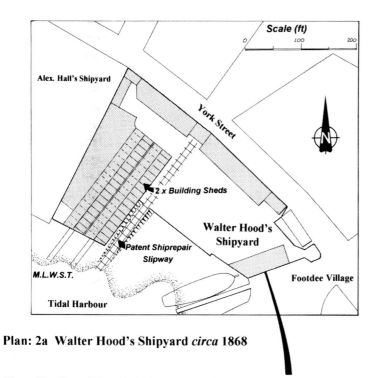

Plan: 2a Walter Hood's Shipyard *circa* 1868

Plan: 2b Site of Hood's Shipyard within Aberdeen Harbour 2000

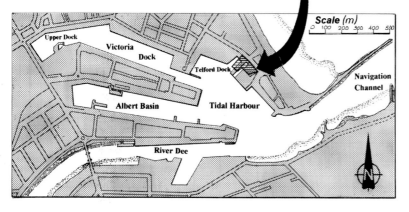

Plans of Hood's shipyard at Footdee; based upon feuing plans and Aberdeen Harbour Board charts.

was formed in 1830, the Royal Copper Mines of Cobre, to work the mine, with money raised by a group of Swansea copper smelters, among others. The mine initially was open cast, 'simply worked as a common English Quarry', but the introduction of Cornish mining technology materially improved production; when fully operational the mine yielded a monthly profit of not less than £12,000.

In 1836, another mining company, the Royal Santiago Mining Company, received a grant of mineral property adjacent to the Cobre company.[12] The new company again had backing from Welsh smelters, particularly Michael Williams, principal of Williams, Foster & Co., at Morfa. Williams had as co-venturers Alderman William Thompson, forge master, and Isaac Lyon Goldsmid, bullion dealer.

In 1838, the mines were worked by some 900 labourers, half of whom were slaves, while the balance came from Cornwall and the Canary Islands. The Cornish men rapidly fell to the scourge of yellow fever, and in short order, Cornish involvement in the mines was limited to skilled mine captains. The ore was crushed to a coarse powder by two steam-driven primary crushers and brought down to the port of Santiago in two hundredweight loads by an army of some 500 horses, mules and camels.[13] In the 1840s, a railway was installed for transportation of the crushed ore to Santiago.

Smelting of copper ore in the Swansea area had first started in the late sixteenth century, but the birth of the industry in the Lower Swansea Valley came in 1717, when Bristol smelting expertise was introduced with the construction of a smelting works at Landore. The abundant availability of high-quality coal close alongside the River Tawe-based smelting works was the economic attraction of the industry to Swansea. Early smelting processes required 3 tons of coal to render each ton of ore; improvements in smelting methodology resulted in 18 tons of coal being required to render 13 tons of ore to yield one ton of copper. Another important factor in the location of copper works was the availability of water to power the hammering process by means of which sheet copper was produced. By the early 1800s, at least thirteen copper works were established upon the banks of the River Tawe, owned in the main by family companies – the Morrises, Grenfells, Pascoes, Vivians and Williams – many of them Cornish.

The Industrial Revolution fuelled the burgeoning need for copper. The importance of the metal in the eighteenth and nineteenth centuries was enhanced by the increasing use of copper or a copper alloy produced in Swansea known as Muntz metal, before the advent of effective anti-fouling paints, for sheathing wooden ships' bottoms to protect the wood against the ravages of boring worms.[14]

In August 1839 GTJ deployed the brigantine *Flamingo* into the Cuban copper ore trade; it was the first of five GTJ vessels so employed over the next eight years. *Flamingo* was followed successively by:

- June 1840, *Alexander Harvey*, barque, 292 tons, the first ship to be built for GTJ by Hood's yard, and named after GTJ's late long-standing co-shipowner Alexander Harvey, farmer of Drums to the north of Aberdeen, who had died in September 1837;

- May 1841, *Michael Williams*, brig, 272 tons named after the principal of Williams, Foster & Co., the largest copper smelting works in Swansea;

- October 1841, *Agnes Blaikie*, barque, 385 tons, named after the wife of Thomas Blaikie, Lord Provost of Aberdeen, who was a shareholder in the ship; and,

- February 1843, *Jane Boyd*, barque, 388 tons, named after GTJ's daughter.

GTJ's ongoing commitment to the copper ore trade into Swansea was marked by his purchase as sole owner in May 1842 of the 280-ton brigantine *Mayflower*. Built at Miramichi, New Brunswick, in 1841 by an expatriate Aberdonian shipbuilder, William Rennie, the vessel was committed for her maiden voyage under GTJ to a copper ore run from Valparaiso to Swansea. Two days out on her laden homewards voyage, *Mayflower* had to put back to Valparaiso leaking, and she was delayed at that port for a further three months effecting repairs before she could resume her voyage for Swansea. Clearly, the softwood hull of a North American-built ship was not as well suited to the rigours of copper ore carriage around Cape Horn as Hood's hardwood-built vessels, and she was subsequently deployed on less arduous trades. Along with the 269-ton barque *Margaret Hardy*, she made one voyage to Cuba in the 1840s, but loaded at Santa Cruz in the west of the island for London, probably uplifting rum, sugar or mahogany.

With the exception of *Mayflower*, all the foregoing vessels were built by Walter Hood. *Alexander Harvey* and *Margaret Hardy* were virtual sister flush-hulled barques. With the progressive increase in size, poop decks were introduced, the first being in *Agnes Blaikie.*

An analysis of these vessels, together with the Hood-built brig *Anemone*, which was employed on the West Coast South America (WCSA) copper run to Swansea, demonstrates them all to have been single-deckers, with hold beams fitted at about one-third of the deck beam stations. The beam to length ratio on the earlier ships was 1:4.2, extending in the later ships to 1:4.6; while their depth to length ratios were 1:5.8, extending on the later ships to 1:6.3. The scantlings of their timbers were noted in the various Lloyd's Register build certificates as being 'much larger than the Rules require', as befitted the rigours of the trade.

Agnes Blaikie was the first of a number of ships owned by a consortium headed by GTJ comprising Alexander Jopp (advocate), Thomas Blaikie (plumber), Robert Shand (advocate), Alexander Anderson (advocate) and Henry Paterson (banker). With the exception of Shand, the members of the consortium were also stockholders in the Aberdeen and Great North of Scotland Railway and directors/manager of the North of Scotland Bank. We will see the significance of these (unsecured) shareholdings in the affairs of the North of Scotland Bank and GTJ towards the end of the decade.

Analysis of sighting reports from *Lloyd's List* and the *Aberdeen Journal* demonstrates that outward bound, once clear of the Bristol Channel, the vessels shaped a course south-west to pass between the Azores and Madeira until such time as they picked up the north-east trade winds between 32° to 30° North latitude, according to the season; once in the trades, course was shaped for Cuba passing north or south about Haiti in the final run to Santiago, according to the season. Homeward bound, the deep-laden vessels followed the Gulf Stream through the Straits of Florida, passing between mainland America and Bermuda, before shaping a rhumb line sailing for the Bristol Channel, a route that generally optimised prevailing winds and current. This was before Maury published his systematic work on ocean winds and currents, but long European experience in the West Indies trade, and the sheer impracticality of butting the elements, would have dictated the routes taken. The tracks followed by the ships engaged on the Cuba–Swansea copper ore trade are shown in Chart 2.

An average round voyage occupied 155 days, with the laden homewards passage averaging thirty-seven days in summer, fifty in winter. At Swansea, before the days of locked dock systems

Barques ALEXANDER HARVEY
MARGARET HARDY

Reconstruction of barques
Alexander Harvey and *Margaret
Harvey*. (PHK)

Scale Feet

and ore yards, incoming ore vessels lightened into barges at the mouth of the River Tawe, before proceeding upstream to discharge the balance of their cargoes at tidal river berths alongside the smelting works.

The trade was arduous, both on ships and crews. The very high density of the copper ore (4.2) made it necessary to raise the centre of gravity of the cargo in stow, and thereby reduce the vessel's metacentric height, by introducing elevated trunks along the length of the vessel. In his classic tome on *The Stowage of Ships* (commonly known in the industry as *Stevens on Stowage*) Stevens, quoting Swansea sources, described the outfitting thus:[15]

all vessels regularly engaged in the foreign copper ore trade have the main keelson raised to the height of about four feet above the skin, on which is laid the platform, which should run as far as possible fore and aft, as many cases have occurred of vessel straining in consequence of the shortness of the platform, and the weight falling too much on one part. The trunk prevents the cargo from pressing against the sides, and generally slopes inwards about three feet. At the top it may be about one-third the breadth of the vessel.

A ship will not conveniently carry more of this ore than will fill one-third of the cubical contents of her hold.

Without the introduction of the trunk, a copper-ore-laden vessel would have carried a dangerously high righting moment with ensuing violent rolling motion in a seaway, making her working by the crew dangerous, and straining the fabric of the vessel; in particular, she would run the risk of rolling her spars out. The ship-side space afforded by the trunk facilitated daily inspection of the shoring and structure of the trunk and repose of the cargo by the carpenter in the course of the voyage. In the figure below, a reconstruction of such a trunk arrangement is made, based on the Lloyd's Register build survey report on **Alexander Harvey**, a ship built for the trade; and illustrations and text appearing in *Stevens on Stowage*.

The copper ore ships had to be inherently strong, with minimal rise of floor to accommodate their lying aground and leaning against each other in a laden condition at Swansea. A unique impression

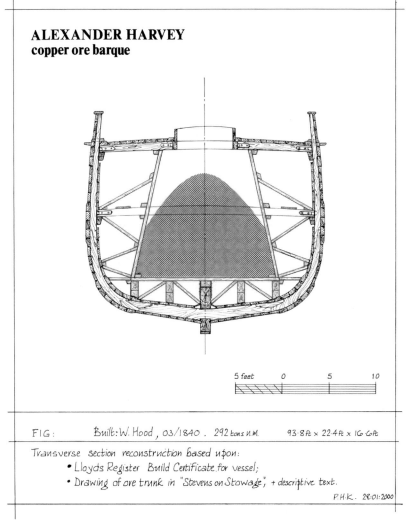

ALEXANDER HARVEY
copper ore barque

5 feet   0   5   10

FIG: Built: W. Hood, 03/1840 . 292 tons N.M.   93·8 ft × 22·4 ft × 16·6 ft

Transverse section reconstruction based upon:
• Lloyds Register Build Certificate for vessel;
• Drawing of ore trunk in "Stevens on Stowage", + descriptive text.

P.H.K. 28:01:2000

Reconstruction of cross section of **Alexander Harvey**, with ore trunk installed.

of such ships and the conditions alongside in Swansea before the introduction of wet docks may be gained from the paintings and pioneer photographic work of the Rev. Calvert Richard Jones (1802–1899).[16] One such photograph shows the bows of the 376-ton barque **Ellen Simpson**, built by Hood's in March 1841 for another Aberdeen owner, Henry Adamson, 'for the copper ore trade [from] Cuba'; this is almost certainly the earliest photographic image of a Hood-built ship. The **Ellen Simpson** would have been very similar to GTJ's **Agnes Blaikie** built seven months later.

The Cuba run carried specific risk for crews over and above the accepted perils associated with small, heavily laden ships operating in the North Atlantic. Yellow fever, or 'Yellow Jack' as it was known among seamen, was endemic to Cuba, and the Swansea press routinely reported the numbers of deaths and sick upon vessels entering from Cuba. On several occasions, water in the casks of ships entering Swansea brought with it yellow-fever-bearing mosquitoes from Cuba, and Swansea suffered a number of outbreaks of the killer fever.

These five ships variously engaged in the copper ore trade from San Jago de Cuba (Santiago) on the south-east shore of Cuba to Swansea until the end of 1847, the last Cuban copper cargo lifted by a GTJ ship being landed at Swansea from the **Alexander Harvey** on 30 December 1847. In that time, a total of forty-six cargoes were uplifted from Santiago de Cuba to Swansea by GTJ ships. It is not clear why Thompson's involvement in the Cuban copper trade suddenly ceased. The UK-based copper mine proprietors had been facing increasing hostility from the British government in respect to their use of slave labour in the Cuban mines, and it may be that the high moral principles of GTJ and Wm. Henderson may have revolted against their ships continuing to support the trade.

In May 1840, GTJ became subscribing shareholder with a 40/64 interest in the newly built 205-ton Hood brig **Anemone**. Contrary to assertions in *The Sea Carriers*[17] and subsequent publications, **Anemone** did not apparently visit Melbourne in 1840. Her maiden voyage from the Clyde to Valparaiso occupied 105 days, which would have precluded her visiting Port Phillip en route; her outwards voyage almost certainly took her by way of Cape Horn. In Chile, she back-loaded copper ore for Swansea. Thereafter, she was constantly on the WCSA nitrate trade for the next six years, trading to and from Liverpool, London and Leith and on occasion carrying South Wales coals on the outward passage.

From the first ore cargo uplifted by **Anemone** in 1840, importation of copper ore to Swansea from the WCSA ports of Coquimbo, Copiapo and Huasco employed GTJ ships concurrent with, but on a much smaller scale than, the Cuban copper ore trade. A Cuban trade ship could anticipate uplifting two, sometimes three, cargoes a year, while the scale of distance and other difficulties inherent to the WCSA trade meant that a round voyage could occupy from nine months to a year. The WCSA bulk trades usually involved an outwards cargo of coal from the Tyne or South Wales ports destined for the Pacific Steam Navigation Co.'s coal depots on the west coast at Valparaiso or Coquimbo; indicative of the size of the PSNC's coal requirement, in 1841 alone the company chartered seventeen colliers to support its needs. WCSA ships invariably cleared inwards and outwards at Valparaiso, where a homewards cargo was fixed. Graph 1 (p. 56) demonstrates the involvement of GTJ ships in the 1840s copper ore trades.

If **Anemone** did not venture to Melbourne and Australia, George Thompson Jnr's sights were certainly set on the island continent, for in August 1841 he advertised, along with Jopp and Shand,[18] the sailing of the new 500-ton barque **Australian**, which was to have been on the berth by 12 October, commanded by Captain Alex Duthie, a veteran with twelve years' experience in the Australian trade. The advertisement, addressed from GTJ's office now back at 40 Marischal Street, implied the first of 'A Regular Line of Packets for Port Phillip and Sydney, New South Wales' from Aberdeen, with the second sailing projected in March 1842. Significantly, although the advertisement specified the **Australian** as being 'nine years A.1. at Lloyd's', no vessel bearing that name, with that description or size appeared in Lloyd's Register within a bracket of years spanning 1840 to 1845. With no subsequent advertisements in evidence, it would seem that the initial advertisement did not generate the support anticipated, and that the venture was premature. **Australian** probably appeared under another name, possibly the barque **Agnes Blaikie**, for although somewhat smaller than advertised (385 versus 500 tons), she commissioned in October 1841, was classed nine years A.1. and was commanded by Captain Duthie, recruited into the company from command of the **Bengal Merchant** on the Australian trade. Perhaps most significantly, as we have seen, **Agnes Blaikie** was the first of a number of ships in which Messrs Jopp and Shand had a shareholding; the coincidence would appear to be too much.

The diverse tramping nature of many of GTJ's shipping initiatives at this time can no better be illustrated than the engagement for three years from the end of 1839 of his barque **Mungo Park** in the salt trade to, and the hide trade from, Montevideo. The River Plate ports were major exporters of hides, together with associated slaughter house products – tallow, bones, horns and hair. The successful carriage of hides required large quantities of brine, and hence salt. Vessels importing salt had to guard against being used upon arrival in Montevideo as convenient storage warehouses for their cargo while salt was drawn down as required to load outward ships, involving much demurrage[19] (a charge levied against the charterer by the shipowner to cover the cost to the owner of delays incurred by the charterer).

The stowage of hide-laden vessels had to take account of the significant weight and likelihood of damage to hides. To raise the centre of gravity of the hide stow, pipes of tallow, each weighing approximately half a ton (a pipe was a large cask of approximately 100 gallons capacity) were loaded as a ground tier, over which a level floor of bones was laid to receive the hides. The hides were carefully laid, hairy sides up, on the bed of bones and a generous salt pickle applied between successive layers to ensure the wet hides did not rot in transit. It must have been a ghastly job for the crew involved!

Mungo Park initially brought a salt cargo down from Lisbon to Montevideo; thereafter, she twice ballasted back to the Cape Verde Islands for salt before loading a Montevideo cargo of hides back to London. From England in early 1842, she loaded 395 tons of coal out to the East India Company's coal store at Mindelo on the island of Sao Vicente in the Cape Verde Islands (CVI)[20] (later to become the Royal Mail Line's coaling station for its South American service), probably loading a further cargo of salt at Boavista CVI for Montevideo. From Montevideo, she again loaded hides for England, arriving in London on 15 December 1842 to complete that tranche of her trading life.

GTJ further strengthened his interest in the North American emigrant/timber trade by taking an 8/64 interest in 1841 in the 440-ton barque **Lord Seaton**, built in Castleton, New Brunswick, in 1840. An interesting insight into a voyage on board a well-run emigrant ship may be found in *From Aberdeen to Ottawa*, the diary of Alexander Muir, who took passage on **Lord Seaton** in 1845.[21]

In June, GTJ's name was associated with a small 187-ton auxiliary paddle steamer *Iris* (sometimes referred to as *Queen*), built by Alexander Hall and engined by William Simpson for initially the Catto/George Thomson (I) consortium, but according to Hall's yardbook, recontracted and delivered to George Thompson Jnr.[22] It is likely that GTJ was acting in a shipbroking capacity; certainly, he does not seem to have operated the vessel, which was sold upon commissioning to the Aalborg Steamship Company of Denmark. It operated her between Copenhagen and Aalborg for the next fifteen years.

In June 1842, GTJ disposed of his 16/64 interest in *Sir William Wallace* upon the sale of that ship to Robert Anderson.

The steady increase in the size and competence of GTJ's ships was no more manifest than Hood's launch in June 1842 of the 583-ton barque *Prince of Wales*. Built at a cost of £5,750,[23] this vessel marked GTJ's move into liner trades, and his entry into the major league of overseas shipowners; his partners in ownership were Shand, Jopp, Anderson, Blaikie and Paterson. Originally destined 'to lay on for Madras and Calcutta', on her maiden voyage, she was in fact chartered upon arrival in London by Edward Gibbon Wakefield's New Zealand Company for an emigrant and supply voyage to Nelson and Wellington, New Zealand. In a letter to his brother, Wakefield described the *Prince of Wales,* following inspection for suitability, as 'a fine ship'.

The paddle steamer *Iris*.

Under the command of Alexander, formerly of **Sir William Wallace**, 43 cabin and 158 steerage passengers, 67 of whom were children,[24] were embarked in the **Prince of Wales** to the account of the New Zealand Company, for a passage money of £16 per head.[25] There were also a number of private fare-paying passengers, among whom was a young Jewish man from Streatham, south London, Samuel Aaron Joseph, bound for Wellington.[26] Joseph was to quickly establish himself in business as a shipbroker in Wellington, in partnership with a Mr Samuel; more particularly, he was to become fluent in the Maori tongue, and was to prove of great service to Governor Grey in negotiations leading to peace with the Maoris. Our interest in Joseph lies fifteen years hence when, having transferred to Sydney, he became the Aberdeen Line's much respected managing agent in that port.

Prince of Wales' voyage out to New Zealand was accomplished in 110 days, sailing east-about. Ninety-eight days out, off King Island in the Bass Strait, she ran in with HM Sloop **Ferret** bearing dispatches from China for Sydney. These announced the cessation of the Opium War between Britain and China. Under the ensuing Treaty of Nanking, China ceded Hong Kong to Britain and opened up five Treaty Ports – Canton, Foochow, Amoy, Ningpo and Shanghai – to free trade without the necessity of dealing through intermediary Hong merchants. This was to have a far-reaching impact upon British trade in the area, and upon GTJ's future development.

Indicative of the caring and disciplined nature of the New Zealand Company's emigration policy, **Prince of Wales** had a former Royal Navy surgeon, Mathew Kearns, embarked as surgeon superintendent to tender to the health and welfare of the passengers, assisted by an assistant superintendent/schoolmaster, a matron and two constables drawn from among the passengers. In the course of the voyage, there were four births (one immediately prior to sailing) and fifteen deaths, twelve from dysentery. The vessel arrived at Nelson on 22 December 1842, where she landed the main part of her immigrants and settlement cargo, including a timber saw mill for a Captain Thoms. She sailed on New Year's Eve for Wellington, arriving at that port on 3 January 1843 with the balance of her thirty-six immigrants and passengers, including S.A. Joseph. The New Zealand Company's settlement situated on the shores of Port Nicholson had initially been named 'Britannia', but at the request of Wakefield had been renamed 'Wellington' in honour of the Duke's earlier services in support of the foundation of the colony of South Australia.

The economic scourge of early Antipodean voyages, before the development of rich pastoral, agricultural and mineral resources in the colonies and before the opportunities offered by refrigeration, was the distinct imbalance between the wealth of ships outward bound with emigrants, convicts and support materiel, and the dearth of paying cargo offering homewards. The early pioneer work of John MacArthur with merino sheep had laid the foundations for the vast wool industry in Australia, but wool was both seasonal and offered at extremely low freight rates. In the early 1840s, the China tea trade had yet to emerge as potential homeward employment and two options presented if no ready homeward cargo offered in the colonies: either to strike up to the East Indies or the Indian sub-continent for cargoes of teak, rice or sugar; or ballast over to the west coast of South America for copper ore, or a newly emerged cargo, guano (Spanish: *huano* = manure arising from the excrement of sea birds). In those days before the extension of the telegraph to the Antipodes, the initiative in respect to choice of cargo usually lay with the individual commander, undoubtedly briefed by owners in terms of options before departure from London.

New Zealand at that time offered virtually no prospects of homeward cargoes; accordingly, after discharging the balance of her passengers and cargo, *Prince of Wales* sailed from Wellington on 18 January 1843, ballasting across to Sydney, presumably in the hope of catching the tail end of the wool season. After a three-day stay in Sydney with no prospects of a paying cargo, she sailed again in ballast on 31 January 1843 for Valparaiso. She would have been GTJ's first ship to visit Australia, but for the apparent intervention of the 259-ton Duthie-built brigantine *City of Aberdeen*, in which GTJ took a 52/64 interest in December 1842, while the vessel was

in Sydney following a voyage from Manila. GTJ may in fact have held an 8/64 interest in the vessel from her commissioning in 1826, but the shareholding grouping and nomenclature in the Register persuades me to believe the earlier interest was in fact held by George Thomson (I). *City of Aberdeen* left Sydney on 22 January 1843, for Auckland with eighty-eight passengers including troops, six days before the arrival of *Prince of Wales.* From Auckland she ballasted to Valparaiso, but was wrecked on Topocalma Shoal off her destination on 25 March; fortunately, all her crew were saved.

Valparaiso in the mid-nineteenth century was an entrepôt for ships arriving on the WCSA seeking cargoes. *Prince of Wales* arrived at the port on 14 March 1843, and her movements over the next fifteen months provide a fascinating conundrum reflecting trading conditions of the time. Cornford[27] has her loading an illegal cargo of guano in Peru, being chased by a Peruvian warship for her troubles, and making her escape through the Straits of Magellan; in fairness, Cornford qualifies the story by earlier stating that the history of the voyage had been lost. She appears to have dallied in Valparaiso for three-and-a-half months before sailing for 'China'[28] (almost certainly the Chincha guano islands off Peru) on 30 June. She arrived back in Valparaiso from Pisco (the clearing port for the Chincha Islands) on 19 August, sailing again after a month for San Antonio, but arriving in Buenos Aires two months later on 22 November. She then moved up to Rio de Janeiro, arriving there on 14 December 1843.

Prince of Wales sailed from Rio on 27 January 1844, nominally back to Valparaiso again, but arrived at Aberdeen via Cork on 12 June 1844 with a cargo of guano from the south-west African offshore island of Ichaboe. Assuming a forty-eight-day passage via St Helena, this would have seen the vessel completing loading at the end of the third week in April 1844 at Ichaboe. The evidence points strongly to the cargo, which was landed in part or in full at Dundee, *Prince of Wales* having touched off at Aberdeen en route, as having been sourced at Ichaboe;[29] whether part of the load had been taken in at the Chincha Islands, or whether cargo loaded at the Chinchas had been discharged elsewhere in the interim, we will probably never know.

However, after what by any standards was an eventful maiden voyage, discharge at Dundee added an intriguing twist to the tale. The Dundee Harbour Trustees meeting of 8 July 1844 complained that the owners of the *Prince of Wales*, discharging in the river off Ferry Port on Craig (now Tayport), had refused to pay port dues in respect to cargo discharged.[30] The problem had earlier been detailed in a letter to the finance committee of the Trustees of the Harbour of Dundee by Mr Robertson, the Collector of Shoredues, in which he complained:

> … a vessel belonging to Aberdeen called the PRINCE OF WALES of 582 tons register has arrived from Africa with a cargo of Guano: has anchored in the River opposite the South Ferry, and has commenced to tranship her cargo into small vessels for other ports without having paid shore dues, or even entered at this office. The South Ferry passage boat went alongside of said vessel today; received about 14 tons Guano came direct up and landed same at the Craig slip for Peter Dalgairns & Co.; it was carted up to their warehouse west shore, weighed and sent away to the country. Mr John Low Jun is acting as agent for the vessel; and it is reported that the whole cargo is to be discharged as above, and without paying dues on ship or cargo. Being a novel case I am at a loss how to proceed …[31]

Evidence quoted by Cornford[32] from the company's account books shows her as having landed 737 tons of guano, which was sold for £7 10s per ton, yielding a freight of £5,533 5s, from which Captain Alexander was paid a bonus of £100. The fact that the cargo was brought in to GTJ's account points to its origin as having been Ichaboe, where the crew themselves would have dug and loaded the cargo. Whatever the source(s) of her cargo, the significance of **Prince of Wales**' homewards voyage was undoubtedly the entry of GTJ into the guano trades, trades which were to have very significant impacts upon the economic life of the British merchant service of the times, and in which GTJ actively participated over the next twenty years.

Ichaboe – Father of all Dung Heaps[33]

Ichaboe lies off the coast of south-west Africa in latitude 26° South, 200 miles north of the Orange River. Its guano deposits were first recorded by an American sealing captain in 1832; a decade later, the significance of his report was noted by a Liverpool master mariner, Andrew Livingstone, against a growing national interest in the qualities of guano as a prime fertiliser. ▶

▼

Livingstone mustered support to mount a three-ship expedition under conditions of commercial secrecy to explore and exploit the island's potential. Only one of the three ships brought a guano cargo back to the UK, landing it at Dumfries in July 1843. The secret was out, and a marine stampede ensued, which at its height eighteen months later saw 460 vessels loading or waiting to load off the island.

The guano obtaining on Ichaboe was not of the same high quality as that arising from Peru; occasional rain on the former leached out some of the ammoniacal salts in the guano, which were so beneficial as fertilisers. However, Ichaboe had the distinct advantage that it was not a sovereign territory, and accordingly no controls or taxes impacted the exploitation of its guano. The prospect of working Ichaboe for the shipmaster was not attractive; a loading master in a letter to his owners quoted in the *Nautical Magazine*[34] described the adjacent coast and outlying island:

> Conceive a barren, desolate, sandy coast; but **so** barren, **so** desolate, **so** sandy! without a soul, or a bush, or a stream near, where it never rains, where the dew wets you through, where it is so cold one gets the horrors, where the air is so clear, that one cannot see the land till you are a mile or two off. An enormous surf beating over the shore, rocks, reefs, shoals, in all directions; conceive a barren rock of an island off this coast, to be covered to a depth of 30 feet, with a beastly smelling bottle sort of mess, looking like a bad snuff mixed with rotten kittens; conceive 132 ships lying packed between this island and the aforesaid sand and surf; fancy 132 masters of merchant-men, with 132 crews, and 132 sets of labourers, all fighting; conceive a gale of wind on top of all this, and you will then only have half an idea of the rum place I have at last got into.

He did not mention that the holding ground was lousy too!

Initially, the guano was worked by ships' crews using ships' boats. Makeshift loading stages were erected from spare spars and planks, which had to be dismantled and returned to the ship before she sailed. As berths became tight, so an arriving ship ▶

would assist the loading of a ship 'on the berth' in order to stake a claim on that vessel's berth and quarrying pit upon her departure. Later, the large merchant houses chartered ships and established labour, supervisors and supercargoes on the island to secure their interests, to the detriment of the freelance owners. This led to bitter clashes on berthing priorities, quarrying rights and labour availability, involving intervention by the Royal Navy on a number of occasions to enforce order and support the authority of the ad hoc committee of shipmasters, which on a rolling membership basis, attempted to regulate the trade on site.

An illustration of loading operations at Ichaboe. (ILN)

The chaotic situation on Ichaboe worsened when it became apparent that guano stocks on the island were finite, and would not support the loading of all the ships presenting at the island. The phenomenon of Ichaboe lay in the fact that from a first cargo in 1843, exports to the UK leapt to a peak of around 208,000 tons in 1845, and fell away to 5,000 tons in 1846 with the reserves spent. The brief but spectacular life of Ichaboe as a guano producer makes interesting comparison with the developing WCSA guano trade.

The discovery of guano on Ichaboe coincided with a major downturn in British shipping, arising from a glut in speculative building in the period 1839 to 1841 to match corn import require-ments; ships were under-employed and their value severely depreciated as a result. The discovery of Ichaboe and the prospects of high-paying cargoes with low overheads had a brief but very important impact upon the economic fortunes of a number of British shipowners.

Prince of Wales was to make one more voyage to Ichaboe from Aberdeen, arriving back on the Clyde in March 1845, where Captain Alexander reported:[35] 'Left at Ichaboe about 250 sail of vessels and about 100 sailed in ballast. A serious misunderstanding had taken place between the shipmasters and agents; the result was unknown as the 'POW' had left prior to its being adjusted.'

She was not in fact the first GTJ ship to visit the island. *Mayflower* also diverted from the WCSA copper ore trade and began loading at Angra Pequina on the mainland just south of Ichaboe before mid-January 1844. Angra Pequina was a source of inferior guano, and a number of ships began loading there in the early days of the rush, only to jettison their cargoes in favour of the higher quality product to be obtained on nearby Ichaboe. *Mayflower* loaded at the island in late January 1844, making her among the first twenty ships to exploit the island. An advertisement in the *Aberdeen Journal*[36] advised:

AFRICAN GUANO

The brig 'MAYFLOWER' Captain Hutcheson, of this port, was
loading a cargo of superior GUANO, in January last, and
is expected to arrive here by the end of this month, or beginning
of April, when the whole will be sold from the ship, on most
reasonable terms.

Parties wishing to purchase will please apply to:

GEORGE THOMPSON JUNIOR
Aberdeen, 8th March 1844

Mayflower was to make two voyages, the second arriving back in Aberdeen in February 1845, whereafter she undertook one Cuban run, possibly for rum, before settling down to the Peruvian guano trade until her disposal by GTJ in 1849. One other GTJ ship was engaged in the short-lived Ichaboe trade; *Flamingo* detached from the Cuba–Swansea copper ore run to undertake at least one voyage to the island in mid-1844. Thus completed GTJ's involvement in Ichaboe. His ships had lifted about 1 per cent of the total exploitation.

On 4 July 1843 GTJ's third son, Cornelius, was born. Cornelius Thompson, who was to graduate from Aberdeen University and study shipbuilding at John Elders's (later to become Fairfields) on the Clyde, would play a leading role in later life in the management of Walter Hood's shipyard and the design of some of that yard's finest ships, before, as a partner in the shipping firm, heading up its London office.

In early 1845, GTJ was joined in the office by a young clerk, William Henderson. Henderson was born at Aberdour on 10 April 1826, the son of a farmer, James Henderson, and Helen Thomson. Henderson had served his apprenticeship in banking with the North of Scotland Bank at its Fraserburgh branch in 1840. We must assume that he had come to GTJ's attention as a director of the bank and, realising his potential, GTJ probably head-hunted him for his own service when he had completed his apprenticeship. Henderson was to rise rapidly in GTJ's employment, graduating successively from clerk to partner, son-in-law and, upon GTJ's retirement, senior partner, Lord Provost of Aberdeen and a knight of the realm.

GTJ's partner in the ownership of the brigantine *Flamingo*, Captain Falconer, had died in 1842, and his 32/64 interest in the ship had been sold to Edinburgh interests. In April 1845, this interest was sold back to the Aberdeen merchants Alexander and William Nicol; at the same time, GTJ sold twenty parts of his 32/64 interest in the vessel to the Nicols, who in turn sold 16/64 to a third party; The Nichols thus held a 36/64 controlling interest in *Flamingo*. The vessel made a trip to the Davis Strait in the summer of 1845, returning with a cargo of black lead. She was then outfitted for sealing and for the next four seasons engaged in Greenland sealing expeditions during the summer, and the coastal coal trade in winter. She was one of only four such vessels operating out of Aberdeen in what was seen as a brief revival of the Aberdeen whale 'fishery'. In 1846, she landed 900 seals, but no oil; 1847, 1,900 seals and 40 tuns of oil; 1848, no record of her catch, but a bad season for casualties, injuries, frostbite, scurvy and fever among the crews; and 1849, 1,400 seals and 20 tuns of oil.

Reference has been made earlier to the imbalance of trade between Great Britain and the Australian colonies. Before the development of wool, meat and other major return cargoes, alternate homeward cargoes had to be found for ships that failed, by virtue of speed or timing, to fix a cargo in Australia; guano provided such a cargo, albeit ships had to ballast trans-Pacific, with the possibility of a part cargo and passengers to New Zealand (which was still at that stage, a dependency of New South Wales) en route, to secure a load. The petrified excrement of millions of sea birds feeding on the fish teeming in the cold Humboldt Current that runs up the entire west coast of South America south of the Equator, guano had

accumulated over tens of thousands of years on the arid coastal areas of mainland Peru, and in particular on its offshore Chincha Islands to the south-west of Pisco. While the Incas had been well aware of the agricultural value of guano as a fertiliser, it was not until the pressures of the population explosion arising alongside the Industrial Revolution that the need for improved crop yield became critical in northern Europe. This was never more so than in the Grampian region about Aberdeen; indeed, the enthusiasm of the Grampian farmers for the new fertiliser may be judged from the regular analyses of the landed product published in the *Aberdeen Journal* and by the following report:[37]

Guano. We have been informed that about 2,000 tons of this valuable manure have now arrived at several ports in this district; yet such is the prospect of demand for it, that it is believed that the above supply will hardly suffice to carry farmers through the ensuing season.

While **Prince of Wales** may have loaded guano in the Peruvian Chincha Islands, albeit illegally the previous year, the 343-ton Hood-built barque **Neptune**, which had joined GTJ's service in August 1844, made the first recorded GTJ loading at the islands on her maiden voyage. Sailing out from Newcastle with a coal cargo for Rio de Janeiro en route, she arrived at Callao on 15 January 1845. GTJ vessels were to be regularly engaged on the Chincha Islands guano trade thereafter until 1865, when alternative fertilisers were available and the core Australian trade had developed, paying homeward cargoes better suited to the quality ships then making up the bulk of GTJ's operation. In later years, GTJ's ships engaged on the guano trade tended to be vessels that had passed their prime as line ships.

An analysis of position reports of vessels engaged on the WCSA guano, copper ore and nitrates trades shows them:

Outward bound tracking south-west by south to pass close west of the Canary and Cape Verde Islands, taking advantage of the Canary Current setting towards the south-west and the north-east trade winds. Crossing the Equator close to the east of St Paul's Rocks and picking up the south-east trade winds, they then hugged the Brazilian coast, gaining the advantage of the Brazilian Current, setting towards the south-west, before swinging away from the coast below the River Plate to avoid the Falklands Current, setting

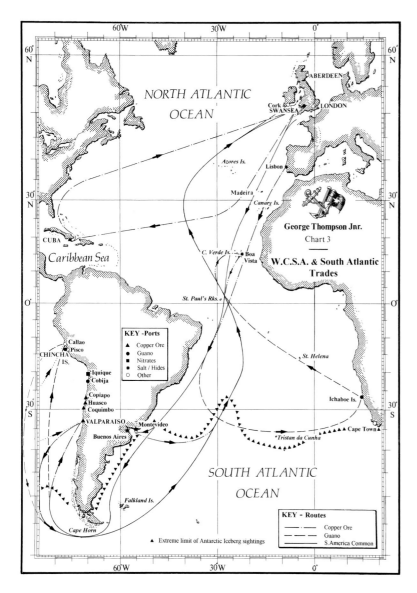

Chart 4 WCSA and South Atlantic Trades.

Homeward bound, vessels headed out into the Pacific until in longitude 90° West, before heading south for the Horn, thereby avoiding the Humboldt Current setting towards the north. Once round the Horn, they headed out into the South Atlantic to optimise the easterlies and the north-east-setting Southern Ocean Current before turning with the south-east trade winds for the Equator, passing close east again of St Paul's Rocks, and north-west across the north-east trade winds until in latitude 30° North, longitude 40° West. From this position, with westerly wind systems taking over, the vessels tracked north-east, passing west of the Azores, for the Western Approaches.

The hazards of navigation and sailing conditions in the Drake Passage to the south of the islands forming the southern tip of South America, of which Cape Horn is the best-known feature, were exacerbated by the risks posed by drifting icebergs that were swept up the south-east coast of South America by the Falklands Current, swinging eastwards across the South Atlantic on the latitude of the southern tip of Africa in all seasons. The tracks described above, along with those followed by ships on the South American salt, and the Ichaboe guano trades, are shown on Chart 3.

The Peruvian Guano Trade

A 2-ton sample of Peruvian guano had first been shipped to Britain in 1840 by the Lima house of Quiros, Allier & Co.; the first full cargo of guano to be shipped out of the Chincha Islands arrived at Callao in T & J Brocklebank's British brig **Bonanza** on 14 February 1841. Thus started an extraordinary trade, which was to survive for three decades, with Britain as the principal recipient.

At all times, title to the guano rested with the Peruvian government; however, extraction, shipping and sale of the product was contracted out to various local and expatriate entities. Initially, extraction from the Chinchas was undertaken by a contractor employing a mixture of slaves from his estates ashore, army deserters and contract labourers. From 1852, the labour of extracting the guano was progressively taken over by indentured Chinese labour, recruited in China and brought to the Chinchas, shamefully, in British-flag ships. The conditions under which this indentured labour force worked was akin to slavery in its worst form, such that in June 1854, a group of

towards the north-east. Rounding Cape Horn, they stood out some miles into the Pacific before striking north, to avoid the lee shore offered by the southern extremity of Chile, thereafter heading in for their initial WCSA destinations, usually Valparaiso or Callao.

nine British shipmasters recently returned from the Chinchas were moved to petition 'the Right Honourable the Lords of the Privy Council of Trade' with a view to Britain intervening to address the situation.[38] The petition described the routine flogging close to death of hapless labourers who had failed to achieve their daily digging quotas, and mass suicides by broken Chinese labourers, not to mention the constant danger of death by collapsed working faces. The petition would appear to have had the impact of enforcing a temporary change of digging contractor, and the expulsion of the overseer responsible for the worst excesses. In 1856, the importation of Chinese indentured labourers was suspended, but new legislation in 1861 once again permitted the introduction of Asiatic colonists, giving rise to one of the most infamous episodes in the labour trade, the 'recruitment' of an estimated 6,584 labourers from the Polynesian islands under circumstances of extreme deception, of whom 2,950 died of disease directly attributable to the recruitment activities on their home islands, a further 3,125 died in Peru or en route to Peru, and only 148 were eventually repatriated alive to their home islands.[39]

Initially, the contract for the charter of vessels, storage and final sale of the guano was vested by the Peruvian government in Quiros, Allier & Co., but in 1842, the prime contract was secured by the British firm, Gibbs Crawley & Co. Peru was at that time at war with Bolivia, and the proceeds from guano sales were used to finance that war; additionally, under early contractual terms Gibbs was required to secure advances to the Peruvian government and provide uniforms for cavalry units of the Peruvian army. Gibbs was to hold the principal guano handling contract until 1861; in the course of this period it worked with other agents, including Quiros, Allier & Co., and Meyers in Liverpool. For a time, following the exposure of the excesses of labour abuse on the Chinchas, Gibbs was also contracted to quarry guano and load ships at the Chinchas, but this did not last long in the politics of Peru.

Quarrying of the guano and loading it into the waiting ships was a primitive, dangerous and wasteful process. Exploitation of the guano was entirely by hand tools; from the working face, the guano was carried in barrows or on a primitive hand-propelled railway system to cliff-top canvas shoots, known as *mangueras*. Two large (ship) and two small (boat) *mangueras* were provided; ships either warped directly under the *mangueras* or loaded by way of boats fed from the shoots. Either way, the loading system was extremely wasteful, an estimated 12 per cent of the guano being lost in dust and sunken loading boats;

there was also constant risk of damage to ships loading under the *mangueras* rolling their spars against the cliffs. It was not until the latter end of the trade that the Peruvian government invested in a loading jetty. The labourers were tasked with daily extract quotas, variously reported, but in the region of 4 tons per day. Work in the arid conditions was extremely arduous and dangerous; working face falls and unblocking choked *mangueras* claimed many lives.

Ships engaged in the guano trade were either chartered in Europe, at Valparaiso or Callao. About one-third of all ships loading at the Chinchas were ex-Australia, and about half had carried an outwards cargo to the west coast of South America. All vessels had to initially be cleared inwards at Callao by the government and thence to Pisco, where they picked up bags and water. Owing to the high instance of ship loss among those engaged in the guano trade, from 1854 Lloyd's Register undertook a structural survey of all vessels at Pisco on behalf of Gibbs, before they went on charter. Once arrived at the Chinchas, a vessel initially exchanged its ballast for guano loaded by way of the ship's boats, and then had to wait its turn to go under the *mangueras* or for the availability of boats to trans-ship cargo out to it; delays, which could often run to months, could be exacerbated by heavy swells preventing loading operations. At times more than 150 ships could be waiting off the islands to load. Supplies were brought out to the waiting ships from Pisco by local boats. It is interesting to note that William Russell Grace, founder of the famous American Grace Line, made his initial fortune capitalising upon the opportunities offered in the Chinchas by running a store ship out of Pisco.

To protect the ship from the injurious effects of guano, the hold had to be carefully dunnaged, both to keep the pumps clear, and to raise the centre of gravity of the cargo mass; it was usual to line the hold with bagged guano before shooting in the bulk product. Local labour was used to level the bulk guano into the wings of the hold.[40]

Once loading had been completed, vessels had once again to clear out through Pisco and Callao, a time-consuming process much resented by the masters. Under the terms of the charter, masters were permitted to uplift at Callao whatever additional cargo to owners' account they might have capacity for before dispatching. Homeward-bound vessels invariably called at Queenstown or Cork for orders; from thence the cargo was routed either to London's West India Docks (70 per cent), or to one of the 'outports' of the trade, Liverpool, Bristol, Hamburg, Leith, Glasgow, Aberdeen, etc.

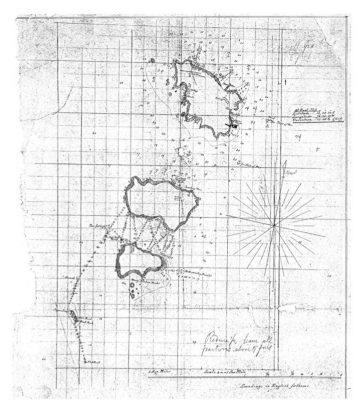

Above: Reproduction of Sketch Survey of Chincha Islands by the master of HMS *Alarm*, 1857.

Below and right: Reproduction of three etchings of the Chincha Islands from the *Illustrated London News*.
1. Manguera (canvas shoot) used to load boats, North Island.
2. North Island guano workings.
3. Shipping massed between North and South Island.

The guano trade from the Chinchas to Britain peaked in 1858, with 302,207 tons imported; a further high of 243,434 tons occurred in 1870, but thereafter the trade steadily declined, petering out in the 1880s. Its demise was a combination of Peruvian government greed in respect to prices demanded, resource depletion, and the development of artificial fertilisers, especially super-phosphates, which were cheaper and more effective. At its peak, the trade provided employment for a large number of British ships.[41]

The guano charter party allowed vessels to load a weight of guano no more than one-third above the vessel's (new) register tonnage, unless specific permission had been given by the charterers following survey; this was a curious multiplier, given that register tonnage was based on a measure of internal volume, and had only indirect correlation to deadweight. An analysis of Gibbs' Guano Registers[42] demonstrates this in respect to GTJ ships loading at the Chincha Islands:

Ship	Register Tons	Loaded	per cent over GRT
Jane Boyd	387	532	37.5
"	387	509	31.5
Lord Metcalf	510	686	34.5
Oliver Cromwell	478	753	57.5
Alexander Harvey	292	342	17.1

Oliver Cromwell, as we will see, was the first Hood-built ship for GTJ with an Aberdeen bow. The high excess of deadweight over register tonnage in her case is a clear indicator of the efficacy of the Aberdeen bow in minimising registered tonnage within a given size of ship.

Birth of the Australian Service

Following her Peruvian guano voyage, **Neptune** undertook a single Mauritian sugar run prior to embarking in 1846 upon the first sailing of a GTJ ship from London to Sydney, arriving at that port on 30 November. The days of GTJ's ships operating on the Aberdeen Line berth in their own right were yet ten years hence and **Neptune** was chartered for the extent of the outward voyage to the Australian Line of Packet Ships, promoted by Henry & Calvert Toulmin of 31 Great St Helens Place and Devitt & Moore of 9 Billiter Street, one of several non-vessel-owning lines operated out of London to the Australian colonies by loading brokers; the same outward loading brokers were used by Duthie's ships. **Neptune** loaded at the London Dock.

From advertisements in the *Sydney Morning Herald*, we can gain a fascinating glimpse of the cargoes carried on the trades to and from Australia at that time:

Neptune Inwards [Sydney] – 30 November 1846:	
Spanish wine	25 pipes, 70 hogsheads, 90 quarter casks
Madeira wine	15 hogsheads, 3 quarter casks
Brandy	4 hogsheads
Bottled beer	291 casks
Beer	175 casks
Geneva	100 cases
B.P. rum	21 casks
Bottled Vinegar	25 casks, 20 half hogsheads
Ginger	11 casks
Vermicelli	2 cases
Refined sugar	20 hogsheads
Mustard	20 cases
Currants and raisins	13 casks, 4 barrels, 6 bundles
Almonds	6 bundles
Split peas	9 casks
Sardines	2 cases
Tobacco	15 kegs
Thread	6 bales
Canvas	9 bales
Tinplate	50 iron casks, 90 boxes
Iron	565 bars, 34 bundles
Phosphorus	1 case
Vitriol	6 carboys
Isinglass	1 bale
Aquafortia	1 case
Gunpowder	19 quarter barrels, 24 kegs
Shot	4 casks
Millstones	6
Pipe boxes	100
Boilers	34

Camp ovens and covers	150
Ranges	9
Wheels	97
Merchandise and effects	20 kegs, 94 casks, 8 hogsheads, 9 crates 155 cases, 94 bundles, 59 bales, 12 packages
Stationery	3 boxes
Books	6 cases
Neptune Homewards – 22 February 1847	
720 bales wool	
251 Hides	
72 casks tallow	
2,000 horns	
60 bags bones	
85 bags hoofs	
9 cases leather	
135 casks black oil	
97 bundles whalebones	
34 casks coconut oil	
2,400 spokes	
1 case gum	
3 cases shoes	

Significantly, **Neptune** must have been considered a fast enough ship to be designated the homewards Post Office Packet for February 1847. She also had 'good accommodation for passengers'. The black oil and whalebones would have arisen from whaling operations 'on the line' (the Equator) and 'bay' whaling along the east coast of New South Wales and Tasmania. Coconut oil frequently formed part of early return cargoes from Australia. Before the technique of drying coconut flesh to produce copra had been developed, whereby the added value of the residual flesh was secured, coconut oil was extracted by primitive pressing methods in the Pacific Islands and trans-shipped in casks through Sydney.

Following the commissioning of **Neptune**, GTJ went for nearly two-and-a-half years without introducing a new ship. Walter Hood's yard in this time built just four small coastal vessels for other owners; times were clearly hard. Over the period spanning the end of 1845/beginning of 1846, GTJ disposed of his 32/64 interests in **Amity** and 64/64 ownership of **Margaret Hardy**. Then 20 years old and colonial-built of softwood, **Amity** no longer

represented the class of ship upon which GTJ was building his future. Her sale had been advertised in the *Aberdeen Journal* two years earlier:

FOR SALE

As she presently lies in the Harbour.

The well known brig Amity, 312 tons O.M.

Colonial built and substantially doubled with American Elm a few years since – is a very handy vessel carrying upwards of 400 lasts and well adapted for the lumber trades; can be sent to sea with little expense except for provisions.

For particulars apply to Captain Dempster on board

March 1843   George Thompson Junior

Margaret Hardy, on the other hand was a relatively new, well-found vessel. Leaving Port Talbot under tow on 25 January 1845, she suffered the misfortune of going aground on the bar at the harbour entrance. The ship was outward bound for Calcutta with a cargo including 320 tons of coal, cases of copper, wine and India pale ale. She was pulled off, but sank in way of the end of the breakwater, blocking the harbour access channel. With more than twenty ships trapped within the harbour and a further twelve outside awaiting a berth, emotions ran high as attempts were made to clear the channel and restore the port's trade. Charges of misdemeanour were filed against the master, Captain Johnston, the pilot and a tugmaster, but were later dropped. She was finally raised on 10 March, her holds having been filled with empty casks to achieve the necessary buoyancy. About 4ft of her stern had broken off in the interim, and her bowsprit and cutwater had been removed to help clear her obstruction of the channel. Her hull, spars and sails were advertised for auction on 1 April 1845, but the auction did not materialise. GTJ clearly considered repairs to be a viable option, at least as a means of realising some value from his only partially insured asset. GTJ disposed of half of his interest in the vessel to Robert Anderson, shipmaster, in September 1845, and the balance to Anderson in January 1846; in the interim, the repaired vessel had made a voyage from Aberdeen to Danzig. The vessel traded on for a further eleven years under Anderson's ownership before stranding in the River Plate in October 1857, where she was sold to foreign owners.

The year 1847 saw a renewed burst of shipbuilding activity with the commissioning of the 478-ton Hood-built *Oliver Cromwell*, GTJ's first ship-rigged vessel and the first of a trio of near-sister vessels designed for the liner trades. *Oliver Cromwell* was the first GTJ/Hood vessel designed with an Aberdeen bow, and her internal construction also introduced iron diagonal knees to Hood buildings. Her hull form is vividly described in an account of her subsequent arrival in Sydney in the *Sydney Morning Herald*:[43]

The peculiarity of [her] construction consists in adaptation of the fine, projecting entrance (previously confined to steamers), with an additional alteration in the stem, which is placed at a great angle with the keel; by this means the bow is run up into a strong and solid **beak**, such as the Roman war-galleys of old are represented to have had. On the apex of this beak, whose elongated prow supersedes the usual **outside** rails, the figure-head is placed, in firm and graceful prominence; and such is the distance betwixt the foremast and this point that, in stowing the fore-top-mast staysail, the hands so employed are completely within-board. The beam of the ship appeared to be disproportionate to her length, but Captain Alexander assured us that this was by no means the fact, and spoke in the strongest terms of her stability and weatherly qualities, affirming that, in sailing by, her peculiar prow imparted immense advantage, the edge, as it were, of the axe, instead of the heel, dividing the opposing sea through which the vessel **draws** with comparative ease and silence, as contrasted with the **boring** of the common bluff bowed ship, which groans and grinds and works amidst the crumbling crests' yeasty billows. The solidity of this conformation was warmly advocated by Captain Alexander, who averred that ships so constructed are much less liable to leak at the wood ends, whilst they, at the same time, possess a superior capacity and stability with a lesser degree of immersion.

While *Oliver Cromwell* and her two succeeding sisters had extremely finely shaped fore bodies and significantly raked masts, their heavy overhanging square poops, which were a marque of Hood-built ships for some years, detracted in my view from their otherwise handsome profiles. They were nonetheless distinctive liner service ships, designed for speed.

Oliver Cromwell's first voyage was on the Sydney service, under the command of Captain Alexander Alexander, formerly of the

SALE OF QUEBEC TIMBER.

There will be exposed for sale, by public roup, on the ground at the back of Messrs CATTO, THOMSON, & Co.'s Rope-work, on WEDNESDAY 26th July current,

THE Cargo of TIMBER now discharging from the Barque "LORD METCALFE," from Quebec—consisting of
20,000 Feet YELLOW PINE.
2,500 „ RED PINE.
3,000 „ ELM.
3,000 „ WHITE OAK.
500 SPRUCE DEALS.
1 M. 5 C. PIPE STAVES.
1 „ 5 „ W. I. W. O. STAVES.
3,000 Running Feet of DANZIC DEALS.
A few Fathoms of HEMLOCK LATHWOOD.

The Timber is of a very superior description; the Yellow Pine being of the same quality as that imported by the Lord Metcalfe last Fall, which was so much valued by the Trade. Sale of the Staves and Lathwood to commence on Water-loo Quay, at 11 o'clock; and of the Timber at 12 o'clock noon. Credit will be given as usual.

GEO. THOMPSON, Jun.

Aberdeen, 11th July, 1848.

Aberdeen, 10th July, 1848.

FOR QUEBEC.

THE BARQUE LORD METCALFE, 510 Tons Register, A. 1 at Lloyd's, WILLIAM ROSIE, Commander, Is now on the Berth for QUEBEC, and will be despatched on SATURDAY the 29th July current. This splendid Trader has excellent accommodation for Passengers, and is well-known for her fast sailing qualities. For Passage Fares, apply to Captain ROSIE, on board; or to GEO. THOMPSON, Jun., 40, Marischal Street.

Aberdeen, 12th July, 1848.

Timber sale and sailing advertisement from the *Aberdeen Journal*.

Prince of Wales; again outward loading was brokered by Henry & Calvert Toulmin and Devitt & Moore. After discharge in Sydney, she ballasted to Valparaiso, thence to Cobija in Bolivia, where she loaded guano for Liverpool. Thereafter, for the balance of the decade, she was engaged on the WCSA trade from Britain, carrying home guano from Peru or nitrate of soda from Iquique.

The otherwise inland state of Bolivia was in those days connected to the Pacific by the province of Antofagasta, of which Cobija, lying on the Pacific shore of the Atacama Desert, was its development port. The success of Cobija was critical to the economy of Bolivia, which otherwise had to pay exorbitant tariffs on imports and exports crossing Chilean or Peruvian territory. In the 1840s, English and Chilean finance had been invested into exploiting the guano deposits at Cobija, and GTJ ships uplifted a total of six cargoes from that source in the period 1845 to 1847. In the War of the Pacific 1879 to 1884, Bolivia lost the province of Antofagasta to Chile, and thereby her direct access to the sea, for all time.

With the delivery of **Oliver Cromwell**, GTJ disposed of his 52/64 interest in **Queen Victoria** and 64/64 interest in **Mungo Park**. At the same time, he bought all the shares in the 1845 495-ton barque **Lord Metcalfe**, and placed her on the Quebec timber trade, filling the void created by the sales of **Amity** and **Queen Victoria**. GTJ was thus progressively replacing his earlier tonnage with larger and more competent units.

A new master was appointed to **Jane Boyd** in April 1847, Captain Isaac Merchant. A newcomer to GTJ's service, he had probably come to notice in 1839, when half-owner and master of the vessel **Happy Return** working in the coastal trade out of Aberdeen. Merchant was to feature broadly in the marine, commercial and personal affairs of the Thompson and Henderson families over the next half-century. In the short term, he commanded a number of GTJ's prime ships, and would marry William Henderson's sister, Isobel, in May 1851.

In May 1847, GTJ commissioned the 478-ton Hood-built clipper barque **Phoenician**; built with a pronounced Aberdeen bow, she rapidly established a reputation as a fast sailer and probably marked GTJ's entry into the 'racer' market for which his later clipper ships would become so renowned. A virtual sister of **Oliver Cromwell** apart from her barque rig, she was clearly an outstanding ship of her time, for she attracted a number of depictions both in paintings, an etching in the *Illustrated London News*, and at least one model. She was described five years later in the same periodical:[44]

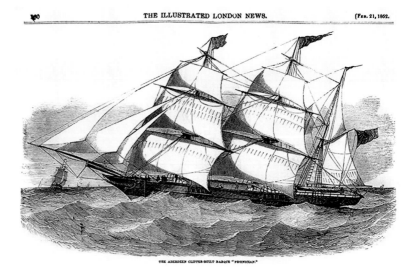

An etching of the barque **Phoenician** from the *Illustrated London News*.

Her length of cut keel is 122 feet; rake of stem, 25 feet, rake of sternpost, 7 feet; extreme breadth, 27 feet 5 inches; depth of hold 19 feet 1 inch. Sailing and carrying powers were never more happily combined than in this vessel, which has discharged 780 tons of deadweight, and invariably made such passages as have not been surpassed either by British or American-going ships.

It is curious that having ship-rigged **Oliver Cromwell**, GTJ should revert to barque rig for **Phoenician.** I can only surmise that the company wished to compare the efficiency of the two rigs in a pair of sister vessels; certainly, all new tonnage built for the company post- **Phoenician**, was ship-rigged.

Phoenician was commanded for her first four-and-a-half years by Hugh Sproat, a commander new to GTJ's service but one who brought with him a wealth of experience on the Australian trade and who, significantly, was known to F.G. Dalgety,[45] ship's agent and trader in Melbourne, who was to develop a very long-standing relationship with Thompsons in the future. However, her initial three voyages saw her running out successively to Manila, Mauritius and India before settling down and building her reputation on the Sydney run, where she was to serve until sold in 1861.

A model of *Phoenician*.
(The Parker Gallery)

Phoenician sailed on her maiden voyage to Sydney on 18 April 1849, arriving at that port on 21 July, after a creditable passage (for those days) of ninety-four days. Following discharge in Sydney, the vessel then made a round trip to the central Pacific slands, carrying a light load of provisions out to Tahiti, returning with a cargo of Pacific Island produce from Tahiti and Upolu in the Navigator Islands (the island upon which Apia, the capital of Western Samoa, is now sited). To a former commander of a Pacific Islands trading vessel, the reconciliation of her inwards cargo manifest reads (and smells) as fresh as the day it was loaded – 8,900 coconuts, 137 casks coconut oil, 89 casks black oil, 19 tons pearlshell, 10 tons arrowroot and 101 bundles of whalebone.[46] One can almost reminiscently savour the nip of the copra bug; almost ...!

Departing Sydney for London two months later, on 19 January 1850, *Phoenician*'s first homeward cargo manifest from the colony reflects an interesting blend of early colonial pastoral and industrial development immediately before the discovery of gold in New South Wales, and Pacific Island trans-shipment produce, some, if not all, of which she had brought in from her recent Pacific Island voyage:[47]

4,511 ingots	Copper
315 bags	Copper ore
1,606 bales	Wool
310 casks	Tallow
7,636	Ox horns

1 case	Pearls
5,000	Treenails
20 tons	Old iron
128 casks	Coconut oil
104 bundles	Whalebone
71 casks	Black [whale] oil
19 tons	Pearl shell

Wool exports from New South Wales had increased fourfold over the previous decade, reflecting the development of the merino wool industry based on the pioneering work of John MacArthur, a former officer of the renegade New South Wales Corps; tallow was a by-product of the sheep industry.

Treenails, hardwood spikes used for fastening plank strakes to frames on wooden ships, and ox horns, to be ground on delivery for fertiliser, were utilised as dunnage to fill the fine ends of the ship and to provide a bed and chocking for other cargo.

The discovery of coal in the colony had facilitated the local smelting of copper ore mined in the Orange area into copper bar form, pre-dating by many years the demise of Swansea as a copper smelting location.

On 30 December 1847, **Alexander Harvey** berthed at Swansea with the last cargo of copper ore that a GTJ ship would carry into that port from Santiago de Cuba. Fourteen months later, **Agnes Blaikie** docked from Huasco with the last cargo of copper ore by a GTJ ship from WCSA, closing an era in the development of GTJ's foreign-going business. Over the course of eight years, five of GTJ's ships had found employment on the run from Cuba to Swansea, bringing in a total of fifty cargoes of copper ore; over the concurrent period, eight copper ore cargoes had been uplifted from the west coast of South America and one from South Australia.

Shortly into 1848, **Michael Williams**, outward bound coal-laden for the WCSA, was burnt out at sea off Patagonia. She had fallen prey to one of the most serious hazards afflicting merchant vessels – spontaneous combustion of a coal cargo, usually associated with loading the coal in a wet condition. Luckily, there were no casualties, the crew being landed safely at Montevideo; GTJ had held a 32/64 terminal interest in the ship.

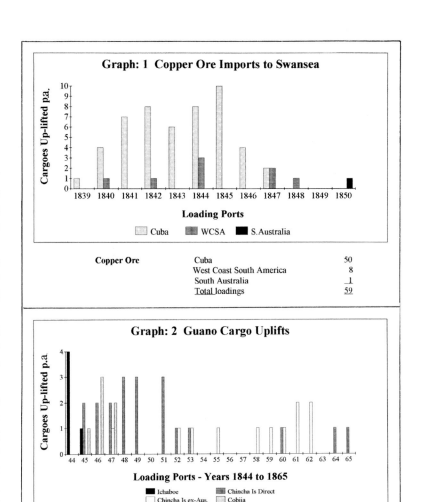

Graph: 1 Copper Ore Imports to Swansea

Copper Ore	Cuba	50
	West Coast South America	8
	South Australia	1
	Total loadings	59

Graph: 2 Guano Cargo Uplifts

Guano	Ichaboe		5
	Chincha Is direct	20	
	Chincha Is ex-Australia	11	
	Chincha Is sub-total	31	31
	Cobija		6
	Total loadings		42

4
PASSING SQUALLS WITH BRIGHT PERIODS –
1848 TO 1859

While clearly a leader within the community, George Thompson Junior was by nature a retiring man and it took significant solicitation to persuade him to enter public life with his election as Dean of Guild in 1840. In November 1842, he was elected to Aberdeen City Council as councillor for the First Ward. His three-year term of duty seems to have passed without particular note, and when completed he did not seek re-election. However, in November 1847 he was again elected to the council, and was immediately invited to become Lord Provost[1] and Chief Magistrate. He served with distinction as Lord Provost for three years, but though pressed to accept a second term, he declined. He continued in the council for a further two years without office.

His term of office as Lord Provost was notable for the initiation of a number of schemes that underscored his compassionate nature, including the laying of the foundation stone for the city poorhouse in 1848. Other significant occasions at which GTJ presided included centennial celebrations commemorating the opening of the Robert Gordon's Hospital; the commissioning of the southern branch of the Aberdeen Railway in 1848; and the granting of the freedom of the city to Sir Robert Peel at a banquet in the old Town Hall in October 1849.

The high point of GTJ's tenure of office as Lord Provost and Chief Magistrate, however, was undoubtedly the arrival of Queen Victoria in Aberdeen en route to Balmoral for her first visit to her new holiday home on Deeside. The Queen, accompanied by Prince Albert and their three children, embarked in the Royal Yacht *Victoria and Albert* on 5 September 1848, and after a triumphal (but seasick) voyage up the coast, arrived off Aberdeen at 0800 in the morning of 7 September, a day ahead of schedule and without notice. Preparations were not completed for the Queen's arrival; a triumphal arch erected on Waterloo Quay was still in scaffolding; a special wooden jetty built out from Waterloo Quay to accommodate the Royal Yacht had not been red-carpeted; the Lord Lieutenant of the county, the Earl of Aberdeen, was a 15-mile horse ride away at Haddo House; and Lord Provost Thompson was asleep in bed. Contingency plans were put into effect to save the situation; GTJ boarded the Royal Yacht and sought the Queen's intentions. Luckily for the embarrassed burghers, she decided not to disembark until the following day, and that afternoon received civic and academic loyal addresses n the Royal Yacht. Prince Albert received the freedom of the city; later, he went ashore and received honorary doctorates from King's and Marischal Colleges.

The following day at 0830 hours, the Queen and her royal party disembarked to be received by Lord Provost Thompson, the Earl of Aberdeen and municipal, military and academic dignitaries. An estimated 80,000 Aberdonians turned out to wish their Queen well on her way to Balmoral, the first time a sovereign had passed through Aberdeen since Charles II in 1650. The ceremony of the

Queen's disembarkation was recorded by the local artist, Peter Cleland, in the form of a diorama, the original of which now hangs in the Town House; GTJ features in the right middle foreground and Alexander Nicol (of whom we shall hear more in Chapter 5), Master of Shoreworks and Provost of Old Aberdeen, is in the left middle foreground. The triumphal arch erected upon Waterloo Quay for the occasion subsequently fell into disrepair, and was re-erected at GTJ's country seat at Pitmedden near Dyce. Cleland's diorama is reproduced in the Colour Section.

We may gather an insight into the public character of GTJ from Lachlan Mackinnon, who relates a story told to him by his father, of GTJ presiding as Lord Provost at a formal dinner. After the interminable speeches (Mackinnon estimated twenty) so beloved of that time, GTJ divested himself of his chains and badge of office, and slamming them on the table before him, audibly sighed 'Lie ye there, Provost Tamson', indicating thereby his wish to conclude the evening on an informal note. Mackinnon describes GTJ as a tall, slightly lame, dignified, but kindly and approachable man with a mischievous sense of humour, who enjoyed good company, good conversation, and in all moderation, a good bottle of wine. 'If he drew a half bottle of port for me in own house, he was imperative that – while his own age might stand in the way – the younger man at least should leave no "heeltaps".'

Storm clouds were, however, gathering on the horizon of GTJ's business life. The Factory Act of 1844 had reduced the working hours of children to six-and-a-half hours per day and those of women and adolescents to twelve hours per day. This seriously impacted upon the economic operation of the mills, which largely derived their labour from these categories of workers. In May 1848, Aberdeen's two largest textile firms, Leys, Masson and Co. and Alex Hadden and Sons, both failed, depriving 3,000 people of their livelihood; both were heavily indebted to the North of Scotland Bank. Repeal of the Corn Laws in 1846 (in the movement towards which, GTJ had played an active part), precipitated by the potato blight in Ireland, permitted cheap corn imports, depreciating the price of home-grown grain. A general recession hit the Aberdeen economy; shipbuilding was badly hit and railway work was partially suspended. In all, sixty-one firms failed, mostly corn merchants and cotton spinners; with losses aggregating £25 million, the North of Scotland Bank found itself in serious trouble.

The key to many of the bank's troubles may be found in the preamble to a libel action successfully pursued by the Bank in 1857 against John Duncan (arising from a railway battle between the Great North of Scotland Railway Company, of which GTJ was a director and the Aberdeen, Peterhead and Fraserburgh Railway Co. promoted by Duncan), in which it was averred that:[2]

a few years ago, the character, credit and stability of the [North of Scotland] Bank were seriously affected, in consequence of the very large losses it had sustained through the mismanagement and mal-practices of the manager at that time, and some of the persons who had been for some time, and particularly in or about 1846, in the management and direction of the affairs and business of the Bank. The parties alluded to, it was discovered, had been in the practice of drawing from the funds of the bank large sums of money for the purposes of their individual speculation, and of allowing large advances to be made to others, without giving or obtaining any security, or adequate security, therefor [sic]. The consequence was that it was found that considerably more than one half of the capital of the bank had been lost, over and above the whole of what was called the 'reserve fund'.

The 'liberal principles' upon which the bank had been founded had caught up with it! On 9 May 1848, Henry Paterson was sacked as manager. He had unsecured drawings on the bank of £44,050 – a significant sum for an official earning a salary of £500 per annum; he was subsequently jailed. Paterson owned shares in a number of GTJ's ships, and these shares were subsequently either sold or placed in the trusteeship of the comptor of the prison. Paterson was but one of a number of bank directors and officials who had invested in the Aberdeen and Great North of Scotland Railway Company using borrowings from the bank. These included:

William Adam	£10,000
Thomas Blaikie	£15,000
George Thompson Jnr	£10,000
Alexander Anderson	£15,000
Alexander Jopp	£10,000
Henry Paterson	£22,500

It is interesting to note the commonality of this shareholding pattern reflected in a number of GTJ's ships at that time and, perhaps not altogether surprisingly, in early 1849 Shand, Blaikie, Jopp and Anderson disinvested themselves of their shareholdings in *Agnes Blaikie*, *Prince of Wales* and *Neptune*.

The dismissal of Paterson was but the start of the remedial work necessary to secure the future of the bank. Textile failures had cost it £160,000, while advances to enterprises promoted by Adam & Anderson amounted to more than £200,000, of which £100,000 was unsecured, bad debt. William Adam and Robert Johnston left the board with Paterson; significantly, GTJ remained on the committee of management. Then, in a further shake-up at a shareholders' meeting in November 1849, Anderson, Jopp, Alexander Milne and GTJ left the board. Whether GTJ resigned on a point of honour or was removed is not clear, but given his character and his position in local society, I sense the former; certainly his co-shareholdings with a number of the key players in the bank's problems must have been an embarrassment. Significantly, he returned to the board of the North of Scotland Bank in 1862 and remained a director until 1881; none of the other former directors were so invited.

Ship		Built	Tonnage (New)	Length				Breadth		Depth	Notes
				'36 Rules	'54 Rules	Overall	Keel	'36 Rules	'54 Rules		
OLIVER CROMWELL		1847	478	148.5	148.7			24.6	27.3	18.9	1
PHOENECIAN		1847	478	146.0	147.0	*154*	122	24.6	27.4	19.1	2
JOHN BUNYAN		1848	467	137.3	150.3			25.0	27.7	18.3	3
WALTER HOOD	Register	1852	918	179.2			161	30.2	*32.9*	20.9	4
	Lloyds Reg.		918	172.2				30.2	*32.9*	20.9	5
	"Empire"					204	170		33.0	21	6

Notes:
1. 1836 dimensions ex-Aberdeen Register of Ships
2. Keel length from article in I.L.N.; Overall = keel length + forward rake + after rake (dimensions ex-I.L.N.)
3. 1836 Registered Length in fact probably length for Tonnage Measurement (MacGregor and see below)
4. Given length of keel ex-Register, unlikely that '36 Length is in fact Register, more likely to be length for Tonnage Measurement (see below). '54 Rules breadth reconstructed from L.R. Build Certificate.
5. The difference in L.R. length aloft with the Register Length is curious, and given identical other dimensions, is thought to be a clerical error.
6. Information derived from Sydney newspaper "Empire" 09:08:53, probably based on information given by Commander. Length overall is probably measured from taffrail to fore side of figurehead. Disparate length of keel from that in Register is curious; possible difference of interpretation of cut-off between raked stem and flat of keel.

PHOENECIAN / WALTER HOOD   Relationship of Dimensions   (Development of work by D.R.MacGregor)

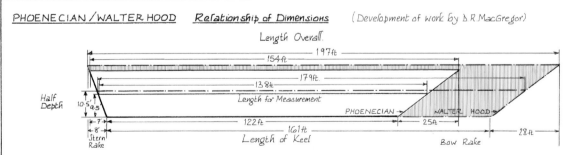

Assumptions
1. The dimensions are developed about rude trapeziums reflecting vessels with Aberdeen Bows.
2. The dimensions for PHOENECIAN / OLIVER CROMWELL / JOHN BUNYAN are in accordance with data recorded in the Aberdeen Register of Ships, and an article on PHOENECIAN contained in the *Illustrated London News*, 21:02:1852.
3. The dimensions for WALTER HOOD are in accordance with data recorded in the Aberdeen Register of Ships and an article contained in the Sydney NSW *Empire*, 09:08:1853. The length of keel for the vessel is per the Register of Ships.
4. WALTER HOOD's form has been extrapolated on the basis of length of keel and register depth, assuming the same angle of rake of bow as PHOENECIAN (the vessel being described as an 'improved sister' of that vessel).

A reconstruction of dimensions attributed to Hood-built vessels with Aberdeen bows.

If GTJ's other business interests had taken a downturn, shipping continued to develop apace. In March 1848, he had taken delivery as subscribing owner (32/64) of **John Bunyan**, together with her very slightly larger sisters **Phoenician** and **Oliver Cromwell** the previous year. This marked GTJ's progression from small, heavy freighting ships suitable for uplifting bulk high-density cargoes, to those with the emphasis on speed and optimised internal capacity, suitable for the emerging Australian liner and China tea trades. The various published dimensions of **John Bunyan**, her two sister ships, and indeed later vessels built with the Aberdeen bow, give rise to significant confusion, and are indicative of the breadth of interpretation available to the various interested parties. MacGregor initially believed the **John Bunyan** to have been lengthened in later life,[3] but came to the inevitable conclusion that within the same published depth, an almost identical tonnage could not be contained within the ship's originally published length and breadth envelope, and that those dimensions were in fact measurements made for tonnage calculations as opposed to register dimensions; his reconstruction of these measurements along register dimension lines convincingly demonstrate them to be nearly identical to measurements later attributed to the ship under the 1854 Tonnage Rules; as such, **John Bunyan** had near identical dimensions to her two immediate predecessors.[4] In the above figure (p. 59), I have developed MacGregor's work to include the even more confusing dimensions variously attributed to **Walter Hood**, built as an enlarged sister of the earlier trio, some four years later.

John Bunyan was described in her Lloyd's Register build certificate as:

> a highly credible vessel either as regards workmanship, materials or design; has the projecting [Aberdeen] bow carried to a moderate extent with full length figurehead, raised quarterdeck about 3ft in height run over main deck for the space of one beam.

In fact, an annotation on the side of the certificate clearly shows the raised quarterdeck extending over two beam spaces.

John Bunyan's construction utilised iron hanging beam knees to both hold and deck beams, and iron staple rather than wooden lodging knees squaring the hold beams, both devices to reduce weight and, in the case of hanging knees, to optimise internal volume. Her hull was constructed from oak main members, with American elm, Stettin and British oak and teak planking successively from the keel. Her decks were Quebec yellow pine, presumably for lightness.

Under the Charter Act of 1833, the Honourable East India Company had lost its monopoly on the China trade. Technically, foreigners were still debarred from the import trade into the United Kingdom, but there had been progressive relaxations of the strictures on trade imposed by the Navigation Acts, especially for Americans. The repeal of the Navigation Acts in 1849 for all but the UK coastal trades opened the prospect of stiff competition for British shipowners on the China trades, especially from the Americans. Gold had been discovered in California in 1848, and for Yankee clippers engaged in the transportation of people and supplies from the east coast to the west to furnish the rush, the relatively short ballast run to China thereafter provided the potential for a valuable, fast cross trade cargo on the homewards run.

The British shipowner, shielded from competition by the Navigation Acts, had been slow to capitalise upon new shipbuilding and outfitting technologies, and the incentives created by revised tonnage regulations, which hitherto had wagered against fast hull forms. The Americans, on the other hand, had been forced to embark upon new technologies and labour-saving devices. They had an abundant source of cheap natural materials for building ships, albeit their softwood ships became waterlogged after a time and lost their fighting edge. According to Lubbock,[5] an American ship could be built for less than £12 per ton, while a British-built ship would cost £15 per ton or more.

GTJ was one of the very few British shipowners who strongly advocated free trade and the abolition of the Navigation Acts. In **John Bunyan** he had a ship that measured up to the challenge thrown down to the British shipowner by the Acts' repeal and he placed his new vessel on the China trade under the command of Captain John Thomson (ex-**Mayflower**). When **John Bunyan** slipped from Woosung on 26 January 1849, with the first tea cargo to be carried in a GTJ bottom, competition from Americans entering the trade was close over the horizon.

John Bunyan was to serve exclusively on this route for the next seven-and-a-half years, developing a reputation from the outset as one of the fastest carriers on the trade. Her outward passages from London often took in Hong Kong as a discharge port, and thence Shanghai and/or Woosung, some 12 miles upstream from Shanghai. Passage times were very much governed by the prevailing monsoon winds in the China Sea. From October to April, the North-East Monsoon provided a strong passage wind particularly during December and January, for ships making down towards the Sunda Straits between Java and Sumatra; the South-West Monsoon, however, blew from May to September, forcing ships to beat to windward down the China Sea, often occupying an extra month to make the signal station at Anjer in the Sunda Strait. Some ships during the South-West Monsoon would take the eastern route by way of the Ombai Strait to the west of Timor. All but one of *John Bunyan's* eight voyages on the China tea trade were progressed through favourable monsoons. Her performance, though never surpassing her second voyage, nonetheless held out well when measured against the average of the remainder of the tea fleet sailing in the same monsoon periods, until her latter three voyages on the China tea trade when ship and commander were apparently becoming tired:[6]

Season	John Bunyan	Tea Fleet Average	Best of Class
1848–49	110	128	109 (Liverpool)
1850	102	118	102
1850–51	112	114	99 (US)
1851–52	108	114	92 (US)
1852–53	124	124	105
1853–54	178*	127	96 (US)
1854–55	121	111	91 (US)
1855–56	122	114	92

* Adverse monsoon.

The average figures for the rest of the tea fleet reflect the general technological improvement of the fleet over those early years of a newly unregulated trade.

The US east to west coast trade via Cape Horn demanded fast, strong ships of a size significantly larger than their British counterparts. The first American ship to enter the China trade into London was the clipper *Oriental.* Her performance on her maiden voyage from New York to Hong Kong and return, coupled with her record outward passage to Hong Kong on her second voyage, caught the eye of brokers, such that she was offered a London freight of £6 per ton of 40 cu.ft, compared with the going rate of £3 10s per ton of 50 cu.ft being offered to British ships at that time, a premium of 114 per cent per cubic foot loaded. The vessel made a

record passage to London, port to port, of ninety-nine days with a cargo of 1,618 tons of tea with total freights of £9,600 (US$ 48,000) equal to 69 per cent of her original US$ 70,000 build costs.[7] She attracted much favourable comment when she berthed in the West India Dock on 3 December 1850, and such was the interest in the vessel that when she subsequently dry-docked in Richard Green's Blackwall yard following discharge, her lines were measured on behalf of the Admiralty by a surveyor, later to become Secretary of Lloyd's Register, Bernard Waymouth, assisted by another Lloyd's surveyor, Cornish. Waymouth was later to be consulted in the design of GTJ's tea clipper masterpieces *Thermopylæ* (I) and *Salamis*.

John Bunyan's performance on her second voyage went largely unheralded in Britain at the time, but with national pride now bruised, a champion was sought and found in that ship. True, her 102-day voyage had enjoyed a favourable monsoon, while *Oriental* had headed into the monsoon on her record-breaking passage; however, *John Bunyan* had sailed from Shanghai, some 860 miles further up the China coast. The *Illustrated London News* of 21 February 1852 eulogised that:

> The JOHN BUNYAN is burden per register 525 tons old and 446 new measure, and she invariably discharged 716 tons of tea, while the ORIENTAL and other fast American clippers only carry a trifle over their register tonnage. Here, then, the British build realise the desideratum of combining fast sailing with large carrying powers, and this it is which gives them the strongest claims to preference.

Clearly shipbrokers who fixed homeward tea clippers did not have the benefit of reading the *Illustrated London News*!

While GTJ's sights were undoubtedly centring upon liner trades to the east and Australia, his commitment to the North Atlantic emigrant and timber trades continued. Early in 1849, he purchased outright the 401-ton barque *Richibucto*, built at Richibucto, New Brunswick, in 1836. With his new ship came her long-time commander, Captain Herman Gansen, an officer well experienced in the Quebec timber trade, a trade in which the ship was to continue to GTJ's account for the next twelve years. *Richibucto* replaced the *Lord Metcalfe* on the Quebec trade, which in turn had displaced *Queen Victoria* two years earlier.

Whether to balance the books and generate cash to face calls from the North of Scotland Bank, or as part of a general trade realignment to concentrate on his emerging core business (I sense the latter), GTJ then disposed of a number of his smaller units hitherto engaged in the copper ore and peripheral trades. In 1849, *Agnes Blaikie* (22/64), *Mayflower* (64/64), *Anemone* (40/64) and *Neptune* (12/64) were sold, to be followed six months later by *Flamingo* (12/64). *Agnes Blaikie* was to be successively owned by Swansea, Bristol and London owners, and was finally lost off Balaklava while on an Admiralty Crimean War charter, run down by the paddle warship HMS *Medina*, on 14 June 1855.[8]

These sales were offset by the 639-ton Hood-built ship *Centurion* joining the fleet in January 1850, with GTJ subscribing owner (24/64). *Centurion* was initially placed in the eastern trade under the command of Captain William Edward.

In March 1850, Walter Hood delivered two interesting brigs to the account of the British Admiralty, specifically built to participate in a belated search for Captain Sir John Franklin, missing since July 1845 when he had last been seen off Lancaster Sound at the start of his ill-fated attempt to find the Northwest Passage to the Orient. The 201-ton brig *Lady Franklin*, named after Franklin's wife, Jane, who was the driving force behind the search effort, and the 113-ton support brig *Sophia*, were built along the well-proven lines of arctic whalers. They were placed under the expedition command of the leading Aberdeen whaling commander, William Penny, at the behest of Lady Jane Franklin, who held Penny in high esteem. The two brigs formed part of an international expeditionary force totalling fifteen ships that in the period 1850–51, searched for traces of Franklin's expedition and his two ships, *Erebus* and *Terror*. Two ships attempted to penetrate the Northwest Passage from the westward, while the remaining thirteen, including the two Hood-built brigs, attempted to follow Franklin's last known track by way of Lancaster Sound. By the close of 1851, hearing rumours of Franklin's expedition having perished at the hands of Eskimos, the expeditions disbanded; *Lady Franklin* and *Sophia* took up commercial whaling on behalf of the Aberdeen Arctic Company.[9]

In early 1850, *Alexander Harvey* (Smith), which since the demise of the Cuban copper trade had been tramping to the Baltic and to Quebec, undertook a single voyage out to Adelaide from Leith with a general cargo including 10,000 fire bricks and building timber. Copper had been discovered in South Australia in the early 1840s, but unlike the Sydney and Melbourne trades, Adelaide suffered a shortage of ships to export the ore. This was initially blamed on the restrictive impact of the Navigation Acts, which precluded the use of German emigrant ships, but in point of fact owners were reluctant to present their ships for what was perceived as a cruel cargo that 'tears our ships to pieces'. *Alexander Harvey* was built for such cargoes and at Adelaide she loaded 400 tons of copper ore for Swansea,[10] sailing on 23 August; nine days later, she put back into port leaking badly after heavy weather had shifted her ore cargo. She was in Adelaide for a further month undergoing repairs. For her cargo to have shifted, she presumably had not erected a trunk (which would have been removed while the vessel was engaged in the timber and general cargo trades). Captain Smith's one voyage in GTJ's service finished upon completion of the voyage, and Captain Middleton took command for the vessel's final voyage under GTJ's colours out to the Chincha Islands for guano.

With his shipping business growing, its centre of activity increasingly London, and with the distractions of his public duties, GTJ took his clerk William Henderson into partnership on 1 January 1850. Thus gelled a remarkable relationship that was to see members of the Thompson and Henderson families jointly associated with the management of the Aberdeen Line in its various forms for at least the next 120 years. Henderson cemented the bond between the two families by marrying GTJ's eldest daughter, Jane Boyd, on 17 February 1852. The match did not apparently meet with initial parental approval, and a charming family story casts GTJ as the unwitting communicant between his home in Golden Square and the office in Marischal Street of *lettres d'amour* between the two lovers, secreted in the lining of his silk top hat.

The discovery of gold at Ophir in New South Wales was declared in April 1851 (the presence of gold in the colony had been known for some ten years but the news had been suppressed for fear of destabilising the fledgling colony), followed shortly thereafter on 8 September 1851 by the Ballarat gold field in Victoria. The first Australian gold rush got under way, with a profound impact upon shipping to the colonies. Almost overnight, more and faster ships were needed to satisfy the outward requirements; against this, the fledgling colonial economy had little to offer in terms of homewards cargoes and there was thus a severe imbalance created, necessitating all but the fastest ships ballasting out of the Australian colonies in search of paying homewards cargoes. The gold rush posed problems for the colony's pastoral economy, and in particular for the masters of ships arriving in the Australian colonies, whose crews deserted en masse to join the bonanza. The situation was graphically described by Captain G.H. Heaton, master of Phillips, Shaw & Lowther's Alexander Hall-built ship **Thomas Arbuthnot**, in a letter to his owners dated 20 August 1851 from Pernambuco. It was published in *The Times* and subsequently reprinted in the *Sydney Morning Herald*:[11]

> Gentlemen, I suppose you have had rumours of the extensive gold fields discovered in New South Wales, causing as sudden a revolution as I believe ever could have visited any country. The colony is completely paralysed. Every man and boy who is capable of lifting a shovel is off, or going off, to the diggings. Stations are in many parts completely deserted; consequently sheep and cattle are left to go and do as they like. Nearly every article of food has gone up, in some cases 200 per cent; and seeing that a great reduction in the grain crops next season must ensue, for want of labour, it will necessarily follow that maintenance for man and beast will be both scarce and high. No doubt there will be extensive emigration from all parts of Europe when once the news gets wind.
>
> We have on board about £800 worth of Australian gold [253 oz[12]], the first shipped from the colony. It was purchased on the spot (in fact dug up before their eyes), by four gentlemen, managing partners of different mercantile firms in Sydney. It is all in lumps, nearly pure, the largest weight 4 lb. less 2 oz. When this was brought down there was a large amount at Bathurst waiting for a military escort, which the people were in hopes the Government would allow them. What we have on board was brought down by four gentlemen, they being armed to the teeth.
>
> I had great difficulty in getting away from Sydney. Although I promised my crew double wages, some six or seven left me as soon as the affair became known. Foreseeing what would most likely be the case, I got a steamer and towed the ship down towards the Heads. I placed two armed policemen, night and day, one at each end of the ship. Still those that could swim got off somehow. All this caused much expense. I left the Lady Clark ready for sea without a soul on board but the captain. I believe he was about starting, with his articles in his pocket, on the road towards Bathurst, thinking he might induce some sailors to return and ship. They were coolly (I mean what sailors were left in Sydney) asking £80 for the run home, and a guarantee of procuring them a ship to return direct to Sydney. I paid £5 and £6 per month for what I wanted.
>
> *Yours, very faithfully,*
> *G.H. HEATON*

Phoenician (Sproat) sailed from Sydney on 11 November 1851, with what has widely been misrepresented to have been the first gold cargo out of the Australian colonies; this was not in fact so, for **Thomas Arbuthnot** landed her consignment in September 1851,[13] and there had been nineteen subsequent sailings with gold aboard. **Phoenician**'s was probably the first significant, formalised cargo of gold dust, which brought attention upon the ship not only for the size of her consignment (seventy-four packages of gold dust weighing 22,909 ounces and valued locally at £74,455)[14] but also for the speed of her homewards passage, eighty-three days from Sydney to Falmouth.

Specific precautions attended the shipment of gold from the Australian colonies to ensure its security. These are described in some detail in Robert White Stevens' masterpiece *On the Stowage of Ships and their Cargoes,* and in so far that it is known that Stevens based many of his observations upon input from GTJ's commanders, it is worth quoting from that volume (commonly known in the profession as *Stevens on Stowage*):

> When the cargo is nearly complete, the master attends at the different banks daily, at stated hours, to see the gold weighed; after which it is placed in small strong wooden boxes, made for the purpose, holding generally 1,000 oz. each; they are screwed down in his presence, sealed with his seal, and that of the bank, where the boxes remain until a day or two previous to sailing, when all is taken, at an appointed hour, and conveyed to the ship. As the gold comes over the gangway, the chief mate takes the ordinary account, and it is then ranged along the cuddy deck, where it is again counted as it goes down, and also as it goes into the safe; when deposited and the safe locked, the key is delivered to the master. Usually the most trustworthy officers, petty officers, quarter master, &c. are selected for this duty; the seamen are employed in other parts of the ship and aloft. There are two keys, one in charge of the master, and the other of the mate, until all the gold is deposited, when the mate's key is delivered to the master, who places a seal on the key-hole, and makes periodical inspections of the safe on the homewards passage. Agents from the banks come with the gold and present their bills of lading to the master for his signature.
>
> On arrival in London docks, and when alongside the quay, the safe is unlocked, and the gold passed into the cuddy, where it is counted as before. It is then put into a cart or wagon, in charge of the master, whose responsibility does not cease until it is safely lodged in the bank.

Sir William Henderson, in a speech at the Aberdeen Town Hall in January 1899 when accepting a portrait of himself by Sir George Reid from the Earl of Aberdeen on behalf of the city, gives an interesting insight into trading practice in those early Australian trade days:[15]

George Thompson and Co. are, I think, the oldest shipping and trading firm to Australia in this country now existing, they having sent vessels there long before the gold fever of the fifties. Well do I remember upon the interesting occurrences which took place, on the arrival of our ships in London from Australia, in those days. They had to bring home their distant freights with them then in foreign specie [coinage] or gold dust, and this had to be taken to the Bank of England or assay office to be converted into the real value, and frequently I went with it in the conveyance which took it to the Bank, saw it melted and weighed, and received its sterling value.

Phoenician, under Sproat, had indeed built up a much-publicised reputation for speed in the service of Marshall and Eridge's line of Sydney packets, on whose outward berth she worked. Homewards, her managing agents in Sydney were Montefiore Graham. A shipping advertisement from the *Sydney Morning Herald* (found pinned to the top of a letter dated 22 November 1852 from GTJ to Henderson), advised:

TO SHIPPERS OF GOLD DUST
Notice
THE clipper PHOENICIAN,
will sail from Sydney on the 11th September.
This vessel made her last passage to England in 83 days.
MONTEFIORE GRAHAM & CO
Sydney, July 16th 1852.

With the servicing of **Phoenician**, Montefiore Graham & Co. became GTJ's agents in Sydney, and were to remain such for many years. Jacob Levi Montefiore was born in Barbados in 1819 and came from a well-regarded Sephardi Jewish family. Well educated, he joined his uncle J.B. Montefiore, an established and much respected businessman, in Sydney in 1837, but shortly thereafter commenced trading to his own account. In November 1846 he merged his firm with that of a wealthy Scot, Robert Graham, to found a shipping agency business in Sydney, expanding rapidly to branches in Brisbane and Melbourne. Montefiore was to become one of the most respected figures in New South Wales, being nominated to the Legislative Council in 1856; amongst other interests, he held directorships of the Bank of Australasia and the New South Wales Marine Assurance Company, and was chairman of the Sydney Chamber of Commerce on two occasions. He was a very significant landowner, philanthropist, and a leading member of the Jewish community in New South Wales. His choice as GTJ's representative in Sydney is remarkable, and formed part of the close relationship with Jewish interests for which GTJ was noted. This manifested itself in the choice of names for a number of subsequent GTJ ships and was undoubtedly behind GTJ's reputation for carrying high-value, low-deadweight cargoes sourced from Jewish merchants on the outwards berth.

A further interesting connection between the Montefiores and GTJ may be found in the early business grounding given by Montefiore's uncle to Frederick Dalgety. Dalgety, who was to found the international agricultural conglomerate that bore his name until its international fragmentation in the late 1990s, served with J.B. Montefiore for six years upon his first arrival in New South Wales (during which time he would have worked alongside Montefiore's nephew), before branching out in business to his own account in 1840 in Melbourne. Dalgety later acknowledged that: 'It was at Montefiore's that I gathered my mercantile experience, or rather my mercantile education.'[16] In due course, Dalgety was to become inexorably linked with the fortunes of GTJ's Aberdeen White Star Line in Australia.

The steady development of larger, faster ships suited to the Australian and eastern trades continued, with Hood's delivering the new 918-ton ship **Walter Hood**, in January 1852, with GTJ as subscribing owner (32/64). The significant increase in the initial shareholdings that GTJ was personally taking in new ships would seem to indicate that whatever financial pain he may have suffered as a result of the North of Scotland Bank problems was now behind him; Walter Hood also now appeared as a shareholder in new tonnage. The warm relationship that must have existed between GTJ and his master shipbuilder is reflected in the choice of name for the new ship. **Walter Hood** undertook an initial voyage to India and China, and thereafter was employed on the Australian trade under the command of Hugh Sproat (ex-**Phoenician)**. On her eighty-day maiden voyage to Sydney, the new vessel attracted considerable favourable comment; she was described as a near-sister of **Phoenician**, 'but of an improved model, embracing in a higher degree the requisites determined by the experience of the builder, for fast sailing and sea comfort'.[17] *Walter Hood*, with a length overall of 206ft, had carrying capacities of 1,500 tons of measurement cargo, and 1,300 tons deadweight. The write-up in *Empire* gave very detailed spar dimensions; her standing suit of sail spread 3,363 yards of canvas.

Walter Hood was followed in September of that year by the 627-ton Hood-built ship *Wooloomooloo*, commanded from the outset on the Australian trade by Charles Stuart (ex-*Neptune*). To offset these two new vessels, GTJ disposed of his 64/64 interests in *Wanderer* (April 1852) and *Alexander Harvey* (October 1852).

In July 1852, GTJ re-entered public life, this time as member of Parliament for Aberdeen, having campaigned on an Advanced Liberal ticket. GTJ set out his pitch in an open letter in the Aberdeen press, addressed from his home at 5 Golden Square. An extract from the letter gives an interesting insight into his politics:

> My political views – generally well known to my fellow-citizens – are those of Progressive Reform, carried out in the consolidation and improvement of the Constitution under which this country has, for so long a period enjoyed such signal and enduring prosperity. My aim would invariably be to renovate, not to destroy; and to improve, as far as possible, the usefulness of institutions which the lapse of time may have impaired. While anxious to facilitate trade and commerce with other countries, I would, at the same time, be ever ready to support whatever had a tendency to increase the comfort and welfare of the great body of the people. In short, to promote the best interests of the country, as well as those of this city and locality, would be my earnest endeavour, should I have the honour of becoming your Representative.

In securing the seat, he displaced the long-standing Tory incumbent, Sir Andrew Leith-Hay, polling 682 votes out of a total cast of 1,160, a majority of 204. The election campaign elicited various charges against GTJ from columnists and leaflet writers, targeted against his involvement with the Aberdeen and London Steam Navigation Company and in particular his insurance dealings on behalf of that company. These were vigorously rebutted by his agent, and did not arise again, but they give an indication of the breadth of his business involvements.

In a reflection of the times, GTJ's letter was addressed 'Gentlemen', and he undertook not to trouble the electors by canvassing them personally. Editorial comment following GTJ's success was generally positive, though his Free Church doctrines were not appreciated. GTJ served as MP for five years, a good constituency member but otherwise undistinguished. I sense that his presence in London on parliamentary duties gave him an opportunity to oversee his increasingly important London-based interests.

Hitherto, GTJ's ships engaged in the Australian trade had run exclusively on the Sydney service. Now on 29 April 1853, *Lord Metcalfe* made the first recorded visit by a GTJ ship to Hobson's Bay, or Port Phillip as the port of Melbourne was then referred to in shipping circles. (Cornford claimed that *Anemone* visited Melbourne on her maiden voyage in 1844, but this is not borne out by research.)[18] In a letter from GTJ in London dated 22 November 1852, to Henderson in Aberdeen, GTJ makes reference to the Melbourne visit, which was clearly seen as a better option than a guano charter with Gibbs to the Chinchas:

> I have your note of the 20th, and I suppose we must let the Lord Metcalfe take chance at Port Phillip as Gibbs people won't give more than £2. 15/- and I think it is not worth our while to fix her at this later in Jan. Will therefore let Capt. Cargill know and he must do his best.

GTJ concluded a strictly business letter with a touching reference to his daughter's forthcoming confinement with her first child: 'I am delighted to hear of Jane's progress and that her appetite is good. I trust she will gather some more strength before her confinement takes place.'

The build-up of ships engaged in the Sydney trade continued in November 1853, with GTJ taking a 32/64 share in the Hood-built 665-ton ship *Maid of Judah*. GTJ's involvement in this new ship is of particular interest, for while he owned half of the ship, and she formed an integral part of his fleet, her subscribing owner was in fact Captain Isaac Merchant, her commander. Significantly, judging by a watercolour by D.M. Little, noted for his accuracy, the ship is depicted with a black hull and a blue/white/blue horizontally divided defaced house flag. GTJCo. was subsequently to take over the ship in 1858. Little's watercolour is reproduced in the colour illustration section.

Tragically, in the latter stages of her construction Hood's master carpenter, George Cay, was killed. He had been ascending a ladder out of her hold and fell 25ft on to stones and iron ballast. The *Maid of Judah*'s figurehead, executed by a Mr Hughes of York Street, was said by the *Aberdeen Journal* to be 'the first one produced in Aberdeen for our large clipper vessels'.[19] On her maiden voyage to Sydney, she carried out the New South Wales Royal Mint.

GTJ's eldest son, Stephen, was admitted as a partner on 1 January 1854, and at this stage the partnership appears to have become reconstituted as a company, although not a limited liability concern. Stephen's accession appears to be the start of a period of rapid transformation, which was to lead in the next two years to the establishment of the company as a liner operator on the Australian trade in its own right.

As part of an ongoing process of trimming his non-core interests, GTJ disposed of his 12/64 in **Lord Seaton** in January 1854; his interest in the vessel had not been managerial and while his disinvestment marked a diminution of his involvement in the North American timber and immigrant trade, he was to hold on to this trade with successive owned ships for a further twenty years.

William Henderson and Stephen Thompson moved to London in 1854 and established themselves in rented office accommodation in a property owned by the Leather Sellers Company at 12 St Helens Place, off Bishopsgate, adjacent to the heartland of London's shipping and insurance activities. This was a clear signal of the company's intention to enter the Australian liner trade in its own right. Hitherto, GTJ's ships engaged on the Australian trade had loaded out of London on the berths of various non-vessel-operating clipper lines established by loading brokers – Mackay & Read, Devitt & Moore, James Thomson & Co., Marshall and Eldridge, and Henry & Calvert Toulmain to name but a few. In September 1854, **Maid of Judah** (Merchant) loaded for Sydney on the berth of W.O. Young, a loading broker operating out of Liverpool, Manchester and London. On 4 December, an advertisement appeared in the shipping columns of *The Times* for **John Bunyan** loading for Sydney, jointly in the names of W.O. Young and George Thompson Jnr. Such joint advertisements continued for eleven months, the last appearing on 6 November 1855, promoting:

WALTER HOOD – For SYDNEY (last shipping day December 8), the well-known Aberdeen clipper ship WALTER HOOD, 936 tons register, JAS. DONALD, Commander; lying in the London Docks. This favourite vessel has made the quickest and most regular passages in the Sydney trade, and offers peculiar advantages to both passengers and

shippers. First and second cabin passengers only will be taken, and an experienced surgeon accompanies the vessel. For freight or passage, apply to W.O. Young, Sun Court, Cornhill; or to George Thompson Junr. and Co., 12, St Helen's place, Bishopsgate.

As part of a restructuring programme designed to better shape the company for its establishment as a trading line in its own right, in June 1855 GTJ transferred his shareholding in all the main line ships into a new joint ownership comprising himself, William Henderson, and Stephen Thompson (hereafter referred to as GTJCo.). GTJ continued to hold and develop interests in non-line ships to his own account. With these transformations completed, on 3 January 1856 the first shipping advertisement for the Aberdeen Clipper Line appeared in *The Times*:

FOR SYDNEY. – The Aberdeen Clipper Line. – The following favourite clipper SHIPS, all built at Aberdeen, by the well known firm of Walter Hood and Co., will be dispatched for SYDNEY direct, with the greatest punctuality:-

Ships	Commanders	Tons Burden	To Sail
Walter Hood	Donald	1,500	Dec. 10
Phoenician	Jamson	900	Jan. 10
Star of Peace	Sproat	2,000	Feb. 10
Omar Pasha	Thomson	2,000	Mar. 10
John Bunyan	Henry	900	Apr. 10
Centurion	Edward	1,100	May 10
Maid of Judah	Merchant	1,100	Jun. 10
Wave of Life	Stuart	1,700	Jul. 10
Wooloomooloo	Ross	1,100	Aug. 10
Oliver Cromwell		900	Sep. 10
New Ship [*Damascus*]	Alexander	1700	Oct. 10

These superior vessels have splendid cabin accommodations and offer peculiar advantages to shippers and passengers. For particulars apply to the owners, George Thompson, jun, and Co., St. Helen's-place, Bishopsgate-street.

The advertisement is particularly interesting insofar that it gives an indication of the burden, or deadweight carrying capacity, of the vessels, and it also names vessels under construction yet to be commissioned. The new line uniquely offered a monthly service to Sydney, the only line to so offer it at that time.

(It should be noted that, contemporaneously with GTJ's Aberdeen Line of Clippers, John Rennie of 43 Marischal Street, was advertising sailings to Australia, also under the trading name of the Aberdeen Clipper Line, and in fairness to Rennie, his early sailings were from Aberdeen! Rennie in fact settled onto the South African trade, and finally sold out his shipowning interests to Liverpool's T. & J. Harrison in May 1911. Rennie's, now part of the Bidvest Group, continue to this day as leading shipping agents in South Africa, and was indeed to become GTJ's agents in that country. For years, the two lines were colloquially known in the shipping industry as 'Thompson's Aberdeen' and 'Rennie's Aberdeen'; to further differentiate between the two fleets, Thompson's tended to be referred to as the 'Aberdeen White Star Line', a reference to the white star that formed the centrepiece of the Line's house flag.)

To service the Line's build-up, GTJ had taken delivery, as subscribing owner, of four further ships over a three-year period from Walter Hood:

Omar Pasha, 1,124 tons register (36/64) on 13 May 1854;
Star of Peace, 1,114 tons register (40/64) in September 1855;
Wave of Life, 887 tons register (40/64) in May 1856; and,
Damascus, 964 tons (36/64) in March 1857.

In the same period, he disposed of his interests in two older units, *Lord Metcalfe* in April 1855 (48/64) and *Prince of Wales* in August of the same year (32/64). Both had served with distinction in the formative years of GTJ's early involvement in the Australian trade, but had reached an age, and were of a size and speed that were no longer compatible with GTJ's emerging requirements.

Pressures to remain competitive by reducing operating costs were clearly exercising the minds of owners such as GTJCo., in particular crew costs. To achieve such, labour-saving devices were introduced whereby manning levels could be reduced. *Star of Peace* was fitted with Cunningham's patent self-reefing topsails, the first of several GTJCo. vessels to be so fitted. In Cunningham's system,[20] the topsail rolled around its yard, the yard being rotated by a parbuckle chain lift arrangement engaging a whelped boss at the centre of the spar. To facilitate the sail rolling around the spar in way of the lift chain

at its centre, the sail had to have its centre cloth omitted for about two-thirds of the depth of the sail, the gap being closed by a bonnet when the sail was set, giving a characteristic 'ladder' effect to the sails so fitted, portrayed in many contemporary paintings. Using the gear, a sail could be reefed, or a reef shaken out by three men and a winch in less than a minute. Cunningham's self-reefing gear was, however, awkward in action and prone to jamming; it was relatively short-lived, being superseded by the introduction of American-style double topsails. From initial patenting in 1850, more than 4,000 ships were fitted with Cunningham's self-reefing systems by 1865. Cunningham, a former naval officer, went on to patent a number of other labour-saving devices that we will see fitted on GTJCo.'s later ships.

In January 1858, emphasising the emerging importance of London as the prime centre of activity, Captain Isaac Merchant was brought ashore from his command of **Maid of Judah** and appointed as the company's shipminder (marine superintendent or operations manager in modern parlance) in London.

I sense that it was at this stage that the 'Aberdeen Green' hull, which was to become such a distinguished and beautiful marque for ships committed to the Aberdeen Clipper Line, was introduced. Such illustrations of early GTJ ships as have survived from before

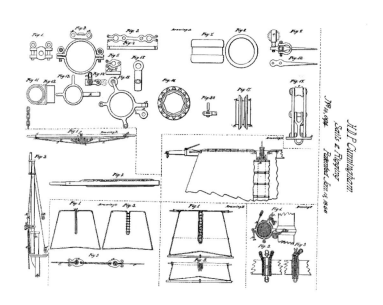

Patent drawing of Cunningham's self-reefing gear.

the advent of the Australian Line all show either black hulls, or black with painted ports. A painting dated 1850 in the Aberdeen Maritime Museum shows **Phoenician** with a green hull, but it also shows her as being ship-rigged, which she was not; a detailed watercolour of **Phoenician** by Frederick Garling in the National Library of Australia dated 185[-]?) shows her with a green hull. The Aberdeen Green livery comprised a beautiful green/blue hull (Jimmy Henderson's father confirmed that there was a distinct blue tinge to the green), set off by a golden yellow sheer line ribband and guilded work at bow and stern. At a later stage, some ships also sported a white ribband between the boot-topping and topside paint. The livery was completed by white-painted lower masts, doublings, yards, blocks, figurehead and bowsprit. The copper-sheathed wooden-hulled ships at the prime of their ascendancy, sported the top two strakes of copper tingles burnished – doubtless a job for apprentices armed with ground pumice and colza oil! GTJCo.'s houseflag comprised a square flag, horizontally divided, red over blue, with a white star superimposed in the centre. Initially the star was eight-pointed, but later this became six-pointed; Hume gives the date of the change as being 1869, and reasons that the change was made to the better to discern the star as such from a distance.[21]

Lubbock waxed lyrical about the presentation of the Aberdeen Line ships:[22]

> No ships that ever sailed the seas presented a finer appearance than these little flyers. They were always beautifully kept and were easily noticeable amongst other ships for their smartness; indeed, when lying in Sydney Harbour or Hobson's Bay with their yards squared to a nicety, their green sides with gilt streak and scroll work at bow and stern glistening in the sun, their figure-heads, masts, spars and blocks all painted white and every rope's end flemish-coiled on snow-white decks, they were the admiration of all who saw them.

The suggestion has been made by some authorities that Aberdeen Green hulls were the marque of Aberdeen-built ships in general. This was certainly not the case; rather, Aberdeen Green was the livery of ships managed by GTJCo. and trading under the auspices of the Aberdeen Clipper Line. From 1863 this included ships owned by Alexander Nicol, which loaded on the Aberdeen Line berth outwards to Australia, and whose ships carried the Aberdeen Line livery and houseflag until their latter three ships, when it would appear that Nicol broke away from GTJCo.'s management.

On the family fronts, William Henderson's second son, George Thompson Henderson, was born on 27 October 1856; his naming in honour of his maternal grandfather started a charming tradition that has survived through the first-born sons on the Henderson side of the family to this time. Stephen Thompson's first son, Stephen Thompson Jnr, was born shortly afterwards on 19 January 1857. Both boys were to become distinguished partners of the company in later years.

A Question of Paint …

Aberdeen Green paint was manufactured by the local Aberdeen firm, Farquhar and Gill. Founded by Alexander Gill in 1815, the company operated out of premises in Drum Lane. According to F & G's former chief chemist, Tom Grieve, Aberdeen Green paint comprised:

> a pigment of mid-chrome and Prussian blue ground together;
> a vehicle of standoil (linseed oil heat-treated to thicken) and barytes;
> white spirit thinners; and,
> manganese and lead dryers.

The materials were initially passed through an edge runner (a large roller propelled around the inside wall of a large mixer drum); then through triple granite rollers (made locally); and finally thinned out and run through a single roll mill and drummed. Prior to 1865, the paint was sold as a paste for thinning on board; subsequent to 1865, F & G pioneered canned ready-mixed paints. The tops of the early cans of ready-mixed paint were soldered closed to ensure they were air tight.

Farquhar and Gill went on to manufacture the cream-coloured paint used on all external surfaces above the green hull of the Aberdeen Line's steamers, and such was the quality of the product that F & G's black ilmenite enamel was used on the Royal Yacht **Victoria and Albert**.

GTJ retired from parliament in 1857 and set up his country seat in the beautiful estate of Pitmedden, situated on the on the south bank of the River Don, to the north-west of Dyce, while retaining 5 Golden Square in Aberdeen as his town house. The Pitmedden estate had originally been fenced out of the thanage of Kintore in 1508, and had had various owners over the intervening period, including in 1612–14 the noted doctor of medicine and medical benefactor, Prof. Duncan Liddell. GTJ initially leased the estate from John Humphrey and over the period 1859 to 1860 built the present house on the site of an earlier one; GTJ appears to have purchased the estate, comprising the mansion house, pleasure gardens, woodlands, home farm and gardens, and the farms of Guildhall, from Humphrey in 1862.[23] The driveways approaching the house were laid along the line of the former Inverurie canal. The Aberdeen and Great North of Scotland Railway, of which GTJ was a director, wound its way along the northern border of the estate and, conveniently, there was a halt arranged in way of Pitmedden for GTJ to embark or disembark. The present Pitmedden House was designed for GTJ by the architect William Henderson, who had been responsible for a number of Union Bank buildings in the North-east. The house was built in a neo-Jacobean style, and was originally harled with granite bordering; it was clearly a reflection of GTJ's tastes, with the centrepieces of the ceilings in each of the public rooms featuring beautiful plaster casts of clipper ships in full sail.

At this stage, GTJ clearly withdrew from public life and began disengaging from the mainstream management of the company in favour of William Henderson, who moved back to Aberdeen in 1862 leaving Stephen Thompson in charge of the London office. Henderson purchased Devanha House from John Blaikie as his Aberdeen home. Situated on the north bank of the River Dee overlooking the Victoria suspension bridge, Devanha was to be Henderson's much-loved home until his death. The house had been built in 1813 around an old brewer's house; rebuilt in 1840, the architect Simpson added a Doric arch on the front and rounded the ends of the house. In the grounds, Henderson established exotic plants and kept animals brought back from foreign parts by the Line's commanders.

With the vast majority of the company's business by then being conducted from London, and at a critical stage of the Line's

Pitmedden House, Dyce; George Thompson Jnr.'s country seat.

Devana House; Sir William Henderson's Aberdeen residence. (PHK collection)

development, the decision that William Henderson should move back to Aberdeen to take eventual overall charge of the company's affairs based in that city, must be seen as an early portent of the parochialism that was to eventually be the downfall of the company as a family-owned entity. However, it should be said that Thompsons rightly took enormous pride in its Aberdeen roots. In his valedictory speech in 1899, which I have earlier quoted from, Henderson noted that:

> 41 vessels have been built in Aberdeen, at a cost of £818,195; in addition, a considerable portion of the yearly outfit and upkeep of these vessels has been sent from this [Aberdeen], thus materially contributing to the prosperity of the city.

If George Thompson Jnr had begun withdrawing from mainstream shipping and public life, he was by no means retired! He was active in local charities; he also took an interest in the agricultural management of his new estate, and was successful in 1868 to the point of winning the Silver Medal of the Highland and Agricultural Society of Scotland for 'the best managed Green Crop, District of Donside'. GTJ continued to invest in his own right in various ships outside the main line of the company. Many of these investments were made with former commanders from his employ, and one senses the hand of the master shipowner giving support and financial credibility to his old trusted servants and friends. One such investment was 8/64 in the 790-ton Quebec-built ship *Forth*, which he entered into in January 1857. *Forth* was engaged in the Quebec trade, but proved a short-lived investment as she was lost in December the following year. One of GTJ's residual private investments, the schooner *Mansfield* (12/64), was wrecked off Peterhead in September 1879.

For the company, business was burgeoning. Its position on the Quebec trade was strengthened by the delivery from Hood's yard in June 1857 of the 614-ton ship *Transatlantic*, in which GTJCo. was a subscribing owner (40/64). Under the command of Captain William Edward, ex-*Centurion*, the new ship succeeded *Jane Boyd* on the North American trade. The latter ship was put on to general tramping, including a run from Moulmein to Aberdeen, and a load of guano from Peru. Moulmein was the principal export outlet for Burmese teak, and it is likely that her cargo was teak for the local shipbuilding industry, possibly to GTJCo. or Hood's own account.

The *Transatlantic* from a watercolour by D.M. Little. (National Library of Australia Vic H26898)

Ship requirements for the Australian trade were boosted by the delivery in August 1858 of the Hood-built ship *Moravian*, 966 tons, with GTJCo. subscribing shareholders (36/64). William Edward, transferring from *Transatlantic* after only one year in that ship, took command of *Moravian* on her maiden voyage to Sydney. Her outward passage was executed in a creditable seventy-six days, and upon arrival in Sydney she found herself in company with five other GTJCo. ships, *Damascus*, *John Bunyan*, *Star of Peace*, *Wave of Life* and *Walter Hood*. *Moravian* and four of the other ships were berthed at Circular 'Quay'. In those days, port facilities at Sydney were distinctly primitive. Sydney Cove's Circular Quay, where most of the loading and unloading was carried out, was effectively a series of stages about the perimeter of the cove. Ships did not in fact berth alongside the 'Quay', but moored off the stages. The berthing operation could occupy a day's hard work for the crew. Two anchors were dropped on the offshore side to spring the vessel off and mooring lines passed to the shore. Two trees, 80 or 90ft long, were laid out from the quay to the ship and lashed to the rails; a platform was built on to the trees to form a bridge for loading and unloading operations.

Moravian was only to undertake one voyage to Sydney, for having returned to London in an equally creditable seventy-seven days, her next voyage inaugurated the company's service to Port Phillip, or Melbourne as the port became known, arriving there on 11 December 1859. Her outward cargo included two 'entire' horses, two Clydesdale mares and eighteen thoroughbred rams 'of very superior description and very large framed', all of which were delivered in fine condition.

Although heralded by the Melbourne *Age* as the pioneer of a new line of packets, it would be a further four years before sufficient suitable tonnage was available to commit more than four sailings a year to the new Melbourne service. From the outset of the Line's involvement in Melbourne, the company's managing agent in that port was Dalgety, whom we have earlier seen in Sydney serving his mercantile apprenticeship with Montefiore. Dalgety was to be managing agent of the Aberdeen Line, initially at Melbourne and Geelong but later throughout Australia, over the next seventy-four years; it is appropriate to dwell at some length on the firm's background.

Frederick Gonnerman Dalgety had moved from Sydney to Melbourne in 1840, where he joined the newly founded firm of Griffith, Borradaile and Co. as manager. The company was established to import and sell merchandise; to purchase wool or make advances on consignments to their friends, John Gore and Co. in London; insurance; shipping; wool scouring; and short-term loans (to trusted squatters).[24] The company acted as shipping agents for Green's celebrated line of Blackwall frigates and Marshall's line of clippers (on whose berth many of the early GTJCo. sailings to Sydney were made). John Gore provided the London connection for the sale of colonial produce, especially wool, and for raising short-term credits necessary for obtaining merchandise destined for the colonies.

A measure of the economic growth of Victoria in the period during which Dalgety established his business may be derived from the following statistics:[25]

	1836	1850	1855
Settlers	177	26,000	300,000
Sheep	26,000	> 5,000,000	> 6,000,000
Exports		just > £1,000,000	c. £13,000,000

The explosion in the early 1850s was a direct outcome of the discovery of gold at Bendigo and Ballarat.

Dalgety was made a partner of the firm in 1844. Already, however, there were problems with the other partners; Griffith withdrew from the partnership, and with it his capital, in March 1845. Gore's son, Harry, was nominated to take his place; however, John Gore would not advance his son's £5,000 capital and Dalgety refused to accept him as a partner. Following a visit by Borradaile to London, John Gore declared that he had 'a strong disinclination, amounting to a determination, not to be connected with any concern in which George Borradaile is concerned'.[26] Borradaile withdrew in March 1847, and the company was renamed Dalgety, Gore and Co. In the period 1846–47, wool, to which the company was heavily exposed, went through a sharp depression, with consequent heavy strains on Dalgety's capital resources. However, the diversity of his operations carried him through, especially his shipping agency business. In 1847, he loaded four ships for Gore and Marshal, grossing £20,000 freight and passage money. Ships agency was not without its problems; in an 1847 letter to an irate client, who had been affronted by a maritime martinet, Dalgety advised:[27] 'I am aware that ship's captains are a very disagreeable class of men to manage, but it is one of the penalties of business, and in your capacity as merchant you must act as circumstances dictate ...' (Casting my mind back to halcyon days in command, I confess to no small amusement at Dalgety's impression of my profession – we had our own views about some ship's agents!)

Much of his business involved squatters, the somewhat unfortunate designation by which settlers who had appropriated free land and developed it on a pastoral basis were known. The 'squatocracy' had developed immense flocks of sheep, but depended upon the likes of Dalgety to advance them credit to keep them in food and provisions between the wool clips. In a letter to Gore in London, he commented:[28]

The [Victorian] squatters themselves are enterprising men of business habits, who supervised their own stations, and not like the sheep farmers of Sydney or Van Diemen's Land who have been spoiled by having convict labour for nothing, built themselves fine villas near the town, attending only to scheming and financing, leaving their stations to be managed by overseers and consequently heavily in debt.

Dalgety, with a reputation for integrity in his dealings with the squatters, developed close personal relationships with his clients, ties that were to survive the short-termism of the gold rush.

The discovery of Victorian gold in 1851 materially changed the economics of pastoral Victoria. Almost overnight, spiralling inflation beset the economic order of the colony and, as we have seen in New South Wales, labour deserted the farms to seek potential quick riches on the gold fields. Dalgety wrote to Montefiore in Sydney:[29]

Things here are getting to such a pitch that in a short time no respectable man will be able to live here. It is impossible to get things done, pay what you will – wood is £4 a load and water 5/- a cask. Cottages containing four rooms cannot be had even at £200 a year. The price of land is going up at a fearful rate.

Dalgety was on the return passage from London, where he had been seeking additional capital, when the gold bonanza broke, and while the economic chaos that ensued was undoubtedly not to his liking – 'Victoria in her golden age has not the same attraction for me she had when Wool and Tallow were her staple commodities' – nonetheless his agents on the ground were quick to exploit the potential offered by the gold rush in terms of the provision of supplies, short-term finance and dealing in gold. Dalgety's Melbourne and Geelong companies now described themselves as 'General squatting agents, gold buyers and financiers'. On at least one occasion Dalgety bought tea in Canton with gold dust and sovereigns and sent it profitably to London for sale.

In 1852, Dalgety took J. Alexander Burnett (Melbourne manager) and Charles Ibbotson (Geelong manager) into partnership as part of a strategy whereby he could return to London, find a suitable wife, and conduct his business from that city, comfortable in the assurance that his core colonial businesses were in good hands. Unfortunately, Burnett died on 25 May 1853, and Dalgety had to find another partner to manage the Melbourne office. To this end, he brought in A.R. Cruikshank from the Portland office as a partner on 1 October 1853. He also took in as a partner at the same time, F.A. du Croz from Launceston.

While the Melbourne company continued trading as Dalgety, Gore and Co., strains were developing between Gore and Dalgety, and in a letter dated 1 August 1853, Dalgety had advised Gore of his intentions to break up the partnership and trading relationship. An irate Gore responded by placing Dalgety, Gore and Co. into liquidation. Faced with the prospect of no London connection and the urgent need to re-establish his Melbourne trading base, Dalgety founded with du Croz, a new company in Melbourne, Dalgety, Cruikshank and Co., and in April 1854, he and du Croz took passage to London to found their own trading house in that city, Dalgety and Co.

Dalgety's intention was undoubtedly to remain in London, but in 1858, Cruikshank resigned from the partnership, leaving the all-important Melbourne office rudderless. Dalgety returned to Victoria, and found in Arthur Blackwood, the then chief inspector of the Union Bank (of which Dalgety had been a director), a first-class replacement. Blackwood, a Scot, brought with him a strong relationship with a number of the wealthier squatters, especially those of Scots origin. The Melbourne company was reconstituted as Dalgety, Blackwood and Co., and it was with this concern that the Aberdeen Clipper Line placed its new Melbourne business in 1859. GTJ and Henderson probably met Dalgety while he was establishing his London office; he would certainly have come with the recommendation of his friend Montefiore in Sydney.

The extension of liner services to Melbourne consolidated GTJCo.'s position as a liner company trading in its own right. By the close of the 1850s, the Aberdeen Line was well established on the Australian trade, with monthly services from London's East India Docks to Sydney, and a quarterly service to Melbourne, supported by first-class managing agents in both Australian colonies. The company maintained a foothold in the transatlantic timber and immigrant trades with two ships, *Richibucto* and *Transatlantic*, but its involvement in the China tea trade had temporarily lapsed from 1856, when *John Bunyan* transferred to the Australian trade. The company had largely pulled out of bulk cargo and tramping trades, although the odd Peruvian guano cargo was still being uplifted by some of the older vessels returning from Australia. The company had also pulled out of the coastal and Baltic trades, although GTJ maintained personal interests in a number of small ships, and his shareholding in the Aberdeen Commercial Company, whose ships engaged in the coastal coal, granite and lime trades.

Heyday of the Clippers – 1860 to 1869

With the company well established on the Australian service, the tonnaging of their Australian trade commitments bears examination. An analysis of the 126 voyages undertaken by GTJCo. vessels on the mainline services to Sydney and Melbourne during the 1860s demonstrates the average ship's round voyage to have occupied 318 days, or 10.4 months. On this basis, to furnish a monthly sailing to both ports would have required a fleet of at least twenty-one high-quality vessels, without making any allowance for casualties or extraordinary stoppages. GTJCo. entered the 1860s with twelve such vessels committed to the Australian trade, some of which were past their prime and required replacing.

To furnish the build-up to a monthly service to Melbourne, the company first switched *Transatlantic* from the Quebec to the Sydney service at the start of 1860. Her initial voyage returned via the Chincha Islands, where she loaded guano, a voyage time that occupied sixteen months and which clearly did little to help liner scheduling; the time factor involved in deviating for guano probably more than anything led to GTJCo.'s withdrawal from that trade. *Transatlantic*'s place on the Aberdeen–Quebec service was taken by *Jane Boyd*, recalled from tramping; she was to continue working steadily on the Atlantic service, two voyages a year, plying exclusively between Aberdeen and Quebec, for the ensuing six years until her sale in 1866.

A steady succession of new, quality liners emerged from Hood's yard over the 1860s to fuel the tonnage requirements on the Australian services and the company's re-emergence in the China trade. Two distinct classes of ship were now being delivered:

- Ships specifically destined for the Australian passenger and wool trade, with gross tonnages moving progressively towards 1,200 tons, and profiles characterised by full-height, round-down poops extending over at least one-third of the vessels' 205ft-plus lengths; and,

- Smaller, non-passenger carrying vessels of between 850 and 950 gross tons, specifically designed for speed on the 'triangular' Australia-out, China-home service. These vessels' profiles typically offered unbroken sheer lines, facilitated by raised quarterdecks built within their bulwark lines aft, surmounted by 'Aberdeen houses' to accommodate the commander and officers without impacting upon cargo space.

The 1,011-ton ship *Strathdon* (GTJCo. 48/64) delivered in February 1860, followed in April 1861 by the smaller 846-ton ship *Queen of Nations*, (GTJCo. 48/64), were typical of this development. Both undertook their maiden voyages to Melbourne. *Strathdon* (Ross) switched to the Sydney service after one voyage, while **Queen of Nations** (Mitchell), after one Melbourne voyage, initiated GTJCo.'s re-entry into the China tea trade with three direct voyages to Woosung/Shanghai from London. The subscribing ownership of **Strathdon** was significant insofar that for the first time GTJ's second son, George Thompson Youngest, then 25 years of age, became a participant in the corporate shareholding block (though apparently not yet a partner), along with his elder brother Stephen, GTJ, and William Henderson. Watercolour depictions by D.M. Little of the two ships appear in the colour section.

Three veterans, **Oliver Cromwell, Phoenician** and **Richibucto**, were sold for further trading in 1861 and 1862. **Oliver Cromwell** (40/64) was sold to Liverpool owners, while **Phoenician** (32/64) went to Belfast; these vessels had initiated GTJCo.'s movement into fast, liner tonnage, and pioneered with distinction the company's entry into the Australian trade. **Richibucto** (40/64) also went to Liverpool owners, but was later sold on to become an element of Christian Salvesen's shipping operation out of Leith. During her twelve years' service with GTJCo., she had been employed exclusively on the North Atlantic trade, turning around more often in Fleetwood and Irish ports than Aberdeen. **Richibucto**'s departure marked a temporary reduction of GTJCo.'s engagement in the North American trade to one ship employed full time.

To further boost tonnage requirements for the Australian trade, and with the capacity of Hood's yard fully committed, the company

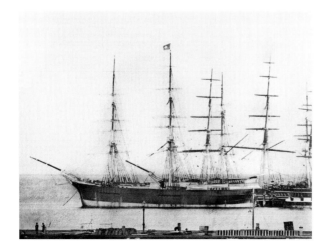

Colonial Empire at Geelong, 1871. (National Library of Australia Vic H91.325/1139)

embarked upon the expedient of buying a suitable vessel, the newly built 1,270-ton ship **Colonial Empire**. The ship had been built in Quebec in 1861 by a renowned local shipbuilder, William Baldwin,[1] who together with Henry Dinning, built ships on speculation and traded them as their 'Empire' ships until such time as they could be sold. **Colonial Empire** was purchased by GTJCo. in Liverpool in May 1861, following her timber-laden delivery voyage, and she was placed under the command of James Ross for her maiden voyage to Sydney in GTJCo.'s service. After her maiden Sydney round voyage, her second such journey returned via the Chincha Islands for guano, before settling on to a regular London–Sydney run until the end of the decade.

Colonial Empire was not to prove a fast passage maker when compared with the company's Hood-built ships. Over the course of the six Sydney voyages she undertook in the 1860s, she averaged 104.3 days on the outward passage and 122.3 days homewards, compared with an average for the rest of the Sydney fleet of 91.2 days and 93.0 days respectively. In consequence, her average round voyage occupied 366 days, compared with 318 days for the rest of the fleet on the Australian service. The voyage turnaround of vessels engaged on the Australian liner trade was a function of many factors; the vessel's fundamental design for speed could be materially impacted by the driving force of her commander and his skill in loading her; port delays, particularly in Australia, often saw a vessel sitting in port 'on the coast' for four months or more, delays usually occasioned by waiting for cargo, especially the wool clip; again, one senses the impact of the personality of the commander and the competence of his agents in Australia in terms of minimising (or exacerbating) such delays. In the case of **Colonial Empire**, she would appear to have been an all-round slow ship!

In 1861, GTJ took two personal 8/64 shareholding interests, one in the brig **Good Hope**, newly built at Garmouth on Speyside, and the other in the barque **Star of Hope**. The **Good Hope**, in which Walter Hood also took an 8/64 interest, had Captain Herman Gansen as subscribing owner (32/64). Gansen had joined GTJ as the 'sitting' master of **Richibucto** upon that vessel's acquisition in 1849, and was last in command of **Jane Boyd** in 1854. Thereafter, Gansen had become a shipbuilder, probably in partnership with William Leslie at Garmouth, Speymouth, and a shipowner in his own right. The **Good Hope** was sold on in November 1861, suggesting that GTJ's involvement was by way of helping Gansen out with a bridging loan.

Star of Hope was built as the **Omar Pasha** at Richmond, Maine, in June 1854; the vessel, which came under the British flag in November 1861, made an initial outward voyage to Sydney from Liverpool, returning via the Chincha Islands. She was thereafter to make two further round trips to the Chinchas, carrying coal on her outward voyages from Cardiff and Sunderland to Rio de Janeiro and Callao, and guano homewards to Hamburg. In 1866, GTJ sold his interest in the ship to GTJCo., and two years later the company acquired a further 20/64. Under GTJCo.'s control, the ship was placed on the outports service to Quebec at the beginning of the 1866 North Atlantic season, undertaking the work formerly executed by **Richibucto**.

While new and purchased vessels went some of the way towards fulfilling tonnage demands, they clearly did not satisfy the short-term market need. The company resorted to voyage chartering suitable tonnage to make up sailings on the outward berth. The choice of such chartered vessels reflected GTJCo.'s intense loyalty to the Aberdeen home market, and in a number of cases was probably tied in with building contracts at Walter Hood's shipyard. Two local shipowners, Henry Adamson and Alexander Nicol, both had ships built at Hood's yard, which were subsequently voyage chartered on the Aberdeen Line's outward berths. In the case of Adamson, whose barque **Ellen Simpson**, an early product of the Hood yard,

we have already seen on the Swansea copper ore trade, the relationship would appear to have been at arm's length, with no cross-shareholding. Nonetheless, at least three of Adamson's ships, **Granite City**, **Gladiator** and **Jason**, were built by Hood's and sailed outwards on the Aberdeen Line berth, **Granite City** serving for three years from 1860 to 1862.

Alexander Nicol was the subscribing owner of twelve vessels built at Hood's yard; in practically all of these, GTJCo., GTJ, James Buyers (shipyard manager) and Walter Hood were also shareholders. Nicol in turn was a participating shareholder in eight vessels built by Hood for GTJCo.

Apart from Nicol's last two ships, **Torridon** and **Yallaroi**, which were built at Hall's in 1885 and had grey hulls with painted ports, Nicol's ships engaged on the Australian service sailed as outward elements of, and carried the hull colours and house flag of, Thompson's Aberdeen White Star Line, in addition to their own rampant lion house flag. Homeward bound from Australia, Nicol's ships were consigned by Dangar, Gedye and Co., Sydney. The warmth of the personal relationship that must have existed between Nicol and GTJ is reflected in the naming of Nicol's Hood-built clipper **George Thompson** and the fact that GTJ took personal shareholdings in a number of Nicol's ships. The following table shows the inter-relationship:

Ships Built for Alex Nicol at Walter Hood with GTJ Group Share Participation

Ship	Date	Type	GRT	A. Nicol	J. Buyers	W. Hood	GTJ personal	GTJCo.
Seaton	Aug 1847	Brig	185	48				
Balgownie	Aug 1848	Barque	379	32	4 + 4	4	8	
Assyrian	Dec 1854	Ship	605	22	8			
Westburn	Jan 1858	Ship	629	22	4	4	8	
Garrawalt	Jan 1862	Ship	702	28	8	8	8	
Glengairn	Apr 1863	Ship	925	32	8		16	
George Thompson	May 1865	Ship	1,294	24	4			16
Glenavon	Oct 1868	Ship	831	36	4		8	
Leucadia	Mar 1870	Ship	944	52	4			
Lydia	Nov 1873	Barque	377	J.V. 64	*	*	*	*
Romanoff	Aug 1874	Ship	1,277	32	4			
Cimba	Apr 1878	Ship	1,174	48	4			

Alexander Nicol was in fact a partner in Walter Hood & Co., along with GTJ. This is evidenced by two share transactions recorded in the Aberdeen Register of Ships in respect to Nicol's barque *Balgownie*:

8th November 1848: Alexander Nicol and Wm. Nicol [shipbroker of Liverpool] trading as the firm Alex and Wm Nicol of Aberdeen, Bill of Sale 24/64ths to George Thompson Jnr, **A. Nicol**, J. Horn, J. Buyers and W. Hood, trading under the name of Walter Hood & Co., Shipbuilders.

22nd November 1852: George Thompson Jnr., **A. Nicol**, J. Horn, J. Buyers Manager and W. Hood, trading under the name of Walter Hood & Co., Shipbuilders, Bill of Sale 24/64ths to Alexander Nicol and William Nicol, trading as A. & W. Nicol.

In addition to Hood-built ships, Alexander Nicol, together with his brother William Nicol of Liverpool, held interests in a number of other GTJ ships.

A. Nicol's shipowning career long predated his association with Thompson's Aberdeen Line. Along with Benjamin Moir and William Hogarth, he had established a line of clipper schooners running between Aberdeen and London in competition with the Aberdeen Steam Navigation Co.; the first unit of this line was the celebrated extreme schooner *Scottish Maid*, pioneer of the Aberdeen bow. He is also credited with being the first local trader to import a guano cargo to Aberdeen, and was one of the first shareholders in the Aberdeen Lime Company. His other business interests included a directorship of the Town and County Bank (critically referred to in the North of Scotland Bank's launch prospectus!), and management of the family's business, the Seaton Brick and Tile Co. Nicol initiated his overseas shipowning business with James Munro as partner; he was then joined by his brother, William, who subsequently moved to Liverpool and set up in business in his own right. In later years, Nicol's shipping business was managed by his nephew, John Blaikie Nicol, and his son, George.

James Buyers, who appears as a shareholder in almost every ship built at Hood's, was Hood's shipyard manager. He came into shipbuilding by way of the Aberdeen Rope and Sail Co., a company that was taken over by Walter Hood. Noted as a shrewd but reserved businessman, it is not clear whether the shareholdings that he took in Hood-built ships were personal investments or if he was acting as a trustee for Hood corporate retained interests that formed part of ship financing arrangements; I sense the latter.

GTJ's personal impact upon the local Aberdeen scene continued. In 1862, the Aberdeen Sailors' Mission was founded, with GTJ taking the chair, and William Henderson a member of council. In the same year, GTJ returned to the board of the North of Scotland Bank, a directorship he held until he retired in 1881. In May 1862, he disposed of his 8/64 private interest in the brigantine *Isabella* upon that vessel's sale to Berwick owners. He had held the same subscribing interest in the ship since she had been built in 1839; she had traded predominantly during that period on the Baltic and Archangel trades, with occasional Mediterranean voyages and seasonal employment on the coastal coal trade.

The build-up of first-class main-line tonnage continued with the commissioning of the 1,192-ton passenger ship *Kosciusko* from Hood's (GTJCo. 48/64) in August 1862. Under the command of Captain Charles Stuart (ex-*Wave of Life*), she undertook her maiden voyage to Sydney, thereafter settling on to the Melbourne run for the balance of the decade. *Kosciusko* was probably the first GTJCo. ship to spread double topsails, an American innovation introduced to reduce the labour of handling heavy single sails high up on gyrating masts; Captain James Holmes, the mariner artist who sailed in the ship as an able seaman, depicted her with double topsails spread on both her fore and main masts.[2] Named after the Polish patriotic leader, *Kosciusko* was a fine-looking ship, with a full-height poop extending over 70ft of her length to accommodate the carriage of cabin passengers. She carried a crew of over forty comprising commander, three mates, boatswain, twenty-two able seamen, six ordinary seamen, eight apprentices, and two or three stewards.

Tragedy struck the Hood shipyard on 27 December 1862 when Walter Hood lost his life in the harbour. He had been visiting the vessel *Good Hope* in the wet dock before she sailed; *Good Hope* was lying outboard of the brig *Rose Hall*, and as he crossed the brow of the latter vessel to gain the quay, he missed his footing and disappeared into the water between the ship and the quay. The vessels were quickly warped off, but there was no sign of Hood, a strong swimmer. In a tragicomic sequence of events the following morning, overseen by Provost Anderson and harbour officials, attempts were made to recover the body. Heavy guns at the Girdleness battery were fired in the hope that the seismic tremors generated thereby might shake his body out of the enveloping harbour bed mud. In the end, David Ogilvie, a noted harbour character, successfully grappled the body near to where it had fallen into the dock. Injuries to Hood's face indicated that he had struck the quay upon falling and had been knocked unconscious. In an obituary, the London *Times* referred to Hood as 'one of the most eminent of Scotland's shipbuilders', while the *Aberdeen Journal* commented:[3]

> We cannot close the account of this most lamentable affair, without noticing the high character which Mr Hood held, both for his eminence as a shipbuilder, and his sterling worth as a man – qualities which not only endeared him to all immediately connected with him in business, but also made his name known and respected in many quarters of the world, where vessels he constructed were accustomed to trade ... his unassuming manner made him many friends, and amongst all classes.

Hood died intestate. He had married his second wife, Jean (sometimes Jane) Valentine Don, the daughter of Alexander Don, a farmer who was also a shareholder in a number of GTJ's ships, on 9 July 1850 in the presence of GTJ and James Buyers,[4] Jean Hood died at their then home, 4 Canal Terrace, Aberdeen, on 15 September 1855. Ann Hood, daughter by his first marriage, who had been living with her father at the time of his death in their last house at 8 Canal Terrace, eventually succeeded to his estate under a letter of confirmation granted to her by the Commissary Court of Aberdeenshire on 2 April 1863.[5] The estate included shareholdings in fifteen ships (4/64 or 8/64); Ann Hood sold two of these shareholdings directly upon the sale of the ships by GTJCo. and transferred the balance of thirteen in March 1867 to a consortium of GTJ, William Edward (one of GTJ's most trusted shipmasters), John Sharp Henderson (advocate) and her late stepmother's father, Alex Don. I suspect that the share transfer was a trustee arrangement established on her behalf by GTJ.

It is interesting to review progress in shipbuilding technology as it applied to Walter Hood's yard during the master shipbuilder's reign as managing partner from 1838 until his death in 1862. In that period, seventy ships had been built, all of wood, and ranging in register tonnage from the little 113-ton brig *Sophia* built for the Franklin search expedition, to the 1,192-ton *Kosciusko*. While the size of vessels built at the yard had steadily increased, reflecting the Australian trade requirements of GTJCo. and Nicol, nonetheless the yard did not specialise, building successively large liner tonnage and small coastal and special-purpose vessels. The yard had followed Hall's with the adoption of the extreme Aberdeen bow in *Oliver*

Cromwell and *Phoenician* in 1847, and continued with this form on its clipper-type vessels, though in later Hood ships, the extreme cutaway of the forefoot characterised in Hall's original model gave way to a deeper forefoot. In fact, the tonnage advantages accruing to the Aberdeen bow had disappeared under new tonnage measurement rules accompanying the Merchant Shipping Act of 1854. These rules, based upon the work of the naval architect George Moorson, finally delivered a scientific method of calculating tonnage, based upon accurate internal volumetric measurement and expressed in tons of 100 cu.ft. The fine forward lines associated with the Aberdeen bow undoubtedly offered fast sailing qualities, but there must have been cargo carriage penalties in terms of broken stowage associated with the fine lines. That Hood's continued to produce ships with a form of the Aberdeen bow until at least 1862 may well have reflected overt conservatism on the part of management and principals. Indeed, even later Hood vessels were still distinguished by carrying the fore part of their hulls further forward above the water line than was normal.

Analysing Lloyd's Register build certificates for construction technology, it would appear that the earlier Hood-built ships did not employ vertical wooden rider knees to support the ends of their deck and hold beams, relying for connection and strength on pairs of horizontal wooden lodging knees to each beam end, and twin bolts extending down through the waterway, beam end and the stringer formed by the shelf and clamp pieces under the beam. Iron vertical hanging knees were first introduced to the deck beams of *Michael Williams* built in 1841; with the commissioning of *Prince of Wales* the following year, the use of iron hanging knees had extended to the lower deck beams as well. The use of wrought iron for strength members at the vessel's extremities – breast hooks and pointers – appeared in *Oliver Cromwell*, built in 1847. The *John Bunyan* built the following year introduced iron staple lodging knees to hold beams, but wood was retained for deck beam lodging knees until 1857. The *Omar Pasha* commissioning in 1854 incorporated pairs of 'malleable iron plates' secured to the end of each beam; a sketch in the vessel's build certificate shows the plates to have been Fell's patent knees. Patented by the well-reputed Workington shipbuilder, Jonathan Fell, the knees, which were installed additionally to lodging and hanging knees, provided a connection between the beam and a pair of frames when the beam landed between the pair of frames.

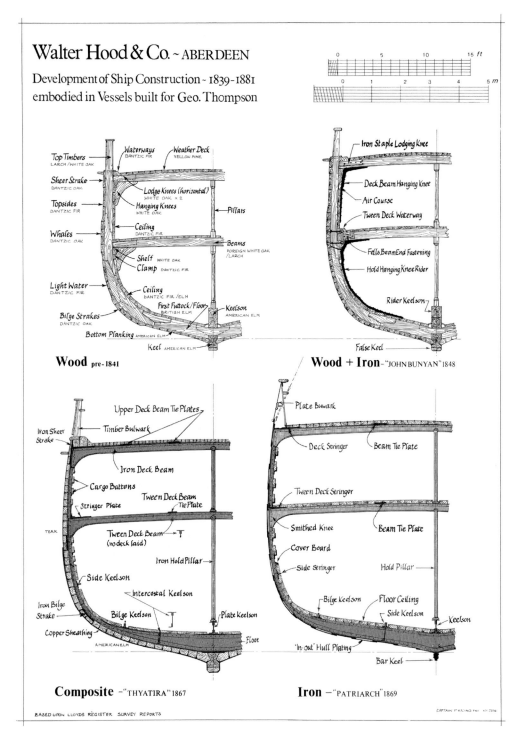

Walter Hood & Co. ~ ABERDEEN

Development of Ship Construction ~ 1839-1881
embodied in Vessels built for Geo. Thompson

Wood pre-1841

Top Timbers LARCH/WHITE OAK
Waterways DANTZIC FIR
Weather Deck YELLOW PINE
Sheer Strake DANTZIC OAK
Lodge Knees (horizontal) WHITE OAK x 2
Hanging Knees WHITE OAK
Topsides DANTZIC FIR
Pillars
Ceiling DANTZIC FIR
Whales DANTZIC OAK
Beams FOREIGN WHITE OAK/LARCH
Shelf WHITE OAK
Clamp DANTZIC FIR
Light Water DANTZIC FIR
Ceiling DANTZIC FIR/ELM
First Futtock/Floors BRITISH ELM
Keelson AMERICAN ELM
Bilge Strakes DANTZIC OAK
Bottom Planking AMERICAN ELM
Keel AMERICAN ELM

Wood + Iron - "JOHN BUNYAN" 1848

Iron Staple Lodging Knee
Deck Beam Hanging Knee
Air Course
Tween Deck Waterway
Fells Beam End Fastening
Hold Hanging Knee Rider
Rider Keelson
False Keel

Composite - "THYATIRA" 1867

Upper Deck Beam Tie Plates
Timber Bulwark
Iron Sheer Strake
Iron Deck Beam
Cargo Battens
Stringer Plate
Tween Deck Beam Tie Plate
TEAK
Tween Deck Beam (no deck laid)
Iron Hold Pillar
Side Keelson
Intercostal Keelson
Iron Bilge Strake
Bilge Keelson
Plate Keelson
Copper Sheathing
AMERICAN ELM
Floor

Iron - "PATRIARCH" 1869

Plate Bulwark
Deck Stringer
Beam Tie Plate
Tween Deck Stringer
Smithed Knee
Beam Tie Plate
Cover Board
Side Stringer
Hold Pillar
Bilge Keelson
Floor Ceiling
Side Keelson
Keelson
'In-out' Hull Plating
Bar Keel

BASED UPON LLOYDS REGISTER SURVEY REPORTS

CAPTAIN PILLING FNI 10-2016

A further extension of the use of iron in an otherwise wooden ship construction manifested itself with the commissioning of **Damascus** in 1857. This vessel incorporated fourteen pairs of diagonal iron plates, each 4ft × 5/8ft, laid inside the timbers, and extending from the upper deck clamps in a diagonal lattice around the hull to the long floor heads. The iron plates were through-bolted to the frame timbers where they crossed them. This construction feature, which was to become a class requirement, was common to all subsequent wooden and composite ships; it provided enormous additional longitudinal and transverse strength to the hull.

The increased use of iron in the structure of the ship was a function of a number of factors. Scarcity of suitable grown hardwood for knees and breasthooks was a key element, as was the constant thrust for improved carrying capacity, which less-bulky and lighter ironwork facilitated. The riders associated with hold beam hanging knees materially strengthened the vessel's structure, and there would also be questions of durability and classification longevity.

The type of wood used in the construction of Hood's vessels also changed significantly over the course of the period. Up to the late 1840s, apart from the strakes of bottom planking between the keel and the bilge for which American elm was used, and key strength member strakes such as the sheer strake, plank-sheer and wales for which Danzic oak was used, the remainder of the hull planking was softwood. Danzic oak, American rock elm and larch were used for key structural members such as the keel, beams and

Walter Hood & Co. development of ship construction, 1839 to 1881, embodied in vessels built for George Thompson.

floors. With the introduction of ships built specifically for long-haul, fast liner services, the more general use of hardwoods for overall construction becomes evident. Thus, **John Bunyan** was the first of GTJCo.'s ships to be built entirely of hardwood with the exception of her decks, for which yellow pine was used; this feature continued even on the later iron sailing ships. With the increasing use of hardwoods, so also the introduction of tropical hardwoods – teak, mahogany and tamarack – became apparent; again a function of material availability in the face of a vanishing native hardwood resources.

The choice of timber used in a vessel's construction had an important bearing upon the initial classification period accorded to her by Lloyd's Register. Paasch in his masterpiece *Illustrated Marine Encyclopedia* explains:[6]

> Vessels built of teak, oak or other superior material are generally (when new) classed on the first Character for terms varying from 12 to 18 years. Vessels built of somewhat lower quality of wood are classed from 9 to 12 years; and those of still less durable timber, for say 6 to 8 years.

In certain of the Lloyd's Register build certificates issued for Hood-built ships, the surveyor annotated the impact on initial class life of the various wood structural elements. The lowest common denominator prevailed in terms of final class allocation. An extra year's initial classification life was granted to vessels built under 'a watertight roof'. The earliest Hood ship so-built was likely to have been **Wooloomooloo**, completed in September 1852. Quite apart from the class credit, there must have been distinct practical and economic advantages attaching to building under cover in the climate of Aberdeen! The use of yellow metal rather than iron for critical fastenings also gained an extra year's initial classification period.

With the death of Walter Hood, James Buyers succeeded as managing partner of Walter Hood & Co. A census conducted at this time showed that Walter Hood's shipyard employed seventy-six men and thirty-nine boys. There was a lull in production at the yard to GTJCo.'s account of some nineteen months following the delivery of **Kosciusko** in August 1862 until delivery of the next Aberdeen Line clipper, the 'lucky' **Nineveh** in March 1864. In the meantime, the yard delivered the 895-ton ship **Glengairn** for Alexander Nicol, and a small 216-ton clipper brig **Fawn** for his brother, William Nicol of Liverpool.

GTJCo. had been absent from the China tea trade since 1856, when **John Bunyan** was taken off the trade to boost tonnage requirements

on the Aberdeen Line's new Sydney service. In the interim, American competition had effectively pulled out of the China trade as a result of the American Civil War. Now, as earlier noted, in July 1862 the company re-entered the trade with the first of three direct sailings by **Queen of Nations** (Mitchell) from London to Shanghai/Woosung. Sailing on each occasion with the benefit of the North-East Monsoon, she averaged 122 days homewards, a fair average for the tea fleets of the time, but not spectacular. The bill of entry reported in the *Mercantile Gazette* (2 February 1865) in respect to her third homewards uplift gives an indication of a typical China cargo:

Tea	chests	4,300
	half chests	4,185
	packages	4,829
	boxes	866
Silk	bales	150
Tobacco	bales	10

Robert Stevens, whose report on the same voyage gives significantly different figures, goes on to give information in respect to the overall loading in his book *Stevens on Stowage*. The vessel stowed 35 tons of [iron] kentledge and took on 230 tons of shingle ballast. In her loaded condition, she drew 16ft 5in forward, and 17ft 10in aft. Her best trim was 4in by the stern, but on this occasion, heavy teas stowed in the after hold impacted adversely upon her trim.[7] The inwards freight agent for her China runs was W.O. Young, who we have seen brokering the GTJCo. sailings to Sydney immediately before the company went independent. Indicative of the esteem with which Stevens was held by the shipping companies for his work, the following testimonial appeared in the fifth edition of *Stevens on Stowage*, dated 7 July 1866:

> We now return your article on the Stowage of Tea, which we think very much to the point, and so far as we know, is correct to the 'Queen of Nations'. To show our appreciation of your work on Stowage, we may mention that we give a copy to each of our Captains – twenty of them – besides having recourse to it here at our office in London.
>
> George Thompson Jnr.

Stevens on Stowage

Robert White Stevens was born in the Barbican area of Plymouth in 1806. The sixth son of John Stevens, a well-known local shipowner, coal factor and owner of the Maritime Inn in Southside Street, Robert was brought up in a family heavily involved in shipping. However, he embarked upon a career in printing and publishing; at the age of 22, he purchased a printers in the Parade, in addition to conducting a business in nautical chart and publications sales.

The first edition of *On the Stowage of Ships and their Cargoes*, as its full title read, was published in 1858; from an initial 172 pages, it grew through seven editions to an 816-page volume as finally reprinted in 1891. From the outset, *Stevens on Stowage*, as it was known in the industry, captured the trust and affection of its mariner and shipowner aficionados. In his great commentary on ships and the sea, *The Mirror of the Sea*, Captain Joseph Conrad accepted it as part of the marine infrastructure of the day:

> 'Stevens on Stowage' is a portly volume with the renown and weight (in its own world) of Coke on Littleton. Stevens is an agreeable writer, and, as is the case with men of talent, his gifts adorn his sterling soundness. He gives you the official teaching on the whole subject, is precise as to rules, mentions illustrative events, quotes law cases where verdicts turned upon a point of stowage. He is never pedantic, and, for all his close adherence to broad principles, he is ready to admit that no two ships can be treated exactly alike.

What was Stevens' secret? I believe it lay in the fact that he based his writings upon the real business of cargo; he corresponded extensively with top-class masters, setting down their proven experience (and mistakes) in many trades. To a high degree, it was a co-operative effort, with Stevens acting as the catalyst. Not only do we learn in detail how to stow a wide range of cargoes for successful out-turn, but we also gain an appreciation of the impact upon the vessels' sailing qualities arising therefrom. To the mariner, this is the stuff of conviction! *Stevens on Stowage* ▶

was not just about stowage *per se*, but combined a compendium of commercial and cargo character information, customs procedures, port practices, etc.; all the information a master before the days of telegraph, let alone satellite communications, needed to successfully prosecute his command.

Predictably, the experience of Aberdeen Line commanders featured prominently in the text. Thus we find:

- JERUSALEM (Largie) loading casks of Western Australian pearl shell out of Melbourne;
- TRANSATLANTIC (Philip), QUEEN OF NATIONS (Mitchell), and OMAR PASHA (Henry) loading wool and colonial produce cargoes out of Sydney and Melbourne; and,
- QUEEN OF NATIONS (Mitchell) loading tea out of Shanghai.

In each case we learn details of ballast, and how the stow impacted draft, trim and sailing qualities; tonnage dues, pilotage rates and other voyage costs.

Stevens died in 1870; his *magnum opus* remained the standard text until displaced by that other great work on cargo, Thomas's *Stowage*, in 1928. In an era when the science of cargo work has been reduced to ubiquitous 'boxes', *Stevens on Stowage* remains a particularly fine read. Stevens' two daughters illuminated the text with some lovely illustrations, both scenic and technical. My own copy is further enlivened by copious marginal notes by its original working owner, indicative of the trusted professional companion status it enjoyed.

Hitherto, GTJCo.'s London office had been in sub-let accommodation in 12 St Helen's Place. With London-based business taking on an increasingly important dimension in the company's affairs, the time had come for larger offices, and the move was made on Sunday, 12 April 1863 to offices at 24 Leadenhall Street in the heartland of London shipping, premises that it would occupy for the next thirty-three years.

In June 1863, the ship **John Bunyan**, which had done so much to establish the company's reputation for fast sailing ships, and which

Nineveh lying at Sydney Cove; note the cargo access ramp. (National Library of Australia SA PRG 1373/3/32)

had effected the turnaround of Britain's fortunes on the China tea trade, was sold for further trading. She had been withdrawn from the main-line Sydney trade at the end of 1859, and after a year on the Quebec trade, had undertaken two voyages to Wellington under charter to Shaw Savill. On the first of these voyages, the crew broached spirits in the cargo and 'mutinied'; the offenders were held at bay by a pistol-armed commander, Captain Allan, before being clapped in irons to await their fate before a magistrate in Wellington. The fact that they only received a six-month jail sentence suggests that the 'mutiny' was a pretty mild affair.[8] *John Bunyan*'s last two voyages under GTJCo. ownership were round trips to New York from London. GTJCo. held a 40/64 terminal interest in the ship at sale to Vanner and Co., London; under her new owners, she was to return to the Australia and China trades.

Two crack clippers commissioned from Hood's yard to the company's account in 1864; in March the 1,174-ton ship *Nineveh* (GTJCo. 40/64) and in August the 839-ton ship *Ethiopian* (GTJCo. 44/64). *Nineveh* was placed on the Sydney service under the command of Captain James Donald, where she was to remain

for most of her GTJCo. working life. She had a reputation for being an extremely lucky ship and a good money earner, both in terms of freight and passengers. The London partner, Stephen Thompson, was later to host a banquet at the Holborn Restaurant in honour of the ship and her subsequent commander, Captain Thomas Barnet, in the course of which he repeatedly toasted the 'Lucky Nineveh'.[9] A virtual sister to *Kosciusko*, she was outfitted 'with all recent improvements, including a steam winch for the discharge of cargo'.[10] It is interesting to note that her average round voyage time over the course of the 1860s was very similar to *Kosciusko*'s, 330 days versus 335 days, and her sea passages were also similar – not an extreme passage maker, but a good all-rounder.

Ethiopian, which followed *Nineveh*, was notably smaller, effectively a sister of *Queen of Nations*. She incorporated a number of design features including for the first time in a GTJCo. ship the use of iron for her hold beams (but not her deck beams, which remained British oak). All her topsails and topgallants were set using a new self-reefing gear jointly patented by John Colling and David Pinkey. Colling's and Pinkey's roller reefing gear was less complicated than Cunningham's, the sail rolling around a light spar mounted forward of the topsail yard, and had the added advantage that the whole sail could be reefed in. Rotation of the reefing spar was achieved by reefing halyards wound around drums at the extremity of the spar. Raising of the topsail yard pulled the sail out of its roll, at the same time winding the reefing halyards on to spar-end drums. When the spar was lowered to reef the sail, tension on the reefing halyards wound the sail on to the spar. The principle was very similar to roller reefing found in modern yachts. Excellent illustrated descriptions of both Cunningham's and Colling's and Pinkey's roller reefing gears may be found in Underhill's *Masting and Rigging*.[11] The ship was also 'fitted with all the modern improvements, having also a steam engine, which does all the laborious work of the ship, such as heaving the anchor up, etc. in addition to acting as a condenser for the supply of fresh water'.[12]

Ethiopian was not fitted up for carrying passengers, 'being intended for the China trade'. This was reflected in her limited accommodation arrangements aft, which comprised a raised quarterdeck upon which was built a 'Liverpool house' giving head room to the interior of the accommodation. The 'Liverpool house', unlike the more conventional 'Aberdeen house', extended across the full breadth of the ship, with rounded-down sides to bulwark level (like a truncated full poop), such that there were no fore and aft access gangways along the sides of the house at deck edge; rather, to gain access from aft to forward, it was necessary to either go over the top of the Liverpool house by way of the ladders provided, or down through the after accommodation doors and out on to the main deck at the forward end of the house – not a popular option in other than fine weather! The Liverpool house occupied the forward length of the raised quarterdeck, leaving a small deck aft upon which was arranged the binnacle, steering gear and wheel. In a following sea, this position was extremely exposed. While providing greater accommodation volume per given length, outside *Ethiopian* and possibly the later *Centurion* (II), the full-width Liverpool house did not gain favour on Hood-built ships.

Ethiopian's maiden voyage to Melbourne under the command of Captain William Edward was accomplished in a record sixty-eight days; she was to prove a consistently fast vessel. After discharging in Melbourne, she initiated the triangular service that was to employ GTJCo.'s crack cargo ships for the next couple of decades, including early steamer voyages. From Melbourne, she loaded coal for Shanghai; upon completion of discharge at Shanghai, she pulled downstream to Woosung, where she loaded tea for London. Her

Harlaw lying at Sydney Cove. (National Library of Australia SA PRG-1373-4-52)

homeward tea passage occupied 122 days, a good time given that she was sailing into the teeth of the south-west monsoon in the South China Sea.

The shareholding grouping of GTJ, William Henderson, Stephen Thompson, and George Thompson Youngest next took a 16/64 non-subscribing owner interest in the 344-ton Hood-built ship *Columba* in October 1865; James Buyers also took a 24/64 interest. This appears to have been purely an investment, for the vessel never participated in the company's main-line trades, being employed in tramping, chiefly carrying coal out of the north-east of England and Newcastle, New South Wales, to Chile, returning with nitrates from Iquique.

In February 1866, a revised shareholding group comprising William Henderson, Stephen Thompson, George Thompson Youngest and for the first time Cornelius Thompson, became subscribing owners (44/64) in the new 894-ton Hood-built ship *Harlaw*. GTJ also took an 8/64 private interest in the ship. The new vessel would seem to have pioneered the use of iron for beams and hold stanchions within a Hood-built vessel. *Harlaw* was built for the Australia and China trades, and indeed she was placed immediately on to the triangular trade to China via Sydney.

In May 1866, all ship shareholdings were transferred to the new shareholding group, marking the retirement of GTJ as senior partner. The exact date of his retirement is not clear. While all accounts have him retiring in 1866, I sense the exact date may have been 31 December 1865 (which would have been in line with subsequent practice); this would explain his exclusion from the subscribing shareholding in *Harlaw*. William Henderson now became senior partner, with Stephen Thompson and his brother George Thompson Youngest managing the London office, and Cornelius Thompson admitted to the partnership. Cornelius by this time was actively involved in the management of Walter Hood, where his skills headed up the design side. George Thompson Youngest appeared as a subscribing shareholder for only two years, whereafter he was dropped, though he frequently appeared as a private shareholder in subsequent ship investments.

George Thompson Junior's reign as senior partner had seen the partnership develop from tenuous beginnings with shipowning almost an aside to a broad-based shipping enterprise incorporating flagship liner services to Australia, transatlantic immigrant and timber trades, a renewed strong presence in the China tea trade, marine insurance, shipbuilding, commodity trading, shipbroking and ship management. GTJ's personal interests extended to banking, insurance underwriting, railway developments and short-sea shipping. The partnership's development in arriving at its latent pre-eminent position in the shipping world had meant it had participated in many facets of British merchant shipping of the time, including the copper ore, guano, British coastal and Baltic trades; now it had changed from an essentially tramp-based operation to a respected liner operator, participating in the Australian, China and North Atlantic trades. The driving force that had seen the partnership through difficult times and set the tone for the future was undoubtedly the adventurous spirit and keen business acumen of the founding senior partner. GTJ's achievement was secured against a background of his having undertaken his full share of civic, public, charitable, church and diverse business responsibilities. I like to feel that the spirit of GTJ may be summarised in his armorial motto *per periculum vivo* – 'through danger I live' (hardly the hallmark of today's analyst bedevilled market!).

GTJ's protege, William Henderson, who succeeded him as senior partner, was a very different man; if GTJ was the piston leading the driving force, Henderson was the flywheel smoothing the drive. He shared many of GTJ's qualities, however. A deeply religious man, like GTJ he was a pillar of the Free Church; he was extremely public spirited, deeply committed to charitable works and a devoted family man. He was significantly more conservative than GTJ, and distinctly self-centred. That said, over the next two decades he was to lead the company through its zenith. If GTJ's armorial motto spoke for GTJ, so Henderson's spoke for the character of Henderson – *sola virtus nobilitat* – 'virtue alone ennobles'.[13]

In July 1866, the company disposed of its 40/64 interest in *Jane Boyd* when the vessel was sold to foreigners. Her place on the Quebec trade from Aberdeen was taken by *Transatlantic*, brought back from the Australian line. *Jane Boyd* had served the company with distinction for twenty-three years on a number of trades, including the Cuba–Swansea copper ore, Peruvian guano, and for a decade and a half, the Aberdeen–Quebec immigrant and timber service. In that time she had been commanded by a number of GTJ's foremost early commanders, including Isaac Merchant, Herman Gansen, John Mann and latterly John Colvin. Concurrent with *Jane Boyd*'s departure, *Centurion* was also taken off the Australian service and undertook a single voyage to Quebec returning to Leith; on her

way in, she struck Carr Rock off St Andrews on 11 November 1866 with apparently no damage, but perhaps significantly she was sold out of GTJCo. service upon her subsequent arrival in Newcastle after discharge at Leith. GTJCo.'s terminal interest in the vessel was 24/64.

Centurion's place on the Australian liner service was taken by the newly built 1,079-ton Hood ship *Christiana Thompson*, commissioned in September 1866 (GTJCo. 44/64). Named after GTJ's wife, along with Nicol's very slightly larger *George Thompson* commissioned in 1865 the pair formed a touching tribute to a man and wife who had done so much for Aberdeen shipping. *Christiana Thompson* was designed specifically for the Australian trade, and incorporated a number of labour-saving devices, including Colling's and Pinkey's patent roller reefing controlling a main topgallant sail above double topsails. Her foreyard was also controlled by means of another of Henry Cunningham's patent devices, a brace winch; such a device was also retrofitted in *Colonial Empire*.[14] *Christiana Thompson* was to initially serve on the Sydney service; her command was vested in Robert Murray (ex-*Damascus)*, who was to remain in control of the new ship for the whole of her twenty-one years with GTJCo. In service, she was to prove a slightly better than average passage maker.

The commanders and officers employed by GTJCo. were 'company's men', most of whom had served their time with the company, often natives of the north-east of Scotland. Standards significantly higher than the norm were required, and this was reflected in the reputation of the ships and their safety record. Command was rarely vested in outsiders unless they brought with them a significant track record, and promotion was based upon seniority. However, an amusing anecdote recounted in MacKinnon[15] attributed to Captain Thomas Ayling Wyness, who served his time with the company and later became a distinguished harbourmaster at Aberdeen, demonstrates that management had an eye for talent – and a sense of humour!

STAR OF PEACE was on a voyage home from Australia [January 1866], carrying passengers, and amongst other things, a consignment of gold for the British Government. Unfortunately, as she was running down to Cape Horn her master [William Mitchell] died, and was buried at sea, and the command was naturally assumed by the First Mate [Robert Algernon Perrett], who was a young and rising officer [a certificated master mariner], but by no means high up as regards seniority in the list of first mates eligible for promotion. [In the South Atlantic] STAR OF PEACE encountered QUEEN OF NATIONS [Thomas Mitchell, commander], whose first mate was senior to Perrett. The two vessels exchanged signals, and the QUEEN OF NATIONS was informed of the death of the Master of the STAR OF PEACE. There was a regulation of the owners that the senior officer of one ship, if on the spot should take precedence over a junior officer of another ship if a vacancy in a command should occur. The mate of the QUEEN OF NATIONS no doubt blessed his good fortune that a vacancy had occurred so unexpectedly in mid ocean, and the QUEEN OF NATIONS now signalled the STAR OF PEACE that her mate would go on board the STAR OF PEACE and take command of her. Not having got any reply to the last signal, the mate of the QUEEN OF NATIONS put his effects together and with them got into a boat, which was lowered to take him to the STAR OF PEACE. When the boat was half-way across he was thrown on his beam ends – so to speak – when he saw the STAR OF PEACE square her yards and sail away, leaving him and his 'dunnage' afloat in the small boat and with no alternative but row back discomfited to resume his subaltern duties on his own ship. The young mate of the STAR OF PEACE, Perrett, had quickly weighed up the situation, and thought that it would be very hard lines on him that his temporary promotion should be baulked by a chance encounter with the QUEEN OF NATIONS and the credit taken from him of bringing the STAR OF PEACE and cargo safely home. And so he 'got away with' the STAR OF PEACE, and as it happened, seems to have 'got away with' his breach of regulations as well.

A search of Lloyd's Captains Register does not indicate the mate of the **Queen of Nations** as holding a master mariner's certificate of competency at the time of the incident, in which case Perrett was well within his rights. Perrett certainly got away with his actions, for he was given substantive command of **Wave of Life** sailing out of London the next voyage, the start of a distinguished career in command in the company's service.

In Australia, the partnership between Montefiore and Graham, GTJCo.'s Sydney agents, had dissolved in 1861, with Jacob Montefiore acquiring the squatting and shipping agency elements of the business. For three years he traded in his own right, before joining with his brother and cousin to form Montefiores & Te Kloot in 1866. By this time, he was a very influential member of the colony's commercial, political and social scene, a director of a number of major banking, insurance, mining and agricultural companies; a prominent promoter of railways and the extension of the electric telegraph; a member of the Royal Sydney Yacht Squadron and a director of the Sydney Sailors' Home; an outspoken free trader; and a leading member of the Jewish community. In all but the latter, he would have enjoyed a close synergy with GTJ!

In 1867, Montefiore formed a new company with Samuel Aaron Joseph – Montefiore, Joseph & Co.[16] We earlier met Joseph when he travelled out to New Zealand as a private passenger in **Prince of Wales** in 1843; after a distinguished career in that colony, he had travelled to Sydney in 1856. In the time that had elapsed since his arrival in New South Wales, he had established a strong commercial base, including directorships in a number of banking and insurance companies. Like Montefiore (and GTJ & Henderson), he was also a convinced free trader, and had won the West Sydney seat in the Legislative Assembly in 1864. Montefiore, Joseph & Co. were to competently serve as the Aberdeen Line's managing agents in Sydney until hit by a general financial crisis that impacted adversely upon New South Wales in 1893.

Two incidents involving GTJCo.'s ships were to swiftly test the new agents' effectiveness. **Ethiopian** (William Faulkner) had cleared Melbourne on 23 February 1867, bound for Shanghai with a cargo of 800 tons of coal. On 1 March, she ran into heavy weather in the Tasman Sea to the south-west of Norfolk Island. The heavy weather continued until by 7 March, in a position close east of the New Hebrides (Vanuatu), she was beset by a full hurricane. The ensuing action, which reflected the finest qualities of merchant navy leadership, courage, endurance, and seamanship, can best be described in Captain Faulkner's own words:[17]

5 p.m.: Blowing a perfect hurricane, with a tremendous sea, and every minute expecting to see the masts go over side. At 5.30 p.m.: An awful gust with a heavy sea struck the ship, which hove her right over on her beam ends, the sea half way over the deck, washing away stock houses, water casks and everything off the deck; floated the pinnace and gig off the skid, and cabin half full of water; ship appearing to be settling down slowly, all hands standing outside the weather rail, expecting that they only had a few more minutes to live. Ordered the mizzen and main masts to be cut away, which only required a few lanyards cut, when they went over the side. Still blowing furiously and tremendous seas; no appearance of ship righting; water up to

the bell on the poop. Cut away the foremast, which appeared to ease her a little. Called the Chief Officer, Mr Anderson, but he could not be found; he was last seen going to cut away the main rigging, when he must have been washed overboard; other three of the crew were washed overboard, but succeeded in getting on board again. Sent the carpenter below to see the state of the hold, when he reported that the cargo had shifted and that the water was up to the stringer of 'tween decks. Sent all hands below to trim cargo over and found that the main mast in falling had broken the stand of pumps. At 7 gale decreasing, but still a heavy sea. Ship still lying over, with the water over the combings of the masts. Found that the water had got into the hold from the fore and coal scuttle hatches, and from the combings of the masts, which we secured with sails. Midnight – Wind from SW with very little wind, and quite clear, but still heavy seas; barometer going up fast, 29.50. During the hurricane the sea was one sheet of foam, and at 6 o'clock it was so dark you could not see anyone standing alongside, with most awful lightning; and with the sea, wind and rain, you could not keep your eyes open a second, for it cut like a knife; the heaviest of it lasted about an hour and a half; and there was not one on board ever expected the ship to come up again; and if the ship had not been a strong one she could not have stood it.

Friday, 8th [March]: At daylight got one of the pumps to work, 7 feet water in hold; people trimming cargo; found the ship a helpless wreck; the three masts gone clean by deck, and only the bowsprit standing; cut away the wreck; impossible to save anything; the ship appears to have received no damage outside; found the inside of forecastle and deck-houses washed clean out; people having lost everything; everything in cabin wet; one of the chronometers filled with salt water and stopped. Noon: Calm, with very hot weather, heavy swell, still pumping and trimming, ship righting, and water decreasing.

Saturday 9th: Midnight; Ship nearly upright, and pumps sucked; let the people lay down until till daylight.

Sunday, 10th: Under way with jury-masts; thanked God that we were left two spare topmasts and a few small spars; still calm and very hot; 700 miles from Sydney, without a mast, which is the only port for us.

At more or less the peak of the hurricane at 6 o'clock on 7 March 1867, the barometer was observed by Faulkner to have dropped to 28.70in (972mb); the subsequent rapid rise of the barometer of 0.32in over the next hour suggests that centre of the hurricane must have passed very close to *Ethiopian*. From 8 to 22 March, there was not a breath of wind; Faulkner attempted to tow the vessel with a boat out ahead, to little avail. A brisk wind picked up on 23 March, and blew until 27 March, when the vessel nearly ran aground several times on New Caledonia. By the morning of Monday, 8 April, the vessel had reached within 12 miles of Sydney's South Head, when the wind turned fickle, and the vessel was driven 100 miles north-east of Sydney, with heavy seas. On 13 April, *Ethiopian* was taken in tow by the French warship *Marceau* (Capitaine Galache), and brought safely to anchor in Neutral Bay, Sydney at 2200 hours that night. Repairs were put in hand, and *Ethiopian* resumed her interrupted passage for Shanghai on 27 July 1867.

The second incident involved *Strathdon* (George H. Pile), which arrived off Sydney Heads on the morning of 29 July 1867; a Southerly Buster (a southerly wind in the wake of an intense cold front moving northwards up the coast of New South Wales), which had passed over that night was blowing a full gale. A pilot cutter under a Mr Robinson put out to the ship to embark a pilot, but was overwhelmed. A butcher's boat, also making for *Strathdon*, witnessed the accident and recovered the crew from the stricken pilot boat, only to be overwhelmed herself in short order. A second pilot boat, observing the fate of the first vessel, put out to the rescue and was also overwhelmed. In all, eight brave persons perished in the tragedy, which became known as the '*Strathdon* accident', even though the ship had been a helpless bystander. In fact, *Strathdon* had problems of her own, for having shortened sail to take the pilot, she now found herself beset in a difficult position, and had to anchor off in Obelisk Bay. Joseph, the newly commissioned partner of Montefiore, chartered the steamer *Hunter* and went out in her to render assistance. With the joint help of the tug *Comerang*, lines were secured to *Strathdon*, and she was towed in from her potentially dangerous position. The public rallied to the tragic loss offshore; Montefiore Joseph opened a relief fund with an initial gift of ten guineas, and acted as a collecting point for further donations, along with the *Sydney Morning Herald*.[18]

The year 1867 was to prove a busy year for GTJCo. and for Hood's shipyard. In March, Hood delivered the small 216-ton brig *Janet* for the Aberdeen–Baltic trade. While the vessel was essentially a Buyers' enterprise, Henderson and the three Thompson sons took a joint 16/64 shareholding, along with Alexander Nicol's 4/64, as an investment. Then in April and August successively, two further clippers designed for the Australian and China trades were delivered; the 901-ton *Jerusalem* and 962-ton *Thyatira*. In each vessel the company had a 44/64 subscribing shareholding. Both vessels were initially placed on the Melbourne service and were not to see China until the next decade. *Jerusalem* (James Largie, ex-*Centurion*) was to prove an exceptionally fast passage maker, reputed within the Aberdeen Line to be second only to the great *Thermopylæ*, but stability-wise tender such that she had to take in sail prematurely to avoid being pressed under. *Jerusalem* was one of the first of GTJCo.'s fleet to be fitted with double topgallant sails.

Thyatira was notable for being the first of only two GTJCo. ships to be built on the composite principle. Composite construction was a short-lived phenomena in the shipbuilding world (Hood was only to build three such vessels), essentially a compromise between the strength, lightness and carrying volume of iron construction, and the ability to effectively anti-foul a wooden hull. Before the development of effective anti-fouling paints, iron shell plating attracted marine growth dramatically quickly, such that to sustain speed over a ten-month round trip, it was necessary to undertake an intermediate dry-docking in the Antipodes (hence the number of fine photographs taken of famous iron clippers in the Williamstown dry-dock, Melbourne, and Lyttleton dry-dock, New Zealand). Wooden hull planking could, however, be effectively anti-fouled by sheathing it with copper or yellow metal tingles (the Royal Navy even went so far as to sheath iron hulls with wood to form an intermediate skin upon which copper sheathing might be attached). Accordingly, a composite ship comprised an iron internal 'skeleton', with hardwood timber shell planking. In the case of *Thyatira*, the planking was of American elm from the keel to the bilge strakes, and there upwards, East Indies teak. Lodging knees were replaced by iron spirketing plates, riveted to plates and frames. We are fortunate insofar that a transverse section of the vessel was appended to the Lloyd's Register build certificate. The vessel was fitted with iron lower masts and spars, patent blocks and wire rigging. The *Sydney Morning Herald*,[19] reporting her first arrival in that port in 1869, eulogised that she was:

Composite built ship *Thyatira* at Melbourne. (National Library of Australia SA PRG 1373/3/39)

one of the finest models that ever floated on the waters of Port Jackson. She may in fact be considered a yacht on a large scale, with this advantage that she has a carrying capacity equal to her tonnage necessary for merchant vessels ...

The whole has been fitted with such an amount of care and attention that it affords a fine illustration of the perfection to which the art of shipbuilding can be brought. ... she is a model of symmetry and good order, and a credit to her builders.

Thyatira was commanded on her maiden voyage by James Ross, ex-*Colonial Empire*, who had more than twelve years' service as master with the company. Sadly, on the homeward passage while running the Eastings down to the south-west of New Zealand, Ross died. Command was assumed by the chief officer, David Bain, until the vessel's arrival in London, when substantive command of the vessel was vested in John Mackay. Lubbock recounts[20] an amusing, but nonetheless telling anecdote of *Thyatira*'s newly joined second mate, Mark Breach, when loading in London for Melbourne. As officer-of-the-deck, Breach came across a stranger smoking a pipe over an open hatch. He remonstrated with the offender, who apologised and put the pipe out. Later, Breach was taken to one side by the mate, Bain, who enquired of Breach if he was aware who the person concerned in the pipe-smoking incident was. In fact, it was Stephen Thompson, who had heartily approved of the young officer's action and prophesied a promising career in the company;

Breach went on to become one of GTJCo.'s best-respected sailing ship commanders.

On 16 March 1868, William and Jane Boyd Henderson's eleventh child, Alexander Duff Henderson, was born. In later life, he was to be one of the last partners appointed to the company as a private company, and was to continue in the restructured company post-1905 as a surviving link with the original entity, until 1929.

Hood's next delivery to GTJCo. was the full-poop 938-ton wooden passenger ship *Ascalon*, delivered in April 1868 for the Australian trade. With *Ascalon*'s commissioning, *Omar Pasha*, one of the original ships of the Aberdeen Line to Sydney, and which had given fourteen years' quiet service to the company, was sold to London owners Taylor, Bethell and Roberts in June 1868; GTJCo.'s terminal interest was 36/64th. Her new owners put her on to a Brisbane service, but her second life was short lived. In the Atlantic, ten days from England on her first homewards voyage, her wool cargo took fire, and despite valiant efforts by her master and crew, the ship foundered; luckily, all sixty-four passengers and thirty-two crew were saved.

George Thompson's Aberdeen Line and Walter Hood's shipyard will be remembered in maritime history, if for no other reason, than for the jewel in their joint crown, the extreme clipper *Thermopylæ*, 991 tons, which was launched on 19 August 1868. The partners held a 48/64th subscribing owner interest in the ship, but significantly no fewer than three company shipmasters, Edwards, Merchant and Henry, also held small shareholdings. Increasingly this would seem to have become the pattern and was, I believe, a clear pointer to the quality and commitment of the company and its people.

While a number of ships built for the Line over the years had been built for the 'Australian and China trades' and had held their own on the China tea trade, *Thermopylæ* was arguably the first GTJCo. ship to truly fulfil the status of a thoroughbred tea clipper; that she was also arguably the finest ever built is a reflection on her owners' ambitions, her design, and her construction. The design of *Thermopylæ* is credited to Bernard Waymouth, a senior Lloyd's Register surveyor, who came to prominence in the mid-1860s for the work he undertook on behalf of the committee of Lloyds Register, framing new rules for the construction of composite-built vessels. Waymouth, whose name is also associated with the design of a number of other famous ships of that period including *Leander* (1867), *Shamrock* (1872), *Melbourne* (1875) and possibly GTJCo.'s *Salamis* (also 1875),[21] was principal surveyor to Lloyd's Register from 1871 to 1872, and thereafter secretary until 1890.[22] In today's market, it seems strange that a servant of an institution committed to professional impartiality was permitted to 'moonlight' on commercial ventures of this nature.

James Henderson, the savant of Aberdeen clippers, was in fact adamant that *Thermopylæ* was designed by Cornelius Thompson, not Waymouth; I suspect that the truth lay somewhere in between, with Waymouth providing intellectual input, and Cornelius Thompson orchestrating Waymouth's output. Certainly, Waymouth generated a couple of plans of the ship, including a sail plan, which included spar dimensions.[23] *Thermopylæ*'s profile and cross section bore a strong generic similarity to the above named ships; further, her cross section was distinctly different to other Hood-built ships of that time, notably *Thyatira*, which preceded her, and *Centurion* (II), which came immediately after, both of whose amidships cross section plans have survived.

Reproduction of the '7ft Drawing' by Cornish. (Lloyds Register Foundation)

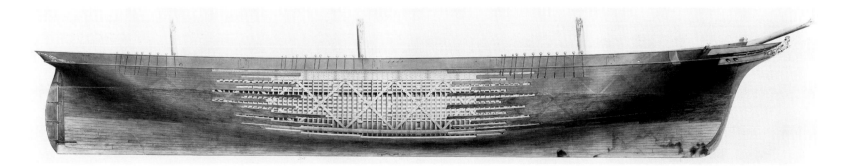

Waymouth's 'Rules for the Construction of Composite Ships' were illuminated by a suite of beautiful drawings executed by a fellow Lloyd's Register surveyor, Harry J. Cornish, who himself went on to become chief surveyor of Lloyd's Register. Outside the main suite of drawings, and incrementally different to a similar drawing within the suite, was a single drawing on a 1:24 scale 7ft long side elevation of a three-masted composite-built sailing ship of about 1,000 tons. The drawing, which had resided in the Science Museum along with the main suite, was returned to Lloyd's Register at the specific request of Cornish in 1925; luckily, the museum photographed it before returning it, for the original has disappeared. The drawing bears a striking resemblance to the known form of **Thermopylæ**, particularly the sweetness of line, fine counter stern and rounded forefoot. Careful extrapolation of dimensions from known sources

and the fact that it was drawn at the same time that Waymouth was designing the ship, tend to confirm my view that the drawing was indeed of **Thermopylæ**, though conclusive provenance has yet to be secured.

Thermopylæ was built on the composite principle, with a topgallant forecastle and a 61ft-long raised quarterdeck; both these structures were contained within the line of her bulwark, to give the side profile of a flush-decked hull. With an eloquent bow, a well-rounded forefoot, and an exquisitely delicate counter, **Thermopylæ** was undoubtedly a beautiful-looking ship, conceived as the 'Company Yacht'. In her design and construction, every consideration was given to speed and optimising cargo carriage. While a comparison of scantlings recorded in Lloyd's Register build certificates[24] demonstrates her to have been generally lighter-scantled than her famous rival

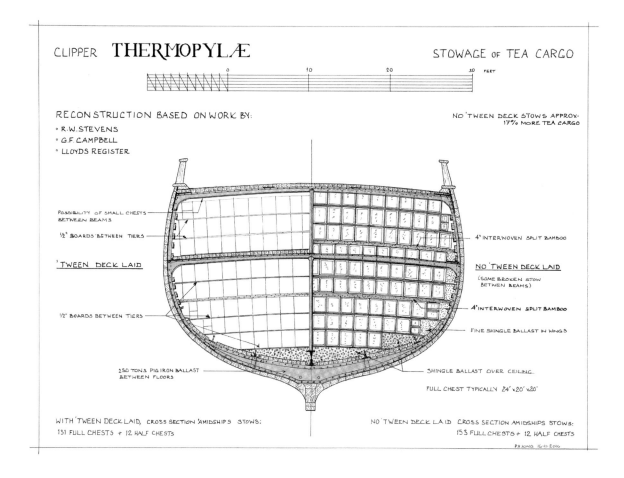

Thermopylæ loading of tea – reconstruction based upon Stevens.

Cutty Sark, further analysis shows that this was achieved without undermining fundamental strength. Strength-critical elements in *Thermopylæ* tended to be heavier than her rival; again, one senses the hand of Waymouth. Unusually, as commissioned she apparently did not have a 'tween deck laid (although a deck is shown on the Lloyd's Register transverse section of the ship); assuming 2½ in yellow pine planking, this would have gained an estimated 13.3 tons deadweight, with net improvement in transverse stability. With a cargo such as tea, there would also have been a significant saving in broken stowage terms by being able to stow up through the beams; by mid-section scale drawing, I estimate a 16.8 per cent gain in the number of standard tea chests that could be stowed. In the modern vernacular, *Thermopylæ* was truly a 'mean machine'.

Given the paucity of recorded information about ships built at the Hood shipyard, we are fortunate that offsets for *Thermopylæ* were recorded in a yard offset book, a copy of which has survived; James Henderson was given access to these offsets, on the basis of which he executed the definitive line drawings on which our current appreciation of *Thermopylæ*'s form are based. These support the popular impression that her hull was devoid of flat surfaces; she in fact had very fine lines forward and aft. Forward, her lines were sharp, carried well aft, very slightly concave below the waterline; there was minimal concavity of the buttock line in way of the counter, again below the waterline. Her hull cross section presented an extremely attractive form and bore the Waymouth marque, with a concave garboard, well-rounded bilge, and a 20in tumble home; her maximum breadth occurred some 3ft below the water line. In service, the vessel had a splendid reputation for going to windward, an attribute that probably found its origin in her depth of keel, which was extended down by a false keel to give a total moulded dimension of 21in (by comparison, *Cutty Sark*'s keel on almost identical dimensions was 17in deep). Her construction materials were such as to qualify her for a basic fourteen years' initial classification by Lloyd's Register; the use of yellow metal fastenings accorded her a further two years; while the fact that she was built under cover added a further year, so that her initial classification life was seventeen years.

Thermopylæ's lower fore and main masts, together with their yards, were of iron; galvanised wire was employed for her standing rigging. Her original sail arrangements are portrayed in a plan prepared by Bernard Waymouth, resting in Lloyd's Register's archives. The plan is annotated with spar dimensions and rake of masts, and notes the application of Colling's and Pinkey's roller reefing gear. Originally, this patent equipment was to be fitted to the main topgallant and mizzen topsails, but a subsequent note in red changed the large single mizzen topsail to double topsails. Double topsails were installed on the fore and main stations. Her profile was very lofty, with long yards. A Cunningham's patent continuous brace winch, which was originally evolved to traverse large naval guns, was installed to control the fore lower yard. Located abaft the

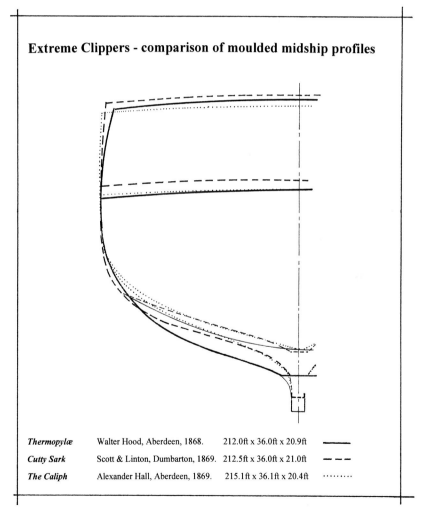

Extreme Clippers - comparison of moulded midship profiles

Thermopylæ	Walter Hood, Aberdeen, 1868.	212.0ft x 36.0ft x 20.9ft	——————
Cutty Sark	Scott & Linton, Dumbarton, 1869.	212.5ft x 36.0ft x 21.0ft	– – –
The Caliph	Alexander Hall, Aberdeen, 1869.	215.1ft x 36.1ft x 20.4ft	··········

Extreme clippers; comparison of moulded sections.

yellow-metal-sheathed over felt. Three iron 8ft panting beams were added forward, and a wooden crosspiece, secured by a pair of wooden lodging knees, was installed under the bowsprit in the forecastle. These additions, which were signed off by Harry Cornish, would seem to indicate that the extreme bow gave rise to excessive panting on her maiden passage south. (In 1884, an additional panting beam was introduced forward, backed by a 19.5ft panting stringer either side. This would seem to suggest that excessive panting remained a problem.)

Captain Edward was not to command the ship on her maiden Australian voyage, however; indeed, he was not to sail in command again, and I believe that having brought *Thermopylæ* 'up' to London, he came ashore to take up a post as the company's ships'

Cunningham and his patent brace winch, originally developed for traversing large naval guns.

mainmast, the winch engaged a permanent chain across the deck, connecting through bulwark sheaves to brace tackles; pulling in on one side paid out on the other, facilitating the adjustment of the fore yard by two men working in safety at the centre line of the ship.

Named at launch by Mrs Hardy Robinson of Denmore, *Thermopylæ* established a new style of naming for GTJCo. ships, which with the notable exception of the first two steamers, was to survive the Line; Greek martial victories blessed most of the remainder of the sailing fleet, switching to Greek philosophers for some of the steamers. *Thermopylæ*'s figurehead on the Waymouth sail plan was depicted as a well-proportioned Grecian goddess, but as commissioned it was a finely carved portrayal of King Leonidas, complete with removable shield and sword, in white and gold. (Leonidas led 300 Spartans in the defence of the Pass of Thermopylæ against an invading 30,000-strong Persian army in 380 BC.) The new ship's Latin motto translated as 'As long as I live, I'll crow'; somewhat presumptively, she sported a gilded cockerel at her mainmast cap. Completed on 17 September, *Thermopylæ* sailed for London with a cargo of granite and whisky on the 21st of the month under the command of Captain William Edward, one of GTJ's most trusted commanders, lately of the *Ethiopian*. Upon completion of discharge in London, she was dry-docked, her bottom cleaned and she was

Clipper *Thermopylæ* at anchor in Sydney Harbour. (National Library of Australia SA 1373/3/43)

Thermopylæ at anchor in Sydney Harbour. (National Library of Australia SA PRG 1373/4/59)

husband [marine superintendent] in London, before becoming a surveyor with the Board of Trade. He was to continue as an active shareholder in GTJCo. tonnage until his death in 1884. Breaking with normal GTJCo. practice, Edward's place for the maiden voyage was taken by a newcomer to the company, Captain Robert Kemball. A Suffolk man, Kemball had originally gone out to Adelaide as mate of the 15-ton coasting cutter *Breeze* in 1848. He had subsequently been mate of the *Orient*, and successively commanded *Fairlight*, *Queen Bee* and latterly the Hall-built clipper *Yang Tsze*;[25] his reputation was probably forged in the latter vessel, for though she was not a notable flyer, he succeeded in 1867 in beating five ships home from China, each with a reputation of being faster than his command.[26]

Departing Gravesend at dawn on Saturday, 7 November 1868, *Thermopylæ*'s maiden voyage under Kemball on the Australia–China triangular service for which she had been designed, established beyond doubt her credentials as an ultimate thoroughbred, and fully justified her owner's choice of commander. On the outward leg to Melbourne, which she reached in the evening of 9 January 1869, she achieved a record passage of sixty-three days (sixty days from the Lizard to Cape Otway). After discharge at Melbourne, she ballasted to Newcastle; en route she overhauled HMS *Charybdis*, whose commanding officer graciously signalled:[27]

'Goodbye. You are too much for us. You are the finest model of a ship
I ever saw. It does my heart good to look at you.'

At Newcastle she loaded 1,200 tons of coal for Shanghai; that such a graceful, beautiful ship should serve as a collier hardly bears thinking about, but the positioning economics were ideal. Her passage to Shanghai took her between the Chesterfield Reefs and New Caledonia – not a track I enjoy given the numerous poorly charted submerged reefs along the way. According to her log, she anchored off Pleasant Island (now the Republic of Nauru, famed for its former phosphate deposits), on 23 February 'to buy a quantity of jugs and coconuts'. Arriving off the Shanghai pilot station north of Ningpo on 10 March, she had established a further passage record of twenty-eight days, pilot-to-pilot.

Upon completion of discharge at Shanghai, *Thermopylæ* moved 500 miles down the coast to the Pagoda Anchorage in the Min River below Foochow, arriving on 2 May to take on her first tea cargo. The Pagoda Anchorage was the favourite loading point for the crack clippers. Navigation of the Min River, including the precipitous gorge of the Mingpan Pass, to gain access to the anchorage was an act of seamanship in its own right. At the height of the clipper ship era, the anchorage must have cut a thrilling sight, with the assemblage of ocean aristocrats taking on the first of the season's tea from sampans lying alongside. Numerous depictions have been made of clippers loading in the Pagoda Anchorage, perhaps none more evocative than a scraper board in George Campbell's *China Tea Clippers*.[28]

The preparation for, and loading of a tea cargo was a highly specialised operation. The hold had first to be thoroughly cleaned (no small job after a coal cargo!), iron work painted and the spaces efficiently ventilated; every attention had to be paid to ensuring that leaks were caulked, bilges sweet, and pumps operated efficiently. This done, preparations were made for receiving the cargo. This initially involved the taking in of a quantity of clean shingle ballast compatible with the ship's stability characteristics and permanent ballast. *Thermopylæ* carried 100 tons of pig iron ballast laid between her floors; no figures are available for the quantities of shingle ballast she took in, but typically a clipper would take in between 150 and 250 tons. Stevens, as ever, describes the modus operandi in wonderful detail, drawing upon the practical experience of an experienced master, Captain R. Little RNR, commander of the clipper *John Temperley*,[29] as communicated by letter:

The usual way of dunnaging a tea cargo in China, is to level the ballast even with the upper part of the keelson – in some cases a little higher, according to the form of the ship. The depth is further regulated by taking into consideration the distance from the under part of the lower deck to the surface of the ballast so that a calculated number of tiers of chests may come in exactly, after the ballast is carefully leveled and rounded down towards the wings; this rounding is done to give the tiers the exact curve of the deck and beams. The distance is measured very precisely with rods, as the ballast is being leveled, and the Chinese stevedores will thus detect the projection of the smallest stone, which is immediately removed. The ballast is covered with half-inch boards, supplied for the purpose by the stevedores at a moderate rate. The ground tier, or flooring chop as it is called in China, is then laid; the lower corners of the wing chests being kept 14 to 16 inches from the bilges of the ship. The wings are then filled in with ballast, which is levelled for the second tier and covered with planks where that tier overlaps the first; the same as under the ground tier. The second tier is laid on the first, and the lower corners of the wing chests are carried out to about 8, 10 or 12 inches from the side, according to the form of the ship and the quantity of ballast required to be stowed away. It is then leveled as before, and the third tier laid; the wing chests are brought to within three or four inches of the sides, the intervening space being filled in with small ballast kept especially for that purpose. When this tier is completed, the hold, in the estimation of a practical and intelligent seaman, has an appearance worthy of being admired – the surface looks like a splendid deck, flush from stem to stern. Above this tier the dunnage used is split bamboo interwoven trellis-fashion, say from two to four inches thick. There is no dunnage of any kind between the sides or ends of the three lower tiers of tea chests and the ballast, which is always very hard stone or shingle – porous sandstone or anything approaching to it being inadmissible. The pump-well, chain lockers, masts, etc. were dunnaged with half-inch boards the same as on the ballast under the ground tier chop. The lower deck was dunnaged with one-inch stuff; sides with split bamboo interwoven, same as below. No matting of any kind was used on the cargo in the main hold or in the 'tween decks. In stowing the tiers they are begun from the sides, and finished in the middle. When fairly entered two Chinamen get on and jamb them down in their places, after which the tier is beaten even at the edges with a heavy wooden mallet about one foot square and the chests are squeezed in so tight that the wing (or end) chests take the shape of the sides of the ship without injury to the packages, when properly stowed.

It was the practice for the flooring chop to comprise chests of the previous season's, or green tea, as an additional safeguard to the new crop being loaded. Stevens illustrated his section on tea with an intricate drawing, which has been much copied. In the drawing on page 88 I have used Stevens' drawing as the basis for a reconstruction of the stowage as it would have applied to the 'tween deck-less **Thermopylæ**.

It was during the time that **Thermopylæ** was taking on her first tea cargo at the Pagoda Anchorage that the famous 'Golden Cockerel' incident occurred. The ship had triumphantly and somewhat cockily arrived at the anchorage with a gilded cockerel surmounting her

mainmast truck; the insinuation was clear and inevitably drew a degree of good-humoured rancour from the other crack ships in the anchorage. One night, when there was some sort of celebratory party under way on board (Lubbock suggests Kemball's birthday) distracting attention, a seaman swam over to the ship, swarmed up the hawse, climbed the mainmast, and stole the cockerel. **Thermopylæ**'s mate at the time, Allan, declared that the incident was plotted by all the officers and crews of the other clippers; Lubbock ascribed the execution of the theft to a seaman from **Taeping**.[30] However, an indignant penciled margin note in my copy of *The Sea Carriers* (margin notes in second-hand books greatly enhance their character and value for me!) states:

> No. The cock was ~~stolen~~ taken by a sailor from Sir Lancelot who swam aboard T on a dark night, and swarmed up to the mainmast truck of the T, took the cock and placed it at the masthead head of Sir Lancelot. Captain Wyness, Harbour Master at Aberdeen who was an officer of the Line is the authority in this. It was no theft but an amusing challenge. The cock was returned to Thermopylæ.

Thermopylæ was towed down the Min River on 3 July 1869, and cleared China on 5 July. On her passage home, she overhauled the clipper **Leander** and Holt's steamer **Achilles**, arriving at Gravesend on 2 October, ninety-one days out from China, a record passage that to Kemball's chagrin was only to stand for two weeks, when **Sir Lancelot** arrived home clipping two days off her time. However, nothing could detract from the vessel's extraordinary achievement of record passages on each leg of the triangular service. In building, outfitting and manning **Thermopylæ**, GTJCo. had undoubtedly embarked upon a project to establish a one-off ship, and this it surely achieved. And her maiden voyage was no one-night stand, for she was to continue to perform among the very best for many years to come, though never quite to the overall superlatives of her first voyage. An analysis of her eleven voyages from London to Melbourne shows an average of 73.2 days on passage, while from China home, she averaged 106.7 days[31] (**Cutty Sark**, with whom she has been principally compared, averaged 117.1 days over eight China homeward voyages). The factors that forged her success were complex, but may be summarised:

- Her initial design and construction, which achieved not just an exceptionally fast ship, but also an effective and relatively safe cargo carrier for servicing her designated trades. There were undoubtedly faster ships on certain points of the wind, but many of these, particularly **Ariel**, were 'over-bred' to the point that they were poor cargo carriers, and dangerous in certain sea conditions. I tend to regard such ships as freaks.

- Her subsequent maintenance; no expense was spared in securing the quality of her hull, with dockings upon each return to Britain, when in particular, her yellow-metal sheathing was either replaced, or rendered fair.

- The quality of her commander and officers. In Kemball, GTJCo. had a first-class commander. He was a good leader, a skilful passage planner, a bold navigator and an indefatigable driver. On the ship's maiden voyage, he was backed by a first-class afterguard; Nathaniel Allan the mate, a cousin of the well-respected Captain Andrew Shewan of **Norman Court** fame, was to enjoy a long career in the company, commanding a number of the crack sailers including **Thermopylæ**, and later steamers; and Charles Matheson, second mate, who was to succeed Allan as mate and then Kemball as her commander, before being killed in a tragic accident in command of the steamer **Aberdeen**. In the quality of her successive commanders and afterguard, **Thermopylæ** stood apart from her arguably more famous rival **Cutty Sark.** In a paper in the *Mariner's Mirror*, John Crosse makes an interesting comparison between the performance of the two rivals in 1872, based upon an analysis of their official log books, and comes to just this conclusion.[32] The successive quality of officer personnel is in turn a telling reflection of the company, borne out by the Aberdeen Line's record, and that of many great shipping company's since those days.

- Luck. **Thermopylæ** was undoubtedly a lucky ship in terms of her winds. Allan confided in his cousin Andrew Shewan that she had enjoyed extraordinarily good winds on each leg of her record-breaking maiden voyage.

Many comparisons have been drawn between the various crack clippers, and particularly between **Thermopylæ** and **Cutty Sark**. Much has been written; Lubbock's three major works, *The Log of the Cutty Sark*, *The China Clippers* and *The Colonial Clippers*, each concentrated on passage making, tending at times to the romantic; David MacGregor's scholarly and dispassionate works, *Fast Sailing Ships* and *The Tea Clippers* give a splendid technical understanding of these thoroughbreds, while George Campbell's beautifully illustrated and technically very sound *China Tea Clippers* is a masterpiece; each help to build up a picture, but Captain Andrew Shewan in his classic book *The Great Days of Sail* gives the seaman's view of an experienced China trade commander. Shewan, after considering all aspects, came out strongly in favour of **Thermopylæ** as being the greatest all-rounder of the clipper era – and I agree with him! Not for nothing was she ruefully referred to by rival commanders as that 'Damned Scotsman!'.

THE LATTER DAYS OF SAIL – 1869 TO 1881

While the diva held centre stage, there was much work for the chorus to achieve. Hood's next new-build for the Aberdeen Line was the 965-ton wooden ship *Centurion (II)*, designated 'an Australian and China Packet', delivered in April 1869. (GTJCo. 40/6). Unlike *Thermopylæ* and *Thyatira* before her, she was not of composite construction, but had iron beams, beam knees, hold pillars and breasthooks; she also had twenty-five pairs of diagonal iron strength members girdling her hull secured to the inside of her frames. The lack of any continuity in construction methodology is difficult to explain, but the answer probably lay in prior commitment of the yard's limited iron-working skill resources to concurrent work on Nicol's 831-ton *Glenavon*, which was delivered six months before *Centurion*.

Glenavon was Hood's first ship constructed of iron; she followed two months after *Thermopylæ* and was committed to the Aberdeen Line's Melbourne berth. Thereafter she continued on the triangular service to China; on her first tea voyage, she achieved a creditable 100-day run home from Foochow against the trade winds. Unfortunately, her service was short-lived, for she was wrecked in the Gaspar Straits, one of the three passages between Borneo and Sumatra, on her third homeward voyage in June 1871.

Centurion was placed on the Sydney service under the command of Captain Thomas Mitchell, formerly of the *Queen of Nations*. Mitchell was another exceptional commander, but from a different mould to the 'bustling' Kemball. While clearly another hard ship driver, Mitchell was also something of an intellectual with an extremely enquiring mind, a noted marine meteorological observer, and an accomplished marine biologist. His documented observations, still held in the archives at the Meteorological Office and by his great granddaughter, Helen Duncan, in Aberdeen, were rated as being of an 'excellent character' by Captain Robert Fitzroy, the then superintendent of the Board of Trade's Meteorology Department. Written in an extremely clear, neat hand, and beautifully illustrated, Mitchell's observations in his meteorological register embraced not only meteorology, but also currents, magnetic anomalies, navigational features and marine biology (a tradition that carried on for many years through the medium of the excellent *Marine Observer* journal published by the Met Office). Mitchell was also an intellectual navigator, not afraid of challenging the findings of Maury,[1] as an extract from his register shows:

By referring to this date it will be seen the Equator was crossed about Midnight in Longitude 22 [degrees] W, 28 days from the Land. I could never make up my mind to go so far to the Westward as that recommended by Lt. Maury at this season of the year, this being the fourth season running that I have crossed either into the end of February or beginning of March between the Longitude of 22 and 24 and have had no reason to regret doing so, as the average passage has been 25 days, longest 30 and shortest 23, besides having carried the NE trade to about 4 North and always found the SE trade before getting to Southward of 2 North, this being the only exception.

Dr Hazel Carnegie's excellent biographical monograph on Mitchell, *Harnessing the Wind*, gives a detailed insight into his work.[2]

From early written reactions addressed to his friend Captain William Edward, Mitchell was clearly not best pleased with his new command. He complained in round terms about deficiencies in *Centurion*'s outfitting, blaming her hurried departure from the building yard; he poured scorn upon the competence of his mate; and he expressed with delicious snobbery, dissatisfaction with *Centurion*'s initial sailing qualities: 'with the wind aft several common Bluff-bowed ships almost kept up ...'

However, as the voyage to Sydney progressed, he became 'hugely' pleased with her sailing qualities, comparing her favourably with *Thermopylæ* in strong winds. She arrived in Sydney on 10 September 1869, after a creditable passage of seventy-five days.

In a letter to Greig, the manager of Hood's yard, while bewailing the fact that she was not going to be an extreme clipper, nonetheless Mitchell reported favourably upon her sea-keeping qualities in all but stern seas. With following seas, the helmsman was very exposed, such that he did not concentrate upon his course; Mitchell recommended that the house should be carried aft to afford some protection to him, without loss of speed and a penalty of only some 5 tons on the deadweight, which he argued would be compensated for by improved steering. Mitchell also commented upon rudder problems on the passage 'up' to London:

> The man at the wheel could hardly hold it for the rudder shaking. I had a deep groove put in the back of it from the water line right down and it is quite steady now. You should not neglect this in your next wooden ship. It is very important as it would soon shake the screw all to pieces.[3]

Centurion's maiden homeward loading at Sydney was especially interesting insofar that she carried the first consignment of the coconut product, copra, to Britain. Hitherto, coconut oil, primitively pressed in the South Sea Islands and shipped in casks, regularly formed an element of homeward cargoes from Sydney; this was to be progressively displaced by copra. The *Sydney Morning Herald* commented:[4]

The first large importation of copra arrived by the [brig] SCOTSMAN, from the South Sea Islands [the Navigators, now Samoa], is about being trans-shipped into the clipper ship *Centurion*. Copra is the kernel of the cocoa nut, which is cut up in small pieces and left to dry, and then shipped home in bulk, where it is pressed, and the oil being extracted, the remains are used for the feeding of cattle. The Messrs Goddeffroy send large quantities to Germany keeping vessels purposely employed for this particular trade. On the hatches being opened on board the SCOTSMAN yesterday, the copra although stowed in bulk was found to be entirely free from heat.[5]

The CENTURION has all her dead-weight stowed. She will take in the dried cocoanuts brought by the [brig] SCOTSMAN (100 tons) and will have quick dispatch in loading her wool ... .

Centurion's homeward cargo comprised 2,166 bales wool, 6 bales skins, 120 bales cotton, 3 bales fibre, 839 casks tallow, 47 casks coconut oil, 2,028 bags copra, 2,285 hides, 256 cases meat and 6 packages of sundries.

Sadly, Captain Thomas Mitchell died at sea, homeward bound during *Centurion*'s second voyage.

On 17 November 1869, the Suez Canal opened for traffic. The impact upon sailing ship owners was not as immediate as many have suggested, but nonetheless, the writing was clearly on the wall for the future of sail on the China trade; after that date, any sailing vessel built for the China trade must have been a short-term investment. Five years on, GTJCo. was to build one further ship nominated for the China trade – *Salamis.*

Centurion was followed five months later by the Aberdeen Line's first ship constructed of iron, the magnificent 1,405-ton passenger ship *Patriarch*. GTJCo. initially took a 60/64 subscribing interest in the vessel, but within two months, the company had diluted this to 44/64 by the extension of 4/64th shareholdings to four of their commanders, including Captain George Henry Pile, who commanded the new vessel for her first seven years' service on the Sydney trade.

Built at a high cost for those days of £24,000,[6] she was widely regarded as the finest iron ship afloat when commissioned. Her length aloft was 230.8ft, beam 38.1ft and depth 22.3ft; a 90ft long, full height, half-round poop was installed. She had very fine lines and a reputation for excellent seaworthiness, borne out by her twenty-nine-year remarkably accident-free record; unusually

Left: The iron passenger ship *Patriarch* lying to a buoy off Gravesend. (National Library of Australia SA PRG 1373/3/47)

Below: *Patriarch* at No. 7 Circular Quay, Sydney, loading from an island trading brig; in the background is Bennelong Point, where the Sydney Opera House now stands. (100 years later, the author discharged the first cargo of Gilbert and Ellice Islands Colony copra to be brought in by a colony ship at the same berth.) (National Library of Australia NSW MSBL 547 d1_47264)

for an iron ship, she was extremely dry. *Patriarch* carried a heavy sail plan, crossing six spars on her fore and main masts to spread course, double topsails, double topgallant sails (probably a later modification) and a royal; she also spread studdingsails outside her square sails, and these continued to be spread long after their use had been generally discarded on other passage makers. Generous accommodation was provided for forty passengers in the 90ft full-deck-height poop.

Perhaps her most notable feature was the innovation of telescopic topmasts. Instead of a conventional suite of three mast elements – lower, top and topgallant – each overlapping in way of their doublings, *Patriarch's* masts were effectively pole masts, each comprising a single lower unit combining lower and topmasts, into which the topgallant mast telescoped, after sending down its rigging. The system had advantages in terms of reductions in weight and windage aloft; however, by the time of its introduction, the widespread use of steel wire rigging had effectively circumvented its advantages. Telescopic topmasts were not perpetuated on other sailing ships, and their application in later years was associated with ships required to pass under bridges on waterways, such as the Manchester Ship Canal.

Patriarch's outward voyage to Sydney was made in a record sixty-nine days from the Downs to Port Jackson heads. Hailing her arrival with customary gushing Victorian-era colonial enthusiasm, the *Sydney Morning Herald* reported:[7]

> During the last twenty-five years the port of Sydney and neighbouring colonies have been visited by many clipper ships whose passages, recorded from time to time, have shown the great advancement that has resulted from the improvement of shipbuilding; but it has fallen to the lot of Captain Pile, of the Patriarch, which arrived on Thursday from London, to totally eclipse anything that has hitherto been made between the latter port and Sydney ... and in fact in all particulars, whether above or below or aloft, a more magnificent ship never entered the waters of Port Jackson.

Patriarch departed Sydney on her maiden homeward wool run on 16 April 1870, and arrived off the Downs on 6 July, a passage time of eighty-one days (not sixty-nine days as given by Lubbock, but nonetheless a good passage). *Patriarch*, under a succession of first-class and universally popular commanders, was to remain a

Patriarch with sails set leaving Sydney. (National Library of Australia Vic H91.220/2959)

firm favourite on the Sydney service for many years. Perhaps the essence of her success was the consistency of her fast passage times, averaging 76.5 days outward and 93.0 days homeward, over the course of her first twenty years' service.

With the delivery of *Patriarch*, GTJCo. disposed of its 36/64 interest and GTJ his personal 4/64 in *Wooloomooloo*, upon that ship's sale to Herman Gansen. Gansen was clearly acting in the role of broker, for he immediately then sold on the majority of the shares to a group of investors, including a personal 8/64 interest to GTJ, and 8/64 to Isaac Merchant, retaining a 2/64 interest for himself. *Wooloomooloo* was to remain under GTJCo. management with a company commander and crew, sailing as an element of the Aberdeen Line, until May 1873 when she was sold to London owners.

Disaster struck for the company twice within seventeen days in 1870, with the losses of *Star of Hope* off Southwold on 9 April and *Walter Hood* off Red Head, New South Wales, on the 26th of the same month. The company had purchased GTJ's personal interest in *Star of Hope* in May 1866, and the partnership had subsequently built up a further 28/64 interest in the ship, such that at the time of her loss, GTJCo.'s overall interest was 36/64 through two shareholding groups. The vessel had had an unfortunate recent career, having been involved in a collision off Anticosti Island with the vessel *Wandsworth* while en route from Quebec to Aberdeen, forcing her to put in to Gaspe on 2 October 1869, 'in a very damaged state' to her stern and rudder. Then on 9 April 1870, while on passage from Shields to Cartagena with a cargo of coke and coal, she was run down by the barque *Archos*, on passage from Sunderland to Venice. *Star of Hope* sank 20 miles off Southwold; *Archos* lost her jibboom and cutwater, and sustained damage to her bows. **Star of Hope**'s crew were landed, apparently intact, at Lowestoft; Captain Talbot, who had commanded the ship for the previous eight years, departed the company's employment, although he does not appear to have been held to blame by the Board of Trade.

The loss of the **Walter Hood** was an altogether more tragic affair in human terms. The ship had departed London for Sydney on 22 January 1870, under the command of the well-respected Captain Andrew Latto, undertaking his fourth voyage in command of the vessel. She had enjoyed a reasonable passage out to Cape Otway; however, having cleared the Bass Straits, she ran into heavy weather, which rapidly deteriorated into storm-force conditions from the south-east. A heavy squall struck the ship at 0300 hours on Tuesday, 26 April, carrying away her topsails, and her first human casualty occurred; replacement jury-rigged sails were bent on, but at 1700 hours, land was sighted to windward on the starboard bow. Efforts to claw the vessel off a lee shore proved to no avail, and at 2000 hours she struck on the south side of Wreck Bay, some 10 miles south of Cape St George, New South Wales. The port anchor was let go and she came head to wind; however, the position was hopeless, and the vessel began breaking up. Andrew Latto, leading the effort to save his command, was swept against the bulwarks forward and broke several ribs; he was carried below to his cabin, where the crew took shelter for the remainder of the night.

Daylight on 27 April found the vessel 150 yards from the shore, but with a terrible sea running between the ship and salvation. Various attempts were made to reach the shore, mostly ending in drowning. Latto came on deck in an attempt to command rescue operations, but was forced below, and shortly after he drifted out of his cabin as the side of the ship broke off and he drowned. On 28 April, with crew members dying of exhaustion but with the weather moderating, the chief and second officers successfully got a line ashore; however, more seamen were lost trying to make the shore. Thirteen seamen remained on board, and were forced to kill and eat the captain's dog in order to sustain life. It was not until the morning of 30 April that a boat from the coastal steamer **Illalong** finally managed to rescue the remaining survivors; in all, twelve souls perished as a result of the disaster, twenty-three were saved. A coroner conducted an inquest on the beach, and the corpses were buried in the bush inshore; shamefully, there was widespread looting of the cargo and corpses. The wreck was sold for £95, while the proceeds from the sale of cargo salvaged by two coasters raised £1,027 and about £400 respectively.[8] GTJCo.'s terminal interest in the ship was 32/64. The wreck site was designated a Historic Shipwreck in 1989, under the Commonwealth Historic Shipwrecks Act 1976.[9]

The last wooden ship to be built for GTJCo. by Walter Hood, the 1,091-ton **Aviemore**, was commissioned in August 1870, and placed initially on the Melbourne trade under the command of Captain Thomas Barnes Ayling, formerly of the **Moravian.** GTJCo.'s subscribing interest in the ship was 40/64, with GTJ taking a personal 4/64 share and the balance shared in 4/64 units between masters and yard personnel. **Aviemore** followed the style for a cargo ship, with a 42ft topgallant anchor deck forecastle, and a 53ft raised quarterdeck. With iron and composite construction well established in the Hood yard, it seems strange that GTJCo. reverted to wood for the construction of **Aviemore**, and I can again only surmise that with Nicol's iron clipper **Leucadia** on the stocks ahead of her, shortage of iron-working skill resources dictated the use of wood. Not a spectacularly fast ship, she enjoyed an unremarkable life, alternating between Sydney and Melbourne as her terminal ports.

Aviemore was followed in April 1871 by the large 1,452-ton iron passenger ship **Miltiades**. The disparate nature of the design of GTJCo.'s ships built at Hood's was never more apparent than when comparing **Miltiades** with **Patriarch**, built some eighteen months previously for essentially the same service. Perhaps the answer may be found in the Melbourne *Age*'s commentary upon her maiden arrival:[10]

[MILTIADES] … is the latest addition to their [GTJCo.] extensive and well known fleet of Australian traders; and in her it would appear as if the builder had studied to combine all the special good points of the many ships which have been launched from their yard.

Unlike the very slightly smaller **Patriarch**, which had a long, full-height poop and forecastle, **Miltiades** had a 52ft raised quarterdeck, such that her main rail running the length of the ship set off an unbroken sheer to perfection. In fact, she did not have an excessive sheer, but she certainly looked a powerful vessel, with her forward hull carried out well under her figurehead. She was heavily rigged, with double topgallant yards on all three masts. On her maiden voyage, she was rigged to carry studding sails, but on subsequent voyages, her stunsail booms were removed.[11] Unlike earlier models, she did not have an Aberdeen house surmounting the raised quarterdeck; rather, she had a small deckhouse mounted well aft. She also had a large deckhouse on the maindeck, in which was incorporated:[12]

a powerful engine fitted up for facilitating the discharge of cargo, dumping wool, condensing water, and other purposes, and the newest improvements have been availed of for easily and expeditiously working the ship. Her half poop deck admits of the saloon being very lofty, and the fittings and decorations, which are all in good taste, pleasingly combine richness with elegance. There is cabin accommodation for 24 passengers, and every requisite for their comfort and convenience has been carefully studied and supplied.

In addition to her cabin accommodation, **Miltiades** could carry large numbers of immigrants in her 'tween decks; while her normal number was given as 250, on a subsequent Shaw Savill outward charter to New Zealand, she carried 470 immigrants below deck.

Her maiden voyage under the command of Captain Robert Algernon Perrett was not without incident. She carried away both her fore and main topgallant masts, an accident attributed not so much to the wind force as her plunging motion in a heavy southerly swell. With her relatively low poop, **Miltiades** had a reputation for being a wet ship on deck in a following sea (notably different to **Patriarch**). This said, she developed an extremely steady reputation for fast, incident-free passage-making over her long career, largely served on the Melbourne trade.

Passenger ship **Miltiades** at anchor, Sydney Harbour. (National Library of Australia SA PRG 173/3/52)

Atrato in her Royal Mail days as a paddle steamer. (National Library of Australia WA SLWA_ b4085455)

Following the commissioning of **Miltiades**, there was a lull in new building activity for GTJCo. of some twenty-nine months. In the meantime, Hood was building the iron ship **Collingwood** for London owners, Devitt and Moore. GTJCo. was busy in other directions during this period, however, acting as managing agents for the government-sponsored emigrant steamer **Atrato** for a single problem-beset voyage to Australia. Built by Caird of Greenock in 1853 as an iron paddle steamer for the Royal Mail Steam Packet Company's West Indies mail service, she had been an outstanding ship of her time. Measuring 350ft overall, with a tonnage of 3,467 gross, she was the largest ship afloat at the time of her commissioning; she had four decks and could carry 224 cabin passengers. Her keel was cast in nine pieces, and her stem and stern posts made engineering history by each being cast in one piece. Outstanding ship though she must have initially been, paddlewheel propulsion had been demonstrated to be inefficient eight years earlier in 1845 by the practical testing of HMS **Rattler** (screw) *versus* HMS **Alecto** (paddle); the use of paddlewheel propulsion in **Atrato** must have been outmoded from the outset. She lasted sixteen years in Royal Mail's service, and was then sold to J. Morrison of London, who converted her into an auxiliary screw steamer, re-engined with A Boulton and Watt compound engine, for the Australasian emigrant service.

GTJCo. advertised her first emigrant sailing under charter to the government of the colony of Victoria, in *The Times* in July 1872, with departure for Melbourne from London's East India Docks in September. Her passage to Melbourne was expected to be undertaken 'at great speed' and to occupy forty-eight to fifty-two days; while a contingent call at Cape Town for bunkers was allowed for, it was anticipated that she would steam non-stop. With 500 passengers embarked, **Atrato** sailed from Plymouth on schedule in September, but off the Lizard she shed the four blades of her propeller and had to return under sail. Dry-docked at Plymouth, repairs were effected and she again got under way on 1 October. At 1400 hours on the sixth day out, in a position off Madeira, steaming at half speed in calm seas, with sails set:

> an appalling crash, and a tremendous shaking from stem to stern, threw all on board into consternation. The scene for the next few minutes was beyond description. From women, of whom there were no fewer than 206 single on board, arose a general shriek, many became hysterical, while others clung to each other in terror. The sensation seems to have been compared only to an earthquake, and the vessel quivered and groaned as if her timbers were being torn asunder [The fact that she was of iron construction seems to have missed the attention of *The Age*'s journalist!]. What had occurred that the vessel should be shaken in this appalling manner while under easy steam and sail, and on a fine afternoon, no one could for a moment conceive. The chief engineer was on the bridge with the captain, and he at once rushed to the engine room, when the truth was discovered that the propeller shaft had broken, and the engines, which were 400 horse power, freed from the strain of the screw, were working at the top of their speed.[13]

Atrato again retraced her steps under sail to Plymouth; sadly three seamen were killed in the course of the passage, washed overboard in heavy seas while trying to secure the jib, which had broken free. Upon arrival in Plymouth, her emigrants were put ashore and housed in the emigrant depot. There followed a prolonged survey by the Board of Trade, accompanied by bitter recriminations, to critically examine the construction of the crankshaft and shafting in her propulsion chain.[14] The lot of her complement of impoverished emigrants provided social and economic problems, but the people of Plymouth rallied to the occasion, providing temporary employment and laying on concert parties for the poor people. Repairs again completed, the vessel left Plymouth on 22 December 1872, and finally arrived in Melbourne on 2 March 1873 after a passage of sixty-eight days, in the course of which she was forced to put into Cape Town for eight days to coal. Despite her problems, the Melbourne press reported enthusiastically upon the ship.

Just what the level of GTJCo.'s involvement in **Atrato**'s Melbourne voyage was is unclear; certainly Stephen and Cornelius Thompson were embarked upon her pre-commissioning cruise down to the Nore on 30 July 1872. The vessel appeared in the Aberdeen Line's regular sailing list, but in specific advertisements, GTJCo. was referred to as an agent. However, *The Age*'s coverage of her voyage refers to her as 'having come out here under the auspices of Messrs George Thompson Jnr & Co.', which suggests a rather more positive involvement by GTJCo. It has been suggested that the voyage was an experiment by the company to test the viability of steam; if so, it had every reason to be frightened off! **Atrato** only undertook one voyage on the Australian emigrant service. Thereafter, she was chartered by Shaw Savill for the New Zealand emigrant trade, with no greater success; nine days out from Plymouth, her low-pressure piston broke and a cylinder cracked; she again had to put back under sail.

In the course of 1873, three older units were disposed of:

- **Maid of Judah.** Captain Isaac Merchant, the original subscribing owner, had sold a majority share in the vessel to the company in 1858. In September 1872, the joint owners drew up a certificate of sale in favour of 'Samuel Aaron Joseph of Sydney, New South Wales, merchant, empowering him to sell the ship for not less than £4,600 within 6 months'.[15] The vessel was sold to Cowlislaw Brothers, Sydney, in February 1873 by Joseph and was subsequently employed on the China trade from Australia, being condemned and broken up at Amoy in 1880. This was the first of a number of instances where Samuel Joseph was entrusted with selling GTJCo. ships upon the completion of their outward voyage to Sydney.

- **Colonial Empire.** In April, the company sold its 40/64 interest in **Colonial Empire** to an Aberdeen shipowner, James Milne, and the vessel was withdrawn from the Melbourne trade upon which she had been serving; the vessel was finally abandoned at sea on 29 January 1880.

- In July 1873, Robert MacKenzie, an attorney in Shanghai, was empowered by the joint owners by way of a certificate of sale, to sell the little barque **Columba**, in which the partners held a 16/64 private investment, and which had been engaged in tramping on the WCSA trade, for a sum not less than £3,800 at Shanghai or any other port in China within twelve months. She was in fact sold on 20 November 1873 to Michael Howlett at Shanghai, who sold her on to Demetrius Sclavo of Hong Kong in May the following year.

The very high standards demanded by GTJCo. of its ships, commanders and officers were a direct reflection of the strong moral and Christian principles to which Thompson and Henderson held dear, and which they infused into the conduct of their business activities; these were in stark contrast to the standards that prevailed in all too great a sector of British shipping, especially in the coastal collier trade, at that time. On to the scene came Samuel Plimsoll – 'the Sailors' Friend'.

Samuel Plimsoll, a coal merchant, who had been elected to Parliament as the member for Derby in 1868, embarked upon an almost single-handed crusade to right a deplorable situation. Plimsoll based his crusade upon the pioneer work of a Tynemouth shipowner, James Hall. He sought to introduce into a revised Merchant Shipping Bill, elements that he (rightly) believed would address the problem of 'coffin' ships, namely:

• Provision for the inspection of all ships unclassed by Lloyd's Register or by the Liverpool Mercantile Marine Association;

• Provision for the adoption of a maximum loadline to prevent overloading; and,

• All shipowners to be prohibited from insuring more than two-thirds of their property in any one ship.

Plimsoll published his famous appeal to public opinion, *Our Seamen – an Appeal*, in December 1872 (ironically, the publishers were Virtue & Co.). Copies were distributed to trade unions, members of Parliament and other influential bodies. The contents were widely debated in newspapers and at public meetings specially convened for the purpose throughout the country. Plimsoll drew on every available source and statistic to support his crusade, making himself thoroughly unpopular with the establishment along the way.

Plimsoll finally had his way, however, and a Royal Commission of Enquiry into Unseaworthy Ships was convened on 28 March 1873. Emergency legislation arising from the Royal Commission came into force with the Merchant Shipping Act of 1876; this provided for every new ship to be marked with a load line to mark the maximum depth to which an owner intended to load the ship. Under the Act there was no prescribed scientific basis for the location of the required load line, the decision being effectively left to the discretion of the owner; the new legislation was accordingly fatally flawed. However, it did establish the platform for much professional debate, which eventually gave rise to scientifically based rules, but these were not to become law until the Merchant Shipping (Load Line) Act of 1890. Plimsoll died after a long illness, worn out by his efforts, in 1898. His enduring monument remains the 'Plimsoll' Line cut into the side of every merchant cargo ship to delineate the depth to which that ship, by calculation, may be loaded, and thereby her safe freeboard.

GTJ and William Henderson were clearly impressed by Plimsoll's work and almost uniquely among shipowners of the time wished to be identified with his name (there may also have been a shrewd interpretation of the emerging political climate). GTJCo. sought Plimsoll's permission for its next delivery from Hood's yard to be named in honour of him, to which, having first checked the Line's bona fides, he gladly acceded. From Plimsoll's standpoint, there could not have been a better reference for his work, coming as it did when he was under siege from all sides.

The new 1,510-ton iron passenger/wool clipper **Samuel Plimsoll**, which bore a carved effigy of Plimsoll as a figurehead (now displayed in the Western Australia Maritime Museum in Fremantle), was launched on 6 September 1873 in the presence of the great man. It would appear that Plimsoll was intended to perform the launching ceremony himself, but at the last moment he graciously delegated the responsibility to the wife of Richard Boaden, her first commander.[16] In a speech at the subsequent reception, GTJ spoke of Plimsoll:[17]

It is lamentable that hundreds – nay, thousands of our brave sailors are yearly sent to a watery grave, chiefly from causes which are preventable. An impression has been made on the public mind by Mr Plimsoll's book which will not be obliterated until a measure is passed to remedy the evils complained of. Mr Plimsoll is engaged in an arduous conflict. Much has been done, much remains to be done. Mr Plimsoll will pardon me for saying that he has to some extent increased his difficulties and raised obstructions which might not otherwise have come in the way by occasionally writing inadvertently and speaking unadvisedly [a view echoed by Lord Shaftesbury in his diaries].[18] Nevertheless his motives are beyond suspicion and the object he has in view is the saving of lives and not the ruin of reputations.

I hope that the successful launch of the vessel is an indication of the ultimate success of the all-important movement in which Mr Plimsoll is engaged. By his labours, he has impressed upon the country the grand principle that human life is of more value than property. A far more emphatic compliment will yet be paid to him than the fleeting one he has this day received. He will be honoured as one who has been highly instrumental in the preservation of human life and in the prevention of human suffering.

The new *Samuel Plimsoll* differed from her two iron-built predecessors by reverting to a 59ft raised quarterdeck surmounted by an Aberdeen house. She sailed from Plymouth for Sydney on 19 November 1873, with 180 emigrants embarked. Before she sailed, the mayors of Plymouth and Devonport held a reception on board in honour of Plimsoll. In a response, Plimsoll rose to the occasion by promising:

I will give myself no rest until there is extended to sailors at sea, the protection that Her Majesty's subjects enjoy on land.[19]

Under Richard Boaden's command, she made a good passage to Sydney, arriving at that port on 1 February 1874, seventy-four days out from Plymouth. Though not comparing with *Patriarch*'s record-breaking maiden voyage, it was nonetheless the best passage of the year, beating *Cutty Sark* by four days and *Patriarch* by five. Her maiden run home to London was the best of the wool fleet for that year, eighty-two days port to port. *Samuel Plimsoll* enjoyed a consistently successful career, with a well-earned reputation for fast passages; her first fifteen voyages were spent on the Sydney service,

Figurehead of clipper *Samuel Plimsoll* in Western Australian Maritime Museum. (Author's collection)

and in 1888 she transferred to the Melbourne run. Her Aberdeen Line service was not without incident, however; she was in time to suffer a serious collision, dismasting and scuttling following fire, but emerged from each to effectively serve another day.

Two months after **Samuel Plimsoll**'s delivery, she was followed from Hood's yard by the small 377-ton barque **Lydia**, owned by a consortium comprising GTJ, William Henderson, Cornelius Thompson, Alexander Nicol and James Buyers, and designated to work on the China coast. Whether **Lydia** was intended as a feeder vessel for GTJCo. and Nicol's main-line ships on the China coast, or whether her original owners had defaulted while she was still on the stocks necessitating intervention by the yard owners, is not clear. Certainly, she did not remain with the joint owners for very long; fourteen months after commissioning, a certificate of sale was drawn up empowering Robert MacKenzie, attorney of Shanghai, to sell the vessel for not less than £6,300 at Shanghai or any other port in China within twelve months. By May 1875, the transaction was completed and in March 1876, she was registered de novo in Shanghai.

Tragedy struck for George Thompson Jnr when on 17 January 1874, his wife of forty-four years Christiana Little (nee Kidd) died, aged 67. As a mother, she had born GTJ eight children, but had suffered the tragedy of seeing one of their daughters die in her third year, and her fourth son, James, die aged 21. She was sustained by her extraordinarily strong Christian faith; her personal diary, a constant dialogue of love for her Maker, dismissed her losses stoically as God's will. Her funeral service on 21 January 1874 was apparently conducted at GTJ's town house at 5 Golden Square, Aberdeen, followed by interment at the Free Church at Dyce. She was laid to rest alongside the two children who predeceased her. Although I have come across little reference to Christiana as a wife, one is left with an impression of serenity, love and quiet support at all times. Her passing must have been an awful blow to GTJ.

In August 1874, **Star of Peace** was sold to London owners, after nineteen years with GTJCo., served exclusively on the main-line Australian trade, the last ten on the Melbourne run. She was to be sold on to the famous Queensland-based Pacific Island trading company, Burns Philp, which ran her for some years before converting her into a hulk at Thursday Island in the Torres Straits. She was finally broken up in 1895.

Diverting momentarily from the Australian trade, the passenger clipper **Miltiades** (Perrett) undertook a single outwards emigrant run to Auckland on charter to Shaw Savill in May 1874. Her passage to New Zealand of seventy-seven days with 470 emigrants embarked was considered smart for the time. Unfortunately however, in the Hauraki Gulf approaching Auckland, between the volcanic Rangitoto Island and Tiritiri Matangi, she missed stays and drifted on to a mud spit off Galle Point. Captain Perrett fired signal guns and a rocket, which attracted the attention of a small coastal steamer, the **Lady Bowen**. Acting upon Perrett's instructions, the **Lady Bowen** laid out a kedge anchor astern, and on the rising tide, rendered towing assistance as **Miltiades** warped in on the kedge anchor with her steam winch; **Miltiades** came off unscathed. The owner of the **Lady Bowen** subsequently made a salvage claim against **Miltiades** in the sum of £10,000, reduced at arbitration to £1,625. After disembarking her emigrants and discharging cargo at Auckland, **Miltiades** took passage back to Melbourne to resume her Aberdeen Line service.

On 17 October 1874, **Transatlantic** docked at Aberdeen from Quebec, at the end of the last transatlantic emigrant and timber voyage to be made by a GTJCo. vessel, ending thereby a record of service on the North Atlantic that had lasted nearly half a century since GTJ's early involvement in the ill-fated **Lady of the Lake**. **Transatlantic** was sold to foreign owners in April 1875. The vessel was rebuilt in 1876, and passed into the ownership of the famous Norwegian shipowner, J.L. Ugland in 1878. She was to survive for a further twenty-one years until foundering in the Atlantic on 15 October 1899, while on passage from Mobile to Stettin.

William Henderson, who five years earlier had become an elected harbour commissioner in Aberdeen, further strengthened his business stature in that city by being elected president of the Chamber of Commerce for 1874. His second son, George Thompson Henderson, born in 1856, had joined the company's service, and on 3 November 1874, took up a post at the London office as Stephen Thompson's assistant. In a charming note to his mother reassuring her that he had settled in well, he described being taken by Captain Merchant to see **Thermopylæ** in the Victoria Docks (discharging tea from Shanghai), and **Wave of Life** in the East India Docks (loading for Sydney).

Despite the opening of the Suez Canal some six years earlier and the inevitable impact upon the tea clipper of the racing tea steamer, the company's next delivery from Hood's was the 1,130-ton iron tea clipper **Salamis**. At launch on 7 May 1875, her bowsprit fouled the rafters of Hood's covered building shed as she came down the ways, bringing down the roof and injuring several people

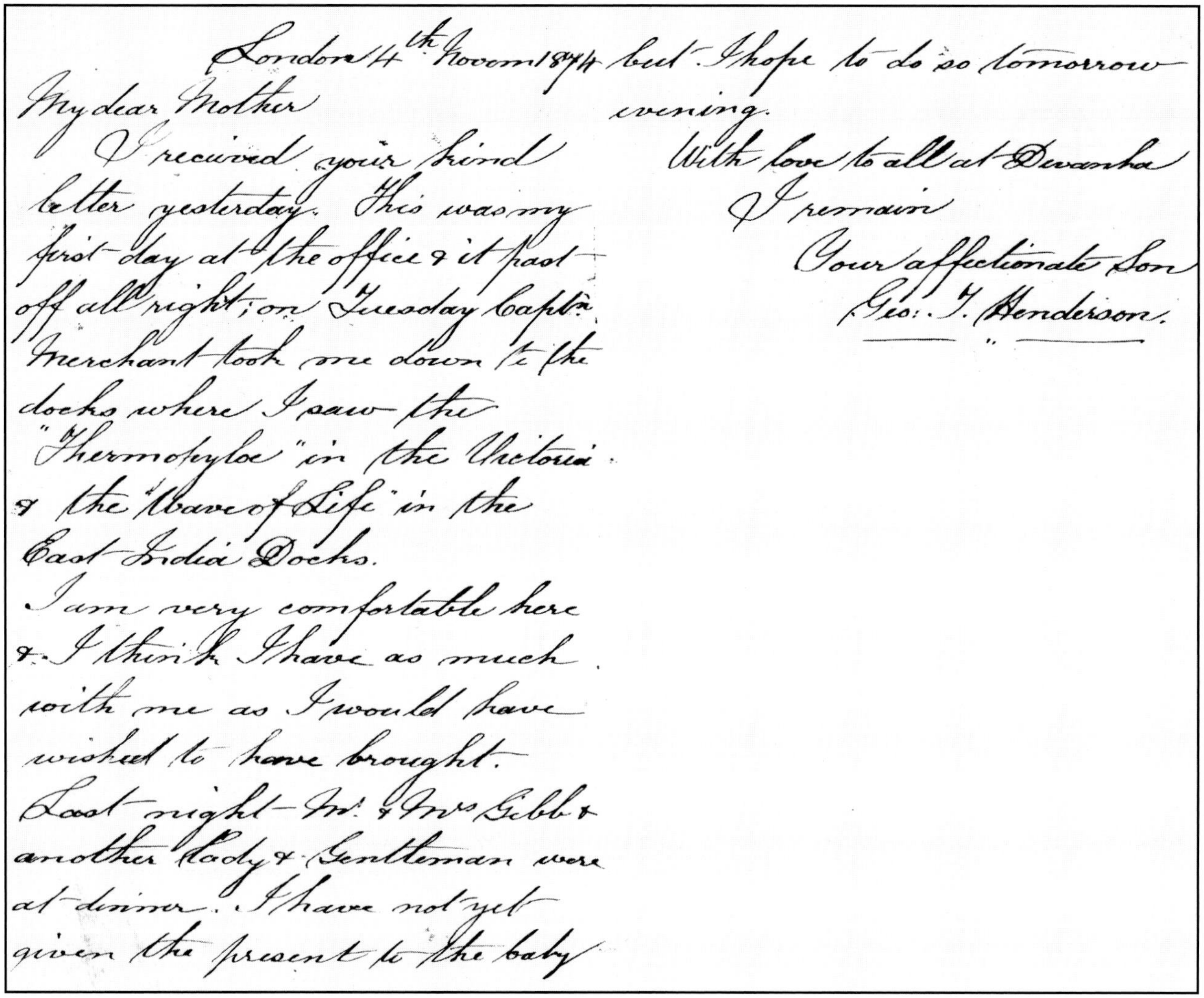

George Thompson Henderson's letter to his mother.

London 14th Novem 1874

My dear Mother

I received your kind letter yesterday. This was my first day at the office & it past off all right; on Tuesday Capt.ⁿ Merchant took me down to the docks where I saw the "Thermopylæ" in the Victoria & the "Wave of Life" in the East India Docks.

I am very comfortable here & I think I have as much with me as I would have wished to have brought.

Last night Mr. & Mrs Gibb & another Lady & Gentleman were at dinner. I have not yet given the present to the baby but I hope to do so tomorrow evening.

With love to all at Devanha

I remain

Your affectionate Son

Geo: T. Henderson.

assembled underneath, two of them seriously. Effectively built on the same mould as **Thermopylæ** but some 10ft longer, **Salamis** was designated for the Australia and China trades. To sustain her speed in the days before effective anti-fouling coatings had been developed for iron ships, she was dry-docked in Australia each voyage after the discharge of her outwards cargo; in this we are fortunate, for some fine photographs were taken of her resting in the Williamstown dry-dock at Melbourne, which give a clear impression of her beautiful hull lines.

Captain Jack Holmes, who sailed in her as an able seaman on her second voyage, wrote of **Salamis** in his autobiography *Voyaging*:

A lovelier ship than SALAMIS it would tax the imagination to conceive. She was glorious to behold. I think she was the most beautiful thing afloat. Her lines and proportions were a joy to the eye – a perfect vision, nobly planned, and a poem upon the water ... She had a billet or fiddle figurehead, with a little Grecian warrior on each side, and the yellow stripe around her green hull was not painted but gilded. [A billet or

fiddle figurehead comprised an inward turned, carved scroll (in this case, carved warriors), in place of a figure or bust. Quite a few Hood ships were so fitted.]

Under the command of Captain William Phillip Snr., formerly of the *Harlaw*, her maiden voyage to Melbourne occupied sixty-eight days, an excellent performance for an iron ship. Indeed, over the course of her first thirteen consecutive voyages to Melbourne, she averaged seventy-five days, pilot-to-pilot, an outstanding record. On her first voyage, she did not go up to China for a tea cargo, but returned instead with a Melbourne wool cargo. Again, she was to prove outstandingly fast for an iron ship, taking ninety-four days on her maiden passage, but overall averaging eighty-seven days over eighteen consecutive homeward passages from Melbourne in the wool trade.

The Aberdeen Line under the strong pastoral as well as commercial stewardship of William Henderson, took extraordinary steps to secure its crews' spiritual well-being. In common with a number of the first-class lines, its outward-bound ships dropped down from the East India Docks on Friday to lie secured overnight to buoys at Gravesend, sailing thereafter on Saturday having embarked London passengers; this was a pragmatic approach aimed at giving their crews time to sober up. However, GTJCo. went one step further; a missionary from the Waterside Mission to Seamen was embarked at the docks to tender to the spiritual needs of the crew on the trip down river. Captain William H. Phillip Jnr recounts in his papers an amusing incident that he witnessed while chief officer of *Salamis*:[20]

We left the East India Dock at 7 a.m., missionary on board as usual. All the men seemed to be as bosky as they could be without being absolutely useless, and the usual shrill 'good-byes' emanated from the galaxy of youth and beauty gathered on the pierhead to see them off. After these last sounds had faded in the distance, I told the boatswain to send the men to breakfast, thinking that they might be in better condition for work afterwards, allowing about an hour for breakfast. The boatswain called out 'Turn to'. As no one answered the call or came out of the forecastle door, he walked over and, after looking in, turned round to me with a broad grin on his face. I looked in also, and saw all the half-drunken men on their knees, with the missionary in the midst of them putting up a prayer. Just as I looked in, I saw a bottle go over the missionary's back. While he prayed they had passed the bottle round and thought it a great joke.

The company had a Bible box placed by each man's bunk. This was much appreciated by the hands; the boxes made splendid repositories for their tobacco and pipes. In Australia, the company also made provision for the spiritual well-being of its crews; for many years GTJCo. paid pew rent for an eight-man pew in the Williamstown (Melbourne) Presbyterian Church. In a letter to Basil Lubbock[21] dated 19 March 1928, Captain Hartley B. Watson commented:

The Aberdeen Line had a few of their own in the local kirk. The 'Boys' respectfully followed the Old Man [Captain William Phillip Jnr.] on Sundays, whether from command or free will I can't say. Several of these Boys are now in our Pilot Service, more than one married to the girl he knew in his half deck days.

I am sure that then, as in my days as an apprentice, the upside of a church service in uniform was an invitation out to lunch and the prospect of attracting pretty girls!

Salamis' second voyage started badly. After casting off her tug, the vessel made out into the Channel, but was struck by a westerly gale, forcing her to seek shelter at anchor back in the Downs. Her anchor carried away with thirty fathoms of cable, and the tug, which was still nearby, was sent up to London to secure a replacement from *Miltiades*, which was on the loading berth. Following the tug's return with a replacement anchor, the gale, which by then was blowing from the south-west, veered suddenly to the north-west with the passing of a cold front, and the riding cable parted at a link on the stem. The third anchor had to be slipped to enable the vessel to beat around to avoid being driven ashore, and she drove down to Dungeness under topsails alone. In the course of *Salamis*' problems in the Downs, a man was lost overside. She fought her way down to Plymouth, where replacement ground tackle was boarded. Her outward passage to Melbourne was not without incident either, for while running her eastings down, a pooping sea carried away the steering wheel. The incident was not without humour, for a Frenchman, one of the two helmsmen at the time of the incident, was washed along the poop still grasping the rim and spokes of the broken wheel crying out 'no more wheel, Cap'n, no more wheel'. It took fourteen hours to dig out the tiller from where it lay under cargo in the fore part of the vessel, and ship it in position as an emergency steering arrangement, all the while with the rudder stock banging about uncontrollably.[22]

Following discharge in Melbourne on her second voyage, *Salamis* ballasted around to Sydney, where she loaded 1,000 tons of coal for Shanghai. No tea cargo was offering in Shanghai at anything like a commercial freight rate, steamers having taken the first of the crop. *Salamis* wasted a month seeking cargo, and then dropped down to Hong Kong, where she loaded a general cargo of 18,000 bags of sugar and cassia, making London on 28 March 1877 after a voyage of 110 days pilot-to-pilot. The voyage was not without incident, for in the Indian Ocean, she suffered a serious leak arising from a number of rivets in her orlop beams forward working loose, requiring tomming and cement boxes to stem the ingress.

On her fourth voyage, following a fast round voyage to Melbourne, *Salamis* made her final sustained bid to secure that elusive tea cargo for which she had been built. After discharge at Melbourne, she carried 1,200 tons of coal up to Shanghai. There, *Thermopylæ* was loading her last tea cargo, but the *Salamis* again failed to secure a tea freight; not only were clippers a dying breed, but there was distinct

Salamis at Newcastle, NSW. (National Library of Australia SA PRG 1373/3/57)

prejudice among the tea shippers towards iron sailing ships, even though *Salamis* had won an enviable reputation as a fast passage maker. Eventually she had to accept a low-paying general cargo for Melbourne and sailed on 28 November 1878, in company with *Thermopylæ*. The two had a close race down the South China Sea, but were forced to anchor along with thirty-seven other ships off the north end of the Straits of Sunda, unable to make headway against a strong adverse current in the Straits. After several ineffectual attempts, *Thermopylæ* was the first ship to break through and report off Anjer, followed by *Salamis*; the rest of the fleet were left at anchor. After discharging at Melbourne, *Salamis* again loaded 1,200 tons of coal at Sydney for Shanghai. This time, she dropped down to Foochow for a tea cargo, but was again confronted by prejudice against her iron construction. She finally succeeded in securing an inferior grade tea cargo for Melbourne, the pick of the crop having been taken by the Alexander Hall-built composite clipper *Black Prince*. *Salamis* sailed a couple of days after *Black Prince*, but to the chagrin of the tea shippers, she arrived in Melbourne three weeks before her rival. To add insult to injury, Melbourne was suffering a tea famine at the time of *Salamis*' arrival, and her inferior cargo sold at a premium, while *Black Prince*'s tea sold on to a glutted market. This was *Salamis*' last tea venture, and thereafter she settled down to a splendid career as a wool clipper, predominantly spent on the Melbourne trade. A reproduction of Spurling's painting of *Salamis* running her eastings down is included in the colour section.

If *Salamis* was late for the tea trade, she arrived on to the back of the burgeoning Australian wool trade to Britain, a trade that was to employ the cream of the British clipper fleet until the last decade of the century; *Salamis*, along with her Aberdeen Line running mates, were just such ships. From an initial trial shipment of Australian wool in 1810, subsequently encouraged by a House of Lords Committee finding in 1825 that the importation of wool should

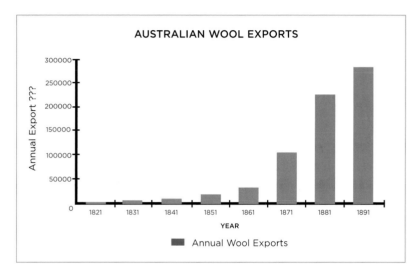

AUSTRALIAN WOOL EXPORTS

be allowed, the scale of growth in the trade may be seen from the accompanying graph.

The Australian export wool trade was organised to coincide with the London wool sales, which took place in January, February and March. Ships were loaded the opposite way around to the China tea trade, with the slowest ships being brought on to the berth to load first, the fastest by reputation loading last, with premium freight rates and the prospect of significant bonuses for the master attaching. This led to the trade being conducted along tremendously vibrant lines, with strong inter-ship rivalry in terms of passage making, and from the commander's standpoint, the responsibility (and prospect of personal gain) of matching the sales to optimise the cargo out-turn by avoiding warehousing costs, interest on cargo lying unsold, and potential falls in commodity price between sales.

The practical business of stowing a wool cargo was not without its challenges. Wool was essentially a volume cargo, its weight in stow improved by dumping the bales, a process culled from the American cotton trade whereby bales were hydraulically compressed and banded before loading to increase their density. Even dumped bales had a relatively low density in stow, and to optimise the quantity that could be stowed, a practice of screwing the bales into stow was used; once the best stow that could be achieved by hand was in place in each tier, planks and screw jacks were introduced between the bales in the hatch square and the screw was applied to force the stowed bales outwards to admit the stowage of extra bales under pressure. The process, often carried out under the personal supervision of diligent commanders, was fraught with hazard, particularly in composite ships, where the forces transmitted by the bales under pressure could spring deck and topside planking. Four bales stowed per register ton of the vessel was considered a good average benchmark; *Thermopylæ* typically loaded 4.89 bales, *Salamis* 5.08, *Patriarch* 4.0 and 4.31. *Patriarch*'s average is surprisingly low considering she was an iron ship, and I can only surmise that as a passenger ship, compactness of stow was compromised to achieve speed of dispatch and schedule keeping; *Cutty Sark*, for all the hype associated with Woodget's command of that vessel and his personal supervision of loading, never economically bettered 4.64 bales per grt. In a number of the newer GTJCo. ships, a steam engine carried in the deck house took care of, among other designated functions, the dumping of wool bales.

Even with dumped bales well screwed into stow, wool was still a light cargo, and the vessel's deadweight, and accordingly her stability on passage, had to be addressed by way of bottom stows of weight cargo such as hides, casks of coconut oil and tallow, and ore parcels (chrome, nickel and/or copper); fine lined vessels such as *Thermopylæ* and *Salamis*, which could not economically stow casks of tallow, still had to resort to a considerable weight of pig iron ballast in their floor spaces to achieve the necessary stability. Stowage was critical in such high-performance vessels, not only in terms of stability, but also to ensure a correct trim upon completion of loading; a few inches' adverse trim could seriously impact the vessel's speed on passage.

The overall loading operation was slow, a situation exacerbated by the small hatch openings in the clipper ships. The loading process was wonderfully recorded for posterity through Dr L. Morris Humphrey's photographs, many taken in *Patriarch*, whose work now forms the Humphrey Collection in the Australian National Library in Canberra.

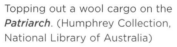
Topping out a wool cargo on the *Patriarch*. (Humphrey Collection, National Library of Australia)

The problems of a wool cargo did not end once stowed. Wool, with its high grease content, had a bad reputation for spontaneous combustion in stow, usually associated with being loaded damp (though I often wonder how often a carelessly discarded wharfie's cigarette was the real culprit!). Wool cargo fires were responsible for the loss of a number of ships, including the former GTJCo. ship *Omar Pasha*. Special care was necessary to ensure that bales were loaded in apparently dry condition (difficult when the wetting may have occurred up-country), and to check deck caulking once the screws had finished their work to avoid leakage damage and the risk of damp-induced spontaneous combustion on passage; dead or slipe wool (i.e.: the wool arising from the sheep killed for mutton) was particularly prone to spontaneous combustion and as a precaution was always stowed in the main hatches where it could be easily accessed. Wool cargoes had another unpleasant side effect; wool brought its former host's fleas on board with it, which rapidly infested the ship, such that the crew were forced to sleep on wet patches of deck to secure a release from their unwanted attention.[23] For all its problems however, wool was a very valuable cargo and only the best ships were chosen to carry it. Cargo underwriters kept careful records of out-turn performance by ship and by commander.

From 1875, a number of the older ships in the Line were rerigged as barques as a crew-saving economy measure. This policy seemed to carry forward into the 1880s when a ship reached an age of 20+ years, but did not impact upon such racers as *Thermopylæ* and *Salamis* during their GTJCo. years; nor were the main line passenger ships re-rigged. There would seem to have been little impact upon the speed of the ships so altered; interestingly, new GTJCo. vessels off the stocks would continue to be ship-rigged.

On 6 August 1875, the first of three accidents occurred to *Samuel Plimsoll* that were to interrupt her otherwise excellent career. The vessel had left Plymouth for Sydney with 360 emigrants embarked; at 23.15 that night she collided with and sank the Italian barque *Eurika* off the Lizard. The crew of the *Eurika* were recovered and landed safely at Falmouth. *Samuel Plimsoll* suffered only superficial damage, and continued her passage from Falmouth on 8 August. The collision did not bring censure or certificate of competency sanction against Boaden, so one can risk an assumption as to where the blame for the collision was attributed.

Hood's next delivery to the Line, in March 1876, was the magnificent iron passenger ship *Aristides*. With a gross tonnage of 1,721, and dimensions of 260ft × 39.5ft × 24.5ft, she was certainly the largest ship built by Hood; she probably represented the limit in size that the yard could accommodate. Although much heralded as the largest ship to be built in Aberdeen at the time of her launch, she was in fact only an average size with her contemporaries in the Australian trade, and small by comparison with sailing ships to come. With a full height, half-round 65ft-long poop and 35ft topgallant forecastle, she was a heavily sparred vessel with what had become a standard GTJCo. sail configuration – deep single royals, double topgallants, double topsails and deep courses on the fore and main masts, while the mizzen crossed a royal, single topgallant, double topsails and a course. No sails were crossed above the royals.

Aristides entered service at a time when steamers offering fifty-day passage times were entering the Australian passenger market in increasing strength, albeit they were yet to achieve economy as cargo carriers. Money Wigram's four passenger-cargo steamers *Durham*, *Kent*, *Somersetshire* and *Northumberland*, names that would be perpetuated in later years by famous ships of the Federal Steam Navigation Company, were offering a regular passenger service via the Cape, returning through Suez; the Colonial Line had started services in the mid-1870s; and Anderson Green's Orient Line was to become a key player from later in the decade. The mighty Peninsular and Oriental Steam Navigation Company serviced its Australian mail contracts and passenger services by trans-shipments from its prime Far Eastern services on to branch-line steamers; following the opening of the Canal, such trans-shipments were made at Point de Galle in south-west Ceylon. P&O's tonnaging strategy had not anticipated the impact of the Canal, and it was slow to take up the opportunities it offered, particularly in terms of direct steamship services to Australia. The first direct P&O steamship sailing via the Canal was made in 1873, but it was not until 1880, spurred on by securing the mail contract for the colony of Victoria, that the company finally settled its sights on Australia as a main-line service with regular direct sailings to Adelaide, Melbourne and Sydney. There were many smaller lines offering direct steamship services, most of which were short-lived. It says something for the loyalty of shippers and passengers to the Aberdeen Line's service that they continued to support a sailing ship investment such as *Aristides*; it may also say something for the conservatism of the company that it continued to commission sailing ships, though it has to be said that steam was by no means an evolved economic proposition for cargo carriers (which the Aberdeen Line primarily was) at that time. There was also, as with the tea trade earlier, shipper reaction to steamers as carriers of the wool clip.

Captain Robert Kemball transferred from *Thermopylæ* to take command of the new flagship, leaving his young chief officer, Charles Matheson, in command of *Thermopylæ*. A very different personality to Kemball, Matheson quickly proved himself to be every bit the driver his predecessor had been; he was to become an extremely popular and well-respected commander. Under Kemball, who was to command the vessel until his death in 1887, *Aristides* was to prove a consistently fast passage maker and a very popular ship. Her maiden voyage was to Melbourne, but exceptionally she followed this with a single round voyage from London to Adelaide. Thereafter, she was on the Melbourne trade until 1889, when she switched to Sydney. In ten Melbourne voyages, she averaged a healthy 77.9 days outwards passage time.[24]

Seven months later, *Aristides* was followed down Hood's ways by the 1,372-ton iron cargo ship *Smyrna*. She was built on fuller lines than hitherto, marking a change in requirement from racing

Duthie's iron passenger ship *Brilliant* at anchor in Sydney Harbour, with *Thermopylæ* in the background. (National Library of Australia SA PRG 1373/24/31)

cargo ships suitable for the China tea trade, whose economy lay in speed and volume cargoes, to freight carriers better suited to a mix of deadweight and volume cargoes. Engaged predominantly on the Sydney trade, *Smyrna* was not a fast passage maker, though I sense she was probably a very satisfactory economic unit within the fleet. Sadly, she did not enjoy a long life; outward bound for Sydney, she was run down and sunk in fog by the steamer *Moto* off St Catherine's, Isle of Wight, on 28 April 1888, with the loss of her commander, Captain Thomas Taylor, and eleven crew.

In July 1877, Hood launched what was to be its last great passenger ship for GTJCo., *Pericles*, of 1,671 gross register tons. An almost identical sister to *Aristides* but 100 tons smaller, fate chose that she was to have a much-publicised rival on the Sydney trade, 'Duthie's Yacht' *Brilliant*, launched from an adjacent Aberdeen yard on the same tide. *Brilliant* had almost identical dimensions to *Pericles*, but instead of a full-height half-round poop, she had a modified Aberdeen poop – a raised quarterdeck with a large house thereon – which made her a wet ship in following seas. *Brilliant* crossed double royals on her mizzen. The two ships, each the product of its owner's respective in-house shipyard, made an interesting comparison in aesthetics. Against *Pericles'* beautiful 'Aberdeen Green' hull with white-painted, half-round poop and

Iron passenger ship *Aristides* under sail off Sydney. (National Library of Australia SA B 12017)

deck housings, *Brilliant* had an enamelled black hull, surmounted by a polished brass rail. Her housings were of polished teak, with demountable fine filigree fretwork panels set inside her bulwarks (when in port!). *Pericles* was outfitted with a boiler and condenser to manufacture fresh water for her passengers; she also had a steam windlass to ease the crew's burden.

Commanded by Captain James Largie, who had been master of a number of GTJCo.'s ships, (most recently *Jerusalem*), *Pericles* took her maiden departure from London on 10 September 1877, calling at Plymouth to embark 489 government-sponsored emigrants. She made Sydney on 3 December 1877, seventy-four days out from Plymouth. *Brilliant* on (Lubbock) corrected times took seventy-nine days for her maiden outward passage, arriving in Sydney two weeks later. From their maiden voyages, the two ships were friendly rivals on the Sydney trade until their disposal in 1904. Much was wagered on their successive voyages; between the two commanders, the traditional wager was a top hat. The record shows that *Pericles*, predominantly a passenger ship southbound, usually excelled on her outward voyages to Sydney, while *Brilliant* took the palm homewards.

On 26 July 1877, GTJ's first son, Stephen Thompson, died in London, aged 44 years. Stephen had become a partner in the firm in 1854, the year he jointly established the company's London office with William Henderson. Three years later, he had taken over as the London managing partner when Henderson returned to Aberdeen. He was very closely involved in the establishment of the Aberdeen Line and was the man on the spot when the company extended its services to Melbourne in 1859. He was clearly a man of significant personality, much respected by the officers of the Line serving through London. Lachlan McKinnon in his *Recollections of an Old Lawyer* tells a story from Stephen's boyhood:

> Stephen Thompson fell in love when a lad with 'Kitty Leonard' – a very pretty girl, while she was yet a boarder at Miss Lambert's school. Miss Leonard having on one occasion mentioned to her admirer that she was hungry, he responded by tying a mutton chop addressed to her on the doorbell of the school. Miss Lambert was not one to sit down with the reflection of 'short commons' on her establishment, and young Thompson was taken by his mother to apologise to Miss Lambert, to the great delight of the young lady boarders, who were observing from the upper landing.

Stephen Thompson was survived by his son, also Stephen, who had joined the company two years earlier and was to be made a partner two years hence, and by five daughters, of whom Jane Boyd was to marry into the Potter shipping family; Anne McKerrell was to marry Captain Charles Taylor of the Line, later to become general manager of the well-renowned Darling Island Stevedoring Company in Sydney; and Theodora was to marry Lachlan McKinnon, the highly reputed Aberdeen lawyer, from whose *Recollections* I have quoted. A couple of months after Stephen Thompson's death, the balance was redressed by the birth of Oscar Stephen Thompson to Cornelius Thompson. Oscar was eventually to become the sole surviving member of the family to be actively involved in the management of the company.

Competition among the sailing ship owners on the Australian trade, with the inevitable outcome of shippers playing one owner against another in the quest for cheaper freight rates, led to the formation of the Associated Australian Owners and Brokers in 1876 in an attempt to regulate the trade. The association, whose membership originally comprised ten owners and brokers including GTJCo., met clandestinely in a hired room over the premises of a Mr Davis (from whom the association derived its nickname, 'the Davis'), who was variously described as a paint supplier, hatter, and most probably a hairdresser, located in various premises in the Minories area of London.[25] The association published its first recorded Freight Agreement in July 1878; the agreement between the signatories and individual shippers, promised a 5 per cent rebate on all net freights on cargoes lifted by the signatories' ships, paid three-monthly through C. Bethell, against the agreement by the shipper not to ship on any sailing vessel outside the agreement without the permission of the signatories. The agreement allowed for the rates of freight to be at the lowest scale rates applicable for the class of cargo, an exception being made for parcels of rough cargoes taken for filling up the vessel, where special rates could be negotiated.[26] The Agreement was 'to be kept strictly secret'.[27]

The Australian Freight Conference, which met with vociferous opposition, especially in Australia, where it was referred to as 'the Ring', was extended to steamships in 1884, when the first agreement on freight rates was established. The Conference was accused, probably with some justification, of orchestrating freight rate increases, estimated by *Fairplay* in an 1883 article to have been between 30 and 40 per cent since inception.[28] Criticism of the Australian Freight Ring and other international freight conferences eventually led to a Royal Commission on Shipping Rings in 1906. The report of the Commission published in 1909, with a final report published in 1923, effectively legitimised the deferred rebate system, while recommending certain controls outside a legislative framework, to guard against abuses of the system inherent in the conference monopoly.[29] The status quo was to exist until the early twenty-first century, when the European Commission intervened on competition grounds, with arguably disastrous impact upon the stability of the liner trades.

Further disaster struck GTJCo. on 31 July 1878 when *Harlaw* (Alexander Stephens) on passage from Sydney to Shanghai with 1,100 tons of Wollongong coal, ran aground and was lost on the Tung Sha Bank in the mouth of the River Yangtsze with the death of fourteen crew. The ship had arrived in pilotage waters the previous evening, and there being no sight of a pilot, Captain Stephens brought the ship to anchor. At 0300 hours on 31 July, Pilot Hume boarded the vessel and she got under way. The weather was heavy, with a very strong tide running. At 0915 hours, the ship struck forward, and after attempts were made to pay her head off, she struck aft, ripping her rudder off and severely damaging her. With the hull rapidly taking water, the commander gave orders for her to be abandoned. Successive boats were launched, only to be swamped with heavy loss of life. Significantly, Stephens' first thoughts were for the salvation of his apprentices, whom he dispatched in the first boat under command of the second officer, sadly to little effect despite the gallantry of that officer. Stephens, the pilot, chief and third officers and nine other persons got away in the fourth (last) boat, and this happily finally reached salvation forty-eight hours after the shipwreck.

A naval court convened at Shanghai by the senior naval officer present and presided over by the vice-consul, subsequently concluded that the loss of the ship was entirely due to the 'undecided and injudicious manner' in which the pilot, John Hume, navigated the vessel; no blame attached to the master and mates for the loss of the vessel; that after the shipwreck, the master and mates did all in their power to secure the safety of the vessel and her crew; and praised the conduct of Second Officer Buyers in his launching of the first boat, and his subsequent heroism in twice attempting to save one of its occupants.[30] Although no blame was attached to Alexander Stephens by the court, it was alleged in evidence that the high death rate was attributable to his ordering

the boats launched while the tide was still flooding strongly; he left the company's service thereafter.

An interesting insight into the trading economics of GTJCo. vessels engaged on the triangular service to China emerges from Captain Stephens' evidence to the naval court. He opened his evidence by stating that *Harlaw*, 'left Sydney, NSW on Saturday, 22nd June with a full cargo of coals **on owners' account**.'

The fact that the coals were carried to owners' account implied that GTJCo. traded the cargo, i.e. it had purchased *Harlaw*'s coal cargo, at its own risk, and would sell it for profit (or loss, depending upon market forces) upon arrival in Shanghai. Presumably Sydney agents would arrange the purchase of the coals on behalf of principals, and it would be up to the commander working with Shanghai agents to secure the best price for the cargo's sale. It might be that the company had a contractual arrangement with the likes of P&O or Ocean for the provision of bunker coal to their fuel depots in the Far East.

In October 1878, the auxiliary barque *Jan Meyen*, a Peterhead whaler of 337 tons register, was purchased by George Thompson Youngest for £3,100. This purchase has been advanced by some authorities as having been an early attempt by the company to assess the potential of steam. In fact, the purchase would appear to have been no more than a private shipbroking transaction by Thompson, for the vessel was sold on a month later to George Welch of Dundee, although Thompson retained an 8/64 interest in the vessel, and Cornelius Thompson subsequently acquired a 4/64 interest from the new owners. The vessel was damaged by ice and lost off Greenland in 1882.

The New Year of 1879 brought with it a further partnership restructuring; a new contract of co-partnership, necessitated by the death of Stephen Thompson and facilitated by the coming of age of the two heirs, was announced. William Henderson and Cornelius Thompson carried over from the previous partnership, while the late Stephen Thompson's son, Stephen Thompson Jnr and William Henderson's eldest son, George Thompson Henderson, were both admitted as partners. If George Thompson Youngest had ever been a partner (his obituary has him made a partner in 1854, when he would have been 18 years old), he was certainly not a member of the new partnership, which also changed the firm's corporate style by dropping the 'Jnr' to become George Thompson & Co. (GTCo.). With the implementation of the new partnership, all the individual ship shareholdings were changed to exclude George Thompson Youngest from the subscribing owners, but the new partnership sold him a private shareholding in each ship, typically 8/64ths, and this situation continued through each successive new ship up to 1900. There is a suspicion within the surviving family that George Thompson Youngest was something of a maverick, whose lifestyle did not fit easily with the senior partner, William Henderson.

On 17 March 1879, *Thermopylæ* docked in London, 110 days out from Shanghai, bringing in the last tea cargo to be carried to London by a GTCo. sailing clipper. GTCo. sailing ships had served with distinction on the China tea trade for forty years, apart from the six years 1856 to 1862 when the company had been concentrating its resources on building up the Australian line. The withdrawal of sailing ships was a response to market forces and did not mark GTCo.'s final abandonment of the China trade, which was to have a brief rejuvenation in steam.

The second incident to impact upon the smooth operation of *Samuel Plimsoll* now occurred, an incident that was to go down in the annals of sailing ship seamanship and bring great credit upon Richard Boaden. Departing Plymouth on 21 March 1879, bound for Sydney with a full complement of emigrants, she was struck down by a tropical squall on 5 April, when close north of the Equator. The force of the squall carried away her bobstay, with the almost inevitable knock-on chain reaction of the bowsprit breaking off at the stem head, the fore topmast breaking at its lower cap, and thereafter the main topgallant mast together with spars. An American ship was in company, also bound for Sydney, and her master kindly offered to help by taking *Samuel Plimsoll*'s passengers on board; this offer Boaden declined.

Over the course of the next two days, Boaden and his crew went about the Herculean task of repairing the damage, using spare spars carried on board for the purpose, salvaged intact gear, superlative application of the seaman's craft, and I sense more than a slight dash of ingenuity. Quite the most formidable initial task was to repair the bowsprit, which was effected by splicing the stump to the broken spar with driven wood splines. Boaden forbore from seeking sanctuary in South America to effect repairs, thereby saving cargo insurers the considerable costs arising from general average. With the damage repaired, Boaden again took passage for Sydney, arriving there on 12 June, an overall passage time of eighty-three days from Plymouth; good by any account, exceptional in the circumstances.

The story had a final twist, which Lubbock delights in telling:[31]

The American arrived a few days later, and as soon as he could get ashore, reported leaving the SAMUEL PLIMSOLL dismasted in the North Atlantic; he also commented upon Captain Boaden's foolhardiness in refusing to tranship his passengers. The story goes that the agent turned around, and rather unkindly imitating the slow drawl of the Yankee, replied with a chuckle, 'If it's Captain Boaden you are talking about, I guess you had better see him yourself. He's in the next room'.

A letter advising on a new contract of co-partnership dated 1 January 1879.

Boaden's feat of seamanship was widely praised, along with his decision not to put in to Brazil to effect repairs. A grateful underwriting fraternity presented him with an illuminated testimonial at a picnic in his honour in Sydney.

Hood's yard had delivered its last ship to Alexander Nicol, the 1,174-ton iron clipper **Cimba**, in April 1878. Widely regarded as Nicol's finest ship, she rapidly established a reputation for herself on the Aberdeen Line's Sydney berth and was almost invariably in the fastest pack of the wool clippers home. **Cimba**'s name was reflected in her rampant Scottish lion figurehead. **Cimba** was followed four months later by her 1,176-ton almost identical sister **Sophocles**, for GTCo. The company's 48/64 subscribing ownership in the ship was joined by a private investment of 8/64 by George Thompson Youngest. Despite almost identical dimensions and sail plan, **Sophocles** was never the flyer that **Cimba** proved to be. The vessel was commanded by two reputable commanders for all her nineteen-year life with GTCo., predominantly served on the Sydney service, the latter seventeen years under Captain Alexander Smith. It is unlikely that her slowness could be attributed to her command, or a change would have been made. I suspect that what she lacked in pace, she made up for in economic return to her owners. **Sophocles** was certainly a beautiful ship to behold.

With **Sophocles** in service, and with ships released from the prolonged voyages that the triangular China service involved, the company embarked upon a rapid rundown of its older ships, a divestment programme that was to see seven famous names sold out of service, and the involuntary loss of an eighth ship over the two-year period 1880–81. Partners also sold their private interests in a ninth ship. The ships disposed of were:

- **Strathdon**, 36/64 sold to a Dutchman 16 February 1880.

- **Wave of Life**, 32/64 sold to London shipbrokers, August 1880 for on-sale to Russian interests.

- **Damascus**, 24/64, sold to Liverpool shipbrokers 'for a sum of not less than £3,500', March 1881, for on-sale to Norwegian interests.

- **Ascalon**, 32/64, sold to James Foot Gibb, London, April 1881; sold on to Trinder Anderson, May 1881.

- **Moravian**, 28/64, sold through Samuel Joseph, Sydney, 20 June 1881 to Sydney owners 'for a sum of not less than £3,250'.

- **Kosciusko**, 32/64, sold to Cowlislaw Bros., Sydney, 22 August 1881; and,

- **Nineveh**, 28/64, sold through Samuel Joseph, Sydney, 20 October 1881, to Sydney merchants (5 December 1881).

The clipper **Samuel Plimsoll** at Sydney, showing the enormous height of her masts. (National Library of Australia Vic H.91.108/699)

Clipper **Sophocles** under sail outside Sydney Heads. (National Library of Australia SA PRG 1373/3/67)

The sale of these ships in relatively short order reflected not only the capacity surplus occasioned by withdrawal from the China trade but also preparation of the Line for the advent of steam. In addition to the foregoing company ships, William Henderson and Cornelius Thompson also divested themselves of their personal interests in the brig *Janet*, which was sold in April 1881. Given the ultra-conservative financing arrangements favoured by the partners, I sense that the sale of these ships would also have generated cash needed to finance the steamship building programme upon which the company embarked in 1880. From the outset, George Thompson and his successors had financed ship acquisitions in cash; at no stage is there any evidence of a GTJ ship being mortgaged, though there may have been private banking arrangements that did not involve security attaching to the ship(s) by way of the Register. After the bank crisis in 1849, which largely arose from unsecured loans, this seems unlikely. As a point of interest, William Henderson replaced GTJ on the North of Scotland Bank's board in 1881 and remained in post until his death in 1904.

Three years after the loss of *Harlaw*, GTCo. suffered a further ship loss, this time *Queen of Nations* on the 31 May 1881, under disreputable circumstances completely out of character with the company's high standards. The ship was under the command of Captain Samuel Bache, a Bristol man who in evidence stated that he had held acting command for five years. He had commanded *Queen of Nations* for her previous voyage when she ran 300 immigrants from the UK to Brisbane; prior to that he had commanded the company's *Strathdon* for two voyages, in which ship he had visited Sydney. Bache does not register as one of GTCo.'s long-serving company men whom one would have expected to have been in command, and while entries in Lloyd's Captains' Register record his two voyages in command of *Queen of Nations*, there are no earlier records of service, even though he had held his master's certificate since 1873.

After initial bad weather, the fateful outwards voyage had passed without undue incident, though Bache was reported in the second officer's evidence at the subsequent Marine Board inquiry to have been eccentric for the greater part of the passage (the crew were less charitable, referring to him as having been drunk on frequent occasions). The ship had last made a landfall off Tristan da Cunha, sixty days previously. No sights had been obtained the previous day, and the vessel was running on dead-reckoned positioning along a coast notorious for its strong south setting currents. Bache and the mate, Robert Anderson, were standing watch-and-watch, the second officer being incapacitated. At 0200 hours on 31 May 1881, Bache was called on deck, lights having been sighted to the westward; the lights were in fact burning coal heaps at the Mount Keira mine and the lights of Wollongong harbour, 45 miles south of Sydney Heads. Passing squalls prevailing at the time gave the impression of flashing lights. Bache mistook the lights for Sydney Heads and ordered the helm over to make for them on a course WNW. At about 0600, as dawn broke, breakers were sighted ahead, and the course was altered to NW by W; the vessel struck five minutes later, with all sail but her main topgallant set. Her wreck site was on Corrimal Beach, 3 miles north of Wollongong Harbour. (It is interesting to note that at the subsequent Board of Inquiry, evidence was volunteered by a coasting master that he had on two occasions in the recent past, redirected overseas ships that were making inshore having mistaken the Wollongong coal fires for Sydney Heads.)

Three seamen attempted to swim ashore during the morning, one of whom was drowned in the attempt. At noon, the balance of the crew came safely ashore in the ship's boat, with the exception of Bache and the mate, who remained on board, reportedly to safeguard the owners' interest in any ensuing salvage action; both were described as acting in an extremely excited fashion, the mate reputedly brandishing a loaded revolver at the crew. Once ashore, the crew made town and 'found means to dissipate their sorrow at the accident'; the petty officers appeared before the police magistrate and swore two separate charges against Bache and the mate of assault and battery; the carpenter had spent the previous night in irons and could not stand his watch because of injuries allegedly sustained. Two attempts were made by a volunteer crew under the local police sergeant to land Bache and the mate, at some substantial risk, but on each occasion one or both men went below decks and refused to be saved. According to *The Sydney Mail*, the two officers were insane, or if the crew were to be believed, both were under the influence of drink.[32]

The inestimable Captain Hixson, President of the New South Wales Marine Board, mobilised the Sydney pilot cutter to the scene of the wreck, and a tug with Captain Ayling, commander of the *Aviemore*, and insurance representatives embarked also proceeded from Sydney when news of the casualty was received. A lifeboat under Captain Ayling put out from the shore next morning, and finally prevailed upon Bache and the mate to come ashore. A salvage operation for the cargo, which was valued at £22,700, was mobilised; the wreck of the ship was sold for £100. Among her cargo, she had a large consignment of Hennessy brandy, which attracted the attention of the local populace, resulting in charges of theft, smuggling and assault on a customs officer. Bache, after failing to appear before the Marine Board on two occasions, finally presented himself on 23 June, by which time the board had ruled against him *in absentia*, using evidence from the crew, which was damning in respect to his sobriety. This charge was countered by the chief and third officers' evidence. The board found that the loss of *Queen of Nations* was caused by Bache's carelessness and drunkenness; it suspended his certificate of competency for twelve months. Apart from one two-month voyage, Bache never sailed again as master, spending the balance of his seagoing career as mate, principally in the Bristol City Line.

In 1991, when bottom scouring uncovered the remains of *Queen of Nations*, the Heritage Branch of the New South Wales Department of Planning undertook a detailed archaeological dive on the wreck, reported in the *Bulletin of the Australian Institute for Maritime Archaeology*.[33] The remains sanded over again by April 1992, and the wreck site was declared a Historic Shipwreck under the Commonwealth Historic Shipwrecks Act in the same year.

In March 1881, Walter Hood delivered the 1,383 gross tons iron ship *Orontes* to GTCo.; *Orontes* was to be the last ship Hood's built. The new ship was a freighter, destined for the Sydney trade. Although Lubbock was somewhat disparaging in respect to her passage making, she was not in fact the slowest of the fleet. Commanded by Captain David Bain for her first twenty-one years, she led an uneventful life until run down and sunk by the steamer *Oceana* off Ostend on 23 October 1903, whilst inbound laden with nitrate.

There is no record to explain the reasons for the closure of Hood's yard, but I suspect it reflected a number of factors, including limitations of slipway length, which curtailed the building of the size of ship needed for the future, and shortage of engine-building skills and facilities in Aberdeen necessary for steamers. The closure was also in line with a general decline in shipbuilding throughout in Aberdeen, which had seen the port's annual gross tonnage delivered decline from 11,000 tons a year in the early 1870s to half that figure by the end of the decade. Over the course of its forty-two-year

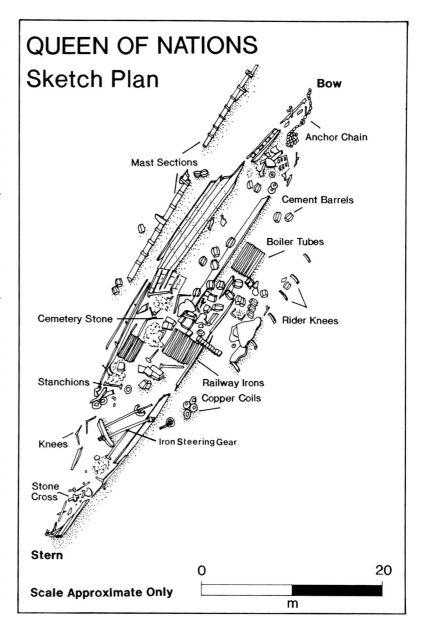

Archaeological site plan of *Queen of Nations*. (Australian Institute for Maritime Archaeology)

Iron freighter *Orontes*; the last ship built by Walter Hood, 1881. (National Library of Australia SA 1373/3/69)

existence, the yard had built 100 sailing vessels of all shapes and sizes, forty-four for George Thompson, eleven for Alexander Nicol and two for Thompson/Henderson private family interests. The yard had built a substantial international reputation for the quality and performance of its ships. With the closure of the firm, the lease on the yard space passed to Duthies, later to become part of Alexander Hall's shipyard when Duthies sold out its shipbuilding operations to that company. Cornelius Thompson, who had been the managing partner in Hood's shipyard, moved to London where he was to direct the Line's operations; he was elected a member of the committee of Lloyd's Register of Shipping.

With the delivery of **Orontes**, GTCo.'s sailing ship fleet comprised sixteen vessels, all engaged on the Australian trade, six of which were passenger and emigrant carriers. The Line had experimented, unsuccessfully with steam; the experience it had gained with the **Atrato** had made it cautious, and thusfar, steam developments were not such as to economically suit its trade. Now however, the company was not only poised to invest in steam, but its entry was to be such as to take the industry technically by force and to universally spell the death knell of sail on the long-haul routes.

A fitting epilogue to the halcyon days of GTCo.'s sailing fleet may be found in Commander Frank Worsley's autobiographical *First Voyage*, when, as a first trip apprentice on the New Zealand Shipping Company's **Wairoa** in 1889, he encountered the outward bound **Patriarch** off the east coast of South America:

A full-rigged, double-topgallant ship, her dark-green symmetrical hull with a yellow ribbon and her white spars proclaimed her to be an Aberdeen White Star clipper, one of George Thompson's Line. Her steel lower masts and topmasts were all in one, and her pine topgallant and royal masts telescoped into the topmast heads, which added smartness and trimness to her appearance aloft. All ships at sea are beautiful, but George Thompson's were particularly so. That ship appeared electric with onrushing power as in radiant beauty her silver-lined tapering towers of canvas heeled to the lilting trades. All that beauty of tropic sea and sky seemed to have been designed to form a setting for her exquisite picture. Her clean green bows, un-disfigured by one rust stain, strained out and upwards, culminating in her white figurehead, which seemed to support the steel and pine that thrust outwards sixty-five feet ahead and carried the slim graceful jibs, the daintiest-looking sails belonging to a ship. Her masts were stayed straight, her yards trimmed to perfection and each parallel to the other. Every halyard was bar taut; every sheet was home and exactly equal to the opposite one; every sail flat, unwrinkled, and better set than a yacht's, and not one 'Irish pennant' marred her flawless beauty and absolute trimness alow and aloft. Nothing was out of place and no fault could have been found with her at an admiral's inspection. Her yards were 'off the backstays', she was going ramping full and sweeping down on us at 9 knots with a bone in her mouth, cutting a feather and hurling a white wave out from either bow ...

From hoisting her number to the last dip of the ensign had been five hectic minutes, punctuated by mental snapshots of the thrilling beauty of the green-hulled outward bounder as she swept past. But those five minutes had left an indelible impression, so that every seaman aboard had registered a mental picture of every trifling peculiarity of rig, or deviation from the normal, aboard the **Patriarch**, to afford endless forecastle argument in the days to come.[34]

This, from a New Zealand Shipping Company ship, a company renowned for operating some of the smartest, best-found ships in the Merchant Navy ... A reproduction of Spurling's painting of **Patriarch** under full sail is included in the colour section.

THE COMING OF STEAM – 1882 TO 1896
'... THAT MESSRS THOMPSON WILL HAVE THEIR REWARD'

The Suez Canal had officially opened to traffic on 17 November 1869. The impact upon sail was not as immediate as many have suggested, although it undoubtedly spelt the eventual death knell of sail on the China trade; any sailing ship built for that trade after that date must have been a short-term investment. Initially, the canal enjoyed a very limited operating depth, severely constraining the size of ship using it, and transit charges were initially set at levels that were economically prohibitive. Further, the efficiency of steam, and the necessary support logistics associated with steam propulsion were not as yet sufficiently developed to capitalise upon the distance-saving potential that the canal offered, except for high-paying, low-deadweight services – passengers, mail, specie – and, in time, tea.

Twin-cylindered compound steam engines, which utilised the economies deriving from putting to work both the relatively high-pressure input steam and the residual low-pressure steam exhausted thereafter, had first been installed in an ocean-going vessel in the mid-1850s, the work of the Clydeside engineers John Elder and Charles Randolph. The high-pressure steam input to such engines was in the region of 30psi, against a furnace consumption of 3.25lb of coal per ihp (indicated horsepower) delivered per hour; as such, they represented an improvement in operating efficiency of some 30 per cent over the norm. A Liverpool locomotive engineer, Alfred Holt, experimented with his own design of tandem compound engine wherein the high-pressure cylinder was mounted over the low-pressure cylinder in a single casting, the prototype of which he installed in the re-engined coastal bulk carrier *Cleator* in 1864. Operating at a steam pressure of 60psi, this engine delivered a fuel economy of some 40 per cent, allowing *Cleator* to extend her economic field of operation from coastal voyages to as far afield as Brazil.

Holt's success lay not only in his innovative design, but also in his persuasive powers in convincing the Board of Trade that high-pressure steam could safely be used in marine applications. He orchestrated his innovation by ordering three tandem compound-engined, barque-rigged 3,000-ton capacity steamers – *Achilles*, *Agamemnon* and *Ajax* – from Scotts of Greenock, at a cost of £52,000 each. Put to work in the Far East trade, these vessels formed the first units of Holt's Ocean Steamship Company, to become world-renowned as the Blue Funnel Line. With a daily coal consumption of just over 20 tons, *Agamemnon* initially dispatched to China via the Cape in April 1866, bunkering at Mauritius en route; an outward passage of seventy-seven days was advertised for the service, with eighty days homewards.

Despite the demonstrably quicker voyage time, prejudice initially wagered against these large steam vessels. However, the opening of the Suez Canal progressively set aside such antipathy, facilitating as it did the potential for homeward runs from China of less than forty days.

Holt's A-class steamer.

In short order, a new breed of racing tea steamers was commissioned into service, dominated by MacGregor's 'Glen', Jenkin's 'Shire' and Skinner's 'Castle' lines offering average speeds progressively increasing to in the region of 14 knots. The ultimate in racing tea steamers was Skinner's *Stirling Castle*, which achieved 18.41 knots on trials. On her maiden voyage in 1882, she made the 10,561-mile passage from Hankow to London in twenty-nine days and twenty-two hours. But with a coal consumption of around 165 tons per day, served by up to 111 firemen, she was not economical to operate, and was sold after her second record-breaking voyage. P&O and Ocean did not participate in the racing voyages; to the

extreme chagrin of Holt's Far East managing agent, John Swire, Holt's Blue Funnel Line ships were markedly slower, with average speeds in the region of 11 knots – but Holt's vessels were significantly more economical in operation.

The opening of the Suez Canal eventually facilitated the economic use of steamers on the high-paying Far East express tea service. However, the development of the steam engine's operational efficiency, and in particular the development of an effective boiler with associated construction steels whereby the higher pressure steam necessary to power more efficient engines could safely be delivered, had yet to reach a stage where steam would economically encroach upon the Australasian long-haul cargo routes.

While steam had reached Australia as early as 1852, heavily subsidised by a Royal Mail contract, it was still far from being an economic means of propulsion for cargo carriers, and sail continued to remain the dominant means of propulsion on the long hauls. Indeed, sail burgeoned as emigration to and trade with the island continent grew. However, in the latter years of sail dominance on the Australian trade, we have seen a shift from the racing clipper style of sailing cargo carrier to a fuller, more cargo-kindly form, evidenced in GTCo.'s **Smyrna** and **Sophocles**.

Higher steam pressures of 60psi in powering compound engines had delivered significant fuel, and thus cargo-carrying, economies; in round terms, a pressure of 60psi in required only about half the coal consumed by the older single-expansion engine. However, it was recognised that above a certain pressure, said to be 70–75psi, no perceptible increase in economy would be achieved with the compound engine. To quote Alexander Kirk in a paper delivered to the 23rd Session of the Institute of Naval Architects: 'The compound or double-expansion engine has relapsed into the condition of the old single expansion one.'

Kirk was convinced that:

> the great success of the ordinary compound engine over the earlier simple engine lay in the range of temperature through which the steam in any one cylinder passed in the course of one stroke, being very much reduced (nearly halved in fact, compared with a single cylinder), it seemed to me that with these high pressures, we must use three successive expansions, and divide the total range of temperature into three parts.[1]

In the 1850s, the Clydeside shipbuilder and engineer John Elder, for whom Kirk then worked, had lodged patents addressing the principle of triple and quadruple-expansion engines. In 1874, John Elder had built a steamer, **Propontis**, for Liverpool shipowner W.H. Dixon, which incorporated a triple-expansion propulsion engine designed by Kirk to match the high-pressure potential of the Rowan and Horton patent boiler specified by Dixon. This was not the first known application of the triple-expansion principle, an earlier craft built for work on the River Seine had been so equipped, but **Propontis** was potentially the first meaningful seagoing application. **Propontis** was also a pioneer insofar that her boiler was the first application of the water tube principle, whereby steam was generated from water passing through tubes heated from flue gases passing through the boiler. This was in contrast to the water being heated by contact with the walls of the combustion chamber, and by tubes bearing hot gases from the combustion chamber passing through the body of the water in the boiler. **Propontis**' boiler, which delivered steam at 150psi, was ahead of its time, and very soon gave trouble, leading to two out of the four boilers exploding at sea. This resulted in the application of water tube boilers passing out of favour for many years, although the engine proved perfectly satisfactory. **Propontis** was reboilered with a conventional flue gas boiler, albeit delivering only 90psi pressure, and the vessel continued to operate satisfactorily for a number of years.

Kirk recognised that high-pressure steam was a prerequisite for capitalising upon the economic potential offered by triple-expansion machinery. However, fruition lay in a package going beyond the triple-expansion concept alone; to successfully and safely achieve high pressures using a conventional combustion gas tube Scotch boiler, the combustion chamber needed radical advancement; an effective condenser was also required. A shortfall in these elements blocked advancement towards effective triple expansion for some seven years following the **Propontis** experiment.

The cylindrical Scotch boiler under pressure was exposed not only to tensile stresses in its outer shell, which current materials and technologies easily addressed, but also more seriously in terms of current technology, compressive, collapsing forces on the furnace flue within. In 1877, a self-made Yorkshire engineer and forge master, Samuel Fox, patented the concept of a corrugated flue. To quote the patent:[2]

> In making this flue, plain sheet metal is first bended into a cylindrical form and the joint welded, after which the cylinder or tube is brought to red heat and the corrugations are formed in the metal either by rolling or embossing or by swaging them.

Tests of Fox's corrugated flues were undertaken in March 1878, a year after his international patents were granted, before invited representatives of the Admiralty, Board of Trade, Lloyd's Register and shipping company officials. The hydraulic destructive tests undertaken on a non-corrugated and a corrugated flue of like dimensions showed the non-corrugated flue collapsing catastrophically at 200psi, while the corrugated flue finally yielded at 450psi, though resistance after initial collapse was long standing, indicating that collapse in service was unlikely to lead to boiler explosion. (Separate tests by the Admiralty had shown yield pressures of 800psi for Fox's corrugated flues).[3]

The first corrugated flues were manufactured out of pig iron at Fox's Leeds Forge, a company in which the shipbuilders Scotts of Greenoch were shareholders and effectively bankers. Early examples of the corrugated flues gained sea experience from 1879. German steel makers were quick to realise the potential of Fox's flues and entered into licensing arrangements with the company. The Germans from the outset manufactured their steel flues with a rolling mill, also patented by Fox, rather than hydraulically swaging or hammering the corrugations as was done at Leeds. It was not until 1880 that finance became available to install a similar mill to roll corrugations at the Leeds Forge.

With the availability of Cox's corrugated furnace flues, Kirk now had to hand the main elements necessary to promote an economically successful triple-expansion engine package, but following the reboilering of *Propontis* after the failure of her original high-pressure water tube boiler, 'the idea still haunted most people that an internally fired boiler was unfit for such high pressures' and he had 'failed to find anyone who cared to make such a long step'.[4] In January of 1881, however, the firm for which he now worked as chief engineer, Robert Napier and Sons, was entrusted with the construction of GTCo.'s first steamship, the SS *Aberdeen*, which was to be engined with a high-pressure, steam-powered triple-expansion engine package to Kirk's design; Kirk commented upon the order: 'and in doing so I hope that Messrs. Thompson will have their reward'.[5]

Kirk surmised that:

> In designing a ship for the long voyage their [GTCo.] ships make from this country to Australia and China, more importance attaches to a small consumption of coal than in ships making shorter voyages, and it was necessary to use every device to attain this end.

No record remains as to why GTCo. chose Napier to undertake the building of its first steamship, but Kirk's reputation must have been a key factor. He clearly understood the company's operational requirements and arguably Napier was the only yard offering the sort of package that stood a chance of success. GTCo. had seen many others fail in extending steamship services to Australia; it had hands-on experience of the problems faced by the *Atrato* under its commercial management nine years earlier. However, the

writing was clearly on the wall, and experienced though it was in sail, the age of long-haul steam was nigh; the mould only had to be broken. The decision to enter steam with an innovative ship such as *Aberdeen* was both a bold step, and one that reflected a careful, if not adventurous thought process, the credit for which was given to Cornelius Thompson,[6] supported no doubt by his father.

If the *Aberdeen* was innovative in terms of her propulsion package, the engine element was reasonably well tried and well understood. Her triple-expansion engine was essentially the same design as that installed satisfactorily in *Propontis* seven years earlier. The three cylinders were arranged over a three-throw crank shaft, whose webs were set at 120 degrees to each other. High-pressure steam at 125psi entered the smallest cylinder of 30in diameter, passed into the intermediate cylinder of 45in diameter, and finally into the largest or low-pressure cylinder of 70in diameter, from whence it exhausted to the condenser, where it was condensed back to boiler feed water. The stroke of the engine was 4ft 6in. The high-pressure cylinder was not jacketed, but the intermediate and low-pressure cylinders, with steam of 50psi and 15psi respectively, were to minimise condensation within the cylinders. The engine drove a single propeller turning at 65rpm.

Two Scotch double-ended 14ft diameter steel boilers were installed, each fitted with six 3ft 6in diameter Fox's corrugated furnaces. The total heating surface of the boiler, corrugated furnace and fire tubes, was 7,128 sq ft. Fox's flues were of steel construction, initially manufactured at the Leeds Forge, but almost certainly corrugated at Essen. The boilers were built to Lloyd's Register rules; these allowed a thinner shell thickness than Board of Trade requirements, but the boiler internals, where most problems would likely be experienced, were more heavily scantled than either Lloyd's or the Board of Trade required. An interesting feature of the boilers, reflecting the requirements of the intended trade, was that variable length fire bars were available. When burning inferior calorific value Australian coal, 6ft fire bars extending the full length of the grate were used, whereas when superior grade English or Welsh coal was burned, 5ft fire bars were used with the remaining length bricked over.[7]

Aberdeen's hull was built of iron to the highest class of Lloyd's Register with dimensions of 350ft × 44ft × 33ft. The vessel was configured with three main cargo holds, two forward and one aft, and a dual-cargo or coal bunker hold immediately forward of the bridge. An open upper 'tween deck ran the length of the ship, in which steerage

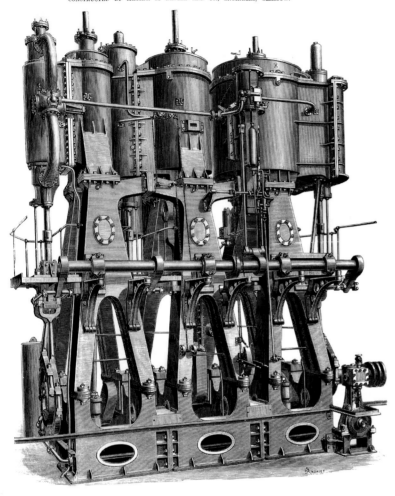

TRIPLE-EXPANSION ENGINES OF THE S.S. "ABERDEEN."
CONSTRUCTED BY MESSRS. R. NAPIER AND CO., ENGINEERS, GLASGOW.

An engraving of *Aberdeen*'s engine from *The Mechanic*.

class passengers could be carried on the outwards voyages, and a lower 'tween deck was arranged in each hold. The vessel's overall cargo capacity was 194,668 cu.ft, while her dual cargo and coal capacity added a further 20,787 cu.ft; reserve coal bunkers were arranged in the upper 'tween deck in way of the boiler room. A total of 1,376 tons of bunker coal could be carried, permitting extended steaming without recourse to coaling. Her registered tonnages were 3,616.23 gross and

2,370.61 net. Her deadweight carrying capacity (which would include coal bunkers), was 4,720 tons. She had three masts and as originally outfitted, she was barque-rigged to capitalise on favourable winds on passage. She was fitted to carry twelve first-class passengers in some considerable comfort in accommodation arranged below the main deck in the stern of the vessel. This was somewhat unusual, for the accommodation must have suffered from propeller vibration. Her upper 'tween deck was arranged with demountable accommodation to carry up to 450 immigrants on the outward passage; upon disembarkation in Australia, the accommodation would be removed to facilitate the carriage of wool homewards.

While **Aberdeen** was technically one of the most advanced steamships of her time, her outward appearance bespoke her GTCo. pedigree. She had a graceful clipper bow, with bowsprit and figurehead. Her pronounced sheer was set off by a golden yellow ribband at 'tween deck level on her Aberdeen-green hull; her superstructure and deck houses were painted cream. Raked pole masts and her raked buff funnel combined to give her a yacht-like aspect.

Aberdeen was laid down on 28 April 1881 and launched on 21 December 1881 by Jane Boyd Henderson, wife of the senior partner, William Henderson and daughter of GTJ. The vessel left the quay for initial sea trials on 19 February 1882. The trials were the subject of intense interest in marine technical circles and extreme measures were taken to establish the efficiency of the new propulsion plant. Kirk's intention was to test the consumption on a six-hour run at 1,800hp, with the ship laden with 2,000 tons of deadweight; in fact, this period was shortened 'by the owner's desire' to four hours. Senior representatives of Lloyd's Register oversaw the trials, the state of the fires and the weighing of the Penrikyber Welsh coal used. The outcome was a consumption of 1.28lb per indicated horsepower per hour; Kirk equated this to 1.5 to 1.6lb of Welsh coal per ihp per hour under sea service. Subsequent trials over the measured mile to establish the vessel's maximum speed showed an average of 13.74 knots on a displacement of 4,753 tons against a mean 2,631ihp, for which fuel consumption was 1.85 tons per hour.

These results, which were not dissimilar to those achieved with **Propontis** seven years earlier, were nonetheless heralded as a breakthrough in marine steam propulsion. **Aberdeen**'s fuel consumption was effectively halved against the norm, and the long-haul routes, hitherto the near-exclusive domain of sail, were

A reconstruction of *Aberdeen*'s boilers and flues. (PHK collection)

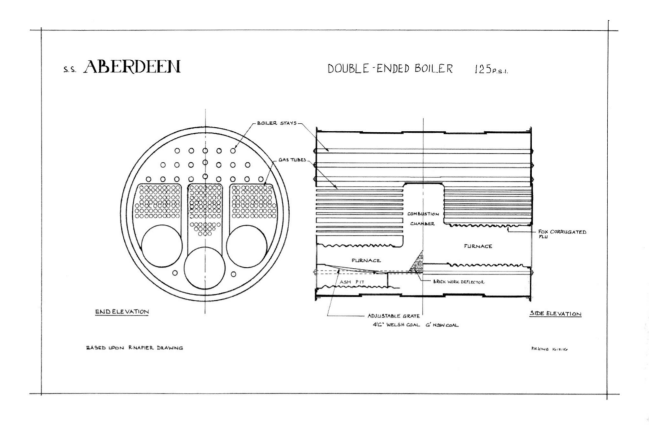

s.s. ABERDEEN — DOUBLE-ENDED BOILER 125 P.S.I.

BOILER STAYS
GAS TUBES
COMBUSTION CHAMBER
FOX CORRUGATED FLU
FURNACE
FURNACE
ASH PIT
BRICK WORK DEFLECTOR
END ELEVATION
ADJUSTABLE GRATE
4'6" WELSH COAL   6' NSW COAL
SIDE ELEVATION
BASED UPON R.NAPIER DRAWING
P.H.KING 15/11/16

opened to steam on an economic basis. With almost immediate effect, practically all new marine propulsion engines were of the triple- or quadruple-expansion configuration, and many earlier compound-engined ships were converted to triple expansion. The accompanying table shows the progress over a period 1872 to 1899 in terms of boiler pressure and consumption:

	1872	1881	1882 Aberdeen	1891 Thermopylæ	1899 Salamis
Boiler Pressure – psi	52.4	77.4	125	160	200
Coal consumption per ihp per hr lb	2.11	1.83	1.55	1.52	1.48

(Table based on J. McKenzie, 'Review of marine engineering during the last ten years' Proc. Inst. Mech. Eng (1901) and personal research)

As a point of interest, *Aberdeen*, in addition to her innovative propulsion system, was also one of the first ships to carry a curve of stability shortly after her commissioning, following the disaster that beset Orient Line's RMS *Austral*, which sank at anchor in Neutral Bay, Sydney, on 11 November 1882 while coaling, with the loss of five crewmen.

Aberdeen loaded her first cargo for Melbourne and Sydney in London's East India Docks and departed on her maiden voyage on 30 March 1882. Captain Charles Matheson, lately commander of the clipper *Thermopylæ*, was in command. In the year prior to taking command of *Aberdeen*, he had served as a supernumerary mate in Anchor Line's steamer *Elysia* on the Atlantic trade, to gain time for a steamship endorsement to his master's certificate of competency.[8] In accordance with common practice of the time, *Aberdeen* broke her passage at Plymouth to take on passengers and immigrants, departing that port with 4,000 tons of cargo and coal on 1 April. She replenished 130 tons of bunkers at Cape Town, and reached

Melbourne on 14 May 1882 after a forty-four-day steaming passage. Her average indicated horse power had been about 1,880, and her coal consumption 1.7lb per indicated horsepower per hour, thus confirming Kirk's prediction. Her daily coal consumption had been 35 tons, and she had averaged 302 nautical miles per day.

The vessel discharged her outwards cargo at Melbourne and Sydney, and loaded a cargo of New South Wales coal at the latter port for Shanghai. From Shanghai, she dropped down to Foochow to load a full tea cargo for home. The Pagoda Anchorage at Foochow was the *sanctum sanctorum* of the tea clippers, and the impact of *Aberdeen*'s arrival can best be described by quoting from a letter written to David MacGregor by Captain Harry Davis, who was in command of one of Killick Martin's clippers waiting to load in the Pagoda Anchorage at the time of her arrival:

> I have vivid recollections of their first steamer s.s. ABERDEEN, barque rigged I think, coming up the Min and anchoring one day at Foochow. We had all to sail and back and fill up the Min from the White Dogs at its mouth, hiring sampans to keep us straight in the very narrow reaches until we got to our anchorages, whilst she came up under her own steam and chose her own berth.
>
> There were eight or ten of our clippers anchored there waiting for tea – glossy black sides, brassworks gleaming in the early sunlight, yards squared by lifts and braces, house flags fluttering at the main

and the glorious red ensign at peak or staff. Some of the ships had been there many days, ours only a few. I think TITANIA was amongst those of us at Foochow waiting for tea, but we did not have time for visiting as our tea was ready for Cape Town and Port Elizabeth.

> Enter the s.s. ABERDEEN of Aberdeen under her own steam. She anchored below all of us and was admired by all, for she looked very smart in her green dress. But although we all admired her I think we resented her intrusion into what had been our freehold and domain for long, long years. She was optical proof to most of us that the day of the tea clipper proper was swiftly drawing to its close. And when at dawn on the fourth day, she hove up by steam, the rattle of her cables and windlass sounded the knell of our lovely vessels as tea-carriers, for she had gobbled up all there was in the go-downs, except ours, for we were loading for Port Elizabeth, Cape Town and East London. We left very soon after and left the fleet waiting for their cargoes that the intruder had swallowed whole. This sort of happening must have broken the hearts of owners, captains and officers.[9]

The understandable resentment and sadness expressed in his letter was probably made the worse by the fact that **Aberdeen**, as opposed to say a Blue Funnel steamer, looked very similar in style and livery to one of their own, and had a lineage that traced in short time back to 'that Damned Scotsman' – **Thermopylæ**, and other great Thompson tea clippers. To compound the agony, **Aberdeen** was commanded by 'one of their own', Captain Charles Matheson, a noted clipper master, fresh from commanding the ultimate thoroughbred. One senses almost a feeling of betrayal.

Aberdeen took passage home via the Suez Canal, calling at Hong Kong and Singapore en route and making arrival in London on 8 October 1882; a round voyage of six months and nine days – a highly successful maiden voyage. In sharp contrast to the inefficiently powered mail steamers, she had carried heavy cargoes on two legs of the triangular voyage, and a record high-volume tea cargo on the third.

That the vessel was designed for and engaged upon the traditional clipper triangular route rather than pursuing a direct run home from Australia reflected the lack of paying cargoes then available in the colony in the Antipodean autumn; it also reflected GTCo.'s long experience in a trade that yielded a profitable round voyage. It did not, however, set the pattern for a truly liner steamship service.

At the time of **Aberdeen** entering service, GTCo. had sixteen sailing ships with an average age of 9.8 years engaged in the Australian trade. The company was unlikely to dispose of an earning fleet of vessels, the operation of which they understood well, and probably at a depreciated value, to make way for further steamers in short order. Probably more pressing was the financing of expensive new vessels. **Aberdeen** was initially owned outright by the partners William Henderson, Cornelius Thompson and George Thompson Henderson; almost immediately in March 1882, the shareholding was diluted when 8/64 were sold to George Thompson Youngest, and significantly, a further 4/64 to Frederick Dalgety. A further 7/64th were sold in May to five new shareholders. Over the course of the next two years, a further 8/64 were sold, the last 4/64 tranche going to Samuel Aaron Joseph, the Line's Sydney managing agent. Financing of the ship had followed the traditional GTCo. route through individual shareholders/ shareholding groups, with no mortgages attaching to the vessel to indicate finance house involvement.

Following her maiden voyage, **Aberdeen** then entered a two-voyage a year trading cycle, which continued for the next seven years, programmed to position the vessel in Australia for the southern spring wool sales, and on alternate voyages, loading coal out of Sydney or Newcastle for Shanghai, and thereafter China tea home. From 1883, her outwards voyages extended up to Newcastle, New South Wales. On her second voyage, which was her first direct homewards loading from Australia, she loaded at Sydney, Melbourne, topping up at Port Victor, 3,400 bales of wool and 3,000 cases of preserved meats. With voyage extensions to Newcastle, copper ingots also formed a bottom cargo for the homewards run.

Aberdeen was a successful, innovative ship. When commissioned, she was arguably the most economical cargo-carrying steamer per deadweight ton/mile in the world, and by the standards of those immediate days, a large cargo carrier. Given GTCo.'s and its Australian managing agents' extensive experience in the trade therefore, it is surprising that **Aberdeen** was not fitted for the carriage of refrigerated cargo. Dalgety clearly foresaw the potential of frozen meat from Australia. As early as July 1880, he expressed the opinion that: 'frozen meat must ultimately become a trade of importance, but that money would be lost before the trade could become remunerative'.[10]

In a letter dated 13 June 1882, Dalgety wrote from London:

I am convinced that frozen meat can be landed and kept here in perfect condition. A cargo of 5,000 was landed from Dunedin last week (out of a sailing ship) in the best condition that of any that has hitherto reached this country. They were in appearance like newly slaughtered sheep, and averaged 70lb to 80lb. Great pains had evidently been taken in slaughtering and shipping them, and in packing them into the chamber on board the ship. The result being that they went off readily at 6½p per pound, and will do much to remove the prejudice that exists against frozen meat.

As a consequence, Dalgety expected much larger imports from Australia and New Zealand, but pragmatically concluded: 'like all new enterprises, it requires time and experience to overcome rural interests and prejudices.'[11]

An Orient Line prospectus dated 21 May 1880, two years before **Aberdeen** was commissioned, stated that:

The export of fresh frozen meat is likely to yield an important addition to the company's [Orient] earnings. A number of applications for space have already been received, and the necessary refrigerating machines are about to be fitted in the steamers.[12]

Other lines followed the Orient Line's first three reefer-fitted steamers in the frozen meat trade:[13]

P&O	1887
Tyzer (Port Line)	1887
Houlder Line	1890
Federal S.N.Co.	1893

However, it was not until 1892 that the Aberdeen Line finally outfitted a ship for the carriage of refrigerated cargo. It may well be that the cost of initially installing refrigerating machinery and associated insulation and trunking was just too expensive for such conservative financing arrangements, where no borrowing was involved, and each ship was paid for from liquid reserves. It is also surprising that the successful **Aberdeen** was not immediately followed by a run of three or four sister vessels. I suspect that overt financial conservatism, possibly a legacy of earlier railway misadventures, and almost certainly reflecting the hand of the senior partner, William Henderson, prevented the company from capitalising upon its experience and fine new equipment, in turn triggering the Line's gradual decline over the next twenty years from the dominant position it had held for so long in the Australian cargo trade.

As originally outfitted, **Aberdeen** had passenger capacity for seventy-four souls. However, following her third voyage, she was outfitted for the carriage of emigrants in her 'tween deck and on her fourth voyage brought out 337 steerage passengers as well as thirteen saloon passengers to Sydney. This pattern would continue.

Tragedy struck at the start of **Aberdeen**'s fifth voyage to Australia. The vessel had dropped down to anchor off Gravesend on 29 February 1884, with Cornelius Thompson embarked, as was his practice.[14] Some 195 steerage and 14 saloon passengers were embarked at Gravesend. When the vessel upgraded her passenger carrying certificate, *inter alia* she had had to upgrade the pyrotechnics carried for use in an emergency, such that she was now required to carry a cannon, fifty cartridges, thirty-six blue lights, thirty-six rockets and fifty friction tubes. In addition, she would have carried pyrotechnics necessary for making the company's registered private recognition signal. In the case of the Aberdeen Line, the company's recognition signal was:

> A red pyrotechnic light burnt near the stern, followed by a Roman candle throwing up three groups of balls to a height not exceeding 50 feet, and each group consisting of a red, white and blue ball, the colours following in the order specified.[15]

Local regulations forbade the carriage of explosives within the dock system, so it was the practice for these unstable pyrotechnics to be landed into the safekeeping of contractors while vessels were in London. The pyrotechnics, contained in a copper magazine, were returned to the vessel by launch on 1 March and formal inspections were carried out by the Board of Trade and Captain Matheson. The magazine was left on deck alongside the chartroom.

Aberdeen got under way in the afternoon of 1 March 1884. The vessel had not cleared Gravesend Reach before the second officer noted that the pyrotechnics' magazine was smoking. Captain Matheson ordered the magazine over the side, and went to help the second officer when a huge explosion occurred; Matheson, blinded, was blasted down on to the foredeck. The Trinity House pilot, the second officer and Captain Matheson were mortally wounded, Matheson dying of his wounds on 4 March, but only

after he had given evidence to the inquiry convened by the Board of Trade from his deathbed. Charles Matheson was an outstanding master, universally liked and respected by all who knew him, crews, passengers, Sydneysiders, Aberdonians alike. His place in command was taken by the new chief officer, James Barclay. The vessel was badly damaged; the bridge, chartroom and master's quarters were obliterated and the officers' accommodation below was damaged.

From September 1884, **Aberdeen**'s next five outwards voyages were undertaken under charter to the Orient Line, carrying emigrants from Plymouth to Australia. An average of 628 souls were carried per voyage on these charters, with the most 670. On the first of these voyages, departing Plymouth 10 September 1884, a defect was discovered in her crankshaft and she put into the refuge of St Helena on 24 September. Here, repairs were effected, the ship's engineers being assisted by personnel from HMS **Opal**, which also happened to be lying off. The 611 emigrants on board, mostly Scots and Irish, were not allowed ashore during the vessel's enforced stay offshore.[16]

Probably unbeknown to those concerned at the time, **Aberdeen**'s loading at Foochow in 1882 was to become a key element in a dispute with far-reaching consequences on the future conduct of liner trades. Under the guiding hand of John Swire 'the Senior',[17] Alfred Holt's Liverpool-based Far East managing agent, the China and Japan Conference had been established in 1879 between the lines serving the direct route from the UK to China and Japan. The Conference sought to regulate the trade for the benefit of its members (Holt, Glen, P&O, Castle, Messageries Maritime and Ben), to the exclusion of outsiders, especially the triangular route traders via Australia. These the members saw as a seasonal anathema seeking to capitalise upon the short but highly lucrative tea season, with alternate voyages catching the Australian wool sales. The Conference members argued, probably with some justification, that they maintained a year-round service to China, balancing the poor out-of-season cargoes with the lucrative tea season. Triangular trade interlopers undercut the rich pickings of the tea season, while taking none of the pain of the down season.

GTCo. could argue with significant justification that it had been engaged in the triangular trade to China for many more years than Holt's and the other Conference members. So too could the Mogul Steamship Company, a shipowning entity of the major shipping agent and freight broker, Gellatly, Hankey and Sewell. Gellatly had effectively inherited its early ships from the famous Duncan Dunbar, whose Australian clippers, like those of GTCo., had engaged on the triangular service home. Gellatly and Hankey had formed the Mogul Steamship Company in 1883 to regularise its shipowning activities, and its early steamships were likewise engaged on the triangular service.[18] The relationship between GTCo. and Gellatly is not clear; I suspect that they shared common loading brokers in China and they certainly operated in close alliance in their fight with the Conference.

Gellatly had been a member of the 1879 China and Japan Conference, and stood accused by Swire of breaking that Conference up insofar that: 'In 1882 [Gellatly's] Captain or Agents at Foochow went behind the Agreement and under-quoted freights that had been arranged.'[19] Swire confronted Gellatly with this accusation at a meeting in April 1885, at which Gellatly was accompanied by 'Mr [Cornelius] Thompson of Aberdeen'. Gellatly, who was seeking a Conference charter for two of his ships, accepted that the 1882 Foochow incident 'was a mistake for which they were not responsible'. (I strongly suspect that it was indeed the **Aberdeen** that was the cause of the rate-cutting row in Foochow when she loaded there in 1882.)

Gellatly then went on to threaten that:

If you won't charter, or allow us to load under the Conference [for the 1885 season], we will send up three Mogul steamers to Hankow, the ABERDEEN will follow, and I can get others to keep up departures. We will smash rates of freights and keep them down during the whole Hankow season. We [Gellatly] could lose some thousands but you [Holt/Swire] will lose £20,000 and the Glens and P&O more, to say nothing of the other Conference Lines.

After Gellatly's threat, 'Mr Thompson simply [said] so far as regards the **Aberdeen** – she will go to Hankow and accept best rates that she can obtain.'[20] In fact, **Aberdeen** and Gellatly's **Pathan** and **Afghan** loaded full tea cargoes at Hankow in June 1885, securing freights of 25/- (£1.25) per ton, compared with 70/- and 60/- secured by the two racing steamers **Glengarry** and **Oopaak**, and a range between 45/- and 30/- for Holts', Castles', Bens' and Glens' non-racing steamers. Against this poor freight, **Aberdeen** was a larger and far more economic ship to operate that any of the others in the season, and several Conference ships went empty.

In Swire's view, they [Gellatly and Thompson] wanted to 'get the cream of two trades. Out to Australia in February and March – and

home from China in May and June'.[21] He was probably right, but at least in the case of GTCo., paucity of cargo for a large capacity steamer home from Australia outside the wool season would have been a major consideration.

As part of the Conference's attempts to squeeze out the Australian trade interlopers, Swire, in a note to Philip Holt in 1884, enquired: 'Will you enter an engagement with P&O, Glens and Messageries Maritime not to send out coal by outside steamer or to purchase cargoes of steamer coal.'[22] It is not clear whether such an embargo was enacted, but it would have had a serious impact upon the viability of the triangular service.

In response to Gellatly's threats and Thompson's obdurate position on **Aberdeen**, the Conference agents in Shanghai issued a circular on 11 May 1885 that restated Conference terms and went on to remind shippers that shipments for London by the SS **Pathan** and **Afghan**, two of Gellatly's ships, and the **Aberdeen**, or by any other non-Conference steamers, at any ports in China or Hong Kong, would exclude those making such shipments from participation in returns to shippers[23] [5 per cent rebate]. On 28 May 1885, Gellatly was dismissed as the Ocean Steamships Company (Alfred Holt)'s London loading agency.

Gellatly responded in August 1885 by taking an injunction out against Conference members. This failed, but Gellatly returned to the fray in autumn 1887 with a high-court action heard before the Lord Chief Justice against the Conference members, alleging that the Mogul ships had been prevented by the actions of the Conference members from carrying on their normal trade and accusing the Conference members of combining together to bribe, coerce and induce shippers to boycott Mogul ships. This action again failed and Gellatly took the matter to appeal; the appeal failed, and Gellatly went to the House of Lords. In a ground-breaking ruling, which effectively gave legitimacy to the Conference system for more than a century until upset by the European Commission, the House of Lords dismissed the appeal in December 1891. Of particular interest arising from the Lords' ruling are the references in Lord Field's judgement to the involvement of Thompsons, the only other shipowner to be named on the appellant's side. Inter alia Lord Field referred to 'Mr Thompson, a shipowner with large tonnage at command, who was also desirous of becoming a member of the conference.'[24]

Aberdeen continued her alternate voyages on the triangular service to China until the 1889 season when, along with the other

GTCo. steamers, she settled into direct services to and from Australia via the Cape of Good Hope with South African ports as line calls, thus ending Thompson's fifty-year engagement in the China tea trade.

In June 1884, GTCo.'s second steamer, *Australasian*, of 3,630grt, was commissioned from Robert Napier's Dumbarton yard. The formal ceremony was undertaken by Mrs Henderson, who cut the fastenings, and Mrs Thompson, who named the vessel. A virtual sister of *Aberdeen*, though with a boiler pressure increased to 160psi, she was barquentine-rigged from the outset. Her ownership pattern followed the model of *Aberdeen*, initially wholly owned by the partnership, with the odd 2/64 later transferred to various shipmasters in the Line, and a personal 8/64 share to George Thompson Youngest in 1888. Interestingly, GTCo. had invited Frederick Dalgety to take a 4/64 shareholding in the vessel, but in a letter dated 5 November 1884, Dalgety advised that while he personally would have favoured such an investment, his board were 'unwilling to incur the risk.'[25]

Commanded by Captain Alexander Simpson, formerly chief officer of the *Aberdeen*, *Australasian*'s maiden outwards voyage was on charter to the Orient Line carrying a total of 643 government emigrants. Over the course of six outwards charters to Orient, five by *Aberdeen* and one by *Australasian*, a total of 3,785 settlers were carried out to Sydney, without apparently the loss of a single life through maritime misadventure. Unlike the *Aberdeen*, the *Australasian* did not engage upon the triangular service to China during the Australian autumn, but tramped coal cargoes to Bombay, Mauritius, Singapore and Batavia, before returning to Australia for the spring wool clip.

On her second outwards voyage, *Australasian* carried among her cabin passengers, William Froude, the noted Victorian traveller, writer and commentator. Froude, who boarded the ship in London on 6 December 1884 and sailed in her to Sydney via the Cape, Adelaide and Melbourne, gives some interesting glimpses into life on board in his book *Oceania*. He clearly regarded himself as God's gift to society in general, and intelligentsia in particular. He wished to make the passage via the Cape, and as such, was limited in his choice of vessel; that he happened by *Australasian* appears to have been a matter of chance, but he was fulsome in his praise for the standard of victuals. A cow was provided for the provision of fresh milk during the passage.

SS *Australasian* lying to buoy at Gravesend. (National Library of Australia)

Upon completion of outwards discharge at Sydney, the vessel went up to Newcastle to load 3,000 tons of coal for Bombay. However, *Australasian* did not go directly to Bombay; she was ordered back to Sydney, where in consort with the Pacific Steam Navigation Co's *Iberia* (which was operating in that company's joint service with the Orient Line), she was taken up from trade by the home government to transport a contingent of the New South Wales Lancers to Suakin in the Sudan to reinforce the imperial response to the dervisher uprising. This was the first overseas military adventure by the Australian colonies; a total of 800 men, their horses and equipment were uplifted by the two ships, sailing from Sydney on 3 March 1885. While the configuration of *Australasian* would have been well-suited for the movement of troops, nonetheless, conditions on board were less than comfortable. A private wrote in his diary: 'It was fearful, as the tween deck was so crowded and the stench was horrable.'

Following disembarkation of the troops, who were destined to be attached to the Guards Brigade, at Suakin on 30 March 1885,[26] *Australasian* went on to Bombay to discharge her coal cargo, and thence back to Sydney to load a homewards wool cargo.

On the home front on 3 July 1885, William Henderson, the senior partner, was invited to give evidence before the Royal Commission of Enquiry on Loss of Life at Sea, under the chairmanship of Lord Aberdeen. Henderson's evidence, if somewhat self-righteous, nonetheless gives a fascinating insight into the management of the Aberdeen Line. Henderson's main theme derived from his experience of running the Line was the importance of not insuring to make a profit from adversity.[27]

From 1886, the steamships began calling at Cape Town outwards bound on an advertised liner basis, rather than irregular coaling stops, thus setting the pattern for outwards sailings that was to endure for the life of the company.

On 31 October 1887, *Damascus*, the Aberdeen Line's third steamer, was launched at Napier's Govan yard; the launching ceremony was performed by William Henderson's daughter, Mary, and the vessel was christened by Annie Thompson, GTJ's daughter. Built as a near identical sister to the first two steamers, she nonetheless incorporated a number of advances. Her propulsion system was more powerful, the three cylinders being 28in, 42in and 70in diameter, driven by a steam pressure of 150psi in (*vs* 125lb for *Aberdeen*). On trials, at a displacement of 4,922 tonnes, she averaged 14.519 knots, against

an ihp of 3,091.4. Her mechanical outfit also incorporated the first commercial application of A.C. Kirk's patented marine distillation plant, one of the first successful such units. Kirk's distiller comprised a cylindrical drum placed in the uptakes of the main boilers, fed with sea water that was converted into low-pressure steam. Part of this output was fed to the low-pressure side of the main engine, while the remainder passed into the condenser, where it was condensed and used to supplement losses in the boiler feed water.[28] Kirk's condenser only produced 3 tons of water a day, but every little helped in the thrust for increased deadweight on long-haul steamers. *Damascus* incorporated a MacIntyre-type water ballast tank under her engine room, a precursor of the double bottom tank standard in modern ships. She was also the first Aberdeen Line ship to be built of steel.

Damascus, of 3,708.56grt, sailed from London on her maiden voyage on 19 January 1888, arriving in Sydney on 9 March 1888; the *Sydney Morning Herald* described her passenger accommodation, which was clearly an advance on that initially fitted to the first two steamers, in the following terms:

> The *Damascus* has every reason to be called a passenger ship, for she has berth accommodation for 41 saloon passengers. The cabins have two berths in each with all the latest improvements, with electric bells and lights in each. There are also cabins which are exceedingly roomy for families. The general decorations are in keeping. The saloon is reached by a substantial broad companionway from a large deckhouse aft. Here is also to be found a social hall for ladies, and abaft that again is a gentlemen's smoking room, both handsomely appointed and upholstered. The whole of the adornments are in excellent taste. Bathrooms, lavatories and such like are also to be found, in fact conveniences of every kind are to be found on board.[29]

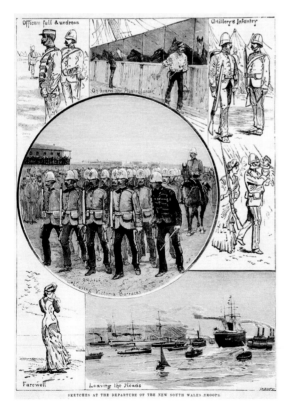

Wood engraving from the *Illustrated Australian News* showing sketches of the NSW contingent embarking in *Australasian*.

Like *Australasian* before her, *Damascus* entered into a two-voyage-a-year cycle, with alternate voyages tramping coal to Bombay, Calcutta and Mauritius from Sydney or Newcastle, New South Wales. In 1889, *Damascus* carried as a passenger, Sir Henry Loch from Melbourne, where he had been Governor of Victoria, to Cape Town, where he was taking up the post of Governor of the Cape Province. In a subsequent letter to GTCo., Loch, later to become Lord Loch, was fulsome in his praise for the standards of passenger comfort and attention obtaining on board *Damascus* and advocated the establishment of a trade from the Australian colonies to the Cape.[30] That the company made specific mention of this letter in a subsequent history of the Line indicates that Loch's suggestion was a moving force in its subsequent settlement into a homeward route via the Cape rather than Suez.

The company was never a member of the South African Conference, maintaining throughout its trading life that the Aberdeen Line had rights to lift any cargo that it liked homewards, basing its argument on the fact that it had served South Africa longer than any of the Conference line members. In the interests of harmony however, the homewards ships tended to lift rough cargo ex-South Africa, and such surplus first-class cargo as the South African Conference lines could not handle.[31]

A succession of losses and disposals reduced the Aberdeen Line's sailing ship fleet over the two years 1887 to 1889 to eleven ships, a net reduction of six vessels since the advent of steam:

- **Centurion** (GTCo. 32/64) was lost off Cannae Point within North Head, while departing Sydney under tow on 16 January 1887. The vessel was beset by a southerly squall while traversing the Heads, and in attempting to take avoiding action from the barque **Manhegan** anchored between the Heads, the tug's line went slack and **Centurion** went aground on the Old Man's Hat, with her anchors out.[32] The wreck site was the subject of a detailed archaeological dig under the auspices of the Marine Archaeological Association of New South Wales, which photographed the remains and prepared detailed plans.[33]

- **Christiana Thompson** (36/64) was sold to Norwegian interests on 25 August 1887. She was renamed the **Beatrice Lines** and continued for a further twelve years until wrecked near Umra off the Norwegian coast on 7 October 1889.

- **Jerusalem** (40/64) was sold to Norwegian interests in October 1887. She was lost on passage from New Brunswick to London in 1893.

- **Ethiopian** (32/64) was sold to Norwegians on 9 April 1888. The old ship was abandoned and condemned off St Michaels in the Azores in 1894.

- **Smyrna** (32/64) was run down and sunk by the steamer **Moto** off the Isle of Wight on 28 April 1888 with the loss of Captain Taylor and eleven crew.

- **Aviemore** (32/64) was sold to Norwegians on 30 August 1888. She worked on for at least another twenty-five years, being converted to a whale oil factory ship in 1910, and was still trading in 1915.

On 22 April 1889, tragedy struck when Jane Boyd Henderson, William Henderson's wife and GTJ's first child, died in her fifty-eighth year; she had borne Henderson fourteen children. Her diaries reveal her to have been a deeply religious woman, accepting each of many personal setbacks as 'God's will', with not a trace of anger or bitterness. She was highly respected in Aberdeen society and a devoted wife to Henderson and mother to his children.

Further reductions in the sailing ship fleet came in 1890–91, when **Thermopylæ** and **Thyatira** were sold for further trading.

The sale of the clipper **Thermopylæ** (32/64) to Canadian interests on 30 May 1890 must have been an emotional wrench for the company. She had served it well as a cargo carrier for twenty-two years, initially in the triangular trade out to Australia and home with tea from China, and latterly on the wool trade. Her last two homewards voyages from Sydney were with cargoes of shale to Rotterdam, reflecting the reduction of the clipper status to tramping cargoes homewards. **Thermopylæ** was sold to Robert Reford, president of the Mount Royal Rice Milling Company of Montreal for £5,000, and for the next five years under the same name worked the North Pacific based out of Vancouver, importing rice from South-East Asia to help feed the Chinese labour population on the west coast, and timber out; to facilitate the latter a bow door was cut in either bow. She continued to make good passages in that trade, until 1895, when, following a timber voyage from Port Blakely in Puget Sound to Leith, she was sold to the Portuguese government, who renamed her **Pedro Nunes**, with a view to converting her into a sail training ship. The Portuguese Navy's plans for the vessel in that role were hideous to say the least, with a topgallant forecastle and poop added and a gun deck with eight cannons installed. Her rig, which had been cut down by the Canadians to that of a barque, was to be restored to ship rig. Perhaps fortunately, advanced rot in her hull stopped the

Pedro Nunes (formerly *Thermopylæ*) being sunk by torpedo off the River Tagus, 13 October 1907. (Portuguese naval archives)

Portuguese short in their ambitions, and she was reduced to a coal hulk, in which role she served until 13 October 1907. On that day, she was towed out into the mouth of the River Tagus and as the highlight of a Navy League regatta in the presence of the Queen of Portugal, she was sunk with two Whitehead torpedoes fired from torpedo boats. Her remains were found by divers in 2005 and ongoing archaeological 'digs' are in progress.

Thyatira (32/64) was sold to Belfast owners J.W. Woodside in 1891. The vessel traded on for a further five years, until 16 July 1896, when on passage from London to Rio de Janeiro she was abandoned off Pontal da Barra on fire.

GTCo.'s disposal of its older sailing ships reflected excess cargo-carrying capacity on the Australian service created by their three, soon to be four, steamers; the remaining sailing ships were either passenger carriers, or iron-built. The running down of the older sailing ships did not mark the end of GTCo.'s love affair with sail, for on 24 July 1890 the company purchased the 5-year-old Harland and Wolff-built steel barque *Queens Island*, renaming her *Strathdon*. The vessel, in which GTCo. had an initial 56/64 interest with the balance held by George Thompson Youngest, was essentially a freighter with no pretence for speed. She carried a mighty spanker and was well regarded as a sailing ship nonetheless.

On 25 November 1891, GTCo.'s fourth steamer, *Thermopylæ (II)*, 3,711 gross, departed London on her maiden voyage under the command of Captain Alexander Simpson. The new vessel, virtually a sister of the three Napier-built vessels, though with boiler pressure increased to 160psi, was built by Hall Russell in Aberdeen at a cost of £70,000. The *Sydney Morning Herald* reported:

Steel barque **Strathdon** (ex-**Queen's Island**); GTJ's last sailing ship, acquired after the introduction of steam. (National Library of Australia Schultze Vic H99.220/2522)

The *Thermopylæ* is the largest steamer ever built at Aberdeen. In point of speed and as a weight carrier, and in passenger accommodation, this vessel ranks as one of the finest liners in the Anglo–Australian trade not flying the mail pennant.

Special attention has been devoted to the finishing of the excellent passenger accommodation. On the main deck aft provision is made for 60 saloon passengers, and 'tween deck 350 voyagers can be housed. Large, airy staterooms, comfortably furnished, are in direct contrast to those provided on some of the weekly boats which cater for a purely passenger trade.

The dining-saloon is a splendid apartment, and elaborately appointed. The saloon is connected to the music saloon by a staircase. This apartment is one of the features of the steamer. The ornamental plate-glass windows fitted in the skylight shed a soft light on the dining-saloon below. The smoking hall is a separate saloon aft of the music room.[34]

Hall Russell's exquisitely executed plans of the vessel show, among other features, a hinged vestigial flap extension to the rudder

located over the trailing edge of the rudder on yokes, and capable of being lifted clear at sea. Apparently this feature was incorporated to provide better steering capabilities in the calm waters of the Suez Canal.[35] However, and surprisingly, the vessel was not fitted with reefer capacity from the outset. A side elevation of SS *Thermopylæ* is included in the colour section.

SS *Thermopylæ*'s outward passage was by way of Tenerife, Cape Town and Albany, arriving at Melbourne on 11 January 1892. Following discharge at Melbourne, Sydney and Newcastle, she loaded a homewards cargo that included 6,152 bales of wool and 2,970 ingots of tin. From the arrival of SS *Thermopylæ*, the four steamers entered into a regular trading pattern between London and Australia, without engaging upon inter-voyage tramping runs from Australia. However, the steamer service was less than regular.

In 1892, both **Aberdeen** and **Australasian** underwent major refits. From Hall Russell's cost book, we know that work on the **Aberdeen** included:

- Two new double-ended 14ft 2¼in diameter steel boilers 19ft 6in long, each fitted with three furnaces, making twelve furnaces in all;

- A new, taller funnel and damper;

- A 20-ton evaporator;

- New steel work and accommodation, which included the plating-in of the after end of the centrecastle deck; and,

- Removal of crossed spars on the main and mizzen masts to reduce the vessel to barquentine rig.

The overall cost of the refit was £9,207; no mention was made of incorporating refrigerated cargo spaces.[36]

In an unusual market research exercise, in November 1892, Captain Alex Simpson, commander of SS *Thermopylæ*, was temporarily relieved of his command in Australia and commissioned by the company to make exhaustive inquiries in Victoria and New South Wales with special reference to the position of the frozen mutton and butter export trades, and to ascertain whether the prospects would justify the company in fitting its vessels with refrigerating

Aberdeen at Melbourne, as subsequently converted. (National Library of Australia NSW PXE 722/11 (3))

appliances and otherwise adapting them to the requirements of the trade. He completed his investigations over a period of six months, in the course of which he visited many of the principal agricultural and pastoral districts of New South Wales, as well as several in Victoria, interviewing large numbers of people interested in the matter, before cabling a resumé of his findings to the company. His sojourn ashore was interrupted when, on 11 January 1893, he accompanied J.T. Cosgrove, Dalgety's Melbourne manager, on board *Aberdeen* to greet Stephen Thompson, who was on a visit to Australia 'to renew his former acquaintance with these colonies'.[37] In a subsequent interview with the Melbourne *Argus* upon completion of his detachment ashore, Captain Simpson gave a fascinating reflection of the shipowner's concerns in respect to the frozen meat trade from Australia, no doubt prompted by Stephen Thompson:[38]

Speaking from the company's point of view, I have discovered that consignors hold very crude ideas respecting the ocean-carrying business. Their paramount desire is to secure the services of large steamers, travelling at high rates of speed, and conveying frozen mutton to the London markets for a half-penny or at the most three farthings, per pound. I pointed out whenever I had the opportunity that vessels of that calibre are not available in Australia, for the reason that very few cargoes are offering for the colonies. The volume of imports is dwindling almost to the point of vanishing, and I am satisfied further reductions may be shortly looked for in that direction. Ship-owners are not prepared to dispatch their fleets to Australia in ballast merely to carry home frozen mutton for three farthings per lb., and thereby sustain heavy losses every voyage. Under existing conditions the homeward cargoes have to bear the cost of the journey both ways. Shippers forget that large steamers, driven at the maximum speed, necessitate heavy outlay in current expenses, and for shareholders to obtain even a small return on the capital sunk in construction consignees must be prepared to pay slightly higher freights than are demanded by the ocean tramps.

Captain Simpson estimated the cost of outfitting a steamer for the carriage of refrigerated cargo to be £6,000. The lengthy interview concluded:

The proposal made in official quarters to give the mail-boats the whole of the butter cargoes was also strongly condemned by Captain Simpson. The suggestion was inexplicable. Any of the other companies who had regular monthly communication with London were in a position to offer shippers facilities and terms equally as favourable for placing their butter on the home market in prime condition, and at the minimum of expense.

Captain Simpson resumed command of SS *Thermopylæ* from Captain James Barclay in Melbourne in March 1893. The *Sydney Morning Herald* reported *Thermopylæ* as having uplifted a 'capital cargo' from Sydney that voyage,[39] comprising:

3,400 bales	wool
930 casks	tallow
96 bales	sheepskins
3,000 bags	ore and matte
7,050 bars	silver lead bullion
9,726 ingots	copper
136 hogsheads	rum

In 1893, financial crisis struck the New South Wales colony, in part associated with severe droughts, which ravished the pastoral industry. P&O managing directors' weekly report to their board based upon communications from their Sydney agent noted on 28 April 1893:[40]

> the freight market is as dull as it can possibly be and at present shows no sign of improvement. Space can be obtained for London June wool sales in sailing ships for un-dumped greasy wool at 5/16d/lb less a rebate and the 4 steamers on the berth taking greasy wool to all ports at 3/8d and giving a rebate of 10 per cent.

The recession led to New South Wales banking institutions crashing. With his wide banking and commercial interests, Samuel Aaron Joseph, who with Montefiore had been the company's managing agent in Sydney during the past twenty-six formative years, was sorely hit, and Montefiore Joseph collapsed, suspending payments on 22 August 1893. At a subsequent creditors meeting, the company's trade debts were said to be £74,632 against assets of £70,777. Such was the respect with which the company had been held, the meeting expressed sincere sympathy.[41]

Samuel Joseph had been a pillar of the commercial, public and Jewish life in Sydney. He had variously been chairman of the City Bank of Sydney; director of a number of financial institutions including the Australian Mutual Provident Society; chairman of the Sydney Exchange Company; founding president of the Commercial, Pastoral, and Agricultural Society of New South Wales; president of the Sydney Chamber of Commerce; member of the board of management of the York Street Synagogue and various other Jewish interests; and a member of the Legislative Council. He resigned from the Legislative Council in August 1893, presumably as a result of financial insolvency. Renowned for his integrity, he had served the Aberdeen Line well as its Sydney managing agent through its formative years as a liner service on the Australian trade. I sense that he enjoyed a very close personal relationship with Thompson and Henderson; a number of GTCo.'s sailing ships were committed to his care for sale in the colony following their final outwards voyages in the company's service. Joseph died at his home in Woolhara on 25 September 1898, a highly respected citizen.[42]

Montefiore Joseph was succeeded as GTCo.'s agent in Sydney by Dalgety. Dalgety appears to have taken over the Sydney agency from Montefiore Joseph by May 1893, when it loaded SS *Thermopylæ* at that port,[43] possibly arising from Stephen Thompson's visit to Australia. Dalgety had sworn not to enter into competition with his old mentor, Montefiore; but with the imminent collapse of Montefiore Joseph, the path was clear, and with his extensive service connections with GTCo. in Victoria, the succession was a natural one. Dalgety was to remain the Line's Australian managing agent throughout its continuing life.

In the outwards trade from London to Australia, the joint P&O managing directors' weekly reports to the board clearly demonstrate a very close, warm working relationship with Thompson's Aberdeen Line, possibly based upon common north of Scotland origins. The board reports make almost weekly comparative reference to Thompson's loadings and the joint efforts to raise freight rates. The Aberdeen Line under Conference arrangements invariably closed at 2/6d per 'fine' rate freight ton less than the mail companies, and their ships almost invariably appear to have sailed full, albeit with volume made up with cargo charged at the 'rough' rate, which the mail companies tried to avoid. Typically over the period 1894–96, in 1894 the mail companies were loading at a fine rate of 40/- per ton fine against Thompson's 37/6d fine and 25/- rough; while in 1896 the mail companies filled at 45/- and upwards, while Thompson's loading alongside secured 42/6d fine and 32/6d rough. An interesting reference to GTCo. in the July 1894 P&O board report, almost by way of an excuse for its own performance, advised:[44]

> The Thompson Line is a very favourite one with shippers; the steamers are much liked, sail to date and providing as they do to Melbourne direct via the Cape delivering their cargoes for that port and Sydney in about mail time.

The refit of the *Australasian* included the installation of refrigerated cargo capacity. While some authorities attribute her as lifting her first cargo of frozen mutton from Sydney on 3 March 1893, the *Sydney Morning Herald*'s detailed list of cargoes uplifted makes no reference to such.[45] However, when she departed Melbourne on 11 March 1893, she had uplifted an 18,600-carcass consignment of frozen mutton at that port, apparently the first to be carried from the Australian colonies by an Aberdeen Line ship.[46] This was some thirteen years after the first trial consignment of 400 carcasses of frozen mutton had been shipped from the Australian colonies.

The entry of 'outsiders' into the refrigerated trades brought a furious reaction from the mail companies – the Peninsular and

Oriental Steam Navigation Company (P&O), spearheaded by that company's chairman and joint managing director, Sir Thomas Sutherland GCMG, and the Orient Line. The mail companies, which in fairness had made early significant investment in refrigerated capacity, regarded the colonial refrigerated produce contracts as their exclusive domain and were prepared to use whatever means that might be appropriate to control the outsiders, while at the same time accepting that they needed the outsiders to mop up contractual surpluses. P&O assessed the 'outsider' refrigerated steamer threat at mid-1894 as being:[47]

> 2 Gulfs, 2 Lunds, 3 Milburns [forerunners of the Port Line] and 5 Thompson steamers fitted or being fitted and all these have been fitted with our consent, some of them in fact at our suggestion because if one thing is more clear than another, it is that the Mail Companies cannot provide sufficient refrigerated tonnage to deal with all of the refrigerated produce which is now carrying from Australia.

SS **Thermopylæ**, having been retrofitted with insulation and refrigerating equipment, lifted her first refrigerated cargo from Melbourne on 24 November 1893, with **Aberdeen** and **Damascus**, also so retrofitted, in 1894. **Thermopylæ**'s initial cargo, which included apples carried on a ventilated, non-refrigerated basis, cheese and 500 tons of butter, some of which was sourced from Tasmania, was beset with problems. P&O's chairman, Sir Thomas Sutherland, gleefully advised George Withers, the Line's managing agent in Melbourne:[48]

> S.S. THERMOPYLÆ. The fruit, cheese and a great part of the butter brought on this ship has been discharged in a most lamentable condition. The fruit was rotting and a large portion of the cheese was floating about amongst the apples in a liquefied state. Some of the butter, we are told, suffered considerably also in one of the holds. From all we can learn, this condition of things resulted from two causes, the first being that insufficient insulation, part of which had been run up at short notice in Australia, while the ventilation was badly arranged; and the other cause was that the packages had been stowed in block, without any dunnage or any provision for a proper circulation of the cold air from the machine, the result being that the air, when introduced into the chamber passed at once through the ventilator on deck and never came in contact with the cases at all. Nearly the whole of the cargo was condemned by the Sanitary Authority.

Sutherland concluded by listing the Australian shippers involved, no doubt with a view to marketing on the back of the Aberdeen Line's adversity. Claims in the region of £2,000 were raised against the Aberdeen Line.

A recurring theme in the mail companies' approach to shippers was 'all or nothing'. In a letter to George Withers, dated 31 August 1894 in respect to butter and fruit shipments, P&O's joint managing director, F.D. Barnes, stated:

> and the fear you seem to entertain that outsiders will be getting a footing in both these trades, we can only repeat what we have said on more than one occasion, that the strongest weapon for the Mail Companies is to insist upon carrying the whole of the shipments or none at all. We cannot believe that it will answer the purpose of shippers to ignore the Mail Steamers all together and entrust their shipment to chance opportunities.[49]

Cornelius Thompson, GTJ's youngest surviving son, died at sea on board the **Damascus** (Douglas), on 18 January 1894, a day south of Ushant while on passage from London to Tenerife. With his naval architect training, he had given invaluable service to the company through the management of Walter Hood. Following the demise of Walter Hood's yard, he had moved to London, where he served as the London managing partner, well known in business and well respected on the company's vessels. He was given credit for being the innovative thrust behind the company's investment in Kirk's application of triple expansion in the **Aberdeen**. He was a member of the management committee of Lloyd's Register of Shipping and represented the company on 'the Davis', the Australian outbound freight Conference. With the passing of Cornelius Thompson, the managing partnership was reconstituted on 15 May 1894 to William Henderson, Stephen Thompson and George Thompson Henderson.

In November 1894, GTCo.'s fifth steamer, **Nineveh**, entered service. Of 3,808 gross tonnage, the company had returned to Robert Napier on the Clyde for her construction. Twelve years had elapsed since GTCo. entered steam so successfully with the **Aberdeen**, twelve years in which the Australian trade had enlarged significantly. Yet **Nineveh** was a virtual sister of the first steamer. Five years were to elapse before further steam tonnage was added to the fleet.

SS *Nineveh*, a virtual sister ship of SS *Aberdeen*, built five years earlier.
(National Library of Australia Vic H99.220/59 Brodie Collection)

With five steamers in service, monthly liner sailings to Australia were established, with return voyages made via the Cape of Good Hope rather than hitherto Suez. The service, though still less than regular, was thus:

Outwards: London–Tenerife–Cape Town–Melbourne–Sydney
Homewards: Sydney–Melbourne–Durban–Cape Town–Tenerife–London

Newcastle, New South Wales, was the Australian terminal port on occasions, and with refrigeration installed, seasonal calls were made at Hobart.

Nineveh was the first GTCo. ship to be outfitted from the outset with refrigerated spaces. The vessel was owned 56/64 by the company and 8/64 by George Thompson Youngest. On her maiden home voyage, she uplifted 13,079 carcasses of sheep and lamb from Melbourne in January 1895.[50] She was also carrying a share of a

400-ton butter surplus for which the mail companies did not have capacity. In a letter to Withers in Melbourne dated 23 November 1894, P&O's Sir Thomas Sutherland commented:

> As far as the NINEVEH is concerned, we are certainly under no obligation to Thompsons, considering the constant attempts by their agents Messrs Dalgety & Co to upset our Butter Contract, but we think now that they find our position is too strong for them to assail, it may be well to give them the opportunity of entering the trade in the only way that we intend that they should and that is by taking whatever share we could give them of any surplus quantities. It will at the same time have the effect of making Dalgety feel they have placed themselves by their actions in a somewhat humiliating position and give them a much needed lesson.[51]

The mail companies, spearheaded again by Sutherland, sought to secure the seasonal fruit uplift exclusively from Hobart. In a communication to Melbourne agent Withers dated 7 September 1894,[52] Sutherland reminded him that, in respect to his forthcoming visit to Hobart, when dealing with shippers the principle of 'all or nothing' carried:

> Shippers to understand clearly that if we are to carry their fruit, they must make it worth our while and that if we are not to have the whole of it, we prefer to have none at all and the Mail Companies will not send a single steamer to Hobart unless these provisions are fulfilled.
>
> We mention this [as] it has come confidentially to our knowledge that Messrs Dalgety & Co are adopting the same tactics in regard to Hobart fruit that they used in regard to our Butter Contract, and they have been making enquiries at this end as to what refrigerated they could get hold of during the fruit season in order that they might make proposals to the Shippers in Hobart.

In the end, the mail companies loaded 125,000 cases of fruit from Hobart during the 1895 season, with surplus carried by the 'outsiders'. The *Tasmanian Mercury* reported:[53]

> The government has chartered the Council of Agriculture to organise ship-ments of 30,000cs by steamers whose carriage must be at least equal to that of the mail boats at the lower freight rates of 3s 9d per case. The Aberdeen Line has been selected as fulfilling these

conditions and the S.S. THERMOPYLÆ takes the first cargo of 6,000 cases. She would have taken more, but the time is early and as with the mail steamers, there has been difficulty filling up the space available. The THERMOPYLÆ will be followed by ABERDEEN on 25:03:95 and the AUSTRALASIAN on 22:04.

Thermopylæ, Aberdeen and *Australasian* each loaded fruit at Hobart in February, March and April 1895, after Sydney. The *Mercury* also reported that Captain Simpson of the *Thermopylæ* was experimenting to secure a better stowage – costing perhaps £300 to £400 to execute. The nature of the experiments are not stated, but given Sutherland's comments, I suspect they centred around dunnaging of the cargo to secure effective cool-air circulation. The apples from the *Aberdeen* landed in London in poor condition, leading P&O's Sutherland to comment:[54] 'Altogether the Aberdeen Line have managed to establish such an unenviable reputation that the fruit Shippers are likely to hesitate before shipping by their steamers again.' There were no more Hobart calls by the Aberdeen Line for five years ...

The mail companies' attempts to control the homewards refrigerated trade as their exclusive right in the face of opposition from Thompsons and Lunds led to an exasperated Sutherland writing to P&O's Melbourne managing agent, George Withers, in March 1895:[55]

The Mail Companies are on the most friendly terms with Messrs George Thompson & Co. on this side, but it is impossible for this feeling to be continued if Messrs. Dalgety & Co. are allowed to attack them at every turn in their business and to do their best to upset every agreement into which they enter.

In a further letter to Withers dated 29 March 1895, Barnes complained:

We are not satisfied with George Thompson's attitude as they are with the enterprising firm of Dalgety & Co. in Australia. They apparently rate at a high value the position that they hold in the Australasian trade, and seem to aspire to occupying a position of equality with the Mail Companies ...

The colonial produce contracts, especially those of Victoria, were organised such that the producers contracted with the government, which in turn contracted with the carriers. It was these contracts to which the mail companies believed they had an exclusive right, and in turn it was these contracts that the 'outsiders' respective colonial agents, especially Dalgety acting on behalf of Thompson's Aberdeen Line and Sanderson acting on behalf of Lund's Blue Anchor Line, were seeking to secure. P&O vitriol was especially reserved for Dalgety, whose power Sutherland clearly feared, such that Sutherland frequently averred that Thompson's could not control its Australian agents.

The individual 'outsider' probably did not have sufficient refrigerated capacity at its disposal to service a large colonial government contract, but by combining their resources they would have. Any such combination was in direct contravention of the Davis Conference agreement; but nothing in the agreement precluded colonial agents tendering in combination in their own names using principals' tonnage, and this Dalgety and Sanderson did, to the intense annoyance of the mail companies. They had been desperately seeking within the Conference to come to a pooling or common purse agreement in respect to refrigerated space, whereby they could still control the trade, while satisfying the refrigerated tonnage investments of the 'outsiders'. They seemed to have almost reached an understanding with Thompsons and Lunds when news came from Australia that the two lines' agents were advertising joint sailings by Thompson and Lund steamers:

... which shows the bare-faced way in which the Conference Agreement was evaded by these two lines:

There is very little inducement to enter into an Agreement with people who have such warped ideas of business morality, but we are still working on in the hope of getting a pool put through, for without such arrangement, rates must inevitably fall to non-paying figures.[56]

A combination of Thompson's and Lund's Australian agents was clearly successful, for a shippers' dinner was hosted by Captain Spalding on board *Australasian* at Melbourne on 4 March 1896 to celebrate a contract entered into between the Aberdeen White Star Line, Lund's Blue Anchor Line and the Victorian government to uplift 60,000 cu.ft of butter per sailing, with the prospect of extending the contract to cover cheese the following year.[57]

Lund's Blue Anchor Line

Wilhelm Lund started as a shipowner in 1869, when his barque *Ambassador* entered the triangular trade, outwards to Australia with general cargo, and home via China with tea. With the eclipse of sail on the China trade, his early ships traded home from Australia with wool. His first steamer, the 1,817-ton barquentine-rigged *Delcomyn*, entered service in 1880, and was placed on the Australian trade via the Cape.

The last Lund sailing vessel was sold in 1890, by which time the fleet totalled ten steamers, loading out to Australia under the brokerage of Houlder Brothers and Trinder Anderson. In 1896, the company took delivery of the 5,078-ton *Narrung*, which inaugurated a new passenger, emigrant and cargo service in the name of William Lund to Adelaide, Melbourne and Sydney via the Cape, with calls at Tenerife. By 1899, the fleet comprised eight modern cargo passenger steamers, operating a monthly service from London and Antwerp to Australia via the Cape; as such, Lund's Blue Anchor Line traded in direct competition with the Aberdeen Line, operating very similar ships.

The Blue Anchor Line's service was disrupted when three of its ships were taken up from trade to support the South African war. In 1904, with the addition of new ships and the war over, a four-weekly service was restored, but now it was jointly with the Aberdeen Line, offering a sailing every two weeks from London and with interchangeable passenger tickets.

In 1906, an order was placed for a new cargo passenger ship, the 9,339-ton *Waratah*; the new ship had passenger accommodation for 128 in first class and 160 in third, with the potential for several hundred emigrants. Though widely lauded in Australia, the new ship was notoriously 'crank' in seamen's terms, and on her second homewards voyage on 26 July 1909, while on passage from Durban to Cape Town, she disappeared without trace and the loss of all on board. Her wreck has never been found despite several serious attempts.

The loss of the *Waratah*, and generally difficult trading conditions, led to the company being forced into liquidation. The P&O, which was debarred from the Australian emigrant trade by virtue of its lascar-crewed main-line vessels, had long viewed the potential of such an enterprise via the Cape using white-crewed ships. Given the opportunity presented by Lund's problems, P&O struck and acquired the assets and trading rights of the Blue Anchor Line for £275,000. The company was soon retonnaged and rebranded as the P&O Branch Line.[58] The old trading relationship between Lund's Blue Anchor and Thompson's Aberdeen Lines does not appear to have survived the P&O takeover of Lund.

During its period of operation in Lund's ownership, the Blue Anchor Line had closely mirrored GTCo.'s Aberdeen Line.

On 11 April 1895, George Thompson Jnr died aged 91. In his long life, he had founded one of the best-respected shipping enterprises in the world; had served his community as a city councillor, Lord Provost and MP; he had been a business leader in Aberdeen, board member of a number of banks, insurance, railway, shipping and shipbuilding companies and a harbour commissioner. He had also been a munificent philanthropist, supporting many good causes including founding president of the Aberdeen Sailors' Mission. He was a devout Free Church man. When he stepped down as Lord Provost in 1850, he was offered the traditional honour of a portrait painted by a leading painter, but he modestly declined. However, in 1880 Sir George Reid PRSA executed a portrait of GTJ at the behest of a large number of citizens grateful for Thompson's many services to the city; accepting the portrait on behalf of the Town Council, the Lord Provost described George Thompson as the *beau idéal* of a good citizen, and as one who had been blessed not only with the means, but with the heart to use them for the benefit of mankind. In his opinion, the portrait of no more worthy man would ever adorn the walls of the city chamber.[59]

Since his retirement from active management of the company in 1866, while no longer a partner, George Thompson Jnr had clearly played a significant behind-the-scenes role. He gave the keynote speech at the launching of *Samuel Plimsoll* in 1873 and appeared as a private shareholder in various new ship investments, often it would seem supporting some of his old commanders who were venturing into master/ownership deals. But he will probably be best remembered within Aberdeen for his liberal support of various charities and medical foundations within the city and university. In

1882, he gave £4,000 to various city charities and £1,000 to the Jubilee Extension Fund of the Royal Infirmary; in the same year he gave £6,000 to the university for nine medical bursaries; and in 1886 he gifted a further £3,000 to the university for the institution of a Travelling Fellowship in Medicine,[60] huge sums when extrapolated to today's financial levels.

He died, revered in his time, Deputy Lieutenant of Aberdeenshire and laird of Pitmedden. He was father to eight children, four sons and four daughters, all of whom, with the exception of George Thompson Youngest, predeceased him. A pillar of the Free Church, he was laid to rest alongside his wife, Christiana, in the quiet beauty of the United Free Church graveyard at Dyce.

Per periculum vivo; The Thompson family tomb, Dyce.

8

GATHERING CLOUDS – 1897 TO 1905

In 1897, the Institute of London Underwriters in conjunction with the Colonial Insurance Companies introduced insurance premiums that penalised homeward cargoes from the Australian colonies carried in iron sailing vessels more than 20 years old. The move provoked an indignant open letter from GTCo. published in the British and colonial commercial newspapers.[1] The letter, clearly crafted by Sir William Henderson, dated Aberdeen, 9 October 1897, complained bitterly, not without justification, that the new premiums took no account of the condition of the ships concerned, their 'ownery' or their insurance record, pointing out that GTCo.'s ships had 'been wonderfully free from claims on Underwriters' during the more than fifty years that GTCo. ships had served Australia.

The letter went on to point out that Henderson in his evidence to the Royal Commission on Loss of Life at Sea (1887) had advised that during the previous thirty-five years:

> The claims on Underwriters by vessels belonging to the Aberdeen Line had come to less than one-eighth of the amount of premiums paid to Underwriters during that period – while the history of our line up to the present time continues as satisfactory as then evidenced.

Five of the company's sailing vessels, the passenger ships *Aristides, Miltiades, Patriarch* and *Samuel Plimsoll* and the cargo ship *Salamis*, were each more than 20 years old, but were 'in as good condition,

by careful looking after and up-keep, as they were upon their first voyage'; these vessels would be affected by the premium increase. The letter went on to draw attention to the fact that:

> According to a reliable statement made up by the largest shippers and consignees of wool carried by our sailing vessels during the last two years, we find that the claims thereon made on Underwriters, from inception of risk, (which in many cases began in distant parts of the colonies before shipment) were £149 1s 7d, which, on 24,867 bales carried, valued at £12 per bale, came to only 1s per cent [0.05 per cent].

According to GTCo.:

> These figures clearly show that age does not affect the efficient carrying of cargo by vessels built as ours have been of superior strength and scantlings, carefully kept up, and treated in every way with a view to the safe carrying of valuable cargoes to and from Australia.

The letter prophetically concluded:

> The arbitrary arrangement of insurance rates homewards which has been made must inevitably drive our sailing ships out of the trade, because Australian shippers are insisting that the ship shall bear the

expense of the extra premium which is sought to be imposed; thus forcing out of the trade those vessels which have been the most profitable both to Merchants and Underwriters.

The increase in insurance premiums probably only expedited the inevitable; the days of liner sailing ships were over. In short order, three of GTCo.'s crack sailing vessels, the passenger ship *Patriarch* and the cargo ships *Salamis* and *Sophocles*, were sold within six months in 1898:

- *Salamis* (GTCo. 48/64) was sold to Norwegian interests, L. Gurdersund of Porsgrund, on 16 May 1898. The fine old ship was used for general tramping and was lost off Malden Island in the Central Line Islands of the south-west Pacific on 20 May 1905, when her moorings dragged while loading guano.

- *Sophocles* (52/64) was sold to Italian interests on 18 June 1898. The vessel was believed to be still trading in 1914.

- *Patriarch* (48/64) was also sold to Norwegian interests, on 2 November 1898. The magnificent vessel was used for general tramping until going ashore off Cape Corrientes, south of the River Plate, in December 1912.

With the disposal of these three ships, the company's sailing ship fleet was reduced to six ships, engaged on the Australia outwards

Salamis aground on Malden Island. (National Library of Australia Vic H91.325/1044 Allan Green Collection)

berth from London, but largely tramping homewards, with cargoes including grain and nitrates. For example, the *Miltiades* (Ayling), following outwards discharge in Sydney, loaded 2,019 tons of coal for San Francisco, departing Sydney 25 August 1896, and arriving in the US on 21 October. Following discharge, she started loading her homewards cargo on 19 November, and completed loading at Port Costa at the mouth of the Sacramento River on 23 December. Her homewards cargo comprised beans, cascara bark, salmon, canned fruit, barley, bran mustard seed, wine, household goods, arms and ammunition, saddlery and pampas plumes. She sailed on 29 December and arrived at London's Victoria Docks on 26 May 1897, 148 days out from San Francisco.

In a letter to his co-partners dated 1 January 1898, Sir William Henderson announced his intention to step down as senior partner with effect from 31 December that year. Henderson had served the company with distinction for fifty-three years, forty-eight of those as a partner, and thirty-two as senior partner. His term of office at the helm had seen the company transform from an operator of crack sailing vessels on the Australian and China trades to a pioneer long-haul steamship operator on the Australian service via South Africa, albeit ever so cautiously, with a number of sailing ships still remaining within the fleet at the time of his retirement. With Henderson's retirement, his son, George Thompson Henderson, assumed the reins of senior partner, with Henderson's fifth son, Alexander Duff Henderson, admitted a partner with effect from 31 December 1898.

Progress, albeit slow, was being made on the steamer front. In 1897, *Aberdeen* underwent a further refit at Hall Russell, Aberdeen, when her cabin passenger accommodation was increased. Then, in 1899 the company returned to Robert Napier for the first of a class of two larger steamships, the 4,573-ton *Moravian*. The new ship commissioned on 14 February 1899, followed by her 4,508-ton sister vessel *Salamis* six months later from Hall Russell in Aberdeen. *Moravian* had registered dimensions of 390.4ft length × 47ft beam × 21.5ft depth, making her some 30ft longer than the first five steamers. Her deadweight of around 5,000 tons compared with around 3,800 tons on the earlier steamers. The new ships were each powered by a triple-expansion steam engine driving a single shaft, served by two double-ended cylindrical boilers delivering steam at 200psi. While of similar general configuration to the earlier steamers, the two new steamers had a trunked cargo hatch on the bridge deck abaft the bridge, and a 105ft double bottom extending along the mid-length.

Moravian, while following very much the profile of the pioneer steamers, had additional passenger accommodation, including 'exceptionally good quarters' provided for sixty third-class passengers. The first-class passenger cabins were placed around the fore and aft part of the saloon, and every cabin was fitted with one or two 14in portholes. 'A large and complete installation of refrigerating machinery was supplied to meet the certain demands of the frozen meat and produce trade between London and the colonies.'[2] On her maiden voyage, *Moravian* carried a trial shipment of preserved lobsters in her refrigerated spaces.

That reefer-fitted ships were finally engaging the thinking of Aberdeen management was evidenced at the launch of *Salamis*, when Sir William Henderson was quoted as saying: 'Frozen butter, mutton and meat brought from Australia in the beautiful white liner in which it was wrapped before being shipped was much cleaner and sweeter than much of what they got at home.'[3] On the non-refrigerated front, he did not think that the first- and third-class passenger accommodation could be surpassed by any steamer afloat. *Salamis* was built at a cost of £94,000.

SS *Salamis* leaving Melbourne. Built at Hall Russel, Aberdeen, she was second of a duo of slightly larger cargo and passenger liners for the Australian service via the Cape. (National Library of Australia NSW PXE 722/3528)

From January 1898, the steamers had been operating a four-weekly rather than a monthly service to Australia via the Cape, with seasonal calls to Newcastle. With the introduction of the two new steamers, the service was improved to a three-weekly frequency from London, commencing with *Nineveh* departing London on 3 January 1899.

The steamers continued to be outfitted as barquentines and were effectively directed as sailing ships when in the Southern Ocean between the Cape and Melbourne. The crossed yards on their foremasts were stowed vertically for the passage out to the Cape, but upon leaving the Cape they were squared and sail set to secure maximum benefit from the westerly winds prevailing in the Southern Ocean. The ships' tracks were directed along great circle routes taking them far south, through the Crozet Islands and past the Isles de Kerguelen in 50° 30' South, rather than the more normal composite great circle tracking along latitude 40° South followed by most steamers on passage from the Cape to Australia. *Thermopylæ* (Barclay) in March 1893 reported:

> The eastern side of Possession Island [Crozet Is.] was coasted along within an easy distance of seeing any signals which might be made from the shore by shipwrecked people. But none were seen, or appearance of recent habitation. Frequent gun-cotton signals were also fired. A course was set along the south side of East Island at a convenient distance from the shore. Numerous sea elephants were seen on several beaches and thousands of sea birds on the rocks. On this voyage the vessel took her eastings in latitude 46.5° South.[4]

Iceberg sightings were common; on her outward passage in 1896, *Damascus* (Douglas) sighted 264 large icebergs in way of the Isles de Kerguelen.[5] While the track followed was shorter, and offered the potential of beneficial winds to optimise the vessels' sailing capacity, the prevailing weather between the Cape and Melbourne must have been thoroughly unpleasant for all but the hardiest of passengers.

On 3 March 1899, *Nineveh* sailed from Sydney with a contingent of 106 officers and men of the New South Wales Lancers, bound for a tournament in London and exercises at Aldershot. Upon departure, they were inspected by Major-General A. French of the Royal Marine Artillery before a crowd of 5,000 well-wishers. At Cape Town, the troops were greeted warmly and entertained ashore. In London, they were again greeted warmly, and marched across the city between railway stations en route to Aldershot, headed by the Coldstream

Guards' band.[6] Upon their return to Cape Town from London on 2 November 1899, again embarked in *Nineveh*, seventy of the troops under Captain C.F. Cox disembarked to a subdued welcome to 'share in the honour of maintaining the authority and dignity of the Empire'.[7] Things were going badly in the confrontation with the Boers and the harsh reality of war was dawning; thirty-six troopers apparently declined to disembark. The New South Wales Lancers were the first of 16,000 Australian colonial troops who participated in the Boer War. Over the next three years, the Aberdeen Line was to be closely involved in troop and war materiel transportation between Australia and South Africa in support of the war.

In May 1899, a development took place that was to set the mould for the future of the Aberdeen White Star Line. Ismay, Imrie and Co., whose Oceanic Steam Navigation Company, trading as the White Star Line, was heavily involved in the North Atlantic trades, and working jointly with Shaw Savill and Albion on the New Zealand trade, decided that the time was right to revitalise its presence in the Australian trade. In the past, White Star had traded sailing ships to Australia following the acquisition of the name, flag and trading rights of Wilson and Cunningham's White Star Line in 1867, but this venture had lost momentum, being sustained with chartered sailing ships, while White Star concentrated its steamship activities on the North Atlantic. Now the company had determined to re-enter the trade with a line of steamers, regardless of cost. The new line would run from Liverpool to Australia via the Cape, returning via the Cape to Antwerp, London and Liverpool. It needed a managing agent in Australia and had invited Dalgety to serve in that capacity. Dalgety's chairman, Edmund Doxat, had discussed the matter with GTCo.'s senior partner, George Thompson Henderson, and then on 18 May 1899, he wrote to the company formally setting out Dalgety's position

SS *Moravian* leaving Sydney with NSW troops embarked for the Boer War.

and effectively putting the Aberdeen Line on notice of its intentions. In his letter, addressed to the company's London office at 7 Billiter Street, Doxat confirmed Dalgety's interest in accepting the agency:

We have long felt considerably handicapped in doing business with Liverpool and Antwerp owing to the difficulty of working Liverpool except thro' the Gulf Line[8] of steamers which at times go there & Antwerp by the German line and we could, we feel sure, do a very large business with Liverpool in many articles like tallow, cocoa nut oil etc., as well as some rougher ones which now either come by sailors to London here to be transhipped on, or by vessels chartered by Lever Bros. to load for Liverpool direct of which some 7 or 8 are now taken up each year. For Antwerp also, we are often unable to ship wool or execute orders for tallow, grain etc., owing to being confined to the German boats, the agency of which is in other hands.

Doxat continued:

Altho' therefore we have by no means solicited their agency and indeed have attempted to dissuade Messrs Ismay Imrie & Co. from the venture, yet as it is an accomplished fact and we feel we can do a considerably increased Liverpool and Antwerp trade by means of these steamers, we are very anxious that the agency should not get into other hands and we think that this would be equally desirable for your sake as for our own as we do not wish to see rates cut down by a wild competition.

Doxat concluded that it was his intention, subject to GTCo.'s concurrence, to accept Ismay, Imrie's invitation to take on the White Star Line's Australian agency.[9] GTCo.'s response is not available, but it can be assumed that the company was in agreement, for henceforward GTCo.'s Aberdeen White Star Line would appear to have become inexorably linked with the Australian service of Ismay Imrie's White Star Line. One senses in Dalgety's relationship with GTCo. a similar one to that which existed between John Swire and Alfred Holt; the trusted and often aggressive overseas agent advising on future trade requirements and policy.

Ismay, Imrie's White Star Line had ordered five new passenger and cargo vessels for the Australian trade from Harland and Wolff, Belfast, in 1897. The first of these new *Jubilee*-class vessels, **Medic**, made her maiden voyage to Australia in 1899. Huge vessels by contemporary standards, they averaged 12,000 gross tons, had large refrigerated capacity, and could carry 320 one-class passengers. Their introduction on the Australian trade caused great excitement, but because they were ideally suited for troop transportation, they were taken up from trade to support the Boer War and did not truly start their liner service to Australia via the Cape until three years later. These five new vessels, put into service over three years, reflected sharply upon the extreme conservatism of George Thompson's approach to tonnaging the Australian steam trade, both in terms of financing (Thompsons had put seven like-ships into service spread over seventeen years) and design, as demonstrated in the attached drawing.

If the new senior partner did not have enough to worry him in terms of unwelcome and vastly superior competition, GTCo. now suffered two major marine casualties in quick succession. On 1 June 1899, a fire broke out in the after hold of **Samuel Plimsoll** (Henderson) while loading for Melbourne in the South West India Dock in the Port of London. The fire was tackled by the London Metropolitan Fire Brigade using three brigade steamers, each with two deliveries, a brigade float with eight deliveries and the dock float with four deliveries[10] The combined hose power could not reach the seat of the fire, and the ship was sunk alongside to extinguish the fire. The ship was refloated the following day and damage was found to be limited to internal fittings in way of the after hold. She was repaired and sailed for Melbourne on 22 July 1899.

Then, far more seriously, **Thermopylæ II**, under the command of Captain William Phillip Jnr, ran aground on Green Point off Cape Town on 11 September 1899 and rapidly became a total loss; GTCo.'s terminal interest was 45/64. The ship was on passage from Melbourne via Natal, making a slow approach to Cape Town, when shortly before midnight, she went hard aground on the Green Point Reef in Table Bay. The night was reportedly calm and the atmosphere clear; Mouille Point lighthouse was less than a mile away. Help was on hand quickly, but any hope of pulling the vessel off would have been in vain. Although only steaming at about 6 knots, the bottom was ripped out of the forward two holds and the engine room. The fifty passengers and the crew were evacuated without loss in the lifeboats and attending tugs before, with a rising swell, the vessel broke in half, disgorging her refrigerated cargo into the sea, to the delight of the local population, to whom Australian lamb and rabbits would have been an unheard-of luxury.

A comparison of design philosophy; ships built for White Star and Aberdeen Line, 1899.

Comparison of design philosophy – ships commissioned in1899
White Star's *Jubilee*-class *MEDIC vs* the Aberdeen Line's *SALAMIS / MORAVIAN* – class.

		MEDIC Jubilee-class	*SALAMIS / MORAVIAN – class*
Length b.p.		550.2 ft	390.4 ft
Breadth		63.3 ft	47.0 ft
Depth in hold		39.9 ft	21.5 ft
Draught		32.0 ft	27.4 ft
Tonnages	G.R.T.	11,984	4,541
	Deadweight	15,400 tons	5,000 tons
Speed		13.5 knots	13.0 knots
Propulsion		2 x Quad. Expansion	1 x Triple expansion
Propellers		2	1
Boilers		2 x double-ended / 1 x single-ended	2 x double-ended
Holds / hatches		7	5
Cargo Capacity	Bale	24,000 bales wool = 480,000 cu.ft	226,286 cu.ft
	Reefer	80,000 ccs mutton = 200,000 cu.ft	73,985 cu.ft
Passenger	First	Nil	50
	One-class	320 / 350	Nil
	Third class	Nil	650

Note: The foregoing particulars are 'best approximates' reflecting the difficulty of securing definitive figures

Thermopylæ was fully laden with a cargo that included twenty cases of gold sovereigns from the Union Bank of Australia worth £100,000 and a further ten cases from the same bank worth £50,000. All this specie was safely transferred to attending tugs. The balance of the cargo was lost; this included: 2,000 cases of frozen rabbits, 5,648 carcasses of frozen mutton and 7,877 ingots of copper. Two famous racehorses, Miora and Chesney, the latter owned by the actress Lilly Langtry, reputedly the mistress of King Edward VII, had been carried in stables on the foredeck. When the vessel broke in half, these two animals escaped and swam ashore, unharmed.[11] The insured value of the vessel and lost cargo was said to be £150,000.

A Marine Board of Inquiry held at Cape Town on 20 September 1899, delivered the following judgement:

SS *Thermopylæ II* wrecked off Green Point, Cape Town.

After careful consideration of the evidence, the Court finds that at 10.20 pm on September 11 1899, when Green Point light was sighted and the course was altered to East of North, no measures were taken by the master to ascertain or to verify the position of his vessel. This could have been readily and accurately done by cross-bearings off Robben Island and Green Point light, and a course set to take the ship safely into Table Bay. Nor did he at any time use the lead to ascertain his position or distance off land. The weather was hazy over the land, but the lights were distinctly visible. The master instead relied upon his own judgement as to his distance off Green Point. We are of the opinion that the vessel was not navigated with proper and seamanlike care by the master after 10.20 p.m. and that the master should have taken cross bearings or used the lead. We find that the loss of the steam vessel THERMOPYLÆ was due to the wrongful act or default of the master, William Phillip Jun. and we do adjudge that the certificate of the said master be suspended for a period of six months.[12]

A fearful blow to any master mariner, but perhaps the more so for Phillip. He had served his apprenticeship with the company under his father, Captain William Phillip Snr in the clipper *Salamis*; he went on to serve through all ranks in *Salamis* to command her for eight years, followed by a period as chief officer of *Damascus* to gain requisite steam time for a steam endorsement to his master's certificate of competency, before assuming command of *Thermopylæ*. He was the fourth generation of Phillip master mariners; at the time of the loss of *Thermopylæ*, his father was in command of the clipper passenger ship *Pericles*. Phillip Jnr was married to a Melbourne girl, in which city he had made his home. A hitherto highly-regarded commander, his service with the Aberdeen Line was terminated, but he went on to become a well-known figure in the Port Phillip pilot service.

On 1 January 1900, Cornelius Thompson's son, Oscar Stephen Thompson, was admitted a partner in the company. He was to serve as partner, chairman and advisor through many changes, until 1932.

In March 1900, *Samuel Plimsoll* (GTCo. 36/64) was sold to Walter Savill, who had separated his sailing ship activities from the mainstream Shaw Savill and Albion. He operated her on the New Zealand trade for two years, but following dismasting in 1902, she was reduced to a hulk, initially serving in Sydney and ending her days as a coaling hulk in Fremantle. In June 1945, in the course of a severe gale, the old lady was struck as she lay alongside a collier by a ship whose moorings had broken and the two careered up the harbour, causing damage to a number of ships and hulks before *Samuel Plimsoll* sank. Her sunken hull was blasted apart by explosives, and her remains were dumped by floating crane on the Beagle Rocks outside the harbour.[13] Her figurehead rests in the Western Australia Maritime Museum, Fremantle.

The problems of sustaining a regular liner service in the face of running a trooping service to the Boer War and the loss of a key vessel were soon to be exacerbated by *Salamis* (Douglas) being taken up from trade by the Admiralty to uplift contingents of the Victorian and New South Wales Naval Brigades to China to support military action against the Boxer Revolt. The ship was chartered by the Imperial Government on 19 July 1900, four days after her arrival in Sydney. Her initial commission, as Imperial Transport 105, was to uplift 200 men from the Victorian Naval Brigade at Melbourne and, following discharge of outwards cargo, she commenced taking on coal for the ensuing round trip and conversion to accommodate up to 500 men was put in hand. The conversion was said to be not as elaborate as that undertaken for troops to South Africa; sailors were accommodated in hammocks, so wooden beds were not required.

Stung by the initiative of the Victorian Colony in providing a contingent to support the Imperial intervention in China, the New South Wales government went into overdrive to field a like contingent from its Naval Brigade. The colonial secretary sent for the inestimable Captain Hixon RN, with instructions to muster a NSW contingent, and this was duly done. Meanwhile, the crew of conscripted and placed under naval discipline for the duration, like it or not. (The same device was used against a striking Australian National Line crew during the Vietnam War.)

Salamis sailed for Melbourne on 29 July, and uplifted the 200-strong Victorian Naval Brigade contingent, together with their heavy guns, ammunition trains and general equipment, on 1 August and returned to Sydney on the 3rd. The *Sydney Morning Herald* reported:[15]

> The SALAMIS looked very handsome as she emerged yesterday morning from the fog and came up the harbour. With the sun shining upon her shapely green-painted hull, the troopship formed a striking picture when she rounded to and shackled to the flagship buoy off Farm Cove. There she was at once surrounded by steam launches and smaller boats, and later the colliers ranged alongside and commenced transferring their cargo of fuel. She takes some 3,000 tons of coal, and as her daily consumption is about 50 tons per day, there will be ample supply on board to enable her to steam to Hong Kong and back without stopping at any intermediate ports.

In the meantime, a NSW contingent of 221 men had been mustered, 203 of whom were blue jackets and the balance stretcher bearers. In turn the men were made up of 110 from the Naval Brigade, sixty Naval Artillery volunteers, and the balance former RN or RNR personnel.[16] (The Australian colonial naval brigades were formed largely for port and coastal protection, against the colonies' preoccupation with the imperial designs of Russia). It is interesting to note that while the

A pencil portrait of Captain Alex H.H.G. Douglas RNR by cartoonist Rene Bull.

Salamis went on strike on 28 July, having been refused enhanced pay for entering the war zone. The ship being now under the control of the naval authorities, the crew was mustered and addressed by the senior naval officer and by Captain Douglas, himself an RNR officer. Dire consequences were threatened if the crew did not resume their duties;[14] suffice to say that a later newspaper report shows the crew in Royal Naval Reserve uniforms, saluting as they went about their duties, so it would appear that they had been

Salamis sailing from Sydney with the NSW and Victorian Naval Brigades, embarked to assist in quelling the Boxer Revolt in China. (National Library of Australia A05042 Australian War Memorial)

naval brigades were embarked as distinct Victoria and NSW colonial units, they were advised that with effect from 1 January 1901, they would all be Australians.

Salamis sailed for China on 8 August 1900, the NSW contingent housed in the forward 'tween decks, and the Victorians in the after 'tween decks, while the officers were quartered in the saloon accommodation and the petty officers in the third-class accommodation; Captain Hixson RN was in command of the NSW contingent.[17] Hong Kong was reached on 26 August 1900, from whence the ship was dispatched to Shanghai, and on to the Gulf of Pechili, where warships and transports from the foreign powers, Britain, Japan, America, Germany and Russia were assembling.

At the western extremity of the Gulf of Pechili, the Peiho River entered the sea, guarded at its entrance by the strategically located Taku Forts, which had been occupied by the allies two months earlier. The Peiho River wended its way above Taku to Tientsing and thence to the east of Peking, both cities under siege from the Boxers. Relief expeditions by the foreign powers were being mounted from Taku. Upon her arrival off Taku, where clearly the Australian expeditionary force was not expected, it was decided that the Victorian contingent would garrison the north-west Taku Fort, while it was deliberated whether the NSW contingent would be sent up to the front at Tientsing. Having disembarked the Australian Naval Brigade contingent, *Salamis* sailed from Taku on 26 October with 500 officers and men of the Welsh Fusiliers embarked. Calling at Chefoo and Wei-Hai-Wei, where nine invalids were embarked, she reached Hong Kong on 2 November, where she disembarked the troops, leaving that port on 18 November. She arrived at Sydney on 6 December 1900, where she resumed her rightful employment as a commercial liner.

The need for the Aberdeen Line to fill the gap created by the loss of the steamer *Thermopylæ* led to it acquiring in 1900 the 17-year-old 4,748-ton White Star liner *Ionic* for a price of £47,500. Built by Harland and Wolff in 1883 as one of a pair of barque-rigged steamers for the White Star Line's joint service to New Zealand with Shaw Savill, she had returned to her builders in 1894. There she had been re-engined with quadruple-expansion engines, served by new boilers and a taller funnel, giving her an enhanced service speed of 14 knots. At the same refit, she had been reduced to barquentine rig, her passenger accommodation had been enlarged and significantly improved, and her refrigerated cargo spaces had been greatly enlarged. In the years immediately preceding her acquisition by the Aberdeen Line, she had been engaged on trooping duties to South Africa, and had been chartered by the Spanish government to repatriate Spanish troops and officials from Pacific Island territories ceded to the USA. Renamed *Sophocles* (II), she entered Aberdeen Line service on 22 October 1900, with no external changes apart from her livery and a new gross tonnage of 4,673; with her straight stem and whale-backed forecastle and poop, she marked a step change in profile from the traditional Aberdeen Line steamer. Whether by coincidence of availability and suitability or otherwise, she also marked the growing ties between Thompson's Aberdeen Line and Ismay, Imrie & Co's Oceanic Steam Navigation Company, owners of the White Star Line.

Moravian undertook one outward Royal Mail voyage to Australia via Suez in March 1901, standing in for the Orient Line's contractual sailing, arriving at Fremantle as the first port of call in Australia.

Reduction of the Line's sailing ship fleet continued over 1902 and 1903 through sale and loss:

- *Miltiades* (GTCo. 46/64) was sold to Italian interests in March 1902.

- *Aristides* (GTCo. 48/64) disappeared on passage from Caleta Buena, Chile, to San Francisco laden with nitrate of soda; last seen on 28 May 1903, never to be heard of again.

SS *Sophocles* (ex-White Star's *Ionic*), purchased to replace SS *Thermopylæ*. (National Library of Australia SA PXE 722/3655-3656)

- *Orontes* (GTCo. 56/64) was run into and sunk off Ostend by the SS *Oceana* on 23 October 1903.

In late 1902, the Sydney trading house, Burns Philp, well known for its Pacific Island shipping and trading activities, established a new service from Sydney to Singapore with its vessel *Moresby*. The company soon found that the vessel could not handle the volume of cargo and passengers, and entered the market in 1903 for a pair of ships to support her. The ageing *Aberdeen* and *Australasian* were considered, together with Eastern and Australian's *Airlie* and *Guthrie*. In the end, Burns Philp bought the latter two vessels.[18]

After a two-year lull in new building activity, in 1902 the Aberdeen Line went to Alexander Stephen at Linthouse for two new steamships, the 6,793-ton *Miltiades* and *Marathon*, at 6,795 tons. With their clipper bows, pole bowsprits and raked pole masts and funnels, the new vessels, arguably among the most beautiful steamships afloat, marked the swansong of Aberdeen conservatism. They were also the last two ships to be built for GTCo. as a private partnership. Of 453ft register length × 55ft beam × 33.1ft depth, their graceful profiles belied a number of significant technical advances so far as the Aberdeen Line was concerned. They were propelled by twin triple-expansion steam engines delivering 6,000ihp, driving two three-bladed manganese bronze built-type propellers to give a service speed of 14 knots; with the added security offered by twin screws, auxiliary sails were dispensed with. The two vessels were configured with double bottom tanks stretching their lengths, including the engine room, the first GTCo. vessels to be so fitted. The five hatches, each served by three derricks arranged on the Hutcheson and Newton principle, were arranged two forward, two aft, and a midships hatch trunked through the accommodation abaft the bridge. The cargo spaces included some 100,000 cu.ft of refrigerated cargo space, served by a state-of-the-art Hall refrigeration plant. They were the first ships in the Aberdeen Line to be fitted with wireless telegraphy. The ships were constructed to Lloyd's Register 100A1 class, under supervision of the Board of Trade in respect to emigrant requirements, and to the special instructions of the British Admiralty Transport Department.

The new ships had first-class passenger accommodation for around eighty persons located amidships, while up to 100 third-class passengers were accommodated in the extended poop. The colonial newspapers were effusive in their praise for the comfort of the accommodation and the luxurious outfitting of the public rooms. Most saloon passengers were accommodated in two-berth cabins, with some single and family cabins available. A feature of the first-class dining room was a stained-glass cupola fitted above it. 'The sanitary accommodation for both classes is very complete.'[19]

Miltiades (Spalding) made her maiden call to Sydney on 14 December 1903, and *Marathon* (Allan) on 26 January 1904.

Back in June 1901, Dalgety's chairman, Edmund Doxat, had communicated with Oscar Thompson recommending the extension of the Aberdeen Line's service to Brisbane.[20] Since 1901, the steamers had seasonally terminated in Newcastle, but now with the service soon to be reinforced by two new steamers, *Damascus* left Sydney on 4 December 1903 to inaugurate Brisbane as the Line's

A side elevation of *Marathon* on builders' trials.

Australian terminal port, to be followed by *Miltiades* later in the month. The lack of a direct service to London from Brisbane had adversely impacted upon the ability of Queensland to develop its export potential. Now with the establishment of the Aberdeen Line's three-weekly service, which the Queensland Butter Manufacturers' Association had helped to promote through Dalgety's, and for which the premier of Queensland, Mr Philp, had offered the inducement of waiving all port dues,[21] the problem was partially addressed. *Damascus* carried the first consignment of Queensland butter to London, which included a box for Mr Chamberlain and one for the Earl of Warwick, gifts from the Darling Downs factories, together with a consignment of cape gooseberry jam in the form of pulp.[22] Subsequent sailings showed a steady increase in butter exports from Brisbane, with *Sophocles* lifting 14,000 boxes in December 1904.

Seasonal calls were also resumed to Hobart with five sailings in 1904, and occasional calls to Portland for frozen meat homewards. Albany continued to be the last regular port of call before leaving Australia for Port Natal; however, an announcement in the *Western Australian* newspaper in October 1904[23] advised of the decision to make Fremantle the last Australian port of call rather than Albany, the first sailing being *Nineveh* (Robb) in January 1905. The same press article noted that only draught restrictions in Fremantle narrowly prevented White Star Line's 'immense' vessels from swapping to Fremantle from Albany. Dalgety's was to be the company's Fremantle agents. It would seem that it was not until 1913 that Fremantle became the first port of call in Australia on the Aberdeen Line's outwards service, supporting the burgeoning emigrant ingress to Western Australia from the homeland.[24]

The company's status in Sydney and its relationship with Ismay, Imrie and Co's White Star Line was further enhanced by the two occupying appropriated berths on Dalgety's new No. 1 Darling Harbour wharf at Millers Point on the south side of the harbour, just inland from the site of the yet-to-be-built Sydney Harbour Bridge, the Aberdeen Line renting 500ft and White Star 600ft of wharf space.[25] The new berths, together with their associated passenger halls, magnificent wool and bonded stores and new access roads, were built by the Sydney Harbour Trust (originally known as the Sydney Harbour Improvement Trust until the significance of that acronym dawned ...) to replace old Millers Point wharves following an outbreak of bubonic plague in the area. The outbreak was ascribed

to the impoverished Millers Point housing, poor sanitary conditions and the dilapidated state of the wharves, which encouraged the breeding of rats. Dalgety described the new facility:

> The wool store and wharf combined make one of the finest water frontage properties in Sydney Harbour. A Liverpool White Star liner and an Aberdeen Liner can berth at the wharf at one and the same time without having to go abreast of each other ... There is no carting from the store to the ship, as the bales are transferred direct from the warehouse into the vessel's hold.

The new wharf, constructed to a rat-free specification, was officially opened by White Star Line's *Medic* in March 1903. The new wool store, built at a cost of £12,833, and proclaimed to be 'the finest building of its class in the port' opened in 1905, with extensions built at a cost of £5,500 opening in 1907, at which time dumping presses with a capacity of 2,500 bales per day were installed. Sample rooms in the wool store, one of the longest and best lighted in Australia, measured 285ft × 129ft; it had a capacity of 40,000 bales.[26]

To service the extension of the Line to Brisbane, and with two new ships in service, late in 1903 Thompson's sought to increase its annual sailings from the UK to Australia from seventeen to twenty-two. This factor, coupled with obvious hostility to the Line's extension to Brisbane from the British India, which had operated a direct service via the Torres Strait by way of BI Associated Steamships since 1881, led to a rift with the Davis members.

Sir Thomas Sutherland, chairman of P&O, in a written deposition to the Royal Commission on Freight Rings, described the working of the Australian Freight Conference – the Davis – as follows:

> This combination, on the whole, works for peace, and if there was none such, shipowners would be worse off than they are now, while as regards the shippers, they would not have such fine fleets at their disposal as they have now, with regular and well-understood rates of freight to work by. Shortly stated all the cargo steam owners pay into the Association account on the basis of 12½ per cent of their freight, and there is no chartering except an occasional sailing vessel in the event of the steam tonnage being insufficient for the requirements of the trade. The contributions to the Association are divided amongst the members according to their shares, and the cargo steamer owners have a pool amongst themselves. The Association has a fixed tariff

of rates which applies to all cargo steamers. The mail steamers' rates are higher than this tariff (except for weight) and vary according to demand for space. They can quote the same rates as the cargo steamers if they wish to do so, but it is understood that they will not quote less. The rates of freight are fixed by the 'Rates Committee of Davis', very often after consultation with the 'Merchants' Committee' in the Australian Trade ... So far, therefore, as our experience goes, our [P&O] connection with 'Davis' does not hinge on its direct profit, but upon indirect advantage accruing from friendly co-operation amongst all concerned in the shipping trade.[27]

Against this background, Davis governed the share of the trade, and accordingly the number of annual sailings to which each member was entitled.

Thompson's move, in December 1903, coincided with Lund's Blue Anchor Line giving notice to the Davis that, with effect from the end of 1903, it would be loading its own ships. Hitherto, Lunds had used the services of Houlder and Trinder Anderson as cargo brokers for its outwards sailings under an agreement that precluded these brokers working for other lines on the Australian service. Trinder Anderson and Houlders immediately began booking cargo on other ships, in apparent conflict with their existing agreement with Lunds.

From December 1903, both lines withdrew from the Davis and from early 1904, GTCo. began a joint two-weekly service from London alongside Lund's Blue Anchor Line. The two lines were closely compatible in terms of tonnage and services, and the joint service made a lot of sense in difficult trading times. The two lines, as has earlier been seen in the homewards refrigerated trades, had been a persistent thorn in the side of the mail steamship lines, and such a union was strictly contrary to the working arrangements of the combine.

The response of the other lines, apparently spearheaded by the White Star Line, was Immediate. Within December 1903, a vicious freight rates war was put in place, with rates slashed by a half, and 'fighting ships' matching each of the joint sailings. In a trade that was already said to be losing money, ships were now sailing in ballast, and neither line had the financial wherewithal to sustain such devastating competition for long. Lunds, by January 1904, was announcing a rapprochement with its brokers and had returned to the fold. Thompson's held out, but at great financial cost.

In contrast to their tempestuous involvement in the Davis on the Australian trade, Thompson's was never a member of the South African Conference, but always maintained that the Line had rights to lift any cargo it liked in South Africa on the unassailable grounds that it had lifted cargo from South African ports for many years longer than the existing Conference lines members. In point of fact, Thompson's maintained a friendly relationship with the Conference members, filling vacant spaces with rough cargo, or on occasions of South African surplus, fine cargo that the Conference line members had not the capacity to lift.[28] Also, homewards-bound vessels bunkering at Tenerife had, since 1900 under the agency of Hamilton & Co., loaded occasional consignments of crated bananas consigned to Fyffes on deck. This trade continued until the outbreak of the First World War.[29]

On 25 March 1904, the sailing ship **Pericles** (GTCo. 46/64) was sold to L. Gundersen of Porsgrund, Norway. Renamed **Sjurso**, she continued trading until broken up at Kiel in August 1923.

Sir William Henderson died on 9 June 1904, aged 78. In his time as an employee, partner and latterly senior partner, he had made an outstanding contribution to the company. Upon his return to Aberdeen from service as the company's London partner, he purchased Devanha House, Ferryhill, in 1857, where he lived for forty-six years until his death, greatly developing the estate, particularly by way of extensive conservatories in which he introduced plants from all over the world. The conservatories now form part of the public Ferryhill Gardens.

In addition to his company service, Henderson had been at the forefront of public life and munificence; he first entered public service in 1869 when he became an elected commissioner of the Aberdeen Harbour Board. Then in November 1885, 'at the urgent solicitation of the citizens, he consented to enter the Town Council and was returned unopposed for Ferryhill Ward' where Devanha House was located;[30] the following year he was 'unanimously and cordially' elected Lord Provost. His three-year tenure of office saw numerous significant public works come to fruition, including new harbour facilities, reconstruction of the Royal Infirmary to celebrate Queen Victoria's fiftieth anniversary in 1887, and the building of the city's public library on the Rosemount Viaduct was also developed under his leadership in 1889. He attended at Westminster Abbey, wearing the newly recreated robe of office of the Lord Provost, at Queen Victoria's jubilee service. He was a director of several

On the social front, he was a founding director of the Aberdeen Sailors' Mission and took over as president when George Thompson Jnr retired from those duties. He was a devoted member of the Free Church of Scotland and for many years was a member of the General Assembly of the United Free Church. Henderson's munificence was on a grand scale, making large donations to charities supporting the poor, the church, educational foundations and medical facilities. Perhaps the most touching memorial to his life may be found in a foreword by his son to a memorial volume prepared for his grandchildren, which reflected upon Henderson, the family man:

Sir William Henderson, circa 1890.

The following pages may give you some idea of your Grandfather's more public activities, but they can give little or no idea of his home life, and of him as he appeared to those grandchildren who knew him at Devanha – of the romps and chasings round the big dining-room table; of the climbing of 'the Mound' to put up flags on a gala day, or to be shown the panorama of the City and river and Deeside hills, or to be rolled down the Mound over and over again, just for the very fun of the thing; of the strolls round the grounds to see the conservatories, vineries, gardens and duly to admire the Big Tree Fern, the orchids and the grapes; of the expeditions to make friends with 'Jacky' the kangaroo, or along the 'Sandwalk' to play at 'the Swings' or round by 'Sandy' and 'the Rookery' to see the golden pheasant, and further on to the stables to see the horses and the big idol from the New Hebrides.

Nor do they describe the summer afternoons when the Sabbath Schools or other gatherings of children or 'grown-ups' were entertained, when tea would be served on the lawn, and then all would disperse here and there to enjoy themselves, and at dark he would summon all together again and finish up the evening with a display of fireworks and perhaps the sending off of two or three balloons – to the infinite delight of the little ones.

At such times he was the life and soul of the party, and endless trouble he took to make sure that each and all had a good time.

commercial companies, including the North of Scotland Bank, whose £5 note bore an image of Devanha House and Ferryhill. Henderson's immense services to the City were recognised when in June 1893 he attended upon his sovereign at Osborne House in the Isle of Wight and was knighted.

Henderson's armorial motto *Sola virtus nobilitat* – Virtue alone enobles – perhaps summarised his approach to life, and makes interesting comparison with that of his father-in-law, George Thompson Jnr: *Per periculum vivo* – by danger I live.

On 3 November 1904, George Thompson Youngest, GTJ's second son and only surviving offspring, died at Pitmedden. While he appears to have been a partner in the firm for a couple of years in the 1860s, he had not been engaged in the mainstream management of the company thereafter. I suspect that his lifestyle did not accord with that of the then senior partner, Sir William Henderson. Nonetheless, he remained an initial participating shareholder outside the subscribing ownership of numerous GTCo. ships, the last recorded being a 3/64 interest in the steamer *Salamis II* in 1899. George Thompson Youngest, though he took no active part in public life, was much interested in the affairs of his native city. He was

A folly tower erected at Pitmedden to commemorate Queen Victoria's Jubilee.

described in his obituary as: 'A man of the most generous-hearted character, he was a liberal donor to many charitable institutions, though few knew this, his gifts always being anonymous.'[31] During his occupancy of Pitmedden House, he caused an attractive folly tower to be built to celebrate Queen Victoria's Jubilee.

With the commissioning of *Miltiades* and *Marathon*, and with the prospect of operating twenty-two sailings a year denied the company by the Davis, the two original steamers *Aberdeen* and *Australasian* became surplus to requirements. *Australasian* was laid up following completion of her forty-fifth voyage, departing Sydney on 8 March 1904; while *Aberdeen* was retained as a reserve ship, undertaking a couple of charter voyages, before departing Sydney on her forty-ninth and final voyage on 30 September 1905. Outstanding ships in their time, they were small and technology had rapidly passed them by.

In January 1905, the *Sophocles*, three days out from Albany homewards, was forced to put back into Fremantle with a fire seated in her refrigeration engine store room, a space containing twenty cylinders of carbonic gas and only separated from No. 4 hold by an insulated wooden bulkhead. The ship's crew under Captain Robert Schleman exhibited conspicuous gallantry in trying to bring the fire under control, but before the days of breathing apparatus being carried on board merchant ships, they were beaten back by noxious smoke, which prostrated several of the officers and crew, including Schleman. In Fremantle, fighting the fire was taken over by the local brigade, but they were unsuccessful, and with the flames now engulfing the refrigerated cargo in No. 4 hold, the hold had to be flooded. Damage to ship and cargo was estimated at £20,000.[32]

After only a year of providing a direct service to Brisbane, in early 1905 the Aberdeen Line began trans-shipping Brisbane-bound cargo at Sydney, even though its ships continued through to Brisbane to load Queensland export cargo. This, predictably, brought an uproar from Queensland merchants. The reason for this change is not clear, but it would appear that it was forced upon GTCo. by the Davis as a quid pro quo for Thompson's readmittance to the fold. Although denied by GTCo., the British India Line was alleged in Australia to be behind the trans-shipment fiasco.[33] The BI clearly saw the service operated by GTCo. as being invasive upon what had always been for it a fragile trade. Under Conference terms, the Aberdeen Line was further restricted to seventeen Brisbane calls a year, and was not allowed to carry frozen meat or hams.

Visiting Australia on board *Miltiades* in March 1905, Stephen Thompson, GTCo.'s London partner, confirmed that it would be impossible to change the system of discharging Brisbane-bound cargo in Sydney, although he accepted that this was anomalous. In response to requests for more sailings to service the burgeoning butter export market, he advised that as the company was losing on its current three-weekly service, it could hardly be expected to increase its loss by offering a fortnightly service. Pressed upon the vexed question of concessionary freight rates for butter, Thompson confirmed that a minimum rate for all Australian ports of ¼d per pound must prevail. Ominously, he also advised that the Aberdeen Line had run at a loss on the Australian trade for the past two years.[34] The timing of Thompson's visit to the Commonwealth was probably significant, a precursor of year-end developments that were to change the structure of the company indelibly.

A further mishap impacted *Sophocles* on her next voyage. Homeward-bound from Melbourne via Fremantle in May 1905, the vessel developed an increasing leak through her stern gland, causing Captain Schleman to put into Albany to carry out investigations. A diver survey under supervision of the local Lloyd's surveyor revealed that one of her propeller blades had broken off. The vibration in the stern shaft occasioned by the asymmetric propeller had displaced the stern gland packing, causing the stern blocks to move, allowing water ingress through the stern tube. Providing divers could remove the boss of the broken propeller blade *in situ* 16ft below the surface, a new blade could likewise be fitted. If, however, they were unsuccessful, the laden ship was too deep-draughted to permit tipping alongside to access the propeller above water, and it would be necessary to move her out into deep water in the sound, with attendant risks. In the outcome, the underwater operation was successful, a replacement blade was fitted, and the vessel proceeded on her interrupted voyage.[35]

Having served Brisbane as the Line's regular Australian terminal port for two years, in September 1905, the company's representative advised the Queensland government that unless the company received a £500 subsidy per vessel, it would have to withdraw its direct service. The Line's trading position in respect to Brisbane had been made the more difficult by the diversion of the immigrant traffic hitherto enjoyed to the Orient Line (Orient had taken the immigrant contract from the Aberdeen at a rate of £16 per head

for Brisbane passengers and £19 for Townsville *vs* Aberdeen's £17 per head all Queensland ports). The Queensland government, while acknowledging the value of the pioneer service offered by the Aberdeen Line, nonetheless considered that its value had been diluted by the advent of the Orient Line, and declined to accede to the demand for a subsidy, while offering a continuance of free facilities.[36] The first Orient Line sailing to Brisbane was made by the RMS *Orotava*, arriving on 1 September 1905.

To prove the point, the Line withdrew its direct service to Brisbane, *Moravian*'s sailing from Brisbane in September 1905 being the last Aberdeen Line visit to that port for a year. It is interesting to record the cargo uplifted by *Moravian* from Brisbane on that voyage:[37]

1,228 bales	wool
120 tons	tallow
2,522 cases	preserved meat
50 cases	extract of meat
1,566 bags	ore
696 boxes	butter
1,806 cases	suet
57 crates	turkeys
100 crates	fouls
10 crates	hares
3 crates	bacon
23 cases	pork

With no frozen meat, such a cargo could not economically support an effectively ballast run north and the 510-mile return voyage to Sydney.

GTCo.'s last sailing ship, *Strathdon*, was reduced to tramping voyages based on Australia. She arrived in Melbourne from Bellingham, Washington, on 24 March 1905[38] before what was to be her last homewards sailing from Australia. On 10 November 1905, she was sold to French interests, Bordes et Gils, renowned for its engagement in the Chilean nitrate trade. Said to be the largest barque of her times, she was renamed *Gers* (III), and continued in the nitrate trade until broken up at Bruges in 1924.

The company's final withdrawal from sail, while inevitable, nonetheless marked the end of an often glorious era. The Aberdeen Line's high reputation in the Australian trade had been forged by its famous clippers; many early New South Wales and Victorian families had been transported to the colonies by the passenger clippers and steamers of the Line. But ultra-conservatism, especially in terms of the financing of the ships, had caused the company to lose its pre-eminent position on the Australian trade. Basil Lord Sanderson, who was to join the company's management in 1921, summed up the situation in his autobiography:

> Unfortunately for the firm, however, though they started the switch from sail to steam at the right moment, they were not so successful in their vision of the type of vessel which would prosper in their new service. The steamers of the fleet were all of one type, beautiful to the eye with clipper bows and green hulls and adequate passenger accommodation both for First Class and for some hundreds of migrants, but their cargo capacity was far too small. They resembled, and indeed were, lovely yachts, but were not economic competitors for the steamers then being built by other shipping companies, who had entered the trade in the days of the pioneering Aberdeen clippers. Progressively the financial position of the company deteriorated, and this could be attributed to a reluctance to move their headquarters from Aberdeen to London, the centre of commercial and shipping services to Australia; for although a London office had been opened quite early on, all important decisions still rested with Aberdeen, who became more and more out of touch with reality. London might make recommendations as to the type of ship required and the type of service necessary, but Aberdeen knew better and provided London with the tools which Aberdeen considered suitable.[39]

A graphical comparison of the first generation of Aberdeen Line steamers built from 1882 to 1904 is shown in the colour section.

NEW OWNERS, NEW SHIPS – 1905 TO 1914

The challenges facing GTCo.'s management team were significant. Market conditions on the Australian trade were difficult, with fierce competition from the mail lines, the other established liner companies – Alfred Holt's Blue Funnel Line, Tysers' Dominion and Commonwealth Line (to become Port Line), the Houlder/Federal/Shire joint service and especially from Oceanic's White Star Line.

In an interesting reflection of the Australian exports trades, demonstrating the Aberdeen Line's decreasing market position when compared with that of the White Star Line, comparative figures released by Dalgety's for the 1903–04 and 1904–05 showed:[1]

	Wool – bales		Fruit – packages	
	1903-04	1904-05	1903-04	1904-05
White Star Line	105,898	103,656	149,782	94,597
Federal Line	84,054	76,775	15,477	19,412
Holt Line	72,330	85,671	92,715	72,028
Lund Line	58,263	49,506		
Aberdeen Line	55,437	54,787		
P&O Line			128,046	119,618
Orient Line			114,143	134,886
Others	130,493	74,177		161,873

Financially, the Aberdeen Line was bleeding; in successive years 1903 and 1904, it had suffered debit balances of £129,988 and £135,114.[2] Thompsons, weakened by the freight rates war precipitated by its fight with the Davis, did not have the financial wherewithal, given its ultra-conservative financing arrangements, to sustain such losses and some form of accommodation with another line on the Australian trade would need to be affected. The White Star Line was the obvious suitor; indeed, according to *Fairplay*, it had precipitated the situation.[3]

As a precursor of refinancing, the hitherto limited partnership was converted into a limited liability company with effect from 15 December 1905, with a capital of £250,000 made up of 150,000 6 per cent preference shares of £1 each; 5,000 ordinary shares of £10 each, and 50,000 management shares of £1 each.[4] The initial shareholders in the new company, each with one share, were:

G.T. Henderson	Shipowner	7 Billiter Square EC
S. Thompson	Shipowner	7 Billiter Square EC
O.S. Thompson	Shipowner	7 Billeter Square EC
Miss M. Thompson		48 Queens Gate SW
W.W. Thompson	Gentleman	48 Queens Gate SW
P. McAuslane	Clerk	7 Billiter Square EC
J. Holland	Solicitor	30 Mincing Lane EC

There was no initial public issue of shares.

The objectives of the company were broad based within the marine mercantile field, including shipowners, merchants, ship and insurance brokers, managers of shipping property, freight contractors, carriers of passengers and goods, barge owners, lightermen, freight forwarders, warehousemen, refrigerating storekeepers and wharfingers.

Then on 1 February 1906, the 'Look-out Man' editorial in *Fairplay*, fumed:

> The rumour that the gigantic octopus known as the Morgan Combine has acquired an interest in the world-famed 'Aberdeen Line' will scarcely be received with joy by the independent lines engaged in the Australian trade. That trade is reputed to have suffered severely through the action of the Combine by its swamping tactics carried out through the White Star Line, and although it is believed that the Combine has not benefited financially by its actions, yet when a concern is run by American millionaires to whom millions are but units, present profit becomes of minor importance when compared with policy; and the policy of our American friends may be inferred by their actions. In good truth, what with American Corporations buying English lines and running them regardless of loss under the British flag; with Emperor William in partnership with German lines and backing them up to any extent; with our government hating the very name of shipping, and our Board of Trade invariably 'agin' shipowners; decidedly the great shipping trade has not over much to be thankful for. In fact, some of the great lines are reduced to such a state that they are only wishing for a buyer to come along and serve them with the Combine sauce.

The Morgan Combine referred to by *Fairplay* was an American railroad and steel conglomerate owned by millionaire banker and financier J. Pierrepoint Morgan. In 1902, Morgan established a holding company, the International Navigation Company, later to become known as the International Mercantile Marine Company (IMM), which was to take over a number of major transatlantic shipping lines, including the Leyland Line, the International Steam Navigation Co. (America Line), the Red Star Line, the Dominion Line and of particular significance, Ismay, Imrie Co's Oceanic Steam Navigation Company (White Star Line). IMM tried, unsuccessfully to take over the Cunard Line, but failed in the face of US anti-trust legislation, and intense hostility from *inter alia* the British Government.

It was not only IMM's shipowning activities that were a cause for concern. In 1902, through the intervention of Oceanic's chairman Bruce Ismay, and as part of an agreement brokered by Harland and Wolff's chairman William Pirrie (later Lord Pirrie), 'all orders for new vessels and for heavy repairs [for J.P. Morgan's International Mercantile Marine], requiring to be done at a shipyard of the United Kingdom [were] to be given to Harland and Wolff' on a cost-plus basis,[5] seriously undermining thereby other UK shipyards, especially those on the Clyde.

At the same time, Pirrie, in association with J.P. Morgan, also negotiated a 51 per cent stake by Harland and Wolf in the Hamburg-Amerika Line, while J.P. Morgan and Co. entered into an agreement with Norddeutscher-Lloyd. Thus the two great German lines were brought under the aegis of the IMM. The 'octopus' activities of the IMM were regarded with great suspicion and hostility by the British maritime establishment, as the *Fairplay* editorial indicated.

With George Thompson and Co. restructured and public shares available, White Star and Shaw Savill moved in to take up the shareholdings under offer. Under the shareholding agreement for George Thompson and Company Ltd struck with the family shareholders, three grades of shareholding were under offer – 6 per cent preference, management and ordinary shares. Specifically, the holders of management shares 1 to 20,000 (White Star) had the right to appoint two directors, one of whom would be chairman of the company; the holders of management shares 20,001 to 33,340 (Shaw Savill) had the right to appoint one director; while the holders of management shares 33,341 to 50,000 (the former George Thompson) had the right to appoint the fourth director. *Fairplay* confirmed that Harold Arthur Sanderson and Edward Lionel Fletcher of the White Star Line, and Walter Henry Savill of the Shaw Savill and Albion Line had been appointed directors of George Thompson and Company Ltd (the Aberdeen Line) in addition to George Thompson Henderson representing management shareholders from the old partnership.

The shareholding structure of the new company was thus made up as follows:[6]

	6 per cent Preference £1 each	Ordinary £10 each	Management £1 each	Capital Issued / Authorised
Oceanic Steam Navigation Co:	£1,200	£10,000 = 20%	£20,000 = 40%	£31,200
Shaw Savill & Albion Ltd	**800**	**6,660 = 13.32%**	**13,340 = 26.68%**	**20,800**
	2,000	16,660 = 33.32%	33,340 = 66.68%	52,000
George Thompson and Co. vis . George Thompson Henderson . Stephen Thompson . Alexander Duff Henderson . Oscar Stephen Thompson	33,597	33,340 = 66.68%	16,660 = 33.32%	83,597
Other Preference Shareholders	<u>114,403</u>			
	£150,000	**£50,000 = 100%**	**£50,000 = 100%**	**£250,000**

The preference shareholders had no voting rights, nor any right to attend the ordinary meetings of the company.

Thus, the Oceanic/Shaw Savill axis secured effective control, with Harold Sanderson, general manager of the White Star Line, appointed the new chairman of George Thompson and Company. The White Star Line and Shaw Savill and Albion had worked together in the New Zealand trade since 1883, when Thomas Ismay entered into an agreement with Shaw Savill whereby the White Star Line provided manned ships into the trade and Shaw Savill and Albion managed passengers, cargoes and schedules. Their joint shareholding in George Thompson was accordingly a natural progression, which in particular gave Shaw Savill and Albion a foothold in the Australian outwards trade, and White Star access to London loading berths. The Shaw Savill and Albion Co.'s annual report dated 3 May 1906 advised shareholders of the company having taken a stake in George Thompson and Co.:

Our valued friends, Messrs Ismay, Imrie and Co. have for some little time been connected with the old, well known firm of George Thompson and Co., who own the [Aberdeen] White Star Line running to Australia, and when Messrs Thompson some little time ago decided to convert their business into a Limited Liability Company, they offered the White Star Company and our Company an interest in the business, with representation on the Board, which offer we accepted, believing that it will prove advantageous and be an additional source of strength to us all.[7]

Just what the pre-acquisition connection alluded to between George Thompson and Ismay, Imrie and Co. may have been is not clear. Certainly, Thompson's had purchased White Star Line's *Ionic* in 1900 to replace the lost steamer *Thermopylæ*, and there had clearly been a close identity between the two lines through their joint Australian agents, Dalgety and Co. Frank Bowen in his history of Shaw Savill and Albion, *The Flag of the Southern Cross*, even went so far as to suggest that at the time of the acquisition, the White Star Line 'already possessed a number of shares' [in George Thompson].[8] I can find no evidence of this, either in the partnership or through individual ship shareholdings.

Management of the new company moved from Aberdeen to its established London office at 7 Billiter Square, off Leadenhall Street, alongside Shaw Savill and Albion. The Thompson and Henderson families continued to be represented at senior management level, with the former senior partner, George Thompson Henderson, serving as general manager and director of the new company, assisted by his brother, Alexander Duff Henderson and cousins Oscar Stephen Thompson and Stephen Thompson in senior management roles. The acquisition of the partnership included the benefit of the underwriting business carried on by George Thompson Henderson and Stephen Thompson, and these two Lloyd's names continued that side of the business until the death of George Thompson Henderson in 1920.[9]

The new company purchased the ship assets of the partnership on 26 January 1906, on the following terms:

Steamer	GRT	Built	No. of 64ths Held	Av. value of shares held in each vessel
Aberdeen	3,684	1881	62	£9,687
Australasian	3,662	1884	64	£10,000
Damascus	3,726	1887	61	£9,531
Nineveh	3,808	1894	64	£15,000
Moravian	4,573	1899	64	£40,000
Salamis	4,508	1899	64	£40,000
Sophocles	4,673	1883	64	£15,000
Miltiades	6,793	1903	64	£130,000
Marathon	6,705	1904	64	£130,000
	42,222	1893		£399,218[10]

As a first act, the new company mortgaged the fleet on 1 February 1906, as security for the issue of £250,000 worth of 4½ per cent preference shares, issued on its behalf by the Law Guarantee and Trust Society. This was the first time in the company's history that a ship had been mortgaged, and marked a sharp change in financial management style. With the capital raised thereby, the new company embarked upon a new building programme.

The four early steamers were becoming distinctly long in the tooth and did not match trade requirements, especially in terms of cargo and refrigerated space. *Aberdeen* and *Australasian* had been laid up for some months, and now in November 1906 the mortgages on the two vessels were discharged and they were sold *en bloc* for £32,000 to The Shipping Agency Ltd, which immediately sold on the vessels, renamed *Halep* and *Scham*, to the Turkish government's Ottoman Company. The ensuing careers of these two ships were fascinating, and are touched upon in the next chapter.

Fleet renewal began with an order at Harland and Wolff, Belfast, for a completely new style of passenger and cargo ship, very much in the mould of White Star's Athenic-class, built at Harland and Wolff from 1901 for that line's New Zealand joint service with Shaw Savill, but with the addition of a short topgallant forecastle. Given the now effective controlling interest in the Line by IMM's White Star Line, there was an inevitability that the order should go to Harland and Wolff.

The new ship, *Pericles*, Yard No. 392, was ordered in 1906 and launched on 21 December 1907. Her dimensions were almost identical to White Star's Athenic-class – 500.6ft × 62.3ft × 31.1ft depth in hold.

Built at a cost of £240,000, she was a quantum leap forward from the *Marathon*, the last ship to have been built for the Aberdeen Line some four years earlier. With a gross tonnage of 10,925, some 50 per cent larger in size than the *Marathon*, gone were the graceful clipper bow and beautiful lines enhanced by a golden yellow sheer ribband of the earlier ship. A straight stem, four masts and funnel raked at a common ratio of 1¼in per foot and the bridge island separated from the main accommodation block, hallmarks of Harland and Wolff, her looks were further diminished by her green topsides being carried up to include the forecastle and bridge deck, thereby denying her long graceful sheer to the eye (In point of fact, before her final voyage, a deck edge yellow ribband was introduced, which greatly enhanced her appearance.)

Aesthetics aside, *Pericles* was a truly remarkable, functional ship. She had accommodation for 100 first-class and 400 third-class passengers, said to be the largest vessel carrying saloon and third-class passengers to Australia at that time. The *Cook Travel Journal* charmingly described *Pericles*' accommodation:

> She carries 100 saloon passengers and the arrangements for their comfort and enjoyment are of a most luxurious character, the dining saloon, smoking room, library, and lounge all being sumptuously

SS *Pericles* as commissioned: sheer line unenhanced. (National Library of Australia NSW a.639109)

S.S. Pericles

A postcard of *Pericles* with a deck edge yellow ribband.

fitted and upholstered; while the third class passengers have been well provided for in every way. The first class dining saloon is a broad, spacious apartment, extending the full width of the main deck; the ample seating accommodation enables all the passengers to dine at one sitting; while a new feature has been introduced in entirely eliminating big tables, replacing them with small ones on the popular restaurant system. The first class library and lounge is a magnificent room ... divided into two parts by a handsome glass screen. The library is fitted up as a reading and writing room and reserved for non-smokers; whereas the lounge is fitted with tables, etc., and smoking is permitted, so that passengers of both sexes may foregather and play cards or otherwise occupy themselves instead of as formerly, the men being banished to the smoking-room and the ladies to the library.[11]

Demountable 'tween deck accommodation for immigrants or troops could be fitted when required.

The new ship was propelled by two propellers, each driven by a quadruple-expansion steam engine, producing jointly 6,000ihp, from a steam delivery of 215psi, generated by three double-ended and two single-ended boilers. Her service speed was 14 knots on a consumption of about 100 tons of coal per day.

In particular, *Pericles* was a great cargo carrier, said to be equivalent to the White Star Line ships, with six holds and hatches, each hatch served by three derricks – the centre one stayed to plumb the hatch, and one of the other two overside according to which side was being worked. The forward two holds and 'tween decks were insulated, with a capacity of around 75,000 carcasses of mutton. Chambers were provided for the carriage of chilled beef.

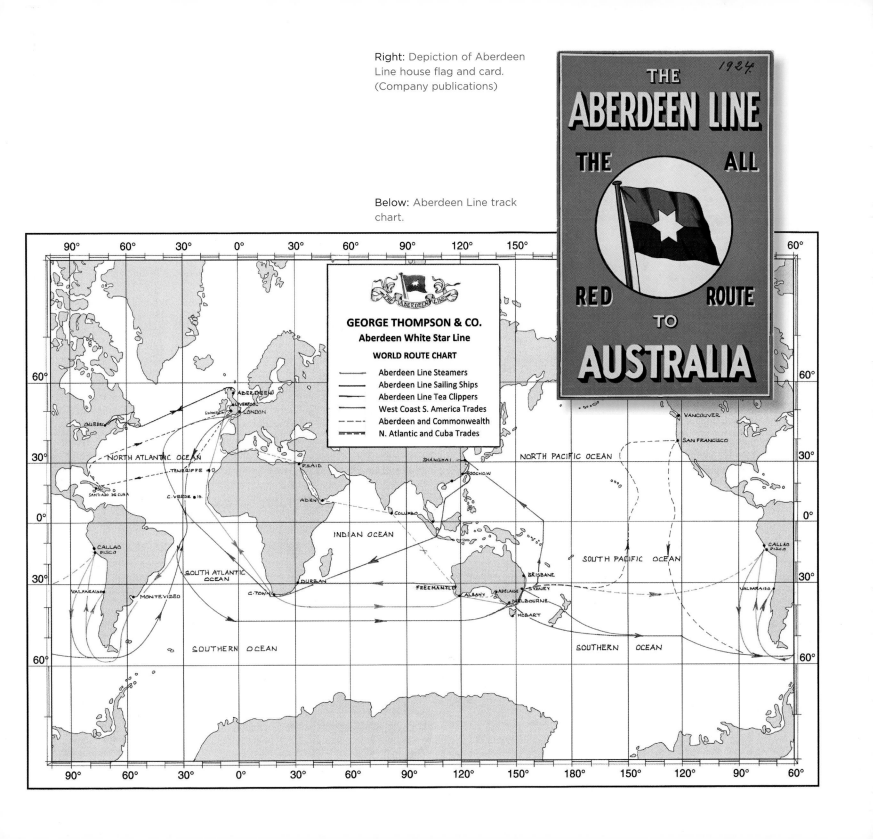

Right: Depiction of Aberdeen Line house flag and card. (Company publications)

Below: Aberdeen Line track chart.

1924.

THE ABERDEEN LINE
THE ALL
RED ROUTE
TO AUSTRALIA

GEORGE THOMPSON & CO.
Aberdeen White Star Line
WORLD ROUTE CHART

Aberdeen Line Steamers
Aberdeen Line Sailing Ships
Aberdeen Line Tea Clippers
West Coast S. America Trades
Aberdeen and Commonwealth
N. Atlantic and Cuba Trades

Disembarkation of Queen Victoria from the Royal Yacht at Aberdeen; Lord Provost George Thompson Jnr in right foreground.

Clipper barque *Phoenician*, watercolour by F. Garling 1806–73. (National Library of Australia PIC Drawer 6881-#R3877)

Above: ***Thermopylæ*** and ***Cutty Sark*** painting by Tim Thomson.

ship "THERMOPYLÆ" ~

comparison with U.T. 704 A.H.T.S.
(drawn to common scale / waterline)

P.H.K. 6/9/87

Comparison of *Thermopylæ* with UT 704 anchor-handling tug/supply vessel, drawn to same scale. The UT704 was the work horse of the North Sea offshore industry in the 1970s, and could be found propping up the Aberdeen quays in numbers.

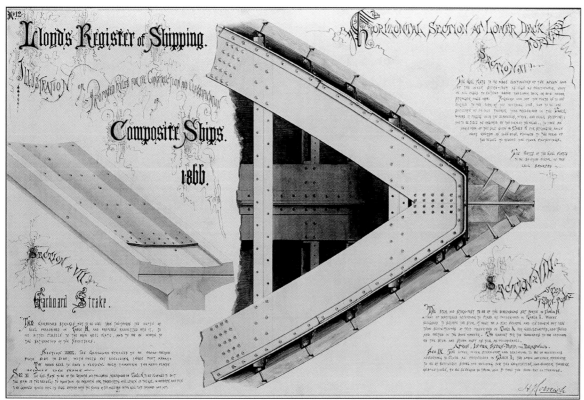

Horizontal section at lower deck – an example of the exquisite draughtsmanship of Harry Cornish of Lloyd's Register, from his suite of illustrations to accompany Lloyd's Register of Shipping's Rules for Composite Built Ships, which Bernard Weymouth, who contemporaneously was designing *Thermopylæ*, was drawing up. (Courtesy of Lloyd's Register Foundation)

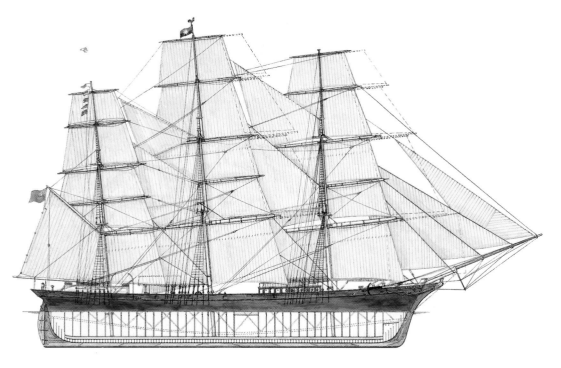

Left: Side elevation drawing – clipper *Thermopylæ*.

Geo. Thompson Jnr. & Co.

Built by Walter Hood & Co., Aberdeen, 1868

While I live, I'll crow!

ship 'THERMOPYLÆ'

Sunk by torpedo off R. Tagus, 1907

Capt. P.H.King FNI 2016

Below: Side elevation drawing of *Thermopylæ*.

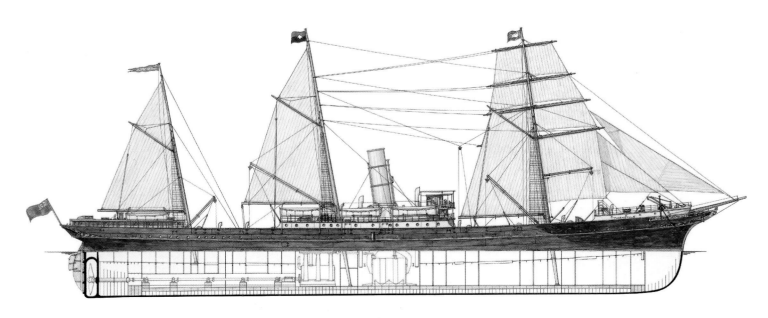

Geo. Thompson & Co.

Built Hall, Russell & Co., Aberdeen, 1891

s.s. 'THERMOPYLÆ' (II)

Wrecked off Cape Town, 11th September, 1899.

Capt. Peter H. King FNI 12/1989

The iron clipper **Patriarch** by Jack Spurling. This would have been very much the vision depicted by Frank Worsley in the extract from his book *First Voyage* at the end of Chapter 6.

The iron clipper **Salamis** by Jack Spurling running her eastings down. **Salamis** was designed along near identical lines to **Thermopylæ**.

Aberdeen Line; the first generation of steamers, built 1881 to 1904

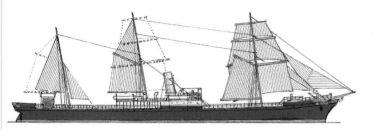

ABERDEEN (Robt. Napier 1882), followed, with progressive incremental changes, by:
AUSTRALASIAN (Robt. Napier 1884), **DAMASCUS** (Robt. Napier 1887),
THERMOPYLÆ (Alex. Hall 1891) and **NINEVEH** (Robt. Napier 1894)
Average G.R.T.: 3,694 Length B.P.: 350.3ft Beam: 44.2ft Depth: 32.6ft

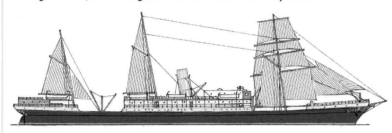

MORAVIAN (Robt. Napier 1899) and **SALAMIS** (Built Alex. Hall 1899)
Average G.R.T. 4,541 Length B.P.: 384.2ft Beam: 47.0ft Depth: 32.2ft

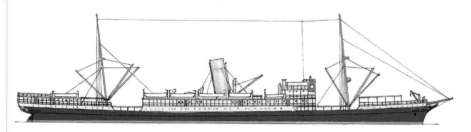

MILTIADES (Alex. Stephen 1903) and **MARATHON** (Alex. Stephen 1904)
Average G.R.T: 6,794 Length B.P.: 454.9ft Beam: 55.1ft Depth: 33.1ft

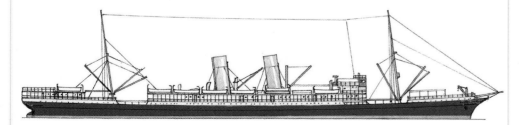

MARATHON (1912) and **MILTIADES** (1913) Following lengthening by Alex. Stephen.
Average G.R.T: 7,831 Length B.P.: 504.9ft Beam: 55.1ft Depth: 33.1ft

Left: Aberdeen Line; the first generation of steamers built 1882 to 1904.

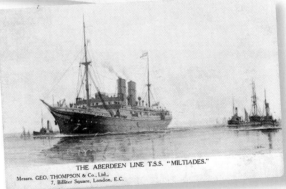

THE ABERDEEN LINE T.S.S "MILTIADES."
Managers—GEO. THOMPSON & CO., Ltd.,
7, Billiter Square, London, E.C.

THE ABERDEEN LINE T.S.S. "MILTIADES."
Messrs. GEO. THOMPSON & Co., Ltd.,
7, Billiter Square, London, E.C.

Above: And as the artist H.B. Freer saw the vessels in his promotional art work: two illustrations of Aberdeen Line ships.

Progressive development of Aberdeen Line steamers built at Harland & Wolff post 1905

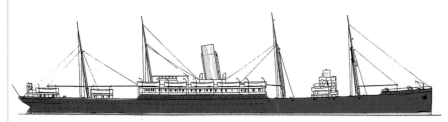

PERICLES (1908)
G.R.T.: 10,925   Length B.P.: 500.6ft   Beam: 62.3ft   Depth in holds: 31.1ft   Reefer capacity: 206,300 cu.ft (approx.)

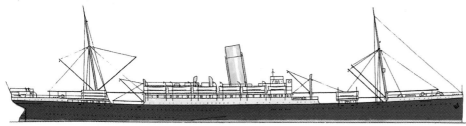

THEMISTOCLES and ***DEMOSTHENES*** (1911)
G.R.T.: 11,232   Length B.P.: 500.6ft   Beam: 62.3ft   Depth in holds: 39.4ft   Reefer capacity: 212,000 cu.ft

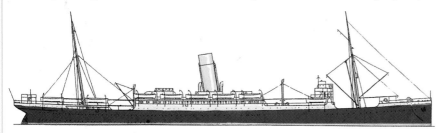

EURIPIDES (1914)
G.R.T.: 14,947   Length B.P.: 550.7ft   Beam: 67.4ft   Depth in holds: 44.1ft   Reefer capacity: 245,593 cu.ft

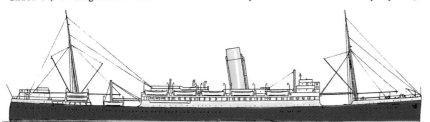

SOPHOCLES and ***DIOGENES*** (1922)
G.R.T.: 12,341   Length B.P.: 500.4ft   Beam: 63.2ft   Depth in holds: 39.6ft   Reefer capacity: 305,184 cu.ft.

Left: Aberdeen Line; post-1905 steamers.

Below: Two more examples of promotional artwork for the Aberdeen Line by H.B. Freer.

THE ABERDEEN LINE Triple S.S. "DEMOSTHENES," 11,400 tons.
Managers—GEO. THOMPSON & CO., Ltd.,
7, Billiter Square, London, E.C.

THE ABERDEEN LINE T.S.S. "THEMISTOCLES,"
Managers—GEO. THOMPSON & CO. Ltd.,
7, Billiter Square, London, E.C.   At Naval Review, 1911.

Pericles ran trials on 6 June 1908, and departed upon her maiden voyage from London on 8 July 1908 under the command of the Aberdeen Line's commodore, Captain Alexander Simpson. This was to be his seventy-seventh round voyage to Australia, all performed over 41½ years' service to the company – he was a highly respected officer both within the Line and on the Australian coast.

Upon her arrival on the Australian coast, the newspapers were fulsome (as ever) in their praise for her appearance, accommodations and carrying capacity:

Interest along the waterfront yesterday was centred in the mammoth 11000-ton twin-screw Aberdeen Line PERICLES ... The great beam of PERICLES seemed to take everybody's fancy, and the noble, commanding appearance of the great liner called forth many expressions of admiration ...

The officers and crew of the PERICLES number 167 all told.

In the meantime, the company was in the process of further disposing of its elderly steamers. On 26 February 1907, *Nineveh* was sold to the Eastern and Australian Steam Navigation Company and was renamed *Aldenham* to replace that company's *Australian*, which had been wrecked near Darwin the previous November. The ship continued to serve the E. and A. on its Australia–Far East trade until the end of 1915, when she was sold to the Royal Mail Meat Transports Ltd and renamed *Larne*. She continued within the Royal Mail Group, serving successively under the same name with the Royal Mail Lines and in 1918, the Zurbaran SS Co. (MacAndrews & Co. Ltd), before being sold for scrap in Wilhelmshaven in 1923.

With the reduction in fleet numbers, the sailing cycle was increased from three weeks to a sailing every four weeks from early 1907. This probably also accommodated a return to calls at Brisbane outwards bound, the first such being *Moravian* in February 1907. In a departure from normal sailings, in June 1907, *Miltiades* took up a round voyage charter to Orient Line to maintain the integrity of that company's mail contract following the breakdown of RMS *Oroya* off Ushant homewards bound, requiring that vessel to be docked.[12] The voyage out and home via Suez was the first Aberdeen Line transit of the Canal in fifteen years.

In April 1908, *Sophocles*, the former White Star ship purchased as a stopgap following the loss of the steamer *Thermopylæ*, was sold for scrapping at Morecambe. *Sophocles* had suffered a number of incidents while in Aberdeen Line service, and must have become an uneconomic unit to operate. The third of the first Napier-built steamers, *Damascus*, which had her saloon accommodation removed the previous year, was withdrawn from service in June 1908, having completed her forty-seventh round voyage to Australia. She was sold to N.G. Pittaluga, Italy, for about £9,000 on 25 April 1910, and was broken in Genoa.

After a relatively settled period in the company's progress, disaster struck when *Pericles*, less than two years old, was lost off Cape Leeuwin at the south-western tip of Australia on the afternoon of 31 March 1910. She was homewards bound on her fifth voyage, and fortunately there was no loss of life. The White Star curse had not been long in manifesting itself! Ironically, the Line's Australian agents, Dalgety's, had received news earlier that day that the company had ordered a sister vessel from Harland and Wolff.

Pericles, under the command of Commodore Alexander Simpson, undertaking his last voyage before retiring, had thusfar undoubtedly been a successful ship. She started her fifth homewards voyage from Brisbane on 9 March 1910. We know from the Australian newspaper archives[13] that she had loaded a valuable cargo in the Eastern States and Tasmania, including 28,007 boxes of butter (15,512 Queensland, 11,899 NSW and 596 Victoria), 35,398 cases of apples from Hobart (where the vessel made a seasonal additional call), 6,000 bales of wool, 900 tons of tallow, 300 tons of copra (trans-shipped at Sydney from the Pacific Islands), 600 tons of lead, 40,000 carcasses of meat, 1,250 crates of rabbits and 500 tons of wheat, in addition to a large quantity of general cargo.

While on passage from Melbourne to Fremantle, *Pericles* allided with an allegedly uncharted rock, 7½ miles south of Cape Leeuwin lighthouse at 1532 hours, 31 March 1910. The impact tore the bottom out of the forward three compartments in the vessel and she began sinking steadily by the head. The commander quickly assessed the gravity of the situation and after initially turning to seaward, turned back towards the shore in the hope of beaching her in Flinders Bay. However, when the situation clearly became hopeless, he put the engines full astern to take the way off the ship and ordered it to be abandoned. In half an hour, all 309 passengers and 156 crew members had taken to the lifeboats in fortuitously calm sea conditions, without loss of life or serious injury, and made for a beach to the east of the lighthouse, now 5 miles distant, which the deputy lighthouse keeper had marked with fires as

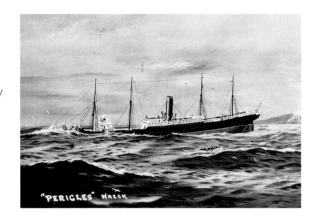

A postcard depiction of **Pericles** sinking off Cape Leeuwin. (National Library of Australia WA b3648362-1)

experienced local masters, and by the chief lighthouse keeper at Cape Leeuwin, the court concluded *inter alia* that:

- Proper care and vigilance were exerted in the navigation of the vessel by the master and officers, and proper steps were taken to fix her position and from time to time to verify such position.
- The vessel was kept on the course steered in the evidence given by the master which course, as set and steered was one which in all the circumstances of the occasion the master was justified in considering a safe and proper one.
- While on such course as stated in the evidence, the vessel struck a submerged obstruction; which was uncharted, and thereby foundered.

guiding beacons. Captain Simpson remained in the vicinity of the ship until she sank at 1800 hours, finally reaching the shore safely at around 2000 hours.[14]

The local populaces of Augusta and Karridale and the surrounding area were spontaneous in giving immediate succour to the survivors, and the Melbourne SS Co.'s steamer **Monaro**, which had been at Bunbury with her fires down, rapidly raised steam and proceeded to the scene. The following day, she embarked the survivors and took them to Fremantle.

Pericles had been delayed in Melbourne for three days by a coal strike, and she apparently had to pick up 150 tons of coal at Fremantle to make up bunkers. This factor, together with the deviation time to Hobart, would have put the vessel behind schedule, raising inevitable accusations of corner-cutting. A preliminary inquiry convened by Captain Irvine, chief harbourmaster at Fremantle, had insufficient evidence to bring charges against Captain Simpson. Accordingly, a formal inquiry was convened by the Crown in Perth under the chairmanship of the resident magistrate, Mr E.P. Dowley, assisted by two nautical assessors, on 8 April 1910.

In evidence, the commander, Captain Simpson ascribed the loss of **Pericles** to the vessel striking an uncharted rock. The vessel's forward draught at the time was 28ft. Simpson was at pains to point out that the vessel was transiting the same route that he had undertaken on eighty-one occasions without mishap.[15]

At the conclusion of the examination on 14 April 1910, in which Captain Simpson's evidence had been supported by two

Undoubtedly, the outstanding reputation of Captain Simpson and the fact that the officer of the watch held an extra master's certificate of competency, would have weighed on the court in coming to their conclusions.

Arising from the conclusions of the court of inquiry, the prospect of an uncharted rock lying on the main steamship route between Fremantle and the East gave rise to serious concerns being voiced in the Western Australian Parliament as to the quality of the hydrographic surveys offshore Cape Leeuwin. As an immediate measure, the Western Australian government tug **Penguin** was dispatched to locate the wreck, which she duly did. An initial survey on the supposed route of the **Pericles** revealed nothing, and a Royal Navy survey ship, HMS **Fantome**, was detached from work in the north-west to undertake a more detailed survey in December 1910, but again after four days' searching, achieved no positive result.[16] The formal position of the **Pericles** wreck is recorded as 34° 25.33'S, 115° 08.24'E in 30m of water.[17] Perhaps significantly, the Australian Hydrographic Service's latest edition of the chart covering Point d'Entrecasteaux to Cape Leeuwin, updated in September 2009, has no indication topographically of the potential for uncharted rocks along the apparent track, and the zone of confidence diagram forming part of that chart covering the waters where **Pericles** was believed to have been navigating has the innocuous annotation: 'Uncharted features hazardous to surface navigation are not expected but may exist' covering the whole sea area outside the dangerous South West Breaker. (The current chart is hardly

A reproduction of a *Western Mail* chartlet.

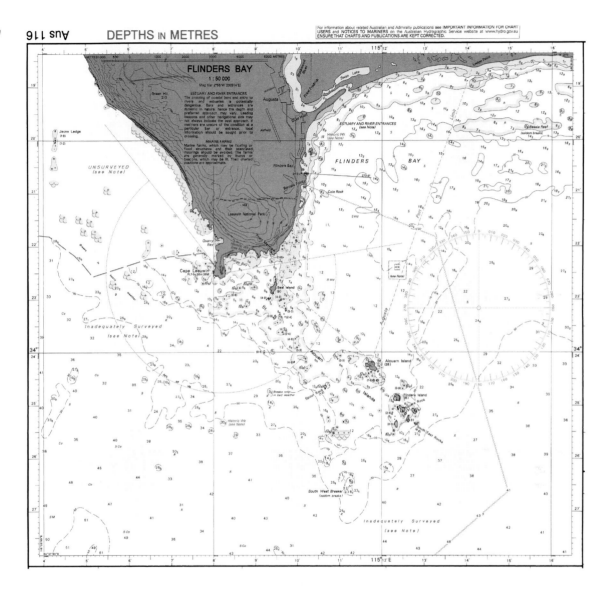

For information about related Australian and Admiralty publications see IMPORTANT INFORMATION FOR CHART USERS and NOTICES TO MARINERS on the Australian Hydrographic Service website at www.hydro.gov.au ENSURE THAT CHARTS AND PUBLICATIONS ARE KEPT CORRECTED.

changed from that reproduced in the *Western Mail*, 9 April 1910, apart from metrication.)

It is difficult, from the reported evidence of Simpson and his navigating officers, to adequately reconstruct the final hours of **Pericles**.[18] Curiously, however, some four months after the Inquiry had given its verdict, an ocean drift bottle launched from **Pericles** at noon on 31 March 1910, was reported recovered by the harbourmaster at Port MacDonnell;[19] this gave **Pericles** off Cape d'Entrecastreaux in position 34° 54'S, 115° 56'E. Projecting the original course declared to the court by Simpson and his officers of N56°W from this position would have taken the vessel's track significantly closer to the dangerous South West Breaker off Cape Leeuwin than the planned 3½ miles advised to the court. That some eighty minutes before the vessel struck, her course was altered outwards half a point (i.e. about 6°) would seem to indicate concern on the bridge that the vessel had been set inside the intended track over the ground.

Predictably, Captain Simpson was heartily congratulated by his friends on the happy issue of the investigation, but the loss of *Pericles* was a hugely sad finale to a distinguished career. Born in Aberdeen in 1849, Simpson had served the Aberdeen Line for 46½ years, embracing eighty-one voyages to Australia. In all that time he had never, until *Pericles*, suffered a casualty of any significance. His career had started in sail as an apprentice in *Queen of Nations*, he qualified as a master mariner in sail in 1876 and rose to command *Samuel Plimsoll* in 1881, before converting to steam as mate of the *Aberdeen*. Thereafter, he successively commanded *Australasian* (the 'blue-eyed commander' in Froude's *Oceania*), *Thermopylæ* (II), and *Moravian* before taking *Pericles* from the builders.[20] In addition to his master mariner's certificate, he held a voluntary engineer's certificate issued by the Board of Trade. He had established a notable reputation for casting ocean drift bottles overboard with position notes contained within, the returns from which formed the basis of scientific research into ocean currents and the foundation for ocean current atlases; his last bottle was cast overboard as he passed Cape d'Entrecasteaux, hours before the grounding. He was also a distinguished ocean meteorological observer. Upon his return to London from Perth, he went into retirement. In a letter to the managing director of Dalgety's penned on his repatriation voyage to London, Simpson wistfully concluded:

> If my owners should ask me to bring out one of the new steamers I will gladly do so; but I am afraid they will think I am getting too old. I can assure you I can run rings around the young ones. They have not been brought up in the school I was brought up in.

Captain Simpson made his sad voyage home from Fremantle as a passenger in the P&O Branch Line (formerly Lund's Blue Anchor Line) steamer *Wakool*, along with some of the passengers and crew from the *Pericles*. A fellow passenger, Captain E. Pusey RN, wrote to the Shipwrecked Fishermen and Mariners Royal Benevolent Society on 7 May 1910 drawing its attention to Captain Simpson's conduct of the evacuation of *Pericles*. The society recognised Simpson's actions when it awarded him an inscribed self-recording aneroid (barograph) at its annual general meeting on 17 July 1910.[21] He died

at Muswell Hill, London, on 17 April 1921. The lighthouse keepers at Cape Leeuwin were suitably recognised for their contribution to the successful rescue by the sister shipwreck society in New South Wales. The insured loss of around £500,000 was the second largest cargo claim hitherto on the Lloyd's market; the claim on hull and machinery was £225,000.

Over a period of time, flotsam from the wreck including butter, wool and casks of oil floated to the surface, to the delight of the people of neighbouring Augusta. A Western Australian government steamer, *Una*, under the control of the receiver of wreck, was sent to the location to salvage what it might. A company was formed to buy the salvage rights, and auctions were advertised for the sale of up to 2,000 boxes of butter and bales of wool. However, it was not until 1957, when an American, Tom Snider, purchased the salvage rights to the lead, that a serious attempt was made to recover the 600 tons of lead that went down with the ship. Working with his boat *Harder*, over the next five years before his death, Snider salvaged between 400 and 500 tons of the metal. It contained traces of gold and silver, which were extracted under contract in Germany. The wreck now remains a popular site for experienced sport divers.

Of specific interest among the flotsam was an oil painting *The Weary Pilgrim, Saint Rocco*, dated 1730–1735, by the Venetian artist Giambattista Tiepolo. The painting had been loaned by its owner, Mrs Heron, to the New South Wales State Art Gallery, but upon that gallery undergoing a refurbishment, all loaned items had been returned to their owners. Mrs Heron embarked in *Pericles* as a passenger, carrying the painting with her. It went down with the ship, but was found washed up on a nearby beach virtually undamaged some weeks later. In 1912 Mrs Heron gifted the painting to the NSW State Art Gallery, where it rests.

It is interesting to note the almost parallel disaster that befell the Aberdeen Line's Cape-route running mate, Lund's Blue Anchor Line, when the previous year that line's flagship, the 9,339-ton *Waratah*, was lost without trace with all hands off the coast of south-east Africa while on passage from Durban to Cape Town on her second return voyage from Australia. The cause of that disaster has never been reliably established, and to date the wreck has never been found. Ironically, *Pericles*, under the command of Captain Simpson, had actively participated in the search for the *Waratah* immediately following her disappearance and Simpson had dined the commanders of the search vessels on board *Pericles*.

The loss of *Pericles* left a significant gap in the company's scheduled liner service, for while a further ship of the new class had been ordered just before the vessel foundered, its commissioning was still many months off. As a stopgap, the IMM Dominion liner *Norseman* was chartered. Built at Harland and Wolff 1898 for the Hamburg-Amerika Line's transatlantic service as the *Brasilia*, she lasted for less than two years with that company before being sold back to Harland and Wolff on 12 February 1900. There, her original accommodation for 300 second-class passengers was replaced with accommodation for 400 third-class and demountable accommodation for steerage passengers; modifications included the fitting of two extra masts to bring her complement up to four. She was sold to the IMM's subsidiary, the Dominion Line, for that company's North Atlantic emigrant service. In size and profile, she was not dissimilar to the *Pericles*, being (post-conversion) 9,546grt, with a length of 516ft and a beam of 62ft (*Pericles* was 10,925grt/518 × 62.3ft).

Norseman left Gravesend on 7 June 1910 on her first voyage in Aberdeen Line service with 460 passengers embarked. Apart from the usual call at Plymouth to embark emigrants, she sailed straight out to Melbourne without a break at the Cape. Interestingly, her chief officer on this first voyage to Australia was Charles Davy Matheson, son of Captain Charles Matheson, who had so tragically been lost in the pyrotechnics explosion in GTCo.'s first steamer, *Aberdeen*, in 1884.

Norseman was to serve the Aberdeen Line under charter for nine round voyages to Australia spanning four years, until relieved by

The Dominion Line's *Norseman*; chartered to replace the lost *Pericles*. (National Library of Australia Vic H81.85/53)

the newly built *Euripides* in 1914. In the course of this service she regularly carried around 1,000 passengers per outwards voyage, mostly immigrants.

The year 1910 saw changes in the corporate structure of George Thompson & Co's 26.68 per cent management shareholder, Shaw, Savill and Albion Ltd. Shaw Savill, whose trade had primarily been to New Zealand, took an interest in the failed Canadian–Australian Line, together with the New Zealand Shipping Company and the White Star Line, against an offer of subsidies from the New Zealand government. While these activities were going on, there was busy trading in Shaw Savill and Albion's shares on the open market, giving rise to speculation that the IMM was poised to make another pre-emptive strike on British shipping, this time the target believed to be Shaw Savill and Albion. In point of fact, the buyer turned out to be Sir John Ellerman, who had quietly acquired 55 per cent of the ordinary shares of Shaw Savill and Albion, and thereby control of the company;[22] within this share acquisition, he purchased the major part of Walter Savill's personal shareholding in the line for £70,000.[23] At the same time as Ellerman's acquisition of Shaw Savill and Albion shares, White Star Line bought a 40 per cent stake in the company.

The order for the Harland and Wolff new-build *Themistocles*, announced the same day as *Pericles* foundered, was followed by one for a second ship of the same class, to be named *Demosthenes*, effectively a permanent replacement for the lost vessel. *Themistocles* was launched on 22 September 1910, and handed over to the Line on 14 January 1911. Under the command of Captain Alexander H.H.G. Douglas RD RNR, the voyage from Belfast to London via Cardiff for bunker coal was something of a shakedown cruise, with various trade dignitaries including the agents general for Victoria and South Australia embarked as guests of the directors. Amongst the guests was a French cartoonist, Rene Bull, whose subsequently published *A Day in my Life on board the Aberdeen Liner TSS Themistocles* gives a vivid if, somewhat bacchanal, impression of life on board on such relaxed excursions.

Themistocles, of 11,232grt, departed London on her maiden voyage for Melbourne, Sydney and Brisbane via the Cape on 16 February 1911. While similar in size and general profile to *Pericles*, the new vessel was in fact a significant advance on the earlier one, both in terms of looks and specification. The centrecastle deck incorporating two hatches was carried forward to the bridge

Cartoons by Rene Bull.

superstructure; a long raised poop was introduced; and Sampson posts replaced two of the earlier vessel's four masts. Aesthetically, her topsides green paint was carried up to the line of the top of the main deck bulwarks, with her forecastle, centrecastle and poop now painted cream, giving emphasis to her graceful sheer; altogether a fine-looking ship.

The new vessel, deadweight 11,000 tons, had seven holds, with about 50 per cent of cargo volume insulated for refrigerated cargoes, and two compartments fitted with overhead hanging rails for the carriage of Australian chilled beef. Her profile, and her dimensions, 500.6ft length × 62.3ft beam × 39.4ft depth of hold, were almost identical to six Royal Mail Line 'D' class vessels that followed from Harland and Wolff.

Passenger numbers vary according to which account one reads, but 103 first-class and 256 third-class passengers seems to be the norm, with the potential for carrying up to 800 emigrants in demountable 'tween deck accommodation. The first-class passengers were accommodated amidships, with single-berth accommodation in the bridge deck and tandem cabins in the awning deck. The third-class passengers were accommodated aft in the poop, main and 'tween decks in one-, two-, three-, four-, six- and eight-berth cabins. A feature of the ship was the provision of single-berth cabins for third-class passengers – the first ship so fitted on the Australian trade. The cost of a single-berth cabin from London to Melbourne was £25.[24] Generous public rooms were provided for both classes, with extensive open deck spaces. The Australian press greeted the new vessel with customary enthusiasm, eulogising over the standards of the passenger accommodation.

Themistocles was driven by twin propellers, powered by two quadruple-expansion, steam reciprocating engines to give her a service speed of 14 knots, with the capability of 15 knots if required. Steam was delivered at 215psi from three double-ended and one single-ended coal fired boilers. Coal consumption was around 100 tons per day with bunker capacity of some 2,600 tons.[25]

In the issue of 4 November 1910, the Melbourne *Argus* announced that the owners of the Aberdeen Line had decided to install Marconi wireless apparatus in all their steamers with the exception of **Salamis**. The vessels were also to be equipped with submarine signalling apparatus.

With **Themistocles'** commissioning, **Salamis** was taken out of service in January 1911 after a successful twelve-year working life spanning twenty-seven round voyages to Australia, which had included her trooping charter to China with the New South Wales and Victorian Naval Brigades embarked in 1900. The relatively short life of the vessel no doubt reflected her small size and premature obsolescence in a rapidly changing Australian trade requirement.

Themistocles.
(*Ships in Focus*, A. Duncan Collection)

Following a year in lay-up in East India Dock, she was sold for about £20,000 to the Bank Line on 21 January 1912 for that company's India–South Africa Line; her name remained unchanged. Bank Line sold her to Canada Steamship Lines of Montreal in 1919, who renamed her *Kamarima*, and she was broken in Trieste in 1924.

Following a successful maiden outwards passage achieved in record time for a Cape-running steamer of thirty-six days, London to Melbourne, *Themistocles* carried back to the United Kingdom some of the contingents who would be representing Australia at the coronation of King George V; these included 183 army cadets from NSW under the command of a Major Wynne. Before embarkation, they were addressed by the NSW State Commandant, General Gordon, reminding them that they carried the honour of their country with them:

> You are embarking upon a serious enterprise. You are all of that age when your characters will be formed for life. You are embarking upon a good ship under a good captain, who has had large experience of taking troops to the Sudan, China and elsewhere; and let me tell you that while nobody will have your interests at heart more than Captain Douglas, he will demand the strictest discipline and obedience to his orders. You are going home as representatives of this country, which is the first portion of the Empire to inaugurate the system of compulsory service. Every eye will be upon you and your every action will be watched. I want you to be an example to the rest of the Empire. Possibly, as they see through you, how national life is being developed in Australia, other portions of the Empire will take the lesson to heart and follow our example. You have, first of all the honour of Australia to uphold, then that of your own families, and finally your own honour.[26]

Themistocles pulled off Dalgety's Wharf at 1600 hours, 21 April 1911, with bands playing, to resounding cheers for the King, Australia and the cadets. The ship was cheered down the harbour from various promontories. En route home, the cadets were entertained at Hobart, and at Durban, where they were taken by special train to the Boer War battlefields.

Upon her return to the United Kingdom, *Themistocles* was chartered by the Admiralty to participate in the Coronation Spithead review. *Themistocles*, wearing masthead Blue Ensigns as befitted Captain Douglas' Royal Naval Reserve status, formed one of the escort of merchant ships with dignitaries embarked, which followed the Royal Yacht *Victoria and Albert* through the lines of British and foreign warships anchored at Spithead on 24 June 1911. A depiction by the artist Freer of *Themistocles* steaming past at the Coronation Spithead Review is incorporated in the colour section. The escorting merchant ships were:

Soudan	(P&O)	Admiralty and press
Eskimo	(Wilson Line)	House of Commons
Rewa	(British India)	House of Commons
Rohilla	(British India)	House of Lords
Themistocles	(Aberdeen Line)	Miscellaneous personages
Ascania	(Cunard Line)	Miscellaneous personages
Mongolia	(P&O)	Indian princes and visitors
Dongola	(P&O)	Colonial premiers and visitors
Plassy	(P&O)	Special envoys

A snap strike by seamen serving in Southampton-based liners, concurrent with a strike by Southampton coal lumpers, precluded such lines as the Union Castle, White Star and Royal Mail from participating in the Coronation Review, and probably explains the heavy presence of P&O and the BI amongst the escorting ships (though these companies had close connections with the Admiralty through their seasonal trooping charters)

Themistocles' near sister vessel, *Demosthenes*, was launched from Harland and Wolff on 28 February 1911, her construction having been expedited to fill the gap left by the demise of *Pericles*, and she sailed from London on her maiden voyage to Australia via the Cape on 31 August that year. With a gross tonnage of 11,233, her dimensions were identical to *Themistocles*, but she differed in her propulsion configuration in that she was triple screw, the wing propellers being driven by triple-expansion reciprocating engines built by Harland and Wolff, while a centre propeller was driven by a low-pressure turbine built by Brown. This combination delivered the same 6,000ihp at the same service and maximum speeds, and it would seem that the change of engine configuration was a live experiment, possibly induced by Harland and Wolff's Pirie, into propulsion efficiency, when compared with the otherwise identical *Themistocles*.

On 20 October 1911, the cargo passenger liner *Gothic*, 7,750grt, was taken on a four-voyage charter from White Star, to facilitate the progressive withdrawal from service for lengthening of *Marathon*

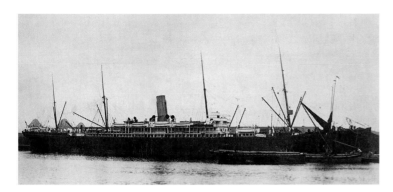

White Star's *Gothic*; chartered while *Marathon* and *Miltiades* were lengthened. (National Library of Australia Vic H25808)

and *Miltiades*. Originally built for White Star's joint service with Shaw Savill to New Zealand in 1893, *Gothic* had proved to be a very popular ship in that trade. However, homewards bound in 1906, a serious fire in her wool cargo had necessitated beaching and hold flooding in the Cattewater, Plymouth, to extinguish the fire. Refloated, but seriously damaged, she was sent to Harland and Wolff, Belfast, where her fire-damaged first-class accommodation was removed, and she was converted to an emigrant carrier. Renamed *Gothland*, she re-entered service on the Atlantic emigrant trade for the IMM subsidiary, Red Star Line, under the Belgian flag. In 1911, she reverted within the IMM group back to White Star under the British flag and her old name for the duration of her two-year Aberdeen Line charter. She again reverted to Red Star Line under the name *Gothland*, in 1913, remaining in that service through severe damage following a grounding off the Scilly Islands in 1914, until withdrawn from service in 1925 and sold for scrapping in 1926.

Marathon, following her twenty-second voyage to Australia, was withdrawn from service and returned to her builders, Alexander Stephen and Sons, on the Clyde on 3 July 1912, to be lengthened by 49ft 10in. The rationale for lengthening the two sisters would seem to have been an economic compromise between building new vessels that were fully compatible with the emerging requirements of the trade or continuing with two relatively modern ships that were prematurely obsolete by virtue of diminished carrying capacity. The lengthening, which involved the addition of a new hold between the bridge and the engine room, gave each ship an additional 83,000 cu.ft of cargo space, equivalent to an additional deadweight

of 1,200 tons; accommodation was also created for thirty additional first-class passengers and forty additional steerage passengers, together with extended external promenade decks.

With the vessel in dry-dock, the process of lengthening commenced with cutting the ship in two immediately forward of the engine casing by 'unstitching' the riveted seams and laps, following the plates in a rough line across the vessel, riveters and caulkers being used to hand cut each rivet – ⅞in diameter in most locations but 1in diameter in the sheer strake and 1¼in diameter in the flat bar keel. The frictional bond between plate laps and seams was relieved by hammering. While the cutting progressed, substantial standing and sliding ways were built under the forward half of the vessel, and a cradle was erected under the forefoot. Heavy palms were attached to each side of the forepart of the vessel in way of the main sheer to take the tackles that would be used to haul the forward half away from the standing part the required distance. Four 20-ton hydraulic jacks were interspersed on either side between the standing and moving halves of the vessel to assist in securing initial movement, and with the ways greased, two triple purchase wire tackles were led to 10-ton hydraulic capstans on either side of the dock entrance to provide the primary motive power.

The job of moving the 2,400-ton forward half of the vessel the required 49ft 10in occupied about five hours, including a meal break, and was executed without a hitch. Once separated the required

Marathon in dock at Alexander Stephen, Linthouse, prior to cutting. (*Shipbuilder* Vol. 7 No: 28, 1912)

Marathon cut – two halves drawn apart.

Marathon cut – cross section looking aft.

distance, the building of a new ship section between the two halves was routine, accompanied by equally routine, almost mandatory, Clydeside labour disputes, which delayed the recommissioning of the two vessels by a month.

No modifications were made to the vessels' propulsion systems, but to balance their previously very elegant profiles, a second, dummy, funnel was added forward of the existing funnel. The resulting profile was pleasing, but the combination of an 'active' and 'dummy' funnel gave successive chief officers a headache in terms of balancing the shades of paintwork on the two funnels; the heated 'active' funnel changing shade relative to the dummy funnel rapidly after each repainting. A comparison of the before and after profiles is given in the colour section.

With underwater and main structural work on **Marathon** safely completed by 12 September 1910, she was floated out of dock, and her place was taken by **Miltiades**, which had been waiting by for a week. Once **Miltiades** had been cut in half, a labour dispute cost more than a month's operational time, and the work was finally completed on a piecework basis pending resolution of the dispute. After trials, **Marathon** re-entered service on the 18 October 1912, with **Miltiades** following on 24 April 1913. The lengthening process, while commonplace in the halcyon days of conventional liner shipping, was at the time in 1912, sufficiently unusual to warrant a six-page

Marathon after lengthening; the chief officer's dilemma – only one funnel heating! (National Library of Australia)

article in *The Shipbuilder* periodical.[27] Once both vessels had been returned to service, the **Gothic** was released from charter.

Gathering storm clouds in Europe increasingly threatened the stability of the region. The emergence of German nationalism, its military, industrial and colonial expansion, and in particular the build-up of the German Navy, threatened the balance of power and Britain's superiority at sea. Against this background, Winston Churchill as First Lord of the Admiralty, announced to Parliament on 26 March 1913, that:

> the Admiralty had called upon shipowners to arm a number of first class liners for protection against danger menaced in certain cases by fast auxiliary cruisers of other powers; the liners were not however to assume the character of auxiliary cruisers themselves. The Government desired to place at the disposal of the shipowners the necessary guns, sufficient ammunition and suitable personnel for the training of the gun crews.

Churchill was at pains to emphasise the defensive nature of the armament, and that no ships would be armed except those directly connected with the food supply of the United Kingdom. In parliamentary exchanges, Churchill pointed out that as the guns were mounted on the stern, they could only be used to fire upon a pursuer. Challenged as to what a defensively armed merchant ship would do if attacked on the bows, Churchill responded, in his most dignified manner, that he could not go into these complicated questions of tactics, but it might occur to the captain to turn his ship around …

Neither the Hague Convention of October 1907, nor the Declaration of London of February 1909, specifically forbade defensive armament for merchant ships, but the defensive arming of selected British merchant ships caused political problems around the world, especially in the United States of America (which *inter alia* controlled the Panama Canal Zone as a sovereign territory of the US). The programme went ahead, but the government had to offer indemnities to participating shipowners in the event of defensively armed merchant ships being detained or otherwise sanctioned against in foreign ports. Up to forty such ships were defensively armed before the onset of war.

On 29 July 1913, the Melbourne *Argus* reported that the Aberdeen liner *Themistocles* had arrived in Melbourne the day before with two 4.7in guns protruding somewhat menacingly over her stern. Each quick-firing Armstrong Whitworth gun, manufactured in the late nineteenth century and obsolete by naval standards, had been tested by the Admiralty before installation, and 'a specially selected 'gun crew' was in charge of the weapons.[28] *Themistocles* was the first ship under Churchill's Defensively Armed Merchant Ships programme to enter Australian waters.

Following completion of her thirty-seventh round voyage to Australia in February 1914, *Moravian*, the last of the original Napier-built Thompson steamers, was taken out of service and the ship was laid up pending sale. On 27 May 1914, she was sold to the Bombay and Persian Steam Navigation Company, a company jointly controlled by the British India Steam Navigation and the Asiatic Steam Navigation Companies, for about £20,000. Renamed *Akbar*, she was placed into the Bombay and Persian's seasonal pilgrim trade – the Haj – from India, Pakistan and Ceylon to Jeddah, and out of season, on that company's trade from India to the Red Sea and Persian Gulf, continuing in that service until she was scrapped in Genoa in 1923. The Bombay and Persian SN Co. became the Mogul Line in 1939 (not to be confused with Gellatly's Mogul Line of earlier mention, which had gone into voluntary liquidation in 1922), and was absorbed into the Shipping Corporation of India in 1963.

An order had been placed with Harland and Wolff in 1913 for a further new passenger cargo ship. To be named *Euripides*, the new vessel was launched on 29 January 1914 and was handed over to the Line on 6 June 1914. The new ship was a development of the *Demosthenes*, but with a gross registered tonnage of 14,947, significantly larger. Indeed, she was the largest ship ever to be built for the Aberdeen Line, and the second largest Eastern-trading liner of her time, only exceeded by White Star's new *Ceramic*, which had immediately preceded her

The new liner *Euripides*; the largest vessel to be built for the Aberdeen Line.

into service. *Euripides*' length overall was 569.7ft (50ft longer than *Demosthenes*), her breadth 67.4ft and depth of hold 44.1ft.

Her profile differed from the *Demosthenes*, with her bridge moved back to form part of the main superstructure block, four holds forward of the bridge, and three aft. An elongated forecastle incorporated No. 1 hold, while No. 4 was trunked through the centrecastle deck, which extended forward of the bridge. Her cargo-carrying capacity was large for the times, with 440,680 cu.ft of general and 248,000 cu.ft of refrigerated cargo space. The Nos 1, 2 and 3 holds were insulated for frozen cargo, while the upper and lower 'tween decks in No. 2 hold and all decks and the hold in No. 3 were fitted with trunked air delivery to facilitate the carriage of fruit or chilled beef.

Euripides' propulsion system followed the triple-screw configuration initiated in *Demosthenes*, with wing four-cylinder reciprocating engines and a low-pressure turbine driving the centre shaft giving a combined 7,500hp. Steam was provided by five double-ended boilers delivering steam at 215psi. While she had a fairly modest service speed of 15 knots, she achieved 17.8 knots, albeit in a light ship, on the delivery voyage to London via Cardiff, where she took on her 2,685 tons bunker capacity of high-grade coal.

Accommodation was provided for 140 first-class and 340 third-class passengers, although demountable accommodation in the 'tween decks enabled her to carry up to 1,100 emigrants. The safety of her enlarged emigrant complement was catered for by nested double lifeboats along the boatdeck and in way of the masthouse between Nos 3 and 4 holds, and aft at the break of the poop. The first-class accommodation was said to be extremely comfortable and spacious, without resort to unnecessary luxury.

Fitted with two 4.7in guns mounted aft from the outset, the highlight of her delivery voyage around the coast from Cardiff, with a coterie of guests hosted by the chairman, Harold Sanderson, was said to have been the firing of these guns. The story goes that the doyen of the press party embarked congratulated Sanderson on building such a magnificent ship when it must have to face so much competition from the railways …

Euripides took up her loading berth in London at Tilbury, precluded by her size from the company's usual berth in the Royal Albert Dock. Under the command of Captain Alexander H.H.G. Douglas RNR, she sailed from London for Melbourne via the Cape on her maiden voyage on 1 July 1914, with a crew of 230 and 963 passengers embarked, mostly emigrants to New South Wales.

Defensive armament; sailor and a soldier grouped around a 4.7in QF naval gun mounted on SS *Miltiades* in 1919. The same type of gun was mounted on *Euripides*. (National Library of Australia PIC/8847/1/63 Terry Collection)

In the years immediately preceding the First World War, George Thompson employed the services of a little-known marine artist, Henry Branston Freer, to produce a series of ship portraits for the company's advertising material, especially for reproduction on postcards for sale on board the company's vessels. Biographically, little is known of Freer; he was said to be a pupil of William Wyllie, and his paintings certainly bore a distinct semblance to his style. He lived in Rochester, Gravesend and Blackheath, and his paintings were largely reflective of the Thames estuary, the Downs and the Royal Docks. He produced a number of Aberdeen Line portraits, including *Marathon* and *Miltiades*, both before and subsequent to lengthening; *Themistocles* and *Demosthenes*, including a portrait of *Themistocles* at the 1911 Coronation Naval Review; and finally *Euripides*, following which his work for the Line stopped and subsequent portraits were undertaken by Jack Spurling. All the portraits that Freer executed for the Aberdeen Line had a mellow charm about them, reflective of an age before the horrors of war broke upon the world. A montage of postcard illustrations of Aberdeen Line ships by Henry Branston is incorporated in the colour section.

10

THE FIRST WORLD WAR AND AFTER − 1914 TO 1921

On 28 July 1914, Austria–Hungary invaded Serbia, precipitating the start of the First World War. Germany followed by invading Belgium, which had refused to give the German forces free passage en route to France, on 4 August 1914, bringing Great Britain into the war, honouring its treaty obligations to defend the neutrality of Belgium. Thus, by the time that **Euripides** docked at the Railway Jetty, Melbourne, on 9 August 1918, the British Empire was at war, a war in which Australia was to play a costly and valiant part.

Developments in Europe had been watched with the detachment of distance in Australia. The assassination of Grand Duke Franz Ferdinand in Sarajevo, Austria's declaration of war on Serbia, Germany's declaration of war on Russia and even Germany's declaration of war on France were all European affairs, reported in the Australian press, but matters that had little apparent bearing on the affairs of Empire. Few in Australia were aware of Britain's treaty obligations with Belgium and the significance of such. It accordingly came as a shock to the people of Australia when on 4 August the news was flashed to all the dominions that Britain, and thus the Empire, was at war with Germany. With dramatic speed, the Prime Minister of Australia replied to London that the Australian Fleet was absolutely at the disposal of the British Admiralty, and that Australia was anxious to send an Expeditionary Force of 20,000 men to any destination desired, the cost of dispatch and maintenance being borne by the Australian government.[1]

On 6 August 1914, the offer of an Australian Expeditionary Force was accepted and the Imperial government requested that it should be dispatched as soon as possible. The Australian Naval Board immediately appointed a committee to deal with the transportation challenge posed by shipping 20,000 men, and their horses, together with equipment, baggage and fodder 12,000 miles to the battle zone. In short order, a list was prepared of all merchant ships in Australian ports, or approaching Australia, and an assessment was made of their suitability/ease of conversion for the intended purposes. Ships were progressively requisitioned on war charter terms once they had discharged their outwards cargoes, with rates of hire to be decided by a special Admiralty Arbitration Court sitting in London. In effect, the vessels taken up from trade were time chartered by the Australian government, with the government paying for bunkers, and extraneous operating costs, while the owner's agents and loading brokers became effectively government agents charged with filling space not occupied by the military, the freight monies from such loadings being credited against the charter hire. Charter hire was in accordance with a scale eventually set out in the 'Blue Book' established by the British government in 1915, with recourse to the special Admiralty Arbitration Court.[2]

Having discharged at Melbourne, Sydney and Brisbane, **Euripides** was taken up from trade by the Australian government in Brisbane as a troop transport on 26 August 1914, at a charter rate of

Australian troops embarked upon HMAT A14, *Euripides.* (National Library of Australia. Australian War Memorial)

Australian troops embarking in HMAT *Euripides*.

Commander and officers, HMAT *Euripides*. (National Library of Australia. Australian War Memorial)

20s 6d per grt per month. The vessel had been built to Admiralty Trade Department requirements with just such a contingency in mind, and conversion to trooping was both anticipated and relatively easy to achieve. Designated 'His Majesty's Australian Transport' (HMAT) with Pennant No. A14, she was converted to accommodate 136 officers, 2,204 other ranks and 20 horses.[3] The 'tween deck spaces were fitted out to accommodate the troops, including the laying of timber sheathing over the steel decks to which tables and benches were secured, fittings for hammocks, additional galley facilities,

piping and pumping to facilitate the use of double bottom tanks for fresh water, storage for baggage, ammunition, food stores etc., and the installation of lighting in the troop decks. Additionally, portable stables had to be provided for the embarked horses, together with spaces for fodder. The vessel was ready to embark troops at Sydney by 18 September 1914.

Euripides was followed by *Miltiades* (A 28) on 27 September 1914, at Sydney, fitted for forty-two officers and 977 other ranks. *Miltiades*, the last of twenty-eight ships taken up from trade to form the first Australian convoy, was also chartered at a hire rate of 20s 6d per grt for an initial 3½ months. *Euripides* took on her complement of 2,269 troops and sixteen horses at Sydney, while *Miltiades* took on 656 personnel, mostly Imperial Reservists called back to the colours, at Sydney and a further 109 at Melbourne, before proceeding for the assembly of Convoy 1 in King George Sound, Albany.

Convoy 1 comprised three Australian divisions embarked in twenty-eight ships, and a New Zealand division in ten ships; the Australian ships retained their original commercial livery, but the New Zealand ships had been repainted in battleship grey from truck to boot-topping. The Australian fleet anchored in three lines off Albany, by division, orientated on Mount Clarence (Divisions 1 and 2) and Strawberry Hill (Division 3), with the New Zealand fleet anchored in two lines to the south-east of the main body of ships. The convoy flagship was the Orient liner *Orvieto* with the convoy commodore embarked, heading up the 1st Division; the 2nd Division was headed by the Bibby liner *Wiltshire*; while *Euripides*, by far the largest element in the convoy, with the Australian 1st Brigade embarked, headed up the 3rd Division.[4]

Detailed convoy naval orders were drawn up by the captain in charge of the convoy, Captain A. Gordon Smith RN. These *inter alia* detailed signalling procedures, station keeping, procedure on sighting the enemy, darkening of the ship, and use of wireless telegraphy. Apart from *Orvieto*, the only two ships permitted to transmit on wireless telegraphy were *Euripides* and *Wiltshire*; the other ships were to maintain wireless telegraphy listening watches. *Orvieto* was to be 'guide of the fleet', with other vessels conforming with her course and speed.[5]

Such a large fleet of ships taxed the limited resources of Albany, the work of the only three tugs available being further hampered by stormy weather conditions. As the convoy assembled, so the ships came in successively to the inner Princess Royal Harbour to take on coal bunkers from the deep water jetty or from coaling hulks, allowing the embarked troops to exercise ashore.

The assembled fleet would have been an impressive and very emotional sight. After the war, Albany was the venue for the first ANZAC Day dawn service, and each year from 1930, on ANZAC Day, a dawn service is held at the ANZAC Desert Mounted Corps Memorial on Mount Clarence overlooking the anchorage in King George Sound where the convoys assembled. I have myself stood at the Memorial overlooking the sound – a truly moving experience.

The destination of the first convoy was initially Europe via Suez, the route changing to via South Africa, where it was planned that the troops would be available to quell latent Boer unrest if required; however, on 30 October 1914, shortly before the convoy's intended departure, Turkey entered the war on the side of Germany and the convoy's destination was changed to Egypt.[6] At 0600 hours, 1 November 1914, the first division of nine ships raised anchor and put to sea, followed at half-hour intervals by the other two Australian divisions, uplifting in all 21,529 Australian troops, with the New Zealand division uplifting a further 8,427 troops, bringing up the rear. *Euripides* took up her position as lead ship of the right-hand column of ships; *Miltiades* brought up the rear of the same column. Once assembled in convoy formations off Albany, the first Australian and New Zealand convoy took passage for Egypt, where the troops would disembark for training prior to engagement in the Gallipoli campaign. For far too many, this would be the last sight they would have of Australia.

The departure of the convoy from Albany, originally planned for 22 September 1914, was delayed by concerns for the adequacy of the escort. The New Zealand government had gone as far as threatening to resign if adequate cover for the New Zealand division was not provided. In the outcome, Convoy 1 was escorted from 6 miles ahead by the heavy cruiser HMS *Minotaur*; on the right flank by the Japanese battle cruiser HIJMS *Ibuki* and on the left flank by the light cruiser HMAS *Sydney*; while 4 miles astern was the light cruiser HMAS *Melbourne*. The Japanese ship, which had earlier escorted the New Zealand sub-convoy across the Tasman Sea with HMS *Minotaur*, in fact joined the main body of the convoy a couple of days after the convoy had departed from Albany, having been detached to escort two ships out of Fremantle, where she had taken on additional coal bunkers from the hulk of the former Aberdeen Line clipper, *Samuel Plimsoll*.

The threat facing the first and subsequent convoys was not submarines; the Germans were not thought to have any operating east of Suez. Rather, the very real threat came from surface raiders and in particular the light cruiser SMS *Emden*, which was known to be operating in East Indies and possibly Australasian waters. Commanded by the brilliant Commander Karl von Müller, SMS *Emden* had enjoyed a highly successful war thusfar. An element of Von Spee's German East Asia Squadron, she had been detached as a commerce raider to harass allied shipping on the East Indies and Australasian routes while the main body of the squadron under Von Spee had headed for South America and the battles of Coronel and the Falklands. Over the course of two months of independent operation, supported by excellent intelligence, SMS *Emden* had held up twenty-one British merchantmen, sinking sixteen; abducted four colliers; shelled the Burmah Oil depot at Madras, causing a huge fire; and made an audacious hit-and-run raid on Penang, wherein she had sunk a Russian light cruiser and a French destroyer.

The former Aberdeen Line clipper, *Samuel Plimsoll*, reduced to a coaling hulk in Fremantle Harbour. (National Library of Australia – State Library of WA)

Now, in an attempt to frustrate communications between Australia and the United Kingdom, and thereby the search for his ship, Müller landed a raiding party on Direction Island in the Cocos (Keeling) group on the night of 8 November 1914, with orders to destroy the Eastern Extension, Australasia and China Telegraph Company's wireless and cable station located thereon. The cable station managed to transmit an SOS message naming the *Emden* before it was overrun. The message was intercepted by Convoy 1, steaming north close by at 9½ knots, and HMAS *Sydney* under the command of Captain John Glossop RN was detached to engage the *Emden*, which she did at 0915 hours on 9 November 1914.

In the ensuing battle, HMAS *Sydney*'s superior gun range was decisive, *Emden* was crippled and run ashore on North Keeling Island; HMAS *Sydney* then detached to sink the *Emden*'s attendant collier, *Buresk*. Von Müller surrendered to Glossop the following day, but only after an apparent disregard for HMAS *Sydney*'s signal to surrender had led to a brief but heavy shelling of the crippled ship with attendant large loss of life. Von Müller tendered his sword in surrender; Glossop chivalrously refused to accept it. *Emden*'s landing party under First Officer Hellmuth von Mücke commandeered an island schooner and, in an epic voyage to the Red Sea, finally made good their escape to Constantinople by 23 May 1915. HMAS *Sydney* caught up with Convoy 1 at Colombo on 15 November 1914. At the specific request of Glossop, out of sensitivity for the heavy loss of life in SMS *Emden*, HMAS *Sydney* was not cheered into harbour; but the troops embarked upon all the troopships were given a half-day's holiday as a mark of celebration of Australia's first major naval victory.[7] *Euripides*, along with two other transports, took on *Emden* survivors for transportation to eventual imprisonment in Malta.

The crowded conditions for the embarked troops were far from pleasant, especially as the convoy passed through the tropics. *Euripides*' troops had suffered an outbreak of influenza, impacting 160 men at Albany, and on passage pneumonia struck, with two soldiers dying. While embarked, the troops went through a daily routine of drills and lectures; when the convoy arrived at Colombo, not without some cause, the Australian troops did themselves and their country little credit by their behaviour ashore.

Euripides, along with the other ships of the first convoy, disembarked her first contingent of Australian troops at Suez and Alexandria, where the troops went into intensive training in the desert to acclimatise them for the crags and ravines of the forthcoming Gallipoli campaign. *Miltiades*, with Imperial Reservists embarked, went on unescorted to Plymouth.

Following disembarkation of troops at Alexandria on her second trooping voyage, *Euripides* proceeded to the UK via Malta, and embarked troops of the Herefordshire Regiment for the Gallipoli theatre at Devonport on 16 July 1915. On 7 August 1915, at around 0600 hours, upon arrival off Mudros Harbour on the western side of the Greek island of Lemnos, the advanced staging port for the Gallipoli campaign, she grounded on the edge of the reef. *Euripides* apparently suffered only superficial damage, but all personnel had to be transferred to other ships, mostly to the *Snaefell*. (Mudros was later to be the location for the signing of the armistice between Britain and Turkey on 30 October 1918.)

Thompson's other ships were progressively requisitioned by Australia upon arrival there and continued in more or less continuous service under requisition until 1917:

Themistocles (A 32) taken up in December 1914;
Demosthenes (A 64) taken up in July 1915; and,
Marathon (A74)   taken up in May 1916.

Marathon was the last British ship so-requisitioned by Australia; she had earlier been taken up by the UK government as an Expeditionary Force Transport from 30 July 1915. In all, thirty-five convoys left Australia under Australian control in the period up to November 1917. Thereafter a further six ad hoc Australian convoys using Liner Requisition Scheme ships sailed from Australia up to mid-1918. The five ships of Thompson's Aberdeen Line made twenty-seven Australian-controlled convoy sailings carrying troops, horses and equipment to the European and Middle East battlegrounds. The ships taken up from trade by Australia served not only to move troops and military stores from Australia to Europe but also to carry Australian produce to Britain and France, vital to maintain the Australian economy. A committee of agents in Australia was charged with filling all spaces not required for military purposes on the homewards run, all net freights received for such cargo being submitted to an Arbitration Court as a credit against the amount paid as charter hire. Outward bound between Australian trooping sailings, Thompson's vessels participated in the company's outwards sailings to Australia from the UK, albeit under charter to the Australian government with freights credited against charter hire. They also undertook short sub-charters as required to the Imperial government.

The 'Blue Book', which covered government charter and freight rates, was based upon rates prevailing in the years immediately preceding the outbreak of war. In the case of charter hire rates, these were said to be struck to provide a return on capital of between 6 and 7 per cent and depreciation of 6.5 per cent. With the immediate scarcity of tonnage arising from losses to U-boat activity and the need for war materiel movements, rates on the free market soared, leaving those owners pinned to government requisition rates at a significant financial disadvantage; Thompson was one such owner, with all five ships eventually subject to government requisition.

At a meeting in London in March 1915 between the Imperial Director of Transports and Ship-owners' Representatives, attended by the Commonwealth shipping representative, a case was advanced for improved rates for the Australian requisitioned ships over Blue Book scales. The arguments advanced included:

- The ships were fitted out in Australia instead of being fitted out in the UK and sent out from England, the Commonwealth thereby gaining to the extent of half a voyage

- The ships had all been engaged upon very remunerative work, which requisition had interrupted; cargo was carried on the transports, the freights from which were credited to the government; this might impinge upon commerce

- The ships requisitioned were generally of a very high standard; passenger liners, refrigerated liners, fast cargo liners, etc.

Three shillings per ton was proposed above Blue Book rates; in the outcome, the rate of hire payable by the Commonwealth ranged from 15s 9d to 19s 6d, with only six ships exceeding 20s per ton, including the five Aberdeen Line ships at 20s 6d per ton.[8] This rate was reduced to 17s 0d per ton from September 1915.

With the main-line ships periodically at least committed to Australian trooping requirements, the Aberdeen Line, under the direction of George Thompson Henderson, somewhat quaintly referred to as 'the Secretary', supported by his brother, Alexander Duff Henderson and cousins Stephen Thompson and Oscar Stephen Thompson, strove to maintain monthly sailings to Australia. For this it often used chartered-in vessels, mainly sourced from George Thompson's parent shareholders. Sailings continued to be advertised to Melbourne, Sydney and Brisbane, but increasingly outwards sailings were designated 'On Government Service'; thus in 1915, only six sailings seem to have been under the direct control of the Line; in 1916 and 1917, this reduced to five sailings; and in 1918, four, though the London office acted as loading brokers for the government-chartered ships. The various owned and chartered ships continued to maintain individual identifying voyage numbers, whether under requisition or company service.

An interesting aside to the main theme of the war effort as it applied to Thompson was the sinking of the Aberdeen Line's first two steamers, *Aberdeen* and *Australasian*, then under the hostile Turkish flag, supporting that country's defence of the Gallipoli peninsula. In 1915, British E-class submarines were conducting an extremely heroic 'private' war against the Turks in the Sea of Marmara, harassing the Turkish supply lines to the Gallipoli front. The exploits of these E-boats are chronicled in the book *Dardanelles Patrol* by Peter Shankland. The submarine E-11 under the command of Commander Dunbar Naysmith VC RN, entered through the boom defences and minefields guarding the entrance of the Dardanelles on the morning of 4 August 1915, and after sinking a Turkish transport and avoiding a gunboat, settled to the seabed for the night. On the morning of 5 August, E-11 came across a number of enemy ships off Akbas-Liman, including the three-masted, clipper-bowed steamer *Halep* (formerly the Aberdeen Line's first steamer *Aberdeen*). A torpedo from E-11 struck the *Halep* on the starboard side below the mainmast, causing her to sink in shallow water. According to Turkish naval archives, she was refloated the next day and returned into service [This seems improbable!].

On 25 August 1918, the transport *Scham* (formerly the Aberdeen Line's second steamer *Australasian*) was damaged by a torpedo from E-11, beached and later towed to Istanbul. In 1923, ▶

the *Scham* was towed to Izmit and used as a coaling hulk for a new naval base under construction at Gölcük. She was finally broken at Savona, Italy, in 1955.

The *Halep* was apparently again damaged by E-11 on 28 August 1915 off Akbas, beached, and scrapped where she lay in 1920.[9]

Halep in a sunken state. (Turkish naval archives)

Scham in a salvaged state. (Turkish naval archives)

Tonnage losses to submarine warfare had, by February 1917, led to a crisis situation whereby action had to be taken on the home front to ensure the continuity of supplies; one of the devices used to optimise tonnage availability was the diversion of vessels usually serving long-haul routes on to shorter hauls. The UK Liner Requisition Scheme came into effect, whereby most liner tonnage came under the direct control of the Imperial Shipping Controller of the Ministry of Shipping, the scheme being administered by a committee of shipowners; initially, ships previously requisitioned by the Australian government were specifically excluded from the scheme, but in short order, these were also taken over by the Imperial government. Arrangements were made with the Australian government in respect to redelivery and refurbishment costs. Ships were progressively taken over under the scheme upon completion of inwards cargoes in the UK. The first such vessel to be taken over from Australian requisition was Thompson's *Euripides* on 2 June 1917.[10]

In effect, ships requisitioned under the Liner Requisition Scheme were chartered by the UK government under Charter Party T.99 terms. It was the intention that the vessels would generally stay on the trades for which they had been built, managed by their owning companies, but the government had the sanction to place them where the national need dictated. This was particularly the case with passenger vessels needed for trooping. Charter rates and incidental costs were enshrined in the Blue Book, subject to appeal to a special Arbitration Court. In the case of the five Aberdeen Line ships, transferred to the Liner Requisition Scheme between June and November 1917, the monthly charter hire was 17s per gross revenue ton. In the case of *Euripides* this would have yielded £12,679.45 per month plus an allowance for refrigerated capacity of £368 5s per month;[11] under Australian requisition her earnings had been 20s 6d. per grt, or £15,694.35 per month.[12] Where Australian troops were now carried, the Australian government was charged per capita passage money, £40 for officers, £22 for NCOs and £17 for other ranks.[13]

With the progression of the war in Europe, the need to concentrate available shipping resources on the support of Britain and France by way of shorter-haul supply routes impacted increasingly severely upon the Australian economy. By 1916, 2 million tons of Australian wheat were waiting to be transported to markets on the other side of the world, with little prospect of shipping bottoms being

Euripides with a paravane minesweeping boom on her starboard bow. (This is curious, given that she is flying two house flags at the main and is apparently in peacetime livery. The flying of two house flags – White Star and Aberdeen did not come into effect until 1926). (National Library of Australia Vic H91.250/1685)

available. Indicative of the problem of tonnage supply to serve Australia, available overseas tonnage had shrunk from around 2 million tons pre-war to 880,000 tons towards the end of the war.

As early as 1906, a Royal Commission established by the then Australian Labour government had recommended the establishment of a federally owned and operated deep-sea fleet. The commission stated: 'The isolated position of Australia, and the many leagues of ocean which separate us from other countries, render the carriage of mails and perishable produce to distant markets a question of paramount importance.' Reflecting Australian paranoia at the perceived control over exports exercised by the British Shipping Ring, the report concluded that the establishment of a federally owned shipping entity would 'check any exorbitant charges which might be made by private carrying companies.[14]

The 1914 speech from the throne to the Australian parliament had included the incorporation of a state-owned shipping line as soon as possible, but nothing had been done in the interim to act upon the commission's recommendations; with the exigencies of war impacting upon the Australian economy and a Labour government in power, interest was accelerated.

Desperate to alleviate the situation created by the progressive withdrawal of an estimated 252,000 tons of shipping from the Australian trade to support the European war effort, twelve German-owned ships interned in Australian waters at the outbreak of war were pressed into service under the Australian flag. Then in March 1916 the Australian Prime Minister, William Morris Hughes, travelled to London to plead the case for more tonnage to serve Australia with the British Prime Minister, Herbert Asquith. Hughes had succeeded as Australian Prime Minister in 1915, when Andrew Fisher had resigned from the post. Following his resignation, Fisher had been posted to London as Australian High Commissioner, and in him, Hughes found an able co-conspirator.

Hughes was received courteously by Asquith, but to no avail. He was successively passed down to Walter Runciman, the President of the Board of Trade, to Sir Joseph Maclay, Director of Shipping, and finally to the committee of shipowners. Hughes was sympathetically received on each occasion, but the net outcome of his pleas for an increased share of the available tonnage to serve the Australian need was a flat 'impossible'. The feisty Hughes is reported to have left the meeting with the committee of shipowners with the comment: 'Nothing is impossible in times of war, and if you won't help me, I'll help myself.'[15]

With the active collusion of High Commissioner Fisher, in what appears to have been a well-planned pre-emptive strike, Hughes, in great secrecy, set about purchasing twenty-five ships through the intervention of a shipbroker introduced by Fisher. The ships were all under charter to the British government, but cancellation clauses in their charter parties provided a let-out in the event of change of ownership. When news of the sales broke, the British government was furious, and pressure on owners led to the sale of ten of the prospective ships falling through; however the sales of the balance of fifteen vessels had progressed to the point of being irreversible. Walter Runciman, the president of the Board of Trade, threatened to have each ship requisitioned when next it touched Britain, but quieter judgement prevailed from Asquith, who accepted an assurance from Hughes that no further such activity would occur.

Ten of the ships purchased were owned by one-ship companies under the control of Scottish tramp shipowner William Burrell. Burrell had a penchant for investing heavily in modern, technically advanced ships at the bottom of the market and selling them off on the top. In 1905, from a position of owning no ships, he had invested in the construction of thirty-two new ones, thirty on the Clyde, where shipbuilding was in deep recession. The ships were built to a standard design, 376ft length overall × 52.2ft beam × 25.5ft depth, with a gross tonnage of 4,400 and powered by triple-expansion steam engines. The prices Burrell paid for the ships, between £40,500 and £42,500 each, often did not cover construction costs. Now, Burrell sold ten of his 'Strath'-ships for around £145,000 each to Hughes.[16]

Hughes did not have Australian government approval for the expenditure of the £2,047,000 needed for the acquisition of the fifteen ships, nor technically did he have to have such approval. Under the War Precautions Act of 1914, as Prime Minister he could commit the Commonwealth to expenditure necessary for the war effort, and thereby he could requisition the funds necessary to purchase the fifteen ships, in cash, from the Commonwealth Bank. The fifteen ships were renamed with the prefix Austral-.[17] The Commonwealth Government Line of Steamers got its ships – and Glasgow would get its art gallery.

Standard-built *Australrange* purchased from Burrell by Hughes for the Australian Government Line in 1916. (National Library of Australia NSW PXE 722/343)

The activities of Hughes and his Australian Commonwealth Government Line would have had little immediate impact upon Thompson's Aberdeen Line, whose ships were running under government charters, and whose cargoes in peace time were essentially liner cargoes, as opposed to the tramp cargoes for which the Australian ships were suited. Had the Commonwealth Government Line's life been limited to a wartime contingency, as the purchase of the ships had been brokered to an astonished Australian government, they would have been disposed of when hostilities ceased and normal trading patterns returned; under such circumstances Thompsons would have had nothing to worry about. However, as time would prove, this was not to be.

By mid-1916, the war was not going well for the Central Powers led by Germany. The Western Front was bogged down, and the British naval blockade of Germany had led to severe food shortages in that country. The German Navy had long advocated unrestricted submarine warfare on allied merchant ships as a means of forcing a conclusion to the war on terms favourable to Germany. From time to time thusfar during the war, effectively unrestricted submarine warfare had been conducted within UK home waters, but Kaiser Wilhelm II was opposed to the general use of such a weapon, preferring moderation instead.

Following the outright rejection by Britain of German peace overtures in December 1916, Admiral Henning von Holtzendorff, Chief of the Admiralty Staff of the Imperial German Navy, addressed a memorandum to the Royal Field Marshall (the Kaiser) and to the army chiefs of staff, again advocating the use of unrestricted submarine warfare against British merchant shipping as a means of defeating Britain or at least driving its enemy to the negotiating table. The Holtzendorff Memorandum, dated 22 December 1916, identified from the outset that the British backbone, which needed to be broken for German victory, lay in its merchant tonnage, delivering as it did essential imports necessary for the country's survival. The memorandum argued that:

- France and Italy were effectively worn out; only the vigour of Britain sustained the war;

- There had been a disastrous cereal crop in 1916, leading to a severe shortage of supply from the USA and Canada, necessitating long-haul supply chains from Australia and Argentina;

- The British merchant marine was already stretched to the limit, unrestricted submarine warfare would further reduce it within six months by an estimated 39 per cent;

- Neutral support for the supply chain would wane in the face of unrestricted submarine warfare, further reducing essential supplies to Britain; and,

- Timing of the commencement of unrestricted submarine warfare was critical – the impact must be felt before next year's harvest alleviated the food situation.

Holtzendorff recognised that the implementation of unrestricted submarine warfare might well precipitate the USA's joining the war on the Allied side, but argued that the impact would be too swift for America to mobilise sufficient war effort to meaningfully change the tide of the conflict on the Western front.

The Holtzendorff Memorandum was considered by the German Chiefs of Staff meeting at the castle of Prince Pless on 8 January 1917, prior to which the Kaiser had been pressured into agreeing to the principle of unrestricted submarine warfare. A declaration of intent to commence was made on 9 January, and the threat was carried into effect on 1 February 1917, despite intense US diplomatic pressure.

With increased merchant ship losses attributed to the resumption of unrestricted U-boat warfare, every effort was made to restrict the impact of the U-boat and surface raider. The adoption of dazzle camouflage, originally advocated by scientist John Kerr in 1914, but actively progressed by a team led by the distinguished artist, Lieutenant Commander Norman Wilkinson RNVR in 1917, impacted more than 400 British merchant ships, including Thompson's five ships engaged on trooping duties. The concept of dazzle camouflage, whereby vessels were painted overall in bold patterns of blue, green, white and black, sought not to render the vessels invisible, but to confuse the sighting enemy as to the target vessel's aspect and speed.

The USA, with a large German immigrant population, and weary of wars with Spain and Mexico, was opposed to entering into what was seen as a European war, even though 159 US citizens had died in the *Lusitania* outrage on 7 May 1915. With the implementation of unrestricted submarine warfare, by 21 March 1917, seven US-flag neutral ships had fallen victim to U-boats, bringing America closer to war, but the final straw was the interception by Britain of the infamous 'Zimmerman cable'.

Anticipating that the resumption of unrestricted U-boat warfare on 1 February 1917 would draw the neutral USA into the

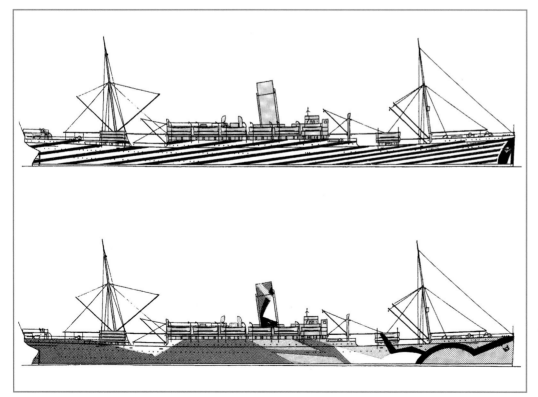

Euripides; two phases of dazzle camouflage.

war on the side of the Allies, the Foreign Secretary of the German Empire, Arthur Zimmerman, cabled the German ambassador in Mexico, Heinrich von Eckardt, instructing him that if the USA appeared likely join in, he was to approach the Mexican government with a proposal for a military alliance, with funding from Germany. By way of reward for collusion, Mexico was promised territories in Texas, New Mexico and Arizona. Eckardt was also instructed to urge Mexico to help broker an alliance between Germany and the Japanese Empire. The telegram, which was forwarded in code on 16 January 1917, was routed via the German ambassador in the USA using secure US diplomatic cable facilities to which the Germans had access. In the outcome, Mexico, unable to match the US military, ignored the proposal and (after the US entered the war), officially rejected it.

The cable, which amazingly was routed through a cable relay station at Land's End in the UK, was intercepted by Room 40, the code-breaking arm of UK naval intelligence under Admiral Reginald 'Blinker' Hall, Director of Naval Intelligence. The British were careful to avoid alerting the US to the fact that British intelligence was intercepting US diplomatic traffic, and an elaborate cover was developed to break the news to the Americans. Initially, the Americans believed the cable was an elaborate British hoax aimed at encouraging the USA to join the war, but gradually, reality dawned and President Woodrow Wilson, who had long been in favour of America joining on the side of the Triple Entente, was given the ammunition he needed to make the commitment. On 2 April 1917, Wilson asked Congress to enter the war against Germany.

On 6 April 1917, the USA finally joined Britain and France in the '1917–1918 War'. An early manifestation of the changed US status was the first transit of the previously neutral US-military controlled Panama Canal by an ANZAC troop convoy in August 1917; Convoy 33 was led by *Themistocles* in company with *Miltiades*. The last Australian troopship convoy using directly requisitioned ships, Convoy 35 in October 1917, included the Aberdeen Line vessels *Euripides* and *Demosthenes*,[18] albeit they were no longer under direct Australian requisition.

At the time of entering the war, the USA had only a relatively small standing army, whose fighting experience had been limited to the war with Mexico. Responding to desperate British calls for support to shore up the Western Front, the USA embarked upon the truly remarkable feat of training a large army, effectively drawn from reserve and conscript sources, and mobilising such from all parts of the country to the east coast embarkation points of New York, Newport News, Halifax and Montreal. A key element in the success of this operation was the skilful utilisation of the US railway system and brilliant logistics planning.

America also entered the war with a relatively small mercantile marine and military transportation fleet, unsuited for large-scale transatlantic trooping duties. There were, however, 104 German ships interned in US ports, including twenty large, top-class passenger ships of Norddeutscher Lloyd and Hamburg Amerikanische Paketfahrt Aktien Gessellschaft (HAPAG). These vessels were immediately seized as they lay at Boston, New York, Newport News, Philadelphia and Cebu in the Philippines, with a view to pressing them into service as troopships. The German crews had been prior-ordered to sabotage the engines of these ships in accordance with an agreed schedule, the order being passed through the German ambassador in Washington. Holtzendorff had anticipated this action in his memorandum; what he had not anticipated was the speed of American action to undo the damage.[19]

With one exception, the liners were steam reciprocating engine-propelled; the crews had broken the engines' cylinders and castings along with causing some damage to boilers. By any normal standards, repairs to classification and thereby insurance requirements would have involved wholesale mobilisation of new parts or re-engining, a prolonged process occupying at least a couple of years in German strategic thinking; the Americans did not have the luxury of time. The US Navy, unbridled by considerations of classification or insurance, embarked upon a hitherto undreamt of solution – repair of the damaged cast-iron machinery elements by electric arc welding. Within six months, all the damaged ships were back in service.[20]

Another vital German asset seized by America upon that country's entry into the war were the dedicated berths of the Norddeutscher Lloyd and Hamburg-Amerikca Lines at Hoboken on the Hudson River, New Jersey, across the North River from Manhattan Island. These facilities, together with the offices of the two lines, were pressed into service as the focus of embarkation for the US troops for France. The first American troopships sailed for war from Hoboken on 14 June 1917, with the fully assembled convoy leaving US waters three days later.[21]

The first Aberdeen Line ship to be diverted to support the US troop uplift was *Demosthenes*, which undertook a single voyage in

June 1917, concurrent with the first US convoy. The remainder of the fleet continued for the time being to serve Australia under the Liner Requisition Scheme throughout 1917.

However, the German spring offensive in 1918, which was aimed at finally breaking the British and French lines leading to either Allied defeat or a negotiated peace, had led to the exhaustion of the British and French armies at a ruinous rate; the support of America on the front line was needed urgently. The US transport fleet had grown to significant proportions in short order, but was no way near to being of sufficient capacity to match the sudden surge in demand. Britain agreed to provide immediate transport for six divisions if America could provide the troops – a feat of manpower and logistics. America did so provide, and by 1 May 1918, eight divisions had been transported to France; in May there were a further nine divisions, in June seven, and in July 1918, six divisions.[22]

To service this demand, every available passenger ship was thrown at the Atlantic bridge. From January 1918, all five Aberdeen Line ships were diverted to transatlantic troop movements, primarily departing from Liverpool, embarking troops in America and latterly from Canada. This concentrated transatlantic trooping duty by Thompson's ships continued until a final voyage departing St Nazaire to America by *Euripides* in early November 1918. Thereafter, with the war effectively won, the ships reverted under the Liner Requisition Scheme to the Australian service, the first ship back on the line being *Marathon*, departing for Melbourne and Sydney in mid-October 1918.

In a speech on 18 January 1918, President Wilson had set out Fourteen Points, based on a premise that the First World War was being fought for a moral cause and for post-war peace in Europe. His Fourteen Points called for free trade, open agreements, democracy and self-determination as the basis for a new world order. While broadly welcomed by the masses, the war-weary leaders of Great Britain, France and Italy were sceptical.

On 29 September 1918, the German Supreme Command, fearing an imminent Allied breakthrough on the Western Front, informed the Kaiser and the Imperial Chancellor Count Georg von Hertling at army headquarters in Spa, Belgium, that the military situation facing Germany was hopeless and that it should sue for peace on the basis of Wilson's Fourteen Points. On 5 October 1918, Germany asked President Wilson to negotiate terms. As a precondition for negotiations, Wilson demanded the retreat of Germany from all occupied territories, the cessation of submarine activities and the Kaiser's abdication. Writing on 23 October 1918, Wilson stated that: 'If the Government of the United States must deal with the military masters and the monarchical autocrats of Germany now, or if it is likely to have to deal with them later in regard to the international obligations of the German Empire, it must demand not peace negotiations but surrender.'

The uncompromising nature of Wilson's response caused the German High Command to reverse its thinking; however, on the night of 29–30 October 1918, the ratings of the Imperial German Navy mutinied in the naval port of Wilhelmshaven and a socialist revolt spread across the whole country within days. This lead to the proclamation of a republic on 9 November 1918 and to the announcement of the abdication of Kaiser Wilhelm II. After a renewed demand by the Allied Supreme Command on 5 November with harsher terms attached, the new German government headed by Friedrich Ebert accepted the terms of the Entente for a truce. An armistice was declared from the 11th hour of the 11th day of the 11th month of 1918.

The run-up to the Armistice had a twist in the tale in respect to US troop movements to Europe. In October 1918, America had received high-level intelligence to the effect that, as a last-ditch stand, the Imperial German Navy had been ordered to sea to confront the combined might of the Grand Fleet and US Navy, in a desperate victory or destruction mission, which might yet turn the tide of war. America, with victory in sight, was not prepared to run the risk of a potentially catastrophic interception of a US troop-laden convoy by elements of the Imperial German Navy. America was also conscious that, with the end of hostilities, it would be faced with the problem of repatriating 2 million US troops without the help of Allied tonnage, the latter being preoccupied with repatriating colonial troops and prisoners of war to/from other parts of the world. America was not, accordingly, keen to commit more US servicemen abroad than was absolutely necessary.

Despite the fact that the mutiny of German sailors at the end of October 1918, had effectively confounded the High Command order to confront the Allied fleets, America in great secrecy went ahead with a decision to sail the final convoy from the US without any troops embarked. With the active collusion of the British Army embarkation officer based in New York, Major P.A. Curry, the twenty-three troopships waiting to embark troops, among them *Demosthenes* and *Euripides*, went through all the processes of embarkation, but at the last minute, the commanders of seven British ships were ordered to sail without their passengers, the excuse, among many given, being a failure of the US Embarkation Service to marshal the troops in time. Major Curry fobbed off the Admiralty in respect to the empty state of the convoy until a day before its arrival within British jurisdiction; Curry was later awarded the US Distinguished Service Medal for his discretion and services – his subsequent career path within the British military establishment is not clear![23]

Over the course of the five years of the First World War, George Thompson's five Aberdeen Line ships had been fully engaged transporting first Australian and then US troops to the Middle Eastern and European theatres of war. In total, the fleet had steamed 958,491 miles and transported 129,404 troops, without loss.

Summary of First World War service of Aberdeen Line ships

Vessel	Miles Steamed	Troops Carried	Taken up from trade	Aus. Convoys	Liner Requisition Scheme	US/Canada Convoys	Released from LRS
Euripides	208,307	38,439	26 Aug 1914	7	3 Jul 1917	3	3 May 1919
Themistocles	222,784	28,137	21 Oct 1914	8	21 Oct 1917	4	12 Aug 1919
Demosthenes	165,537	20,973	16 Jun 1915	4	17 Mar 1917	7	19 Mar 1919
Marathon	184,379	20,804	30 Jul 1915	3	29 Sep 1917	–	1 Apr 1919
Miltiades	177,484	21,051	21 Sep 1914	5	16 Oct 1917	4	23 May 1919
Totals	**958,491**	**129,404**		**27**		**18**	

Sources

1. *Sea Transport of the A.I.F.*, Greville Tregarthen, (Australian) Naval Transport Board.
2. *Service List Part 1 31 January 1921*, Ministry of Shipping.
3. *Shaw Savill Uncatalogued Manuscripts*, National Maritime Museum.
4. *Aberdeen Line*, Company at Centennial (1926).

Note: Interspersed inter-voyage while under Australian requisition, vessels were on occasion novated to Imperial service for feeder voyages.

Now, with the cessation of hostilities in Europe, efforts turned to repatriating Australian troops and prisoners of war. A total of 331,814 Australian troops had set out for war; of these, tragically, 61,859 (18 per cent) had been killed; many had been returned to Australia in the interim, wounded. In broad terms, the repatriation operation involved 92,000 men from France, 6,000 from the United Kingdom and 17,000 from the Middle East. By September 1919, only 10,000 men remained to be repatriated.

While repatriation was the priority, the five Aberdeen Line ships remained requisitioned under the Liner Requisition Scheme, but as 1919 progressed, they were released back to George Thompson, the last being *Themistocles* in August 1919. Repatriated troops continued to be carried as passengers after individual vessel's date of release from the Liner Requisition Scheme. As a twist to the repatriation of thousands of war-weary Australian troops, the influenza pandemic that was killing millions in Europe led to some sections of the repatriated troops being quarantined upon arrival in Australia. This necessary precaution gave rise to much bitterness among the troops and their dependants, and led to a number of violent incidents at the quarantine stations.

Themistocles (Jermyn) left Plymouth on her last voyage under the Liner Requisition Scheme on 13 June 1919, with 1,172 Australian troops embarked. She left Cape Town on the morning of 3 July 1919, in bright sunshine. However, dense fog set in that night on the port side of the vessel, and just before midnight, she collided with the Norwegian auxiliary barque, *Eddersyde*, coal-laden from Durban to South America. The barque contacted the port side of *Themistocles* about 20ft from the bow, and scraped down the port side, damaging *Themistocles*' hull plates, the bridge, all the port side boat davits, and finally fouling the port propeller. The barque herself, with her port side ripped out, sank very quickly, killing seven of her crew. The thirteen remaining, including the master, took to the water, and were picked up by two lifeboats launched from *Themistocles*. At first light, with further searching fruitless, *Themistocles* took passage back to Cape Town, with tug assistance, for repairs and to land the survivors. The troops were billeted ashore in hutment camps, the Australian mails were transferred to another ship, and the ship was dry-docked in the Royal Naval facility at Simonstown. Repairs were completed by 19 July, the troops re-embarked, and the vessel resumed her passage to Melbourne, arriving there on 8 August 1919.[24]

To boost the repatriation work, three former German passenger ships, seized as reparations under the peace treaty process, were allocated by the Allied Shipping Commission to the management of George Thompson. These were:

- *Adolph Woermann* (6,355 tons) from Adolph Woermann's Deutsche Ost-Afrika-Linie's South and East African service;
- *Bahia Castillo* (9,949 tons) from the Hamburg-Südamikanische Dampf-schiffahrts-Gesellschaft's South American service; and,
- *Chemnitz* (7,542 tons), an intermediate ship from Norddeutscher Lloyd's transatlantic service.

Adolph Woermann undertook one round voyage in 1919 under Thompson's management; *Bahia Castillo* three voyages in 1919–20; and *Chemnitz* three in 1919–1921, all involved in repatriation work.

Adolph Woermann, under the command of the Aberdeen Line's Captain Ogilvie, departed the UK in June 1919, bound for Wellington, New Zealand, with service personnel and war brides embarked. Following disembarkation, she went over to Sydney and Melbourne to load for the UK, her voyage home diverting via Bombay to pick up British troops repatriating from India and Turkish prisoners of war bound for Constantinople en route. She was clearly intended to undertake a second voyage under Thompson's management, but this did not come about, and she was subsequently sold to the Royal Netherlands Mail Line, renamed *Venezuela* in 1921.

The liner *Bahia Castillo* had been employed as a German naval transport in the Baltic in 1917–18. Surrendered to the Allied Shipping Commission on 22 May 1919, she undertook her first voyage under Thompson's management in July 1919. The ship, which had been laid up for some time, was pressed into service as a 'family ship'; her first voyage under Thompson management was to end in an Australian Royal Commission of Enquiry. From 1915, a critical shortage of men to man the munitions factories in Britain had led first Vickers and subsequently the Australian government to recruit more than 6,000 civilian volunteer munitions workers in Australia – the munitions worker tradesmen and war worker navvies as they were known. Under the terms of their contracts, these men, many of whom had married and spawned families during their stay in Britain, had to return to Australia at the end of hostilities. To facilitate this, the British government offered free passages home for the workers and their families on 'family ships' carrying doctors, nurses and facilities for the children.

Bahia Castillo, commanded by a Captain William Bibby, was quickly brought out of lay-up, underwent a short refit and bunkering in Liverpool and, still grimed with coal dust, was pressed into repatriation service, embarking 586 munitions workers, 342 wives and children and 21 Army medical personnel at Plymouth on 14 July 1919. Immediately after boarding the ship, the complaints started; some passengers wanted to leave, but were warned that such action would lose them the right of free passage.

The voyage to South Africa was fraught with technical problems all too common with a ship fresh out of lay-up with an unfamiliar crew – blocked sewerage systems, galley equipment, plumbing failures – and shortage of basic supplies. Relationships between passengers and crew, especially the steward staff, were at an all-time low when the ship docked in Cape Town. There, complaints were telegrammed to Britain and Australia, and a poor situation was further exacerbated by excessive drinking on the part of both camps. The ship went on to Durban to bunker, and shortly after leaving for Fremantle on 23 August, a rowdy gathering of passengers was so threatening that the master decided to return to Durban, where an armed guard of Australian troops was embarked to maintain order during the voyage to Fremantle. The troops had to use force to evict men from the quarters allocated to them; fittings were vandalised in retaliation.

At Fremantle, a further welter of complaints was made, and a number of passengers disembarked, refusing to sail unless the military guard was withdrawn. This the naval authorities refused to do and the ship sailed for Albany with the disembarked passengers' baggage remaining on board. The matter was now becoming a political hot potato; the Hughes government was facing an election wherein it could well do without the distraction of the *Bahia Castillo* in every newspaper. It would have to be said that there was little sympathy in general public circles for the returning munitions workers, who had led well-paid, protected lives in England while the flower of Australia was laying down its life in the trenches a few miles across the Channel. The passengers who disembarked in Fremantle were finally reunited with their baggage in Albany, after promises had been made by the government to convene a Royal Commission of Enquiry into the circumstances obtaining on board the ship. The ship berthed in Melbourne on 16 October 1919.

The Royal Commission, chaired by the police magistrate, Mr P. Cohen, supported by an army and a naval assessor, began taking evidence as soon as the vessel berthed at Melbourne. Its report, made public on 9 February 1920, exonerated the defence authorities, the master and crew of the ship from the many serious charges made against them. Specifically, the commission found that the treatment of patients in the ship's hospital was quite satisfactory and that a child who died on the voyage received proper treatment; that the master of the ship, in the face of insubordination and trouble on the part of a number of passengers, was quite justified in returning to Durban for an armed guard; and that no improper force or roughness was used towards the passengers while ejecting them from that part of the ship required for the guard. There was muted criticism of the allegedly high-handed approach of the master and the embarked military officers.

Thus concluded the *Bahia Castillo* affair. One senses that had the voyage involved returning troops rather than civilian munition workers, the matter would never have occurred. The ship was clearly pressed into service by the government to fill an urgent need and arguably was not fit for purpose. Just how much control Thompsons had over the condition of the ship and the conduct of the voyage is a matter of speculation, but she clearly did not measure up to the company's normal standards of excellence. Captain Bibby does not appear to have been a regular Aberdeen Line commander, and I suspect the crew was a scratch post-war recruitment. *Bahia Castillo* made two further voyages in April and December 1920, returning troops and their dependants, with no further reported troubles. The ship was sold to A.G. Hugo Stinnes fur Ueberseehandel, Hamburg, in October 1922, and renamed *General Belgrano*. Stinnes was taken over by Hamburg Süd in 1926, and the ship was scrapped in 1932.

The *Chemnitz* undertook three round voyages to Melbourne, Sydney and Brisbane, between July 1919 and May 1921, initially primarily repatriating troops and their dependants. On the latter voyage, she loaded outwards at London and Antwerp; homewards, she was advertised for cargo only. At the end of her third voyage, her service under Thompson's management ceased, and she was sold for scrap in Holland in 1923.

Marathon became a casualty on 9 September 1919, homewards bound from Australia, when in thick fog off Dover, she was run down by the Japanese ship *Hejin Maru*. With Nos 1 and 2 holds flooded, *Marathon* was beached 1½ miles off Littlestone, north

Bahia Castillo. A pre-First World War photograph of the vessel at Hamburg; note the lifeboats stowed on athwartships skids in way of the mast houses, needed to accommodate 2,500 steerage passengers on the South American service. (Courtesy Hamburg Sud)

of Dungeness. Her ninety-four passengers were taken off safely by the Dover Harbour Board tug. Attempts to refloat her were initially unsuccessful, but she finally refloated on 14 September and proceeded under her own steam to London. Repaired, on her next voyage she carried out 120 returned New South Wales soldiers, together with an equal number of dependants, and forty-two married Queensland men and their wives. Her arrival at Sydney on New Year's Day 1920, marked the end of the Aberdeen Line's participation in post-war repatriation work.

With the repatriation of Australian servicemen and women completed, *Euripides*, *Themistocles* and *Demosthenes* were sent over to Cherbourg in early 1921 for the refitting of passenger accommodation, the work having to go abroad because of a joiners' strike in the UK. Then, by the last half of 1921, the Line finally returned to a scheduled fortnightly service to Melbourne, Sydney and Brisbane, using chartered vessels from the two parent companies to make up sailings, which included outward calls at Antwerp.

HARD TIMES – 1919 TO 1929

For some lines, particularly Inchcape's P&O group, the First World War had been a highly rewarding interlude, the group having profited from inflated freight rates and generous government compensation on shipping losses – often paid out on superannuated vessels – with scant regard for the human toll arising therefrom. The huge profits made by P&O had enabled it to acquire a number of other shipping companies in 1917, including the New Zealand Shipping Company, Federal Steam Navigation Company, the Union Steamship Company of New Zealand, the Hain Steamship Company, James Nourse, and the Orient Steam Navigation Company, allowing it to emerge from the war, despite enormous losses, with more than 2 million tons of shipping. Likewise, the Royal Mail Group controlled by Sir Owen Phillips, later to become Lord Kylsant, had generated enormous profits during conflict, emerging with nearly £20 million surplus, which Phillips proceeded to invest in new acquisitions, ships and companies. The profits made by some elements of the shipping industry had attracted the attention of the Treasury, which introduced an Excess Profits Duty in 1915, becoming more punitive in 1917.

By comparison, the First World War had not been a 'good' war for George Thompson's Aberdeen Line, for while almost uniquely the company had come through it unscathed in terms of ship and seafarer losses, its five ships had been tied in to government charters almost from the outset for the duration, charters which were far from generous in their reward and which prevented the company from profiting from soaring freight rates available on the open market. Further, following the cessation of hostilities, the five ships were retained in government service for some time engaged in urgent repatriation work, such that the company was not able to capitalise on the immediate post-war shipping boom. By the time the fleet was once again fully restored to its rightful trade, recession had begun to bite.

Stephen Thompson, grandson of George Thompson Jnr, retired from his senior management post in 1919 having served the company for forty-four years. Then, on 3 January 1920, the four original Thompson/Henderson management shareholders from the 1905 takeover relinquished their management shareholdings in favour of the Oceanic Steam Navigation Company, 60 per cent, and Shaw Savill and Albion, 40 per cent. Thus the company was then entirely controlled by these two shareholders.

On 2 June 1920, George Thompson Henderson died in post. He had been a partner of the old company from 1 January 1879 and senior partner from the time of his father, Sir William Henderson's retirement on 31 December 1898. At the time of the company's acquisition by Oceanic and Shaw Savill in 1905, he became a director of the new entity and its general manager. With his passing, Oscar Stephen Thompson, son of Cornelius Thompson and grandson of George Thompson Jnr, took the executive helm and his cousin, Alexander Duff Henderson, was appointed his deputy. Thus, although no longer shareholders, the Thompson and Henderson families continued in senior management roles within the company that continued to bear their grandfather's name.

With the passing of George Thompson Henderson and the retirement of Stephen Thompson, the Lloyd's underwriting business hitherto conducted by these two names under the mantle of the company lapsed. In a court action later brought by the Inland Revenue against the company, the position of the Lloyd's underwriting activities undertaken by Henderson and Thompson were described as a trade distinct from that of shipowning, a view upheld by the appeal judge in a judgement against the Revenue.[1] *Scales vs George Thompson* has been a much quoted judgement in subsequent tax cases.

The management of George Thompson was strengthened on 30 March 1921, when Basil Sanderson joined the company as a management trainee. Sanderson was the son of Harold Arthur Sanderson, general manager of the White Star Line and chairman of George Thompson & Co. Oscar Thompson had noted Sanderson for his boxing prowess at Rugby and Sanderson had clearly left a favourable impression upon him, for now Thompson invited him to join the company. Harold Sanderson was initially implacably opposed to his son joining a company under his chairmanship, but Oscar Thompson went behind his chairman's back direct to Philip Albright Small Franklin, the president of the International Mercantile Marine Company, owners of the White Star Line, and secured his blessing for the appointment; indeed, it was Franklin's personal intervention that finally placated Sanderson Senior. The date Sanderson took up office within George Thompson and Co. is significant; he was scheduled to start work on Monday, 1 April 1921, but Oscar Thompson was keen that he should not take up office on April Fool's day, so on the preceding Saturday, Oscar Thompson broke his weekend routine to receive Sanderson into the company. The bond between Sanderson and Thompson would prove to be very close and enduring.

We are indebted to Sanderson for the only extant description of the company environment that he found himself entering. To quote from his autobiography *Ships and Sealing Wax*:

> The Billiter Street office retained the delightful old world atmosphere of the former partnership background. No member of the management had an appropriate title. All policy and conference work was the prerogative of Oscar Thompson, who was styled 'Secretary'. The Secretarial work and accounts were the responsibility of Duff Henderson, who held the title of 'Manager'. Office organization and management and also passenger problems not dealt with by Oscar Thompson fell to the lot of Raymond Jones, who signed as 'Assistant Manager'... It was a real family atmosphere. To the staff, Raymond Jones, who had been promoted from their midst, was known as Mr Jones. The others, whom I have enumerated were addressed as Mr Oscar, Mr Duff and I was Mr Basil – a most charming atmosphere, almost straight from Charles Dickens – and it worked.[2]

Shortly after his appointment, under Oscar Thompson's close direction, Sanderson embarked upon an extended visit to the company's interests in Australia, extending to a visit to New Zealand. Even at that stage, the group intention was that the Aberdeen Line, which had Australian trading rights, should merge with the Shaw Savill and Albion, which had New Zealand Conference rights, but no rights in Australia. Sanderson clearly deeply appreciated the year he spent on his Antipodean expedition, making many contacts and securing an understanding of the Australian trading scene that would stand him in good stead in the future. A particular impression the visit to Australia left with Sanderson was the deeply engrained hostility towards UK shipowners that existed in that country, particularly the

The ticket office at Billiter Street.

perceived grip of the Shipping Ring, led by Inchcape's P&O group, over the Australian export economy. Sanderson ascribed much of this antipathy to the failure of the British shipowners to communicate properly with their Australian customers.

The Aberdeen Line was in the limelight in 1921 when, on 8 July, **Demosthenes** was the first ship to enter the new King George V Dock in London. This followed a formal ceremony when King George V, embarked in Lord Inchcape's yacht **Rover**, cut a silk tape across the lock entrance.

Before the outbreak of the First World War, the company had planned to build two new passenger cargo vessels along similar lines to the well-proven Demosthenes class, one to replace the lost **Pericles** and one to augment the fleet. Now, with the war over, and with the ageing **Marathon** and **Miltiades** too small and lacking the reefer capacity for the emerging requirements of the trade, orders for two new vessels were placed at Harland and Wolff, Belfast, in 1919. The two identical vessels were slightly smaller and slower than **Euripides**; they were to have cruiser rather than counter sterns, and a single trunked hatch abaft the bridge, which was located at the forward end of the centrecastle deck. The two new vessels were to have registered dimensions of 500.4ft length overall × 63.2ft beam × 39ft depth (effectively the same as

THE ABERDEEN LINE.   S.S. "DEMOSTHENES."—11,250 TONS.
BETWEEN ENGLAND, SOUTH AFRICA AND AUSTRALIA.
Managers—GEO. THOMPSON & CO., Ltd., London. E.C.3.

Demosthenes entering KGV Dock for the first time. The Inchcape yacht **Rover** can be seen in the left foreground

Themistocles), and a deadweight of 11,700 tons. The twin-screw vessels adopted steam-turbine propulsion packages rather than the reciprocating engines hitherto used, each shaft driven by a compound Brown–Curtis turbine, comprising a high-pressure and a low-pressure unit acting through double-reduction gearing. Steam at a pressure of 215lbpsi was supplied from one single-ended and four double-ended cylindrical coal-fired boilers. The propulsion system generated a somewhat modest 5,200shp driving the vessels at 13.5 to 14 knots. The vessels were fitted for 131 first-class passengers in significant comfort and 422 third-class passengers; passenger capacity could be extended to accommodate emigrants in portable 'tween deck berths. The new ships had six hatches served by eighteen 5-ton and one 30-ton derricks, with electric winches. Their insulated cargo space, at 305,184 cu.ft, was some 20 per cent larger than **Euripides** and 30 per cent larger than **Themistocles** and **Demosthenes**.[3]

The first of the new ships, **Sophocles**, was launched on 22 September 1922, and entered into service on 1 March 1922, followed 5½ months later on 16 August 1922 by her sister, **Diogenes**, the latter having the dubious distinction of being the last ship to be built for George Thompson's Aberdeen Line.

The two new ships cost £1,915,000, a high price for such vessels. To finance them, the company entered into a 5 per cent mortgage debenture stock issue on 13 July 1922, secured on the fleet, and unconditionally guaranteed by the Oceanic Steam Navigation Company as parent shareholder; Shaw Savill and Albion, in an internal transaction with the Oceanic Company, sub-guaranteed 40 per cent of the debenture.[4]

Marathon had sailed from Sydney on Voy. 39, her last with the Aberdeen Line, on 31 December 1920, followed by **Miltiades**, Voy. 43, on 8 February 1921, whereafter both vessels were laid up. Then, with the two new ships in service, **Marathon** and **Miltiades**, arguably two of the most graceful steamers ever built, were sold *en bloque*, to the Royal Mail Steam Packet Company on 9 October 1921. It allocated the vessels within group to the Pacific Steam Navigation Company for its WCSA service; **Marathon** was renamed **Oruba** (II) and **Miltiades**, **Orcana** (II). The vessels proved uneconomic in their new service, and after a period of lay-up they were sold for scrapping in 1923–24. The disposal of **Marathon** and **Miltiades** marked the last vestiges of the once great Scottish family shipping line. They reflected at the same time the highest professional standards upon

Diogenes – a painting by Jack Spurling for corporate publicity.

which the Line had built its name, and the overt conservatism upon which it foundered as a private company.

With five modern passenger cargo ships in service, each averaging a 140-day round trip, augmented by chartered Shaw Savill and White Star Line cargo and emigrant-carrying vessels making up about 50 per cent of sailings, the Aberdeen Line resumed a two-weekly service from London and Antwerp to Albany, Melbourne, Sydney and Brisbane, with seasonal calls to Hobart. In 1923, the company's homewards sailings were extended to include Hull as first port of call in the UK, giving better access for Australian wool to the northern mills, and the city was canvassed specifically for Yorkshire emigrants. The first ship so committed was **Sophocles**, sailing from Sydney in February 1923.[5]

The emigrant trade to Australia, which had virtually ceased during the First World War, resumed with different emphasis. Immediately following the conflict and completion of repatriation operations, an acute problem confronted the British government in terms of the employment of thousands of returned servicemen. Emigration to the dominions provided a partial solution, and in 1919 the Overseas Settlement Scheme was sponsored by the Imperial government, whereby ex-servicemen and women, together with their dependants, were offered free passages and other incentives to migrate to the dominions. The Australian government, motivated to expand its agricultural economy, allocated 24 million acres of hitherto uninhabited land to the scheme; 23,000 farms were established throughout New South Wales, Queensland, Victoria and South Australia. The scheme lasted until March 1923, during which time 34,750 ex-servicemen and their dependants migrated to Australia. Then, as an extension of the original scheme, the Empire Settlement Act was passed in 1922 whereby, in collaboration with the dominion governments, private organisations and public authorities, 'any suitable person' from the general public, especially married couples, single farm labourers, single women, and teenagers between 14 and 17 years of age, were given free passages and other assistance to the dominions. Over the duration of the extended scheme, 212,000 emigrants were given assisted passages to Australia.

The life to which these emigrants exposed themselves was tough in the extreme. Many of those carried out by the Aberdeen Line settled in Western Australia, working the karri timber stands in the Northcliffe area. The migrants came in groups via Albany, often from a specific area of the UK, particularly Yorkshire. The shipboard life of one group emigrating from Leeds in **Diogenes** was described in the *Yorkshire Evening Post* in March 1924:

> Although there is an abundance of food of the best sort at meal times, one gets such an appetite from the sea air that a ton of biscuits per family would not go amiss, once the seasickness has been got over. The washing of clothes is quite possible on board, there is scarcely need for more than three changes of underclothing as berth baggage.

Against this background, the Aberdeen Line, with its prime carriers designed for the emigrant and reefer trades, should have been in a relatively strong position, despite the recession. However, this was not to be; unwelcome competition had come from an unexpected quarter. The Commonwealth Government Shipping Line (the Commonwealth Line), formed on the initiative of Prime Minister Hughes as a wartime expediency to move stockpiling Australian produce to world markets, had been expected to be disposed of following the cessation of hostilities, but this did not happen. Shortly after the formation of the Commonwealth Line, Hughes had split with the Labour Party over the question of conscription and together with some of his followers had formed an alliance with the Liberal Party to form a National War government, over which he presided until 1923. Hughes had, since 1918, fostered an intention to retonnage the Commonwealth Line with modern, purpose-built, passenger-carrying vessels to service the immigrant trade and modern refrigerated cargo ships.

On 24 March 1919, the manager of the Commonwealth Line in London, H.G.E. Larkin, announced the formal intention that the Line would trade permanently;[6] then, on 25 June 1919, a ministerial statement advised of the government's policy to continue operating the Line in peacetime.[7] The decision was fiercely divisive politically within Australia, with approval coming from the Labour benches on socialist ideological grounds, and from unlikely bedmates in the Country Party, whose primary producer supporters, while implacably opposed to socialist policies, were keen to do anything to keep freight rates down and break the perceived grip of the British Shipping Ring over the Australian economy. The National government was not so supportive of the Line's continuance; however, Hughes had his way, and contracts were signed with Vickers Ltd at Barrow-in-Furness on 4 July 1919 for three new passenger–cargo steamers, with large emigrant and refrigerated capacities. This was followed on 17 July by contracts for two further identical ships to be built by William Beardmore on the Clyde. (There seems to have been some suggestion that the five new vessels were originally intended to be primarily cargo vessels with accommodation for only twelve passengers, but the specification was upgraded after the first keel had been laid.) The subsequent debate in the House of Representatives on 31 July 1919 centred not so much on the rationale for the continuance of the Commonwealth Line and the building of the five new ships, but on the manner in which the orders had been placed at a cost of £2 million – without parliamentary approval and apparently without having gone out to tender. The House reflected upon Hughes' earlier commitment of £2 million of federal funds for the acquisition of forty-three ships in 1916 without Parliament's approval, but this had been a wartime expediency within his executive authority.[8]

Each of the five new passenger–cargo ships would be named after a bay in the host register state of the vessel. The keel of the first new ship, **Esperance Bay**, was laid in September 1919 by Mrs Larkin, the wife of H.G.E. Larkin, the UK manager of the Line, with delivery scheduled for eighteen months later; subsequent deliveries were pitched twenty-four months and thirty-six months after date of contract.

The stated objective of the Commonwealth Line was not to enter into a freight war with the Conference lines, but rather to secure freight rate stability, 'providing rates were reasonable'. Australian merchants in London, meeting with Larkin, proposed a bringing together of the Commonwealth Line and the Conference lines.[9] The reaction of the British shipping establishment was far from receptive to the idea. *Fairplay*, never slow to advocate the cause of the British shipowner in strident terms, commented that the exemption of the Commonwealth steamers from excess profit and income taxes had enabled the [Australian] government within two years to wipe off the whole cost of the [originally purchased Commonwealth] steamers in two years. *Fairplay* forecast that:

The conditions of the shipping trade when the Commonwealth new boats are delivered will make it impossible for them to pay. Sooner or later the British investor will be asked to lend the Commonwealth the money for the purchase of these ships to enable them to run the English owners, who are large taxpayers, off the trade.[10]

At the annual general meeting of the Peninsular and Oriental Steam Navigation Company on 11 December 1919, the chairman, Lord Inchcape, complained that the Commonwealth government had an idea of becoming a shipowner, competing with private enterprise. While Inchcape was satisfied that the Australian Prime Minister was actuated by the highest motives in starting the government line, he was convinced that Mr Hughes had a wrong conception of what was good for his country. In Inchcape's view, Australia would be infinitely better advised if it followed the British government's example of leaving commerce and industry to private enterprise and individual initiative.

Australian Commonwealth Line Dale-class freighter *Ferndale*. (*Ships in Focus*, A. Duncan Collection)

Hughes was not minded to follow Inchcape's advice; indeed, the Commonwealth Line had also contracted with the government of New South Wales to build two advanced cargo liners at the Cockatoo Island Dockyard, Sydney, with large refrigerated capacity for the home trade. These vessels, the Dale- boats, were 152.4m length overall, with a gross tonnage of 9,570. Powered by twin quadruple-expansion steam engines, coal-fired, they had a speed of 16 knots – fast for cargo vessels of that era but designed to pace the Bay- boats in service. They were fitted with 20,020 cu m of refrigerated space in ten chambers. Each vessel cost £850,000 to build, very high by prevailing standards. The first vessel, *Fordsdale*, was commissioned in March 1924, and the second, *Ferndale*, in October of that year.

Thus, by September 1919, the Commonwealth Line had seventy-six ships, in service or building, as follows:[11]

Austral ships purchased by Hughes in the UK	12
Ex-enemy ships seized by the Commonwealth	17
Sailing ships in commission	2
Steamers building in Australia	26
Steamers building in the United Kingdom	5
Wooden steamers in commission or building	14

While this might seem a formidable fleet, many of the ships were elderly, small and uneconomic to operate, even without Australian manning. The wooden ships built in America and latterly in Australia as a wartime expediency to overcome material shortages proved a disaster; the sailing ships were time expired; and many of the those building in Australia were destined for Australian domestic trades. However, any ship on the home trade, however incompetent, taking cargo and passengers away from the Conference lines was unwelcome competition, which hit the UK shipowners badly at a time of recession. The Aberdeen Line, constrained as it was by Conference agreement to the Cape route, was to be sorely hit by the entry of the five Bays and two Dales, which, free of Conference restraints, were routed on the more direct route via Suez, taking in Aden and Colombo en route.

Following an initial post-war boom, recession set in that impacted all trades, but especially the Australian one. This recession, which was to extend throughout the 1920s, hit UK ship owners from a number of directions – a drop-off in outward cargoes; excessive tonnage capacity, partly arising from the cheap acquisition of government standard freighters; the rise of foreign flag ships on a trade hitherto the domain of the UK flag; and competition from the Commonwealth Line.

Significantly, while the rest of the Conference lines regarded the Commonwealth Line as an interloper, and competition with the Australians was of the fiercest, on a personal basis the Aberdeen Line management extended every friendship to the management of the Commonwealth Line. It argued that it was better to work with the intruders, admitting them to Conference discussions and working with them to secure common freight rates, than to engage in fruitless competition with a state-funded entity. In this, the Aberdeen Line, as so often in the past, was at serious variance with its Conference colleagues. However, the approach was eventually to win the day, and the friendly relationships with the Commonwealth Line's management arising therefrom were to be hugely advantageous in years to come, as events unfolded.

Following his return from Australia and New Zealand, Basil Sanderson became increasingly involved in Australian Conference business, taking over from Oscar Thompson as the Aberdeen Line's member with full rights and responsibilities. He sat on a

Comparison Between Aberdeen Line's Sophocles-Class/Euripides and Australian Commonwealth Line's Bay- Boats

	Dimensions ft. (av)	Gross tons	Deadweight tons	Insulated cu.ft	Speed knots	SHP	Fuel	Passengers 1st class	Emigrants 3rd class (fitted)
Euripides	570 × 67.3	14,947	3,800	245,593	15.0	8,300	Coal	141	388
Sophocles	519 × 63.3	12,351	1,000	305,184	13.5	5,200	Coal	131	422
Bay- boats	550 × 68.0	13,850	2,600	360,000	15.0	9,000	Oil	12	720

number of Conference committees, including a new one set up in 1925 to rationalise shipments of wheat parcels on liner sailings from Australia. The main bulk of wheat exports from Australia were handled as full cargoes carried by chartered tramp steamers and the occasional sailing vessel. However, wheat parcels had for long formed an important filler cargo on liner sailings, especially outside the wool season, and some ships sailed with 2,000 to 5,000 tonnes wheat bottom weight. The commercial columns of Australian newspapers regularly recorded the five Aberdeen Line passenger ships shipping wheat parcels. Parcels of wheat shipped on liner tonnage were outside Conference control, and rates had dropped to as low as 20s per ton, half the rates obtained for bulk cargoes on tramp ships. A prime function of the committee was to bring order to the movement of wheat parcels on liner tonnage. While members representing the other Australian trade liner companies circulated around him, Sanderson was to remain on the Wheat Committee representing the interests of the Aberdeen Line until the outbreak of the Second World War.

The Aberdeen Line had made its last dividend (25 per cent) to shareholders in 1920.[12] Trading conditions for the company and the other Cape-route lines in the Australian service became progressively worse during the 1920s; the two new ships did not operate profitably and competition was fierce, especially from the Commonwealth Line with its Suez-routed ships.

As an interesting trade development, in March 1925, *Sophocles* landed at Hull the first trial shipment of South African peaches, pears and plums.[13] Hitherto, the home sailings of Aberdeen Line ships visiting South Africa had only filled vacant space with rough cargo and such surplus South African Conference lines' cargoes as might be offering. Homewards sailings called at Tenerife for coal bunkers and also picked up bananas for Fyffes.

If trading conditions were not difficult enough, in August 1925 a significant percentage of British seamen went on strike across the UK and dominions, generating huge financial losses within the shipping industry and economic hardship in the dominions. The strike, which was unofficial, was triggered by the National Sailors' and Firemen's Union (NSFU) offering the employers a reduction in pay of £1 per month. By the end of the First World War, seamen's pay had risen to £14 10s per month, but with increasingly stark economic times, this had been cut in four tranches to £9 by May 1923, restoring to £10 per month in 1924.

Perceiving that the owners were about to impose a cut of £2 or £3 a month and against a background of increasing general economic gloom, with pay cuts demanded in the mining and transport industries, Havelock Wilson OBE MP, the president of the NSFU, convened a special conference of (non-elected) delegates on 28 June 1925, at which he argued that rather than be forced to accept an imposed reduction on a far larger scale, it would be prudent to offer the owners a £1 reduction. The motion was carried, the owners were no doubt delighted and the cut came into effect on 1 August 1925. The NSFU was the only representative body of the employees on the statutory National Maritime Board and seamen had to be card-carrying members of the NSFU. to gain employment on British ships; however, there were other unions representing seamen's interests, including the Amalgamated Marine Workers Union (AMWU) and the marine section of the communist-backed National Minority Movement (NMM). These two bodies initiated unofficial strike action against the pay cut, contrary to the will of the NSFU. They also demanded the introduction of a forty-eight-hour week at sea/forty-four-hour week in port, overtime payments, and the provision of bedding and eating utensils,

Strike action was slow in getting under way in the UK, and had not really started to grip until towards the end of August. A large pool of unemployed seamen provided the owners with a ready supply of scab labour, and indeed, many NSFU members were not inclined to strike, accepting the financial reality of the pay cut; critically, the striking seamen were not supported by tugboat men. However, and in particular, the way that the strike impacted the Aberdeen Line, action in the dominions was far more telling.

In South Africa, where the strike carried the support of the Labour Party and the Communist Party of South Africa, indirect action started on 24 August 1925. *Sophocles* (Ogilvy) sailed for Australia from Plymouth on 13 August 1925, without apparent delay, but upon reaching Cape Town, the crew withdrew their labour. The commander attempted to sail with ninety-three crew members locked in their mess room and officers undertaking the seamen's duties; once outside the 3-mile limit, the men were sent to the stokehold and ordered to get on with their duties or face charges of mutiny. The men's response was that they had intimated before they left the anchorage that they would not sail, that they had been taken out beyond the 3-mile limit against their will, and that the charge of mutiny would not stand. Ogilvy was forced to relent and the ship returned to anchor within three hours. The ninety-three strikers were put ashore and were housed initially in the Communist Hall, but later they were billeted in the Wynberg military camp as charges of the government. Eventually, the men along, with about 500 other seamen, were repatriated to the UK by the South African government. *Sophocles* lay off Cape Town for nearly five weeks, finally clearing South Africa on 4 October 1925 with locally recruited labour, said to be the sons of Dutch farmers, making up her crew.[14]

The strike in South Africa, which started in Durban and extended to all ports, caused grievous harm to the local producers. At one stage, nearly 2,000 Australia-bound passengers were stranded in Cape Town. The strike also introduced racial undertones when the Union Castle Line was thought to be recruiting lascar seamen from Bombay to release its strike-bound ships.

In Sydney, seamen at a mass meeting of more than 1,000 British seamen at the Communist Hall on 20 August 1925 voted unanimously to strike in all Australian ports until the £1 cut in wages was restored. The strike, which started the next day following a further mass meeting, was supported by the Seamen's Union of Australia under its president, Tom Walsh. As the strike was unofficial, it did not carry the support of the usually militant Waterside Workers Federation (which was anyway short of funds following a prolonged industrial dispute campaign), and a curious situation arose whereby striking ships continued to work cargo, with striking seamen feeding the donkey boilers to provide steam for the winches. Havelock Wilson entered into a bitter war of words with Walsh over his support for the strikers, and cabled the Australian Prime Minister Bruce in an attempt to prevent the strike spreading. Action was taken by the Australian government to have Walsh, an Irish immigrant, together with his assistant, deported from Australia, but this action failed in the courts.[15]

As the Aberdeen Line's large passenger ships were white-crewed and carried a high profile in Australia, strike action by their men attracted significant local attention. The first signs of trouble emerged at midnight on 20 August when firemen on board *Themistocles*, berthed in Sydney, advised the commander, Captain William Jermyn that they were withdrawing their labour. Jermyn, while sympathetic with their cause, argued with them not to follow this course of action. Three hundred seamen from *Themistocles* returning from a mass meeting on 22 August found the wharf gates locked and they were forced to spend the night on the Domain;[16] later they were housed on the floor of the Communist Hall (the Salvation Army declining to provide support in their halls). In Melbourne, 100 seamen were locked out of *Euripides* on 25 August when they withdrew their labour following the vessel's docking from the UK. On 11 September, the crew of the Shaw Savill steamer *Mamari,* voyage-chartered by the Aberdeen Line, also walked out in Melbourne.

These actions, along with similar lock-outs on other ships in port, served to embitter the mood of the men. Remaining on board was not an option, for the cooks were also on strike, and food was denied the striking seamen by the owners. Locked-out seamen had to depend upon the charitable support of the Australian Seamen's Union and other left-wing bodies. As the names of strikers were cabled home, so their monthly allotments to hard-pressed families were suspended.

The commanders of the strike-hit ships charged striking crew members before the Australian courts with having refused to obey lawful commands under the Merchant Shipping Act of 1894. By 9 September 1925, 329 warrants had been issued in Melbourne alone against 190 seamen from the *Euripides*; by 19 September, 946 warrants had been issued in Sydney. The mass issuance of arrest warrants led to a farcical situation wherein the strikers co-operated with the police in serving the warrants and in generally coming forward voluntarily before the magistrates. Strikers were usually offered the option of returning to their ships and resuming work, or being sentenced to up to three weeks' imprisonment with hard labour. The prison option had attractions, given the conditions under which the strikers had been living, and it relieved the strike fund of the need to pay for their upkeep. The prison authorities were said to take a compassionate view towards their striker guests. The conditions 'enjoyed' by NSW State hard labour convicts and those of seamen employed under the Merchant Shipping Act make interesting comparison:[17]

	Hard labour rations/conditions NSW Government gaols	Merchant Shipping Act scale of provisions
	Per day	Per day
Bread	20oz	16oz
Oaten meal	8oz	1½oz
Meat	12oz	12oz
Potatoes	16oz	13oz
Sugar	3oz	3oz

	Per week	Per week
Soap	3½oz	None
Salt	3½oz	2oz
	5 blankets, cocoanut matting	No bed or bedding
	Hot bath, candles, light, water in cell	No bathing; water 4qts per day
		No eating utensils
	Weekend off	84-hour week

By mid-September 1925, with the strikers facing restrictions on social benefit payments, a generally hostile public and a ready supply of blackleg labour available to sail ships from the UK, the strike in the mother country began to wane; delays to sailings from UK ports became less frequent. Finally, at a mass meeting of 1,500 seamen in London in late October, it was decided by a majority said to have been of one vote, to call off the strike. In the dominions, especially in Australia, where there was significant local support, the strike held firm. Ships of the P&O Line and the British India Line, with largely lascar crews, were not affected. The 'Cape runners' – the Aberdeen Line, Oceanic's White Star Line, Holt's Blue Funnel Line and the white-crewed P&O Branch Line, were particularly badly hit.

Sophocles arrived at Albany from Cape Town on 20 October and sailed from Melbourne on 28 October for Sydney, where the chairman of the seamen's strike committee, C. O'Neill, confidently expected the ship to be held up when her temporarily recruited crew members from South Africa were due to be paid off. *Diogenes* left London on 10 September 1925, her departure from the UK delayed by twenty hours at Plymouth, when her engine room staff objected to the incompetence of eight firemen, who had to be replaced; with *Themistocles* strike-bound in Sydney and *Euripides* strike-bound in Melbourne, *Diogenes* initially bypassed Melbourne on 23 October with the intention of sailing straight to Sydney,[18] but this was subsequently reversed and the ship berthed at Melbourne as planned. Her crew were subjected to daily efforts to embroil them in the strike, but they held firm and she sailed for Sydney on 28 October. *Demosthenes* left London on 8 October making her Australian arrival at Albany on 18 November 1925, at the tail end of the strike in that country. Strikers who boarded the vessel in an attempt to embroil the crew when she berthed at Melbourne on 24 November, were afforded a hostile reception by the firemen; the strikers were unsuccessful in persuading the crew to refuse duty.[19]

The strike in Australia began wavering from the west – Fremantle, Albany and then Adelaide. However, it held firm in Melbourne and Sydney until late in November 1925, finally being called off on 26 November. On 25 November 1925, *Demosthenes* sailed from Melbourne with all 230 crewmen on board; 100 crewmen had returned to *Themistocles* in Sydney on 18 November, and by the next day the majority of the crew had returned en masse, enabling the ship to sail on 28 November. On 19 November, *Sophocles* sailed from Melbourne for the UK, the first Aberdeen liner to make a home departure from Melbourne since 30 June.[20]

The 1925 strike of British seamen across the dominions left no winners:

- **The seamen** had withdrawn their labour in the hope of restoring the £1 reduction in monthly pay, which had come into effect from 1 August 1925. They also sought to secure better conditions of work, working hours and union representation on board ships. They achieved nothing; many were left destitute together with their families; many were unemployed; and a bitter feud existed between the official union, the National Sailors' and Firemens' Union led by Havelock Wilson, which had not supported the strike, and the breakaway, communist-backed Amalgamated Maritime Workers Union led by Emanuel Shinwell. The overtones of the strike were to spill over into the general strike of 1926.

- **The owners**, according to the Reuters news agency, lost more than £2 million in lost freights from Australia alone. They also had to pay harbour dues, fuel, maintenance, insurance and the pay and subsistence of loyal crew members on the strike-bound vessels. When the strike was over, it took some months for the various ships trapped in the dominions to take up a regular trading pattern again. In particular, the strike gave the opportunity to foreign flag ships, particularly the German and French lines, to strengthen their footholds in trades that hitherto had been the near-exclusive domain of the British shipowner. Ironically, the ever-militant Australian Commonwealth Line ships were not directly involved in the strike, further entrenching their position in the home trade.

- The economies of **the dominions** – Australia, New Zealand and South Africa, which relied heavily upon British shipping to take their produce to the world markets, were badly hurt.

1925 centennial poster. (Dixon)

In the midst of the damaging strike, George Thompson's Aberdeen Line celebrated its centenary. On 11 September 1925, arguably somewhat insensitively, Dalgety and Co., as George Thompson's Australian managing agents, hosted a dinner at the Hotel Australia in Sydney presided over by Sir Henry Braddon, Dalgety's superintendent in Australia, to celebrate the anniversary. The governor of New South Wales, Sir Dudley de Chair, was guest of honour, and the guests included a large gathering of senior personnel drawn from NSW's maritime and commercial world.[21] On the home front, the company recorded its centenary by commissioning the author, Cope Cornford, to write a corporate history, privately published as *The Sea Carriers* – a book notable for the fact that the first mention of the Aberdeen Line or George Thompson Jnr appears in Chapter VII ... The Line also commissioned a fine centennial poster designed by Charles Dixon featuring the brig **Childe Harold** and the steamer **Sophocles**.

On 31 August 1925, George Thompson Ltd acquired the White Star freighter **Bardic**, 8,010grt, for her book value of £242,086;[22] the vessel was initially renamed **Hostilius** but was renamed **Horatius** a year later.[23] **Bardic** was built for the shipping controller at Harland and Wolff, Belfast, in 1918, as the G-class fast refrigerated standard cargo ship **War Priam**. She was purchased by White Star Line on 13 March 1919, to replace war losses, and renamed **Bardic**. For her first two years' service, she was engaged on the North Atlantic under transfer to the IMM Group's Atlantic Transport Company, but from April 1921 she served for White Star on its Australian service. On 30 April 1924, the **Bardic** ran aground in thick fog off the Lizard. She was refloated a month later in an epic salvage operation and taken to Falmouth, where she was repaired. Quite why the Aberdeen Line needed the extra vessel at a time of deep depression is not clear; I suspect the sale amounted to an offloading of surplus tonnage forced upon George Thompson by Oceanic.

If trading conditions had been hard for George Thompson in the years leading up to 1925, the seamen's strike was probably the straw that broke the camel's back. The Aberdeen Line was constrained by its Conference rights to ploughing the longer route to Australia via the Cape. The other three Cape runners to Australia – Alfred Holt's Blue Funnel Line, the White Star Line and the P&O Branch Line – had also suffered severely. Consolidation between lines became essential. On 24 April 1926, the Australian press ran headlines:[24]

Freighter *Horatius* (ex-White Star *Bardic*) at Cape Town. (*Ships in Focus*, A. Duncan Collection)

Cape Route – Shipping Merger after heavy losses

Three important British passenger services, the Aberdeen, the Blue Funnel and the White Star lines, trading to Australia via the Cape, have united certain of their activities in a first-class and cabin-class service to England.

Under the new arrangement, the three lines would field eleven ships on the service:

Aberdeen Line   *Euripides*, *Themistocles* and *Demosthenes*
Blue Funnel   *Ascanius*, *Nestor*, *Ulysses* and *Anchises*
White Star   *Ceramic*, *Suevic*, *Runic* and *Medic*

The Aberdeen Line and Blue Funnel would provide first-class passenger accommodation, while the White Star Line would provide cabin class. The Aberdeen Line and P&O Branch Line would separately provide third-class accommodation. The revised service would sail from Liverpool.

Rationalisation of the Cape route was a necessary step, but so far as George Thompson was concerned, with the company effectively insolvent, far more drastic surgery was necessary. In 1926, the following inter-group restructuring was put into effect, with George Thompson's Aberdeen Line effectively being placed into the internal receivership of its senior parent shareholder:

• *Sophocles and Diogenes*, which over the first five years of their trading life had not proven to be successful, having run at an aggregate loss, were taken out of the Aberdeen Line's Australian

Mamilius (ex-White Star *Zealandic*) transferred to operate the Aberdeen Line's London berth. (*Ships in Focus*, A. Duncan Collection)

service and bare-boat chartered to Shaw Savill for the New Zealand trade, **Sophocles** was renamed **Tamaroa** in June 1926, and **Diogenes** became **Mataroa** a month later. Both underwent an extensive upgrade to suit them for their new employment, including conversion from coal to oil fuel at a cost of around £70,000 per ship. It was a change that increased their maximum speed to above 15 knots, improved tourist passenger accommodation and increased refrigerated capacity.[25]

- The balance of the Aberdeen Line fleet (**Themistocles, Demosthenes**, **Euripides** and **Horatius**) were transferred to, and integrated with, White Star Line's Australian service ex-Liverpool, under White Star Line management.

- To sustain the Aberdeen Line's berth rights out of London, the elderly Shaw Savill cargo and emigrant carrier **Waimana** (10,389grt), renamed **Herminius**, and the White Star Line/Shaw Savill joint

service cargo and emigrant carrier **Zealandic** (10,898grt), renamed **Mamilius**, were chartered to the Aberdeen Line.

George Thompson and Co. was reduced to the status of little more than a loading broker, with earnings derived from the charter hire of the two ships chartered to Shaw Savill, the profit/loss on the ships managed by White Star Line, and loading broker commissions.

The first sailing of the joint service from Liverpool was advertised in *Fairplay* on 14 October 1926, with cargo sailings from London.

In January, Basil Sanderson was appointed manager of George Thompson and Co. His promotion was in line with a long-term strategy whereby George Thompson and Co. would eventually be merged with Shaw Savill, with him managing the joint companies. As a presage to such an appointment, Sanderson had first to have corporate management experience under his belt. Although the Aberdeen Line was very much the junior company with only five ships under its pre-1926 control, it punched high above its weight by virtue of chartered tonnage, much of it coming from Shaw Savill,[26] and it had Australian Conference rights.

In April 1927, George Thompson & Co. and its staff moved from its office in 7 Billiter Square, an office it had occupied since 1896, to joint accommodation with Shaw Savill at 34 Leadenhall Street, with job functions merged. Basil Sanderson was appointed joint manager of the two companies under John MacMillan as general manager. Sanderson's early months under MacMillan were not easy – they were two men of immensely strong character, one from a privileged shipping background and the other a self-hewn West Highlander, quick of temper, but with a heart of gold; however, following an 'appalling explosion' when both men lost their tempers and thumped the table, perfect harmony prevailed for the next eighteen years.[27] Oscar Thompson, very much an *éminence grise* of the London shipping scene with his vast experience of the Australian trade, was retained as 'adviser', a post he was to hold until his retirement in 1932.[28]

Events were now to take a turn that would influence not only George Thompson and Co., but the British shipping industry as a whole. As far back as 1917, the British government had approached the loss-making International Mercantile Marine with a view to buying back into British ownership the British tonnage owned by the combine. Sir William Pirrie, chairman of the Belfast shipbuilders Harland and Wolff, and Sir Owen Phillips, later Lord Kylsant, chairman of the Royal Mail Group, were invited to strike a deal with IMM. In 1919, after protracted negotiations spanning three years, a £27 million offer was accepted by the directors of IMM but rejected by its stockholders.[29] Now, on 27 November 1926, with the IMM group in serious financial difficulties arising from the trade depression, and following a joint acquisition attempt by Cunard and Furness, Kylsant struck to secure the whole ordinary share capital of the Oceanic Steam Navigation Company from the IMM. The acquisition took effect from 1 January 1927 and cost £7 million, paid £2million in cash, and the balance in three tranches, £1.25 million in June 1928, £1.25 million in June 1929, and £2.5 million in December 1936.[30] A new company, the White Star Line Ltd, was formed as a vehicle for the acquisition. Financing of the acquisition of Oceanic followed vintage Kylsant lines:

- White Star Line Limited to have a capital of £9 million, made up of 4 million ordinary shares of £1 each and 5 million 6½ per cent cumulative preference shares of £1 each.

- The 4 million £1 ordinary shares to be subscribed by Royal Mail Group companies, of which only £1 million were paid up; in fact, Royal Mail only paid 2 shillings in the pound, seriously reducing the paid-up capital of the company.

- The 5 million preference shares were sold through intermediaries to the public in two tranches of 2½ million, guaranteed as to capital and dividend by the Royal Mail Steam Packet Company (which did not have the necessary reserves to cover the guarantee).

The bringing back of a famous transatlantic line into British beneficial ownership brought significant acclaim from the British shipping industry and the public at large; however, concerns were growing in banking and government circles in respect to Kylsant's financial dealings and the over-expended nature of the Royal Mail Group, which by now embraced Harland and Wolff.

From Kylsant's standpoint, the acquisition of the Oceanic Steam Navigation Company brought two strategic advantages, set out in his report to shareholders at the annual court of the Royal Mail Steam Packet Company on 25 May 1927. Firstly, it gave the Royal Mail group access to the cream of the North Atlantic passenger trade; hitherto, the Royal Mail Line had operated a passenger service from Southampton to New York via the West Indies – the 'comfort route'. Now he had one of the most prestigious lines in the Atlantic trade under his control. Secondly, and of our particular interest, the Royal Mail Group re-entered the Australasian trades, which the group had been absent from for eighteen years following the withdrawal of the Pacific Steam Navigation Company's joint service to Australia with the Orient Line. To quote from his address to the annual court:[31]

Besides the regular service to and from Australia which the White Star Line has carried on for many years, the famous Aberdeen Line to Australia founded over a century ago by Messrs George Thompson and Co. has become one of the associated companies [of the Royal Mail Group], through the acquisition of the White Star Line.

In addition, the acquisition secures us a large interest in the Shaw, Savill and Albion Company Limited, whose vessels jointly owned by the White Star Line, trade with New Zealand.

Lord Kylsant and the Royal Mail Group

Owen Crosby Phillips, the son of a Wiltshire cleric, the Rev. Sir James Erasmus Phillips Bt, was born in 1863. He served a six-year apprenticeship with the Newcastle-upon-Tyne ship managers and shipbrokers Dent & Co. before moving to Glasgow in 1886 to join Allen C. Gow and Co., ship managers and shipbrokers, the partners of which held shares in some of the tramp ships the company managed.

In 1888, in partnership with his elder brother, John, 1st Viscount St Davids, Owen Phillips established his own shipping entity, Phillips and Co., in Glasgow, and ordered the tramp ship *King Alfred*, then building at the Blyth Ship Building Co. Ltd, with money raised by his brother and other shareholders. To own the vessel, a one-ship company was established, the King Alfred Steamship Co., with Phillips and Co. providing the management. The *King Alfred* was successful, such that by the autumn of 1895, with the active support of his brother, a second steamer, the *King Bleddyn* was ordered from Sunderland. The name of the owning company had been changed to the King Line in November 1893.

The shipping skills of Owen, working in tandem with the investment skills and wide field of friends of brother John, were a potent mix, and by the end of the nineteenth century, in addition to the King Line, the two brothers had established the Scottish Steamship Company as a subsidiary with seven tramp ships operating profitably between the two companies. They had also started a finance company, the London Maritime Investment Company, and the London and Thames Haven Petroleum Wharf.

Early into the twentieth century, the King Line took a controlling interest in the Newcastle-based Northern Transport Ltd, bringing with it three further ships, one of which was a tanker that was put to work servicing the Thames Haven Petroleum Wharves. Phillips then turned his attention to acquiring the Newcastle-based Tyne Steam Shipping Co., but in this he was thwarted by Sir Christopher Furness. However, in something of a quid pro quo, Furness, who had been negotiating to buy the Royal Mail Lines, withdrew from negotiations leaving the door open for Phillips.

The Royal Mail Line had been founded under Royal Charter in September 1839, providing services initially to the West Indies supported by an Admiralty mail contract, and extending under further mail contracts to Brazil and the Plate in 1850, the extension to the Plate being initially served by a feeder vessel out of Rio de Janeiro. Competition from other British lines, particularly the Booth Line to the Amazon; Lamport and Holt to the Plate; the Pacific Steam Navigation Company, which started a cargo and passenger service to Valparaiso via south-east coast ports of South America; and latterly by Houlder Brothers, together with complacency borne out of comfortable mail contracts, had hurt the company badly. More particularly, competition following the entry of the German Hamburg-Brasilianische Dampschiffahrtsgesellschaft, later to be taken over by the hugely efficient Hamburg-Südamerikanische Dampschiffahrtsgesellschaft – Hamburg-Süd as we know it today – brought the Royal Mail Steam Packet Company close to its knees by the close of the nineteenth century.

John Phillips had begun buying into the Steam Packet Company through the medium of one of his investment companies in 1901 on the back of Royal Mail's share price collapsing 32 per cent. With the withdrawal of Furness from negotiations, the Phillips moved in. By October 1902, Phillips was in a controlling position, and by January 1903, Owen Phillips and his nephew had taken their places in the court of directors of the Steam Packet Company; it only took until March of that year for Owen to become chairman.

With innovative financing arrangements masterminded by John Phillips, and Owen Phillips' aggressive understanding of the shipping industry, the Royal Mail Group's fortunes were turned around. By 1910, Owen had become a respected figure in the shipping world and a significant public figure, such that in that year he was knighted for his services. He did not, however, have the financial wherewithal to satisfy his ambitions. From an early stage, Owen struck up a friendship with Sir William Pirrie, chairman of the Belfast shipbuilders, Harland and Wolff. We have already noted Harland and Wolff's association with the International Mercantile Marine company and through it involvement with two major German lines. Now, almost the entire new-building business and significant repair work of the Royal Mail Group was placed with Harland and Wolff, and this association provided Phillips with access to funding, not least Northern Ireland government loans and guarantees under the NI Trade Facilities and Loan Guarantee Acts, necessary to achieve the expansion he sought.

Over the course of the next twenty years, Elder Dempster, the Pacific Steam Navigation Company, Glen Line, MacGregor Gow, James Moss, Lamport and Holt, the Shire Line, the Union Castle Line, the Nelson Line, Coast Lines, MacAndrews and Co., and the shipbuilders Harland and Wolff, Belfast, were brought under Royal Mail control, to name just some of the component companies of the group, which included coal and oil bunkering, wharfage, lighterage, oil storage and agency operations. To manage the whole, the individual companies were sub-grouped according to trades, each sub-group having a flagship company. A highly complex system of accounting was developed, with interwoven cross-shareholdings, such that it was difficult to disentangle the financial status of any one company, but the flagship company in each sub-group could always be demonstrated to be profitable. Kylsant personally masterminded the financial affairs of each company, the individual directors often being kept in blissful ignorance of the arrangements being made on their behalf. However, while Kylsant personally controlled high strategy and finance, he left the operational management of the various group companies wholly to the high-quality officers making up their senior management. Roland Thornton, a partner of the ultra-conservative Alfred Holt & Co. described the Kylsant empire as 'a crazy edifice of functionless units, none of which gained any benefit from its association with any of the others'.

Financing of this huge acquisition programme was achieved by fixed-interest debenture issues guaranteed by the various group cross-shareholding companies on the back of their marine assets (sometimes without the direct knowledge of directors), and by guarantees extended under the Trade Facilities Act of 1921. The latter was a facility designed by the Lloyd George government to reflate the economy and provide work for thousands of people by promoting capital investments and the purchase of equipment manufactured in the United Kingdom necessary for such capital investments. A Northern Ireland Loans Guarantee Act offered similar financial guarantees, critical to the financing of Harland and Wolff.

A peerage was conferred on Owen Phillips in the 1923 New Year's Honours List and he took the title Baron Kylsant of Carmarthen. It was as Lord Kylsant that he would go down in history.

Lord Pirrie died in 1924, and Kylsant, who had long been a director, became chairman of Harland and Wolff. He took over an enormous manufacturing entity, heavily indebted to the Northern Ireland government, and effectively bankrupt. With few exceptions, the order book was made up of loss-making contracts. (See Appendix 2: GTCo. Corporate Chronology)

A postcard of *Herminius* at Grand Harbour, Malta.

What was not made clear was the fact that the White Star Line, which was deeply involved in the North Atlantic and Australian immigrant trades, had suffered huge losses in the years preceding the acquisition, arising from the fall-off in immigrant numbers in the 1920s.

In a little-remembered interlude in international history, which involved the Aberdeen Line, on 23 March 1927, Nationalist Chinese troops under Chiang Kai-shek occupied the city of Nanking, driving out Northern forces. The following day, in what was to become known as the Nanking Outrages, five senior expatriate figures from the UK, Italy, America and France were murdered, five further individuals including a Japanese army officer were seriously injured, wives were systematically raped, and the legations were sacked; looting of foreign property was widespread. The Aberdeen Line steamer *Herminius* was taken up from trade in March 1927 to transport the 2nd Battalion of the Dorset Regiment from Hong Kong to Shanghai to support British interests following the Nanking Outrages.[32] She subsequently repatriated the Dorsets to Malta following their engagement in China.

Oceanic had owned 40 per cent of Shaw, Savill and Albion since 1910, the majority balance of 55 per cent being owned by Sir John Ellerman from the same time. Following the acquisition of White Star/Oceanic by the Royal Mail group, Sir John Ellerman, shrewd shipowner that he was, became concerned at the prospect of sharing the ownership of Shaw Savill with Kylsant, whose financial acumen he doubted. In 1928, Ellerman offered his 55 per cent shareholding in Shaw Savill to Oceanic. True to form, Kylsant leapt at the opportunity of a further acquisition and a deal was struck in the sum of £910,820[33] (widely believed to be far too high a price), making Shaw Savill and Albion, and George Thompson & Co., wholly owned subsidiaries of Oceanic, and in turn the Kylsant group. Oceanic did not have the cash to pay for the acquisition outright, and the deal was structured such that Ellerman was paid £310,820 in cash, with the balance in six annual tranches of £100,000.

Harold Sanderson, who had been chairman of George Thompson & Co., since its acquisition in 1906; of Shaw Savill and Albion from 1912; and president of the IMM from June 1913 in succession to J. Bruce Ismay, was displaced by Lord Kylsant from his position as chairman of Oceanic and its two subsidiary companies. Sanderson, in failing health and seriously concerned by Kylsant's financial tactics, resigned from all three boards on 30 June 1928. (He had originally intended to retire in 1912.)[34] In 1929, Alexander Duff Henderson, son of Sir William Henderson and the penultimate member of the original owning families to hold senior office in the company, retired, possibly I suspect for the same reason.

While the boards of Oceanic, Shaw Savill and George Thompson grudgingly accepted that Lord Kylsant at some stage must have demonstrated significant shipowning acumen, he had little or no knowledge of the Australasian trades, and his management style did not accord with the likes of such highly experienced and respected Australasian shipping men as John MacMillan and Oscar Thompson. Of his relationship with Kylsant, Basil Sanderson wrote:

> [Kylsant] was never able to strike the pitch calculated to evoke the proper chords. For me, it was always a weak and unconvincing treble, with no solid base notes in the accompaniment.[35]

Whether they liked Kylsant or not, in 1930 Shaw Savill and George Thompson were forced to move offices from Shaw Savill's hallowed head office at 34 Leadenhall Street to Royal Mail House, 50 yards down the street.

The Australian Commonwealth Line of steamers, competition from which had been a major factor in the decline of the Aberdeen Line, had, after an initial First World War and immediate post-war boom, lost money on increasing scales from 1922 onwards. Despite having preferred status in the Australian emigrant trade, the Line had operated against a background of vastly inflated operating costs occasioned by the employment of seamen under Australian articles, a competitive penalty estimated over the five -Bay and two -Dale ships to have been in the region of £220,00 per annum. Further, the Line had an appalling industrial relations record, which pitched unions against management, with ensuing frequent costly delays and embarrassments. This culminated in a strike by stewards on *Moreton Bay* on 27 December 1927, while acting as Sydney Regatta Flagship, whereby the Governor General as principle guest on board was left unfed. The Line had been reconstituted under an Australian Commonwealth Maritime Board in early 1923, at which time the fleet valuation had been written down to £4,700,000. The board was charged with reducing the loss, and all but the five -Bays and two -Dales were progressively disposed of by the end of 1925. However, losses continued to mount and the Parliamentary Joint Committee on Public Accounts was instructed to conduct an investigation into the affairs of the Line, concluding that it should be sold. When announced by Prime Minister Bruce in late 1926, there was considerable opposition from socialist camps and from those interests that feared that the Australian economy would again be exposed unchecked to the British Shipping Ring. In the year running up to its sale, the ACL lost £895,000.

The board, on behalf of the Australian government, invited private tenders for the acquisition of the Australian Commonwealth Line on 2 January 1928. The tender document stipulated *inter alia* that the five -Bay and two -Dale ships sold would continue to provide a regular service to Australia and should remain on the British or dominion register for at least ten years. Preference would be given to offers containing proposals for safeguarding the interests of Australian exporters and importers in regard to freight rates.[36]

John McMillan was enthused by the prospect of acquiring the ACL. The acquisition of a modern fast fleet, with its trading rights, would significantly increase Shaw Savill's presence in the Australian trade, remove the requirement for building new ships and would remove competition from the Aberdeen Line. He proposed a bid of £1,850,000; undeterred by the parlous state of the Royal Mail Group and the chronic underfinancing of the Oceanic sub-group, Kylsant assured him that the financing of such was well within the capability of the Royal Mail, and the bid went ahead.[37]

On 17 April 1928, Prime Minister Bruce sent a cable to London accepting Kylsant's offer. In an announcement to the House of Representatives on 25 April 1928, Bruce advised that only three bids for the Australian Commonwealth Line had been received by the closing date of 28 January 1928. The White Star Line

Largs Bay in Aberdeen and Commonwealth Line colours and with new lifeboat davits.

bid £1,850,000, subsequently increased to £1,900,000 to cover the cost of repatriating Australian crews as passengers from the UK, estimated at between £60,000 and £70,000 (officers were repatriated as first-class passengers, ratings as third-class). Runciman bid £1,000,000, subsequently increased to £1,250,000 but subject to option conditions, and the Australian Commonwealth Shipping Company, a venture that was to be established to purchase the Line, £1,575,000. In Bruce's opinion, the White Star offer was incomparably the best for Australia, and a contract for the sale was signed on 21 April 1928. Payment for the ships was to be made in the sum of £250,000 cash, prorated as each ship delivered in London, and the balance in ten equal annual tranches, attracting 5½ per cent interest. The outstanding monies were to be secured by debentures attaching as a first charge on the ships and other sections of this part of the White Star business.[38] Bruce had clearly not done his homework on the financial status of the White Star group and its parent!

The five -Bay and two -Dale ships delivered in London from May to August 1928, the last Australian Commonwealth Line ship to leave Australia under the Australian flag being the *Ferndale*, departing Sydney on 19 June 1928. To the consternation of the Shaw Savill/ Aberdeen Line management, the ownership of the acquired line was placed in the name of the White Star Line, and not Royal Mail as it had been led to believe. The Line was renamed 'Aberdeen and Commonwealth Line' under the management of George Thompson and Co.; the ships were given the Aberdeen Line livery of green hull and yellow funnel, but the Bay/Dale names were retained. Threatened blacking of the returning Bay ships by the Australian Waterside Workers and other maritime unions did not materialise. In January 1929, Southampton became the outwards passenger terminal for the Bay ships, rather than London; while homewards sailing of ACL ships now routinely took in Hull after London. Strategically, the acquisition was hugely advantageous to the Shaw Savill/Aberdeen Line sub-group.

Former UK-based ACL staff were absorbed into the UK establishment. In Australia, where Oceanic, Aberdeen and Shaw Savill had hitherto been exclusively represented by Dalgety's, a potential problem existed; however, this was resolved by Dalgety's retaining the residual business of the three lines, while the former ACL offices and staff, under E.A. Eva, former resident manager of the old ACL in London, had responsibility for the Australian end of the Aberdeen and Commonwealth Line. Basil Sanderson visited Australia in October 1928 to ensure a smooth transfer of management and representation of the Aberdeen Line and the Aberdeen and Commonwealth Line under the new arrangements.[39] The previously generated very warm relationships between George Thompson & Co.'s management and ACL were to pay dividends.

In 1931, the passenger accommodation of the five Bay-class vessels was reconfigured. Originally carrying twelve first-class and around 712 third-class passengers, the vessels were converted to one class, with accommodation for 270 tourist-class passengers, which could be increased as need dictated to 540 by the installation of portable cabins in the upper 'tween deck. The conversions also included the extension of the bridge deck forward to incorporate an island deck house, trunking No. 3 hatch thereby, the replacement of deck cranes immediately forward of the bridge with sampson posts, and the replacement of the original 'Australis' lifeboat davits with luffing davits serving nested lifeboats.[40]

Thus, George Thompson & Co. had been handed a lifeline. However, the company's problems were far from over; over-tonnaging on the Australian trade and the worldwide trade depression forced the Aberdeen Line ships operating out of Liverpool under White Star management to be periodically laid up, along with other vessels of the joint service; *Horatius* had been laid up for a few years at Falmouth.[41]

12

'ONLY THE STEAMERS, NAME AND GOODWILL . . .' 1930 TO 1993

For years, Lord Kylsant had contrived to bolster the confidence of investors by demonstrating that his flagship companies were consistently profitable, despite difficult trading conditions, by injecting funds from hidden reserves garnered from the huge profits made by the group in the First World War and its immediate aftermath. He had earned a reputation with investors for financial prudence and conservatism. However, as 1929 drew to a close, the over-borrowed/under-capitalised status of the Royal Mail Group, coupled with the adverse impact upon its South American trade arising from the loss in 1928 of the Lamport and Holt liner *Vestris*, with massive accompanying claims in the US courts, and the financial problems of Harland and Wolff, had driven the group's financial status to such a parlous level that the lending banks, the Bank of England, the Treasury and in particular the Trade Facilities Act (TFA) Advisory Committee, which oversaw the extension of guarantees under the Act, were demanding action from Kylsant to clarify the situation. Kylsant ducked and weaved, but the patience of his creditors was wearing thin. In particular, the intricately interwoven shareholdings of the various group companies complicated the preparation of a consolidated balance sheet demanded by creditors, whereby the overall financial heath of the group could be assessed.

Specific to Kylsant's problems was the repayment of a number of Trade Facility Act and Northern Ireland government guaranteed loans, totalling £9.75 million, falling due in 1930. To the irritation of the creditors, the various group companies had consistently paid dividends from hidden reserves up to 1929, and now there was no money left in the pot to pay off the loans. In Kylsant's opinion, with improving market conditions, the group was viable given a moratorium on loan repayment, and to reinforce his case he effectively tried to blackmail the government by pointing out the adverse impact on employment and the national economy if the group collapsed as a result of his demands not being granted. The government at that time was engaged in the major restructuring of prime industries, particularly the iron and steel and shipbuilding industries, and well knew that it was deeply dependent upon a continuing viable shipping industry for its plans to work. Kylsant tried desperately to persuade the Treasury, the Bank of England, the TFA Advisory Committee and his creditor banks to delay repayments on the loans for at least six months, allowing breathing space for the group to make progress in trading its way out of the problem. While there may have been some sympathy for his cause, given the adverse impact on the economy of bankruptcy, hard heads demanded to see a credible consolidated group balance sheet before committing to any course of action. Kylsant finally yielded and commissioned his auditors, Price Waterhouse, to undertake the task.

In the face of slow progress in preparing the consolidated balance sheet, a Committee of Inquiry was established in May 1930 by the creditor banks, charged with identifying the true extent of the group's indebtedness. The committee of inquiry was headed by Sir William McLintock, senior partner of the accountants Thomson McLintock, assisted by Brigadier General Sir Arthur Maxwell, a managing partner in Glynn Mills and Co. and Frederick Hyde, managing director of the Midland Bank. McLintock, a brilliant accountant with a reputation for creative financial solutions, immediately went to work, and established that the group had liabilities of more than £30 million, broken down as follows:

Unsecured liabilities excluding Harland and Wolff and White Star	£10.3 million
White Star Line liabilities	£10.12 million
TFA/Northern Ireland government guaranteed loans	£9.75 million

This was an unprecedented sum, secured in the main by the value of the combined fleets, set at £14 million (though Kylsant valued the fleet at about 50 per cent of build value of £100 million.)

To avoid the prospect of imminent collapse, with the potentially disastrous impact upon creditors and the economy, immediate action had to be taken by the interested parties. The Committee of Inquiry established a task force of three eminent practitioners, to be known as the Royal Mail Voting Trustees, under the chairmanship of Sir William McLintock; the other two trustees being Sir Arthur Maxwell and Sir Walter Runciman, an eminent shipowner. The Voting Trustees were to be given unprecedented powers over the financial management of each of the group's individual companies. Each company was required to transfer all voting rights to the trustees and to undertake not to enter into financial commitments, declare dividends, nor lend or borrow without the trustees' permission. While Kylsant nominally remained chairman of each company, Walter Runciman was made deputy chairman, with effective executive control. In return for these strictures, a restructuring scheme was to be produced that included moratoria of repayments due to creditors, especially those under the TFA.

The Voting Trustees set to work with urgency, skill and authority, disentangling the inter-meshed shareholdings, finding buyers for the viable companies, and disposing of those that were not. Their task was not easy, for their presence and authority was not welcomed by many of the component boards, especially Union Castle. High on the Voting Trustees' priorities was dealing with the financially crippled White Star Line Ltd, of which George Thompson and the Aberdeen

and Commonwealth Line were wholly owned subsidiaries. The capital structure of the White Star Line Company Ltd was nominally £9 million, broken down as follows:

5 million 6½ per cent cumulative preference shares of £1 each	£5,000,000
4 million ordinary shares of £1 each	£4,000,000
of which only 1 million were paid up	(£3,000,000)
Capital at March 1930	£6,000,000[1]

In 1929, the authorised capital had been increased from £9 million to £11 million.

The White Star Line ordinary shareholder structure since acquisition in 1927 was allocated as follows:[2]

Royal Mail	37½ per cent	£1,500,000 of which £750,000 had been paid up
Union Castle	25 per cent	£1,000,000 of which £100,000 had been paid up
Elder Dempster	25 per cent	£1,000,000 of which £100,000 had been paid up
Nelson Line	12½ per cent	£500,000 of which £50,000 had been paid up
	100 per cent	£4,000,000 of which £1,000,000 had been paid up

The White Star Line Group, owned the whole capital of:

The Oceanic Steam Navigation Co. Ltd

Shaw Savill and Albion Co. Ltd

George Thompson and Co. Ltd

The Aberdeen and Commonwealth Line, acquired from the Australian Commonwealth government in 1928

The cost of acquiring the White Star Line Group had been £9,810,820, broken down as follows:

Shares of Oceanic Steam Navigation Co., from IMM	£7,000,000
Balance of shares in Shaw Savill and Albion Co, from Ellerman	£910,820
Commonwealth Line vessels, from Australian government	£1,900,000
	£9,810,820[3]

The White Star Line debt mountain confronting the Voting Trustees in April 1930 was £10,120,000, comprising the following:

Balance of price payable to the IMM, due December 1936	£2,350.000
Balance payable to Sir John Ellerman, repayable £100,000 pa	£400,000
Balance of price payable to Australian government for the Commonwealth Line, repayable by instalments of £165,000 pa	£1,485,000
Glyn Mills Bank facility	£1,250,000 (of which £525,000 matured for repayment by Sep 1930)
George Thompson & Co. overdraft	£200,000
Existing TFA loans	£2,600,000
Balance of price of vessels payable to Shipping Liquidation, Board of Trade	£85,000
Subtotal	£8,370,000
To which had to be added provision for two further ships building	£1,750,000
Total	**£10,120,000**[4]

The assets of the White Star Line Group were essentially the ships it owned, forty-eight vessels with an aggregate gross tonnage of around 600,000 tons. Two large motor ships each with a gross tonnage of around 27,000 tons were building for the North Atlantic trade, one for delivery in June 1930 and the second at the end of 1931. The group's surplus of assets over liabilities, taking no account of the preference or ordinary share capital represented by the White Star Line Group's ships, depended very much on what interpretation was placed on their current market value:

Book value of all assets as at 31st December 1928	£4,700,000
Substituting for the book value of the fleet, a 25 year life	£5,700,000
Substituting for the book value of the fleet, a 20 year life	£3,900,000

The foregoing made no allowance for goodwill. Technically, the White Star Line Group was not insolvent, but the White Star Line per se and George Thompson were both haemorrhaging monies with little hope of recovery; only Shaw Savill and Albion remained a viable operating company.

George Thompson's Aberdeen Line's position had been hopeless for a number of years, and its status had been one of effective receivership since 1926. The company's balance sheet at 31 December 1930 showed:

	£		£
Share capital, fully paid	250,000	Steamers at cost less depreciation to 31 December 1927	1,593,073*
5% mortgage debenture stock	766,335	5% Mortgage Debenture Holders' Deposit	50,000
Loans, secured/unsecured	580,086	Minor assets	4,353
Trade creditors, accruals & tax	410,157	Trade debtors	70,174
Deferred rebate to shippers	10,942	Insurance premium pre-paid	3,081
	£2,017,520	Cash at bank	466
		Profit and loss account	**296,373**
			£2,0175,520[5]

* The directors considered that the book values of the steamers were in excess of present value under existing conditions.

The secured and unsecured loans included a bank overdraft of £199,000; a parent shareholder loan from the Oceanic Steam Navigation Co. of £175,000 to help keep the company running as a going concern; and £242,086 due to the Oceanic Company in respect to payment for the *Horatius*. In the latter case, the Oceanic Company was given a floating charge to rank immediately behind the 5 per cent debentures, but this had been waived by Oceanic in order to enable Thompson's to secure a bank overdraft.

That just one year later the steamers were valued at a maximum of around £250,000 demonstrates just how overvalued in the then market conditions the balance sheet value of the steamers was (and indeed how unrealistically high the build costs of *Diogenes* and *Sophocles* had been), a problem that carried through the entire Kylsant group.

To help finance the building of *Diogenes* and *Sophocles* and provide working capital, George Thompson had raised £600,000 by way of a debenture stock issued under the terms of a trust deed dated 13 July 1922; a supplemental trust deed dated 18 May 1925 raised a further £270,270 debenture stock. Under the terms of the trust deed, which attracted 5 per cent per annum fixed interest, no provision was made for annual redemptions, but the deed of 13 July 1922 required that the amount outstanding at any one time should not exceed 50 per cent of the assets mortgaged in security, in this case George Thompson's fleet. For calculation purposes, the value of the assets was their original costs less 5 per cent per annum. In effect, George Thompson had an obligation to redeem around £70,000 per annum to address the requirement; this had been done up to and including 30 June 1931.

The hopeless situation confronting the board of George Thompson was set out in a letter from the deputy chairman, Walter Savill, to the secretary of the Voting Trustees, Frank Charlton, dated 28 August 1931.[6] In it he pointed out that the directors had, for some years, recognised the impossibility of keeping the company alive as a separate shipping concern and had recommended that the two parent shareholders, Oceanic and Savill, should take over the ships and secured liabilities under such domestic arrangements as they cared to make, allowing George Thompson and Co. Ltd to continue as a loading broker so as to retain the advantage of its (Conference) rights on the Australian trade and its goodwill, which was deemed to be significant. Walter Savill complained that, despite the formulation of a scheme by John MacMillan, the general manager of both Shaw Savill and George Thompson, for one reason or another this was never fructified (although the 1926 rejigging of the Aberdeen Line services out of Liverpool under White Star management and the chartering of the two loss-making new ships to Shaw Savill would seem to have achieved just that). This seems strange, given that the board of George Thompson and Co. Ltd was made up of directors appointed by the two parent shareholders, and Lord Kylsant. One suspects that 'for one reason or another' possibly reflected the interfering hand of Kylsant.

Walter Savill went on to warn that the position of George Thompson and Co. Ltd was so serious and the need for further financial assistance by the end of the year so pressing that, unless the Voting Trustees could formulate a plan for keeping the company in existence as a going concern, the board recommended liquidation as the best way for extracting it from its entanglements, even though this meant losing significant tax credits accrued over prior year losses. Savill reflected that, despite the good name and valuable connections that George Thompson had earned over

the years in the shipping world and Australian Trade, nonetheless liquidation seemed both advisable and proper.

Two months later, on 26 October 1931, Savill again wrote to Charlton pointing out that position of the George Thompson debenture stockholders was becoming worse by the day. Without taking account of the guarantees of the Oceanic Steam Navigation Company and Shaw Savill and Albion, the deficit stood at approximately £400,000, with the debt to the debenture stockholders £657,000 against a fleet valuation of only £250,000.

In May 1931, charges were brought against Kylsant alleging that he had published false statements in the 1926 and 1927 Royal Mail accounts. Kylsant was subsequently cleared of the balance sheet charges, but fresh charges of issuing a false prospectus in 1928 to support a debenture issue proceeded through the Old Bailey and the appeal court, resulting in Kylsant being handed down a one-year jail sentence in November 1931. The verdict was considered by many to be flawed and politically driven; significantly, Kylsant's London clubs refused to accept his resignation. Basil Sanderson probably summed up the view of the shipping fraternity:

> [Of Kylsant] There was no vice in the man, unless it was conceit, and the twelve months' imprisonment to which he was committed was savage, unless it is held proper to affix the sentence according to the damage inflicted, in complete disregard to the motive behind the offence.[7]

With his imprisonment, Kylsant resigned from the chairmanship of all group companies, including George Thompson & Co. Ltd.

On 5 November 1931, the 20-year-old **Demosthenes**, after a period of lay-up in Rothesay Bay, was sold for scrapping to Hughes Bolckow & Co. of Jarrow for £9,620. **Demosthenes** had served with quiet distinction over a most successful career, including distinguished trooping service in the First World War.

Marginally improving trading conditions excited various outside interests into acquiring the viable elements of the Kylsant group, especially the Shaw Savill and George Thompson/Aberdeen and Commonwealth Line. The Voting Trustees were anxious to avoid being forced to accept bargain-basement offers for the target companies and sought Bank of England assistance to structure financial support for the White Star Line whereby time could be bought in order to secure more favourable sale conditions. In May 1931 offers for Shaw Savill and George Thompson & Co. were

Demosthenes in later years.

received from P. Henderson (who had been Shaw Savill's partner in sail to New Zealand – the 'Albion' of Shaw Savill and Albion) in the sum of £878,100, and from Furness Withy in the sum of £1.06 million. In their strengthened position, the Voting Trustees were able to reject both offers.[8]

In a briefing note to Sir William McLintock dated 6 November 1931, the deteriorating status of George Thompson and Company Ltd was summarised as follows:

- The Company's business had been reduced to that of an agent, subject to receiving charter monies from *Mataroa* and *Tamaroa*; the profit and loss of the ships run by the White Star Line; and management commissions (cargo brokerage/passenger commission) on the BAY-boats.

- The Company was hopelessly insolvent, with debentures only covered by the assets to a comparatively small extent.
- The valuation of the fleet assets in the current market were estimated to be:

Mataroa and *Tamaroa*	£200,000
Euripides, *Themistocles* and *Horatius*	£75,000
	£275,000

- Liquid assets held by the trustees on behalf of debenture holders were:

Cash deposited as security with the debenture trustees	£50,000
Proceeds from sale of *Demosthenes*	£8,900
Less expenses to be refunded	(£400)
	£58,500

- The principal objection to liquidation was the loss of very large unexhausted wear and tear allowances and losses carried forward for income tax purposes.
- The Company had bank loans amounting to about £200,000.
- There was the possibility of substantial claims from the Australian Government for War Profits Tax.
- Despite the loss of Income Tax allowances, liquidation was recommended, with the sale of assets and goodwill to Shaw Savill and Albion.
- The indebtedness of the Company to the Debenture Stock holders was calculated to be:

Debenture Stock outstanding			£715,051
Deduct	Cash in hand	£58,000	
	Mataroa/Tamaroa	£200,000	
	Goodwill and name of company	£10,000	
		£268,500	£268,500
			£446,551

From this sum would be deducted the proceeds of the sale of the remaining three ships and petty debts.

The Voting Trustees proposed to address the company's indebtedness to the debenture stockholders by the following offer:

Total amount outstanding		£715,051
		Per £100 debenture
Cash in hand with trustees	£58,500	
S.S.& A to buy goodwill and name of Company for cash	£10,000	
	£68,500	£9/12/ -
S.S.& A. to purchase *Mataroa* and *Tamaroa* for	£214,500	£30/ - / -
To be satisfied by the issue of S.S.& A. Notes carrying 5½ per cent redeemable by equal instalments at par over 15 years		
OSN Co. to issue Thompson debenture holders income stock for	£393,250	£55/ - / -
		£94/12/ -

The receiver would dispose of the remaining three ships and recover debts.

John MacMillan, general manager and director of Shaw Savill and Albion (and also of George Thompson) in a letter dated 8 December 1931 made an offer to the board of George Thompson for the acquisition of its assets. For this, he was rapped over the knuckles by McLintock for acting without the authority of the Voting Trustees, and at McLintock's request he withdrew the offer and substituted it by a memorandum of like content dated 11 December, addressed to the Voting Trustees.[9] In the memorandum, MacMillan flagged Shaw Savill's interest in acquiring George Thompson's assets and goodwill, but not the company or its liabilities. He made clear that Shaw Savill's prime interest was in securing the *Mataroa* and *Tamaroa*, in which it had invested £140,000 reconditioning for the New Zealand trade, and in which trade it had been operating satisfactorily for some years; MacMillan dismissed the remaining three ships currently trading between lay-ups on the Australian trade out of Liverpool as obsolete and unprofitable.

The utmost Shaw Savill could pay for the five steamers was £270,000, broken down as the following:

Mataroa and *Tamaroa*	£220,000
Euripides	£30,000
Themistocles	£10,000
Horatius	£10,000

A further £10,000 was added for George Thompson's goodwill. The offer, which MacMillan averred was a liberal one and more than any other company would be prepared to pay, stipulated that Thompson's interest in the 'Davis' (i.e. its Australian outwards Conference trade rights) would be transferred to Shaw Savill and was made subject to Shaw Savill being granted a share of the west coast UK to Australia, where the three latter ships were already operating in consort with White Star Line.

At a meeting of George Thompson & Co. Ltd debenture stock holders convened on 27 January 1932, Sir William McLintock[10] reviewed the status of George Thompson and Co. Ltd and its parent Oceanic Steam Navigation Co. Ltd as it applied to George Thompson. His review of George Thompson's financial status mirrored his memorandum of 9 November 1931. McLintock, while declining to place a market value on the Thompson fleet, advised that although the book value at 31 December was £1,545,376, this reflected the fact that depreciation had not been taken into account since the end of 1927; had depreciation been addressed, the book value would reduce to just over £1,000,000, which was still considered to be very much in excess of the ships' value in the market conditions prevailing at that time.

McLintock advised the stockholders that £715,051 of debenture stock remained outstanding; interest on this stock had been paid up to and including 30 June 1931. The company's financial situation was such that it had reached the limit of bank loans and the parent shareholders, Oceanic and Shaw Savill and Albion, were not disposed to increase the substantial loans they had made to keep the company afloat. Accordingly, George Thompson was not able to discharge the debenture interest payable on 31 December 1931.

McLintock dwelt upon the guarantees supporting the debenture, 100 per cent from Oceanic with a 40 per cent cross-guarantee to Oceanic from Shaw Savill. He touched upon the acutely difficult trading conditions facing all operators on the North Atlantic, Oceanic's main trade. Oceanic was in a critical financial position, and McLintock advised that the prospect of the George Thompson debenture holders recovering any portion of the sum payable under the Oceanic guarantee were very remote and counselled that any attempt to enforce this guarantee would only destroy the chance that they might ultimately have of recovering in the future some portion of the amount owing. McLintock further advised that the Shaw Savill cross-guarantee was 'rather an ambiguous document, and there is considerable difference of opinion, not only amongst those connected with the companies but also amongst counsel and solicitors who have been consulted, as to just exactly what the Savill guarantee means'.

McLintock counselled that, in the opinion of the Voting Trustees, the relationship that existed between George Thompson, the Oceanic Company, the White Star Line Ltd and the Shaw Savill and Albion company demanded that the whole position should be very carefully considered in the debenture stockholders' interests, given the 'peculiar relationship which had existed between these Companies for so many years'. McLintock, on behalf of the Voting Trustees, recommended the formation of a committee representing the interests of the debenture holders to confer with the debenture stock trustees, and in turn with the Voting Trustees, with a view to formulating a scheme acceptable to all parties. The Voting Trustees were prepared to do everything they could to help find a solution to the difficulties that surrounded the position of George Thompson as it affected the debenture stockholders.

A committee of four was duly appointed comprising:

H.C. Sugden	nominated by Harold Sanderson, the largest debenture holder;
F.G. Burt	nominated by Sir John Ellerman;
E. de M. Rudolf	nominated by various insurance companies; and,
Mr Carlisle	nominated by various trust companies.

The stockholders agreed that during the deliberations of the committee, the payment of interest upon the 5 per cent mortgage debenture stock should be left in abeyance.

On 19 February 1932, at a meeting of the Voting Trustees, the George Thompson debenture trustees and the debenture stockholders' committee, the Voting Trustees advised that George Thompson and Co. was haemorrhaging financially, £49,500 having been expended in 1931, and recommended that the ships and goodwill should be sold to Shaw Savill and Albion at a fair price. The Voting Trustees undertook to secure an offer from Shaw Savill, further pointing out that the management of the -Bays and -Dales could probably be transferred to Shaw Savill and Albion. To add urgency to the situation, George Thompson's bankers, the Midland Bank, by letter of the same date, froze the company's overdraft at £188,000.

In a letter to the Voting Trustees dated 25 February 1932, John MacMillan, as general manager of Shaw Savill and Albion, intimated that the company would be prepared to make a formal offer for the ships, assets and goodwill of George Thompson and Co. Ltd in the improved sum of £325,000, paid by instalments over ten years, with the outstanding balance attracting 5 per cent interest. George Thompson and Co. Ltd would be wound up and a new company, George Thompson & Co. (1932) Ltd, would be formed, to which as nominee for Shaw Savill and Albion, the goodwill and business of George Thompson would be transferred. The offer would require the Voting Trustees to use their best endeavours to secure for Shaw Savill at least 75 per cent of the Oceanic West Coast berth to Australia, with the possibility that if Oceanic wished to rid itself of this berth, then Shaw Savill would make an offer for *Ceramic*, giving the company exclusive use of the Glasgow and Liverpool berths to Australia.

In a separate letter to the Voting Trustees of the same date, MacMillan confirmed that Shaw Savill would be making an offer for the purchase of the fleet and goodwill of George Thompson and Co., and set out Shaw Savill's strategy in making the acquisition. He began by reviewing the five-ship fleet, dismissing *Themistocles* and *Horatius* as being 'useless except as scrap', and *Euripides* as requiring a very large amount of money spending to equip her for the New Zealand trade, where she could be profitably employed for an estimated five years. (The fact that *Themistocles* remained in service until 1947; that *Horatius* was sunk by enemy action in 1941; and *Euripides*, albeit with significant monies spent on her and renamed *Akaroa*, lasted until 1954, puts in question the impartiality of the assessment of MacMillan, as a general manager of both companies, of the fleet value, albeit the Second World War intervened.)

Shaw Savill's real interest lay in *Mataroa* and *Tamaroa*, bare boat chartered from George Thompson since 1926, and in which a large amount of money had been spent to suit them for the New Zealand trade. 'They are now recognised everywhere as Savill steamers and if they were taken over by others and departed the New Zealand trade, it would mean a very great blank in the present services and for a time would seriously handicap and prejudice us, as we have no other passenger steamers to replace them. It is only on account of these two steamers that we are offering for the fleet, although *Euripides* can be made a fairly satisfactory vessel for our trade.'

MacMillan went on to point out that the goodwill of George Thompson & Co. Ltd in the Australian trade would be very useful to the Savill company insofar that it would give it an entry to the trade, but more particularly it would address the imbalance in outwards and homewards sailings on the New Zealand trade. Whereas New Zealand outwards opportunities were only twenty-three a year, thirty-six to forty homewards sailing were needed to service that trade. By employing Australian outward trade ships crossing to New Zealand after discharge, the need for ballast voyages to New Zealand from the UK would be obviated.

The management of the Aberdeen and Commonwealth Line would pass to a successor company, George Thompson (1932) Ltd, to be incorporated as a wholly owned subsidiary of Shaw Savill and Albion, providing Savills with a further satisfactory proposition.

MacMillan concluded: 'You will therefore see how desirous we are to obtain ownership and control of Thompsons, and we earnestly hope it will eventuate.'

In a letter to the directors of George Thompson and Co. Ltd dated 8 March 1932, John MacMillan, as director and general manager of Shaw Savill and Albion Ltd, made a formal offer for the acquisition of the fleet and assets of George Thompson in the sum of £325,000, along the lines proposed to the Voting Trustees on 25 February. Shaw Savill & Albion Co. Ltd offered to purchase:

- The goodwill of George Thompson's business, together with the right to incorporate a new company under the title George Thompson & Co. (1932) Ltd, or some such similar name, and also the right to use the company's flag and the name by which the company was known in shipping circles, namely the Aberdeen Line.

- The five ships owned by Thompsons, free of encumbrances, together with all gear and stores relating to them, ashore or afloat.

- All quay plant and other chattels and effects around the world belonging to Thompsons.

- All office furniture, books and documents belonging to Thompsons and used in connection with its business.

- The benefit of all existing agreements and arrangements in connection with Thompsons' business as shipping owners, ship managers and brokers.

The offer then went on to detail the timing and process of handing over the assets, insurances, pool adjustments, etc., and the future of the Thompson staff, who were under notice of termination with effect from 31 March 1932.

The purchase price would be paid as follows:

Upon acceptance of the offer and executing bills of sale on the five vessels	£55,000
By equal annual instalments of £30,000, the first to be paid on 1 March 1933.	£270,000
	£325,000

Interest at 5 per cent would be paid on the outstanding monies owing, and these would be secured by mortgages to be taken out on each ship.

The offer anticipated the benefit of Thompson's management of the Aberdeen and Commonwealth Line transferring with the company, but made provision in the event that the Owner (Oceanic) cancelled the management arrangement.

MacMillan followed through the offer with a side letter to the Voting Trustees of the same date emphasising the importance of Shaw Savill securing 75 per cent of the west coast trade to Australia, which had not been incorporated in the offer to purchase Thompson. He further pointed out the hopelessness of the Oceanic Steam Navigation Co. trying to operate the west coast trade with only one steamer, and intimating that Shaw Savill would be keen to purchase the *Ceramic* to secure 100 per cent of the trade.

The committee of the debenture shareholders met with the Voting Trustees on 11 March 1932 and expressed their reservations about a deal that left the stockholders short of some £400,00 on their investment. The proposal on the table was that the shortfall would be covered by the issuance of Oceanic deferred creditors' certificates. The debenture stockholders were particularly concerned to secure the benefit of the 40 per cent Shaw Savill guarantee, but as McLintock stressed, the 40 per cent guarantee, albeit issued in respect to the Thompson debenture stockholding, was between Shaw Savill and Oceanic, and would not be available to the Thompson debenture stockholders. It is a measure of McLintock's powers of persuasion and standing as a man of great integrity that he carried the day, and following the meeting on 11 March, Cecil Sugden of Hill Dickinson, as spokesman for the committee, in a letter to McLintock advised that the committee had agreed unanimously to recommend to the debenture stockholders' meeting on 15 March 1932, that:

- They should accept an offer in the net sum of £350,000 on the general terms of Shaw Savill's offer contained in their letter to the Directors of George Thompson & Co. Ltd of 8 March 1932. [Note that no offer in the sum of £350,000 had been made by Shaw Savill, and McLintock probably fed this sum into the debate as being achievable.]

- Acceptance of Oceanic deferred creditors' certificates for the balance due under the Oceanic Guarantee (in other words, assent to the Oceanic scheme of arrangement).

- The release of any claims that the debenture stockholders might have against the Shaw Savill Company under its counter-guarantee.

- All monies in the hands of the debenture stockholders' trustees to be retained for the benefit of the Thompson debenture stockholders.

- The Oceanic Company to enter into an agreement with the Shaw Savill Company that while any monies were due to the Thompson debenture stockholders, they would not attempt to enforce any claim that they might have under the Shaw Savill counter-guarantee.

On 14 March 1932, Shaw Savill's offer for George Thompson and Co. was finally increased to £350,000, paid:

Down payment	£62,000
Nine equal annual payments of £32,000	£288,000
Total	£350.000

Duncan McKellar was appointed receiver of the assets of George Thompson & Co. Ltd on 6 May 1932, and in a notice to Aberdeen and Commonwealth Line employees, he advised that since management of the Line had passed to Shaw Savill & Albion Ltd, their employment would cease with immediate effect and recommended that they contact the new managers to ascertain whether their services could be retained.[11] On 16 June 1932, Shaw Savill & Albion bought the fleet and assets of George Thompson and Co. Ltd from the receiver of the debenture stockholders.[12]

Ironically, on the same day that George Thompson went into receivership, the Aberdeen and Commonwealth Line freighter, *Ferndale*, was lost by grounding off the coast of North Africa on passage from Brisbane to Hull. The insurance payout arising from the loss was paid directly to the Australian government in part-settlement of monies outstanding from Oceanic's acquisition of the Australian Commonwealth Line.

Under Shaw Savill ownership, work was put in hand immediately to convert *Euripides* for the New Zealand service. The conversion, entrusted to Hawthorn Lesley, followed the pattern established for *Sophocles* and *Diogenes* six years earlier. The boilers were converted from coal firing to oil, 4,450 tons of bunker space was created; the old third-class accommodation was converted to cargo space, and the first-class accommodation was converted to provide for 200 one-class passengers; a swimming pool was installed; and a verandah lounge, so beloved of Shaw Savill, was installed across the after end of the boat deck. Under her new guise, and renamed *Akaroa,* her gross tonnage increased from 14,947 to 15,128, and her speed increased by ½ knot; she made her maiden voyage on the New Zealand trade from Southampton on 28 February 1933, offering a 100-day round trip to New Zealand for £112. She was to prove an extremely popular ship on her new trade.

Themistocles, with her livery changed to Shaw Savill's (Black hull with a white sheer line ribband, buff funnel with a black top), retained her name and continued to serve on the joint service from Liverpool to Australia via the Cape. She did this in consort with Oceanic's *Ceramic* and Blue Funnel's *Nestor*, *Anchises*, *Ulysses* and *Ascanius*, trading initially under the name of the Blue Funnel and White Star–Aberdeen service from 1932 to 1938, and thereafter as the Blue Funnel and Shaw Savill–Aberdeen until the Second World War intervened. The Shaw Savill and White Star cargo ships that had been transferred to the Aberdeen Line in 1926 were returned to, or, in the case of *Zealandic*, sold to Shaw Savill along with the *Horatius* (renamed *Kumara*).

For a number of years, the North-east shipowning and shipbuilding group, Furness Withy, under the chairmanship of Sir Frederick Lewis (later Lord Essendon), had been engaged in grand strategies directed towards the Oceanic group. Furness Withy had survived the Great Depression because, as the *Economist* put it: '... the Group had maintained a reputation for ultra-conservative finance and shrewd reluctance to take anything but the right step at the right time, which went far to explain its acknowledged position as one of the strongest shipping organisations in the world.'

In the summer of 1925, Lewis had suggested to Sir Thomas Royden, the then chairman of the Cunard Steamship Company, that the two companies should jointly acquire the UK-flag ships of the International Mercantile Marine. Cunard later withdrew, leaving Lewis to field an offer of £7 million for the Oceanic Steam Navigation

Company; the deal fell through when Oceanic could not meet Lewis' stipulation that the Oceanic accounts should demonstrate a return of 8 per cent since 1919.

In October 1929, with the Kylsant group on the brink of collapse, Lewis had approached Sir Horace Hamilton, the permanent secretary of the Board of Trade, renewing the concept that Cunard should take over the White Star Line, leaving Furness Withy to purchase the remainder of the Kylsant group, excluding the troubled Lambert and Holt and Harland and Wolff. Following a creditors' meeting of the White Star Line group in June 1930, aware of Lewis' interest in securing Oceanic's Antipodean services, Shaw Savill and the Aberdeen Line/Aberdeen and Commonwealth Line, McLintock advised Lewis of the intention to sell the assets of the White Star Line. In July, McLintock approached Sir Percy Bates, the chairman of Cunard, to sound out whether Cunard would be interested in purchasing the White Star Line jointly with Furness Withy, leaving Cunard to operate the North Atlantic services and Furness Withy the Antipodean services. Cunard, to the irritation of Lewis, subsequently withdrew from this proposal, and proceeded with an offer by itself of £3.25 million for the White Star North Atlantic assets in service (i.e. excluding the new-building *Georgic*) and its goodwill. The offer was rejected by the Voting Trustees.

With the purchase of the assets and goodwill of George Thompson & Co. by Shaw Savill in June 1932, the way was now open for the latter, the only viable company within the Oceanic Group, to further secure its position on the Australian trade by acquiring control of the Aberdeen and Commonwealth Line, which it had been running successfully under the management of George Thompson for the past four years, from Oceanic's subsidiary, the White Star Line.

In a detailed memorandum to the Voting Trustees dated 21 May 1932, John MacMillan set out Shaw Savill's rationale for the acquisition of the ACL by a consortium headed by Shaw Savill and Albion. MacMillan, given his close contacts with the Australian government, was concerned in the first instance that the Australian government, clearly worried by the circumstances surrounding the White Star whereby it defaulted on payments due on the ACL, might exercise its right to take back the steamers by giving seven days' notice and selling them to recover all or part of the £1,320,000 still owing to it. MacMillan had been in discussions with the Australian Attorney General, J.G. Lathan, who was at that time visiting London, and had established that the

Australian government would probably accept a cash offer of Aus £650,000, with the balance of monies owing secured as ordinary creditors against the White Star Line. The Australian government would give Shaw Savill up to 30 September 1932 to find the cash. MacMillan sought the Voting Trustees' authority for him to formally confirm the foregoing to Latham before he left for Australia the following week, with a view to securing an option up to the end of September to purchase the ACL steamers.

A new owning company, the Aberdeen and Commonwealth Line Limited, would be established to own the ships. Participating shareholders whom MacMillan had lined up included:

Dalgety and Company	£100,000[13]
Mr Siley (R.H. Green & Silley Weir)	£100,000[14]
Messrs J. & E. Hall, Ltd, Dartford)	
Messrs Shaw Savill & Albion Co. Ltd	£100,000

MacMillan was hopeful that a further £100,000 shareholding could be secured, with the balance obtained from the banks on the security of a mortgage on the steamers. He expressed confidence in the financial success of the investment, given a very slight favourable turn in the tide on outward loadings, and the significantly improved Homewards earnings arising from better organisation between the lines on the Australian trade. He foresaw the 'subscribers should receive a good return for their money'.

From Shaw Savill's standpoint, control of the Aberdeen and Commonwealth Line was crucial to address the imbalance between the outward loadings on the Australian trade and the homeward loading on Shaw Savill's traditional New Zealand trade. MacMillan advanced the same trade arguments as were contained in his letter of 25 February 1932 to the Voting Trustees in respect to the acquisition of George Thompson.

In August 1932, Furness Withy's chairman, Sir Frederick Lewis, now Lord Essendon, was invited by the Royal Mail Voting Trustees to become chairman of White Star Group. In the same year, Oscar Stephen Thompson, George Thompson Jnr's grandson, and the only member of the Thompson family to remain in a senior management post, retired from his post as advisor, but he clearly remained closely involved in the company in a non-executive role.

Acquisition of the Aberdeen and Commonwealth Line by a consortium of Shaw Savill and Albion and P&O was completed on 10 April 1933, with £500,000 (equivalent to Aus £625,000) being paid in to Australia House in London. The balance of the monies outstanding to the Australian government would be paid in annual tranches, with interest at 5½ per cent on the outstanding balance. A new board was appointed representing the shareholding groups:[15]

Lord Essendon	Furness/Shaw Savill	Chairman
John MacMillan	Shaw Savill and Albion	Managing Director
Walter Warwick	Furness/Houlder Brothers	
H.G.B. Larkin	P&O Steam Navigation Co.	
Charles Cowan	New Zealand Shipping Co./P&O	
Irvine Geddes	Orient Steam Navigation Co.	

Management of the Aberdeen and Commonwealth Line was placed in the hands of a revamped George Thompson and Co., a wholly owned subsidiary of Shaw Savill and Albion, based at 34 Leadenhall Street, London, with Oscar Thompson as chairman; the other directors were given as John MacMillan, Basil Sanderson, Walter Henry Savill and Sir Norman Alexander Leslie. The new company was registered on 13 March 1933, with a nominal capital of £1,000 in £1 shares,[16] with the corporate objective of carrying on the business of merchants, shipbuilders and shipbrokers. E.A. Eva, the general manager in Australia of the Aberdeen and Commonwealth Line, was appointed Australian director of George Thompson and Co.[17] Captain Gambell, a George Thompson master, was appointed marine superintendent of the Aberdeen and Commonwealth Line in Sydney. With the five Bay-boats under Shaw Savill and Albion control, reconfiguring and upgrading of their passenger accommodation was put in hand.

Furness Withy, together with its associated British Maritime Trust, had earlier attempted to acquire the Antipodean trading interests of the Oceanic Steam Navigation Company, and with it a major shareholding in Shaw Savill and Albion, as part of a proposed joint venture with Cunard. This having been thwarted, Furness Withy set about acquiring a majority shareholding in Shaw Savill and Albion by way of buying up the unpaid Ellerman shareholding. This was completed by 22 May 1933. Lord Essendon took over as chairman of Shaw Savill and Albion, with John MacMillan remaining as managing director. Three new directors representing Furness interests were appointed to the Shaw Savill board: O. Maxwell, W.C. Warwick (Houlder Brothers) and J.W. Watts.

With its Australian trade interests consolidated, Shaw Savill set about rationalising the Australian management and agency of its two Australian services. With effect from 1 January 1934, the local branches of the Aberdeen and Commonwealth Line in South Australia, Western Australia and other out ports were absorbed into Dalgety and Co., long-time agents of the Aberdeen Line and the White Star Line in Australia. The transfer was not complete, however, for there was clearly some backtracking, with the closure of the A. & C. Line office in Brisbane being postponed indefinitely.

As part of the restructuring of the Kylsant group, and as a means of facilitating government support for the financing of Cunard's new-building Hull 534 (the prospective *Queen Mary*) at John Brown's Clydeside yard, White Star Line was forced to merge with Cunard to become Cunard White Star Line. This left the Australian service of the Oceanic Steam Navigation Company out on a limb with only one ship so engaged, and Shaw Savill moved to buy *Ceramic*, thereby securing 100 per cent of the group's west coast trade to Australia. This was achieved in 1934, with the first voyage under Shaw Savill colours sailing on 25 August that year. The vessel initially continued without change, apart from livery, on the west coast route to Australia via the Cape, pairing with her running mate, *Themistocles*, within the Blue Funnel/Shaw Savill–Aberdeen Line joint service. *Ceramic* was subsequently taken out of service and placed at Harland and Wolff, Govan, in June 1936, where over the course of a three-month conversion, she was completely upgraded to Shaw Savill standards, with passenger accommodation reconfigured for 480 cabin-class passengers (reduced to 340 in 1938), a verandah café was installed at the after end of her boat deck and the forward end of the bridge deck was glassed in. Her boiler installation was upgraded to incorporate thirty-six corrugated furnaces in six double-ended boilers; this together with the fitting of new propellers and a streamlined rudder gave her an extra knot of service speed.[18] *Ceramic* resumed service on 15 August 1936.

Furness Withy finally acquired the remaining shareholding in Shaw Savill and Albion from Oceanic for £1.5 million on 18 December 1935.[19] The purchase included Shaw Savill buying out the White Star joint interest in several of its New Zealand trade ships.

In 1936, *Esperance Bay*, which had attended King George V's Coronation Spithead review, was sold to Shaw Savill to replace *Ionic* and completely refitted for its New Zealand tourist-class trade, with accommodation for 292 passengers; the conversion included

a verandah café at the after end of the boat deck. The vessel resumed in service renamed *Arawa*, with her first voyage under Shaw Savill colours sailing on 22 January 1937. *Hobsons Bay* was renamed *Esperance Bay* in her place.[20] This left four ships operating the Aberdeen and Commonwealth Line service via Suez and intermediate ports to Australia up to commencement of hostilities in the Second World War in 1939.

Oscar Stephen Thompson, the grandson of George Thompson Jnr, died on 25 July 1937. He had served with great distinction as a partner of the company since January 1900, and as director through many difficult years; he was renowned for giving sound advice and support to successive colleagues within both George Thompson and Shaw Savill and Albion. Thompson was widely respected in shipping circles, both in London and in Australia; his 1921 study and knowledge of emigration led to him becoming the UK shipowners' representative on the Overseas Settlement Committee. He was a senior member of the UK shipowners' delegation to Australia in 1929 for a conference convened by Prime Minister Bruce to discuss the contentious matter of shipping and freight rates. Thompson was closely involved, as had all earlier senior members of the Thompson and Henderson families, in the welfare of seamen and their dependants; over a thirty-year period, he had participated in the management of such charities as the Shipwrecked Fishermen and Mariners Royal Benevolent Society, the Sailors' Home and the Red Ensign Club. His sporting interests included motor car racing, driving his legendary car 'Pobbles' on the Brooklands Track. During the First World War he converted the car into an ambulance and drove it himself in France under the Red Cross. His legacy in Australia included presentation of an 'Oscar Thompson [golf] Cup' to be competed for between the various shipping houses in Australia.[21]

The Blue Funnel/Shaw Savill–Aberdeen Line joint service via the Cape continued in that name until 1937, when 'Aberdeen Line' was dropped from the joint service nomenclature. Thus ended fifty-six years of Aberdeen Line steamer services to Australia via the Cape, although *Themistocles* remained on the service until 1947. Then, following a lay-up in the Blackwater estuary, she was sold for scrapping to Arnott and Young and Co., arriving at its Dalmuir yard on 24 August 1947. Her commander at the time of going to the breakers was Captain G.P. McCraith; he had joined the Aberdeen Line as a boy in *Miltiades* in 1919, and his subsequent professional career led ultimately to him being appointed an Elder Brother of

Themistocles in Shaw Savill colours, on her final voyage to the breakers.

Trinity House. Presiding at the flag lowering was Raymond Jones, who had served in the shore management of the Aberdeen Line since joining as a 14-year-old boy in 1889 through to his retirement in 1945. For a vessel that had been deemed to be fit only for scrap at the time of the acquisition of George Thompson by Shaw Savill and Albion in 1933, she had executed a remarkably successful career on the same trade, apart from disruption by two world wars, over a span of thirty-six sea-going years, in the course of which she completed seventy-nine voyages on the Cape run to Australia; surely a legendary ship![22]

At commencement of hostilities in 1939, *Jervis Bay* was taken over by the British Admiralty and outfitted as an armed merchant cruiser under Royal Naval command, intended for convoy protection. Her epic fight against the vastly superior German battle cruiser *Admiral Scheer* on 5 November 1940 has been well documented elsewhere, and it is not appropriate to dwell further upon her loss in action, other than to pay tribute to the heroism of all concerned. The other three ships served with quiet distinction, *Esperance Bay* and *Moreton Bay* initially as armed merchant cruisers and then as troopships, *Largs Bay* as a troopship throughout. The three remaining Bay-boats returned to merchant service after refits in the period 1947 to 1949, *Largs Bay* being the last in 1949 following repairs to mine damage sustained in the Bay of Naples in January 1944.[23]

Resuming in commercial service, the Aberdeen and Commonwealth Line continued with three ships on the same trade to Australia via Suez. On 26 December 1951, P&O sold its interest in the Line to Shaw Savill. The deal involved the acquisition by Shaw Savill of 255,000 £1 shares held by the P&O Group out of the 500,000 shares issued.[24] A rundown of the ageing fleet ensued, the first to go being the *Esperance Bay*, which arrived for scrapping on the Clyde on 6 July 1955, and the remaining two ships in 1957, the last being *Largs Bay*, which arrived at Barrow-in-Furness breakers on 22 August 1957.[25]

Of the other former Aberdeen Line ships, *Kumara* (ex-*Horatius*), after service with Shaw Savill's fleet, had been sold to Greek interests in 1937. *Akaroa* (ex-*Euripides*), with the commissioning of Shaw Savill's *Southern Cross*, went to the breakers in May 1954 after a much-loved second career on the New Zealand trade; again, not bad for a ship deemed to be fit only for scrap twenty-one years earlier! *Tamaroa* (ex-*Sophocles*) and *Mataroa* (ex-*Diogenes*) went to the breakers in March 1957, again after successful second careers on the New Zealand trade.

Relieved of management responsibilities for the Aberdeen and Commonwealth Line when that entity ceased trading, the name George Thompson and Co. Ltd continued as a Furness Withy subsidiary, and was used for an Anglo–Australian confirming house venture in 1968, the Australian end being headed up by Malcolm Thompson, another great-great grandson of George Thompson Jnr. In a changing market, this venture did not meet up to original expectations; however, the name of George Thompson lingered on within Furness Withy, but I have not succeeded in pinning down its ultimate anchorage. I suspect the corporate entity was used as a vehicle for the launch of another company within the Furness Withy Group.

There was to be a final twist in the tale of George Thompson's Aberdeen Line. When containerisation of the Australian trades came about in 1967, the two senior partners in Overseas Containers Limited's Australian trade, the P&O Group and Furness Withy Group, sought a link with the past and focused upon their earlier joint venture in the Aberdeen and Commonwealth Line. The new container ships were given Aberdeen Green colour hulls, and the Bay-names of the Aberdeen and Commonwealth Line. This link with the past was finally severed when P&O, having bought out the other parties in OCL, repainted what became the P&OCL fleet in 'European Blue' hull colours in 1993.

On 12 June 1980, the remaining shareholders in OCL (P&O, Ocean & British & Commonwealth) purchased Furness Withy's shareholding in OCL against an accepted acquisition of Furness Withy by C.Y. Tung's Orient Overseas Holdings Ltd in Hong Kong; the acquisition went through on 30 September that year. Ten years later, following financial problems within the Tung Group, the Furness Withy element of Orient Overseas was acquired by the German Rudolf A. Oetker Group, trading as Hamburg Südamerikanische (Hamburg Süd). I suspect that somewhere within Hamburg Süd, arguably the most competent shipping line in today's global market, lie the *'name, goodwill and flag'* of George Thompson's Aberdeen Line. (Sadly, at the time of going to press, news has broken that the mighty A.P. Moller Group of Denmark, trading as the Maersk Line, has acquired Hamburg Süd subject to due procedures – strains of the International Mercantile Marine 'octopus' of 1905 and the Kylsant empire?)

POSTSCRIPT

Few would have believed in 1932, with the fall of the once mighty Kylsant empire, that within seventy years, Britain, for long the greatest merchant shipping country in the world, would be reduced to having no line of any significance sailing under its flag (and here I discount foreign beneficially owned vessels sailing under what is no more than a UK flag of convenience). The culture of short-term gain, so beloved in Britain in the Thatcher era and in subsequent years, can find no place for the long-term investment profile that is shipping. With the disappearance of shipowning as a major industry, so too has gone the large expertise bank associated with such activity, such that maritime posts in the UK now have to be filled by applicants from abroad, there being few indigenous qualified personnel available. Such major associated industries as insurance, regulation, maritime law, line management, port operations and marine surveying have to look elsewhere for expertise, and in turn will drift away from the UK for want of same. We have already seen the European hubs of nearly all the major international shipping lines re-establish in Denmark, Germany, Holland or France.

From the outset of his shipping enterprise George Thompson based his success on professional excellence. The standards obtaining among his commanders and officers were among the best in the world – hence the exceptional safety record of his ships. It is tragic to reflect that such expertise and excellence has been frittered away in the succeeding years, victims of a national culture of short-termism and individual greed.

Family tree of the Thompson and Henderson families involved in the Aberdeen Line

the THOMPSON family

PER PERICULUM VIVO

GEORGE THOMSON
of Arbroath, Angus
m. ELIZABETH DEUCHARS 19:11:1764

Rev. Prof. JAMES KIDD
b. 06:11:1761   d. 24:12:1834
Preacher and Academic
m. JANE BOYD

Jean ?
Margaret ?
James THOMSON

ANDREW THOMPSON (b. THOMSON)
b. Angus 08:07:1766 d. Madras 18:04:1807
Royal Regiment of Artillery 23:11:1787 to 30:11:1805
Joined Honourable East India Company as Conductor
Posted to Fort St. George, Madras

Married
13:06:1801

ANNE STEPHEN
b. Old Machar 11:07:1772 d.

William Campbell KIDD
Benjamin Rush KIDD
Jake Allan KIDD
James Little KIDD

CHRISTIANA LITTLE KIDD
b. 12:09:1806   d. 17:01:1875

Married
12:07:1830

GEORGE THOMPSON Jnr.
b. Woolwich 23:06:1804 d. Aberdeen 11:04:1895
Started company 01:11:1825   Retired 05:1866
Lord Provost of Aberdeen 1847 to 1850
Member of Parliament for Aberdeen 07:1852 to 1857
H.M.'s Deputy Lieutenant for Aberdeenshire

Elizabeth ?

Annie CROMBIE
Agnes Elizabeth THOMPSON
Agnes Elizabeth DOAK
James Kidd THOMPSON

CORNELIUS THOMPSON
b. 04:07:1843   d. 18:01:1894 at sea
m. GRACE FROST 21:12:1865
m. AGNES MARION WILLIAMSON 12:07:1870
Partner 05:1866
Managing Partner of Walter Hood to 1881
London Manager of Geo. Thompson from 1881

GEORGE THOMPSON Ygst.
b. 29:08:1836 d. 03:11:1904
m. MARY STEWART 04:09:1860
Partner 05:1866 to 05:1868 (or 01:01:1879?)

STEPHEN THOMPSON
b. 29:06:1833 d. 26:07:1877
m. CATHERINE MARY KNIGHT 20:02:1856
Partner 01:01:1854
London Manager of Geo. Thompson from 1857

Grace THOMPSON
Alice LEGGATT

OSCAR STEPHEN THOMPSON
b. 07:10:1877 d. 25:07:1937
Partner 01:01:1900 to 15:12:1905
Management Shareholder to 03:01:1920
Secretary to 1927; then Adviser to 1932

George Keith THOMPSON
Walter Hood THOMPSON
Muriel Annie THOMPSON
Frank THOMPSON
Harold George THOMPSON

STEPHEN THOMPSON
b. 19:01:1857 d. 10:12:1938
m. AGNES LILIAN LEITCH 16:06:1898
Joined company 1875   Retired 1919
Partner 01:01:1879 to 15:12:1905
Management Shareholder from 15:12 1905

Rosamund Lilian KENNEDY
George Stephen THOMPSON
Catherine Mary GRAY
Richard Leitch THOMPSON

the HENDERSON family

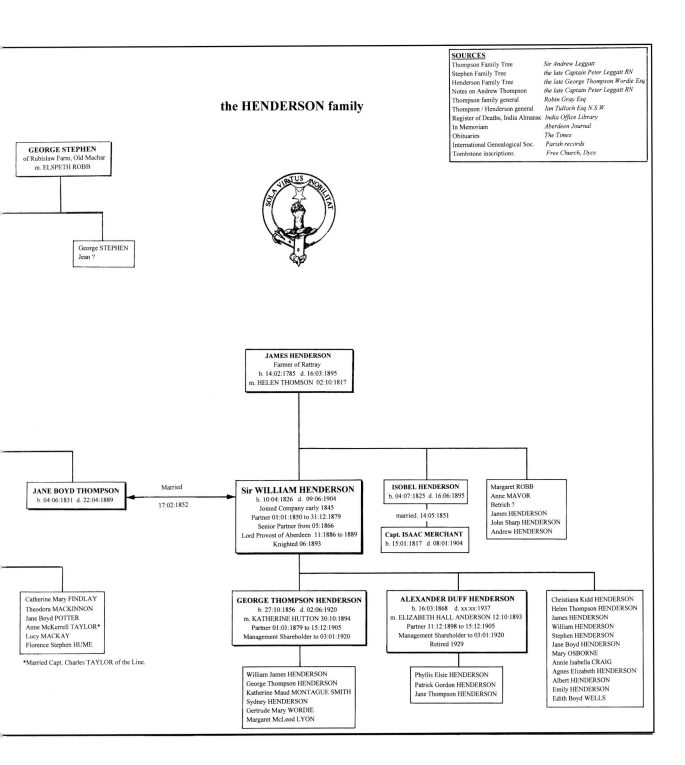

SOURCES
Thompson Family Tree   *Sir Andrew Leggatt*
Stephen Family Tree   *the late Captain Peter Leggatt RN*
Henderson Family Tree   *the late George Thompson Wordie Esq*
Notes on Andrew Thompson   *the late Captain Peter Leggatt RN*
Thompson family general   *Robin Gray Esq*
Thompson / Henderson general   *Ian Tulloch Esq N.S.W.*
Register of Deaths, India Almanac   *India Office Library*
In Memoriam   *Aberdeen Journal*
Obituaries   *The Times*
International Genealogical Soc.   *Parish records*
Tombstone inscriptions   *Free Church, Dyce*

GEORGE STEPHEN
of Rubislaw Farm, Old Machar
m. ELSPETH ROBB

George STEPHEN
Jean ?

JAMES HENDERSON
Farmer of Rattray
b. 14:02:1785 d. 16:03:1895
m. HELEN THOMSON 02:10:1817

JANE BOYD THOMPSON
b. 04:06:1831 d. 22:04:1889

Married
17:02:1852

Sir WILLIAM HENDERSON
b. 10:04:1826 d. 09:06:1904
Joined Company early 1845
Partner 01:01:1850 to 31:12:1879
Senior Partner from 05:1866
Lord Provost of Aberdeen 11:1886 to 1889
Knighted 06:1893

ISOBEL HENDERSON
b. 04:07:1825 d. 16:06:1895

married. 14:05:1851

Capt. ISAAC MERCHANT
b. 15:01:1817 d. 08:01:1904

Margaret ROBB
Anne MAVOR
Betrich ?
James HENDERSON
John Sharp HENDERSON
Andrew HENDERSON

Catherine Mary FINDLAY
Theodora MACKINNON
Jane Boyd POTTER
Anne McKerrell TAYLOR*
Lucy MACKAY
Florence Stephen HUME

*Married Capt. Charles TAYLOR of the Line.

GEORGE THOMPSON HENDERSON
b. 27:10:1856 d. 02:06:1920
m. KATHERINE HUTTON 30:10:1894
Partner 01:01:1879 to 15:12:1905
Management Shareholder to 03:01:1920

ALEXANDER DUFF HENDERSON
b. 16:03:1868 d. xx:xx:1937
m. ELIZABETH HALL ANDERSON 12:10:1893
Partner 31:12:1898 to 15:12:1905
Management Shareholder to 03:01:1920
Retired 1929

Christiana Kidd HENDERSON
Helen Thompson HENDERSON
James HENDERSON
William HENDERSON
Stephen HENDERSON
Jane Boyd HENDERSON
Mary OSBORNE
Annie Isabella CRAIG
Agnes Elizabeth HENDERSON
Albert HENDERSON
Emily HENDERSON
Edith Boyd WELLS

William James HENDERSON
George Thompson HENDERSON
Katherine Maud MONTAGUE SMITH
Sydney HENDERSON
Gertrude Mary WORDIE
Margaret McLeod LYON

Phyllis Elsie HENDERSON
Patrick Gordon HENDERSON
Jane Thompson HENDERSON

Appendix 2
GTCo. Corporate Chronology

1825	**George Thompson Jnr establishes shipping entity in Aberdeen.**
1852	Pilkington & Wilson's White Star Line enters Australian emigrant trade from Liverpool.
1856	**Aberdeen White Star Line established in Australian trade from London.**
1858	Shaw Savill formed; NZ trade.
1864	Henderson's Albion Line formed; NZ trade.
1869	Oceanic Steam Nav. Co. Ltd formed, emphasis on North Atlantic trade.
1882	**First Aberdeen Line steamer *Aberdeen* enters London–Cape–Australia service.**
1883	Shaw Savill and Albion formed; NZ trade.
1899	White Star Line re-enters Australian trade with six Jubilee-class ships.
1902	Oceanic Steam Nav. Co. Ltd acquired by Pierpoint Morgan's Intl. Mercantile Marine (US).
1905	**George Thompson & Co. established as a limited liability company; acquired by Oceanic, 60 per cent, & Shaw Savill, 40 per cent.**
1910	Sir J. Ellerman acquires 55 per cent of S.S. & A. Co. Ltd; White Star/ Oceanic acquires 40 per cent of S.S. & A.
1916	Australian Government Line formed as wartime expedient.
1919	Shaw Savill and Oceanic equalise shareholding in George Thompson Ltd, 50 per cent each.
1922	Australian government establishes Australian Commonwealth Line with five Bay-class cargo/passenger steamers and two Day-class cargo liners.
1926	**George Thompson's operations rationalised with White Star ex-Liverpool.**

1927	Oceanic Steam Nav. Co. Ltd acquired by Kylsant's Royal Mail Group.
1928	Australian Commonwealth Line purchased by White Star Line, renamed Aberdeen & Commonwealth Line.
1928	George Thompson & Co. appointed managers of the Aberdeen & Commonwealth Line.
1928	Sir J. Ellerman's 55 per cent shareholding in Shaw Savill acquired by White Star Line Ltd.
1930	Royal Mail Voting Trustees appointed in face of imminent collapse of the Royal Mail Steam Packet (RMSP) Group.
1932	Shaw Savill acquired ships, assets and goodwill of George Thompson & Co. Ltd.
1932	Royal Mail Lines formed as holding company for RMSP Co. assets.
1932	George Thompson and Co. liquidated.
1933	Royal Mail Voting Trustees wound up.
1933	New A. & C. Line formed with P&O Group and S.S. & A. 50 per cent each.
1933	George Thompson and Co. Ltd formed as subsidiary of Shaw Savill to manage the Aberdeen & Commonwealth Line.
1934	White Star's North Atlantic service merged with Cunard. White Star's Australian service acquired by Shaw Savill.
1935	White Star liquidated.
1935	Shaw Savill & Albion Co. Ltd acquired by Furness Withy Ltd.
1951	P&O shares in ACL acquired by Furness Withy.
1957	ACL ceased trading.
1957	**George Thompson & Co. retained in holding company capacity within Furness Withy.**
1980	Furness Withy acquired by C.Y. Tung, Hong Kong.
1990	In the face of the near collapse of C.Y. Tung Group, Furness Withy sold to Germany's Rudolf A. Oetker Group – Hamburg Süd.
2017	Hamburg Süd sold to Maersk Group.

Appendix 3
GTJ Fleet List

1. Ships in which GTJ/GTJCo. & Family were Subscribing Owners or Managers

No.	Name	Type of Ship	Built	Builder	Builders' / GRT	Dimensions (ft) Register	GTJ / Co 64ths		Remarks / Disposal
							Initial	Max	
1	*Douglas*	Brigtn	1815	Aberdeen	135	69.8 x 21.7 x 12.7	2 / 1825	16	Lost off Portlethen, 25:10:1829
2	*Marmion*	Schnr	1826	Alex Hall	78	56.7 x 18.1 x 10.8	16 / 1826	24	Sold to Stonehaven 19:02:1835
3	*Lady of the Lake*	Brigtn	1827	St John NB	294	96.7 x 26.5 x 5.5	8 / 1827	16	Lost to ice off Grand Banks, 18:05:1833
4	*Childe Harold*	Brig	1828	Alex Hall	116	68.1 x 20.3 x 11.1	14 / 1828	32	GTJ sold interest 08:1838. Lost in Baltic, 06:1845
5	*Mary*	Brigtn	1828	Miramichi NB	134	71.3 x 21.2 x 12.1	8 / 1829	56	Sold to Yule 17:03:1838
6	*James Lumsden*	H'dite	1828	William Duthie	116	65.3 x 20.6 x 11.9	12 / 1831	32	Vessel last heard of 09:12:36, Aberdeen
7	*Struggler*	Schnr.	1827	William Duthie	106	64.7 x 19.7 x 11.7	32 / 1831	48	GT sold interest 25:04:1836; nothing further heard after 1844
8	*Dunnotar Castle*	Brigtn	1833	William Duthie	165	78.8 x 22.1 x 14.7	24 / 1833	32	GT sold interest 08:08:1838. Lost ashore W. France, 23:03:1848
9	*Mansfield*	Schnr	1824	Jas. Anderson	125	69.3 x 21.0 x 12.5	4 / 1834	12	Vessel wrecked near Peterhead, 09:1859
10	*Braemar*	H'dite	1829	William Rennie	120	65.7 x 20.7 x 12.1	64 / 1835	64	GT sold interest 06:1835. Shipbroking deal. Ship lost
11	*Falcon*	Brigtn	1836	William Duthie	132	70.0 x 19.1 x 12.5	32 / 1836	32	Sold to Aberdeen Commercial Co. 09:1837. Lost off Holy Island 26:09:1851
12	*Sir William Wallace*	Brigtn	1824	St Stephens NB	321	100.3 x 27.0 x 19.2	32 / 1825	32	GT sold shares 06:1842. Vessel lost off Belle Isle 1842
13	*Shakespeare*	Snow	1825	Nicol Reid	179	78.8 x 23.0 x 15.0	64 / 1836	64	Sold 03:1838 to South Shields. 1851, no trace in Lloyd's Register

No.	Name	Type of Ship	Built	Builder	Builders' / GRT	Dimensions (ft) Register	GTJ / Co 64ths		Remarks / Disposal
							Initial	Max	
14	*Amity*	Bqtine	1825	Oromocto NB	312	98.5 x 27.0 x 19.1	8 / 1836	32	Sold 02:12:1845. Vessel broken up Stornaway 1847
15	*Flamingo*	Brigtn	1837	William Duthie	185	76.0 x 20.3 x 15.0	32 / 1837	32	Disposed of remaining interest 01:1850; Vessel sold to Hull.
16	*Queen Victoria*	Brigtn	1837	Halifax NS	261	84.1 x 21.6 x 15.1	64 / 1838	64	Vessel sold to James Jobling, South Shields
17	*Wanderer*	Brigtn	1838	Alex Hall	156	80.7 x 18.4 x 12.4	8 / 1838	64	Vessel sold to William Nicol, Liverpool, 04:1852.
18	*Mungo Park*	Barque	1838	Alex Duthie	224	91.8 x 20.7 x 15.6	32 / 1838	64	Vessel sold to Richard Connon, Aberdeen 1850 Sold to Newcastle
19	*Isabella*	Brigtn	1839	Alex Duthie	156	77.5 x 19.3 x 12.8	8 / 1839	8	Vessel sold to Arthur Bryson Gowan Jnr, Berwick
20	*Alexander Harvey*	Barque	1840	Walter Hood	292	93.8 x 22.3 x 16.6	64 / 1840	64	First ship built by W. Hood for GTJ. Vessel sold to Thomas Alan, Banff.
21	*Anemone*	Brig	1840	Walter Hood	205	85.4 x 20.4 x 14.5	40 / 1840	40	Vessel sold 10:1849 to Aberdeen owners; 11:1851, condemned at Callao.
22	*Margaret Hardy*	Barque	1841	Walter Hood	296	93.9 x 22.4 x 16.6	16 / 1840	64	Vessel sold to Robert Anderson, Aberdeen 10:1857, vessel stranded in River Plate
23	*Michael Williams*	Brig	1841	Walter Hood	227	89.6 x 20.9 x 15.0	64 / 1841	64	08:02:1848, Vessel burnt at sea off Monte Video
24	*Agnes Blaikie*	Barque	1841	Walter Hood	385	116.3 x 23.6 x 16.8	12 / 1841	22	Vessel sold to William Jenkins, Swansea 06:1848. Lost in collision with HMS *Medina* off Balaclava
25	*Mayflower*	Brigtn	1841	W. Rennie NB	280	95.3 x 21.2 x 16.3	64 / 1842	64	Vessel sold to John Jamieson, Aberdeen, 07:1849. / Scarborough 04:1853
26	*Prince of Wales*	Barque	1842	Walter Hood	583	133.0 x 25.7 x 18.9	12 / 1842	48	Vessel sold 08:1855 to London; 20:09:1858, sold to foreigner at Callao
27	*City of Aberdeen*	Brigtn	1826	William Duthie	259	90.3 x 25.8 x 17.1	52 / 1842	52	Vessel lost 09:1843 off Peru
28	*Jane Boyd*	Barque	1843	Walter Hood	358	109.6 x 23.8 x 18.1	64 / 1843	64	Vessel sold to a foreigner 08:1866
29	*Neptune*	Barque	1844	Walter Hood	343	104.5 x 22.8 x 16.4	12 / 1844	22	10:1849, Vessel re-registered in Greenock. 05:10:1863 lost, Scharnhorn
30	*Oliver Cromwell*	Ship	1847	Walter Hood	478	148.7 x 24.6 x 18.9	48 / 1847	56	Vessel sold 11:1861 to Holderness & Chilton of Liverpool
31	*Lord Metcalfe*	Barque	1845	Quebec	485	170.6 x 26.1 x 18.2	64 / 1847	64	Vessel sold 04:1855 to Robert Donald
32	*Phoenecian*	Barque	1847	Walter Hood	478	154.0 x 27.5 x 19.1	40 / 1847	40	Vessel sold 03:1862 to London / Liverpool / Belfast. Vessel lost 1863
33	*John Bunyan*	Ship	1848	Walter Hood	467	137.3 x 25.0 x 18.3	36 / 1848	40	Vessel sold 06:1863 to London owners. Lost 25:09:1873 en route Barrow
34	*Richibucto*	Barque	1836	Richibucto NB	401	118.7 x 27.3 x 18.5	64 / 1849	64	Vessel sold to Liverpool, 03:1861. Vessel sold to Ch. Salvesen, Leith 05:1868
35	*Centurion* (1)	Ship	1850	Walter Hood	639	157.0 x 26.4 x 19.2	24 / 1850	24	Vessel sold to William Johnson, Newcastle 03:1867. Vessel lost 1866
36	*Walter Hood*	Ship	1852	Walter Hood	937	179.2 x 30.2 x 20.9	32 / 1852	32	Vessel lost near Jarvis Bay L/H NSW 27:04:1870
37	*Woolloomooloo*	Ship	1852	Walter Hood	627	154.7 x 26.9 x 19.1	32 / 1852	36	Vessel sold 09:1869 to H. Gansen. Wrecked under Spanish flag 1885

No.	Name	Type of Ship	Built	Builder	Builders' / GRT	Dimensions (ft) Register	GTJ / Co 64ths		Remarks / Disposal
							Initial	Max	
38	*Maid of Judah*	Ship	1853	Walter Hood	756	160.7 x 31.0 x 19.3	32 / 1853	40	Sold to Cowlislaw Bros, Sydney, 02:1873 via Samuel A. Joseph. Condemned at Amoy, China 06:1880
39	*Omar Pasha*	Ship	1854	Walter Hood	1271	203.5 x 32.7 x 22.3	36 / 1854	36	Vessel sold to London Shipbrokers 06:1868. Burnt at sea 1869; wool fire
40	*Star of Peace*	Ship	1855	Walter Hood	1114	215.2 x 35.9 x 22.6	40 / 1855	40	Vessel sold 08:1874. Bought by Burns Philp, Sydney. Converted to hulk at Thursday Is. Broken 1895
41	*Wave of Life*	Ship	1856	Walter Hood	887	189.6 x 34.2 x 21.0	40 / 1854	40	Vessel sold to Brazil 08:1880; R/N *Ida*. 03:1897 condemned & broken
42	*Damascus*	Ship	1857	Walter Hood	964	207.9 x 33.9 x 20.8	36 / 1857	36	Vessel sold to Norwegians via Liverpool S/B 04:1881; R/N *Magnolia* Lost off Bersimis, 01:09:1893
43	*Transatlantic*	Ship	1857	Walter Hood	614	152.8 x 29.5 x 17.9	40 / 1857	40	Vessel sold to J. Ugland, Arundal. 04:1875. Sunk in Atlantic 15:10:1899
44	*Moravian*	Ship	1858	Walter Hood	966	199.7 x 33.6 x 21.3	36 / 1858	44	Vessel sold via S.A. Joseph 1881 to Sydney NSW owners. B/U 03:1895
45	*Strathdon* (1)	Ship	1860	Walter Hood	1011	210.0 x 33.8 x 21.6	48 / 1860	48	Vessel sold to Dutchman 16:02:1880. Peruvian flag 'Zwerver'. B/U 1888
46	*Queen of Nations*	Ship	1861	Walter Hood	846	190.9 x 32.5 x 20.1	48 / 1861	48	Vessel wrecked near Woolongong NSW 31:05:1881
47	*Star of Hope*	Ship?	1854	Maine, USA	788	156.5 x 32.7 x 21.2	8 / 1861	36	Vessel run down and sunk off Southwold by *Archos*, 20:04:1870
48	*Colonial Empire*	Ship?	1861	Quebec	1305	198.4 x 38.3 x 22.4	64 / 1862	64	Vessel sold to J. Milne, Aberdeen, 04:1873. Vessel abandoned 29:01:1880
49	*Kosciusko*	Ship	1862	Walter Hood	1192	212.5 x 36.4 x 22.7	48 / 1862	48	Vessel sold to Cowlislaw Bros., Sydney, 22:08:1881. B/U at Canton 1899
50	*Nineveh* (1)	Ship	1864	Walter Hood	1174	210.0 x 36.3 x 22.7	40 / 1864	40	Vessel sold 20:10:1881 to J. Hay Goodlet, Sydney NSW Vessel abandoned N. Pacific 02:1896
51	*Ethiopian*	Ship	1864	Walter Hood	839	195.8 x 34.1 x 20.2	44 / 1864	44	Vessel sold to Norwegians, 02:1888. Abandoned / condemned 10:1894
52	*Harlaw*	Ship	1866	Walter Hood	1055	194.0 x 34.0 x 21.2	44 / 1866	44	Vessel wrecked in SE mouth of Yangtze, 31:07:1878, coal laden
53	*Christiana Thompson*	Ship	1866	Walter Hood	1217	203.5 x 35.2 x 21.7	44 / 1866	44	Vessel sold to Norwegians 25:08:1887, R/N *Betarice Lines* Wrecked near Umra, Norway, 07:10:99
54	*Jerusalem*	Ship	1867	Walter Hood	901	196.5 x 33.8 x 20.7	44 / 1867	44	Vessel sold to Norwegians 10:1887. Last heard of / lost 28:10:1893
55	*Thyatira*	Ship	1867	Walter Hood	962	201.0 x 33.9 x 21.1	44 / 1867	44	Vessel sold W.J. Woodside, Belfast, 21:07:1891. 16:07:1896, lost to fire
56	*Ascalon*	Barque	1868	Walter Hood	938	201.5 x 34.4 x 20.6	44 / 1868	44	Vessel sold to Trinder Anderson, London, 04:1881 Sold to Norwegians 1890. Wrecked at Annalong 07:02:1907
57	*Thermopylæ* (1)	Ship	1868	Walter Hood	991	212.0 x 36.0 x 23.2	48 / 1868	48	Sold to Reford, Montreal, 30:05:1890; rice trade to WCNA Sold to Portuguese navy 1895; sunk by torpedo 13:10:1907

No.	Name	Type of Ship	Built	Builder	Builders' / GRT	Dimensions (ft) Register	GTJ / Co 64ths Initial	Max	Remarks / Disposal
58	*Centurion* (2)	Ship	1869	Walter Hood	965	208.1 x 35.0 x 21.0	40 / 1869	48	Wrecked off N. Head, Sydney, 16:01:1887
59	*Patriarch*	Ship	1869	Walter Hood	1339	230.8 x 38.2 x 22.3	60 / 1869	60	Sold to Norwegians 01:11:1898. Lost off C. Corrientes, 23:02:1912 First iron ship in fleet
61	*Aviemore*	Ship	1870	Walter Hood	1091	235.0 x 36.7 x 22.2	40 / 1870	40	Sold to Norwegians 30:08:1888. Converted to floating oil refinery, S. Shetland. Still trading 1915
62	*Miltiades* (1)	Ship	1871	Walter Hood	1452	246.5 x 39.3 x 23.3	44 / 1871	46	Vessel sold to Italy 06:06:1902. Dismasted, B/U Genoa 1905
63	*Samuel Plimsoll*	Ship	1873	Walter Hood	1510	241.3 x 39.0 x 23.1	40 / 1873	40	Vessel sold to W. Savill, 03:1900. Coal hulk at Fremantle. 09:09:1916 Sunk by drifting ship 18:06:1945
64	*Salamis* (1)	Ship	1875	Walter Hood	1130	221.6 x 36.0 x 23.7	40 / 1875	44	Sold to Norwegians 16:05:1898. Wrecked Malden Island 20:05:1905
65	*Aristides*	Ship	1876	Walter Hood	1721	260.0 x 39.5 x 24.5	40 / 1876	48	Sailed from Caleta Buena with nitrate, 28:05:1903. No trace
66	*Smyrna*	Ship	1876	Walter Hood	1372	232.2 x 38.1 x 22.3	48 / 1876	48	Run down by SS *Moto* in fog off Isle of Wight, sunk 28:04:1888
67	*Pericles* (1)	Ship	1877	Walter Hood	1671	259.6 x 39.4 x 23.7	40 / 1877	46	Sold to Norwegians 25:03:1904, timber trade. Broken Kiel, 08:1923
68	*Sophocles*	Ship	1879	Walter Hood	1176	223.4 x 34.7 x 21.7	48 / 1879	48	Sold to Italians 18:06:1898. Believed to be still afloat in 1914
69	*Orontes*	Ship	1881	Walter Hood	1383	234.8 x 36.2 x 22.5	44 / 1881	52	Last W. Hood ship. Sank after collision, Rugtingen Bank, 23:10:1903
70	*Aberdeen*	Steam	1881	Robert Napier	3684	362.0 x 44.0 x 23.0	64 / 1882	64	Sold *en bloc* to Turks 11:1906
71	*Australasian*	Steam	1884	Robert Napier	3662	361.6 x 44.2 x 21.3	64 / 1882	64	Crippled by HM Sub E11 Sea of Marmara 1915
72	*Damascus* (2)	Steam	1887	Robert Napier	3762	362.0 x 44.3 x 23.6	64 / 1882	64	Sold to Italians 25:04:1910
73	*Strathdon* (2)	Barque	1885	H & W, Belfast	2038	282.8 x 40.4 x 23.6	56 / 1890	56	Sold to Bordes, France, 10:05:1905. R/N *GERS*, nitrate trade
74	*Thermopylæ* (2)	Steam	1891	Hall Russell	3711	362.2 x 44.4 x 33.0	56 / 1891	56	Wrecked off Green Point, C. Town, 11:09:1899
75	*Nineveh* (2)	Steam	1894	Robert Napier	3808	365.0 x 45.0 x 33.0	56 / 1894	64	Sold to Eastern & Australian SN Co., 26:02:1907; R/N *Aldenham* Sold to Royal Mail Meat Transport Co. R/N *Larne*, 1916 Sold to MacAndrews 04:1918. Sold to Germans for breaking, 03:1923
76	*Moravian* (2)	Steam	1899	Robert Napier	4573	390.4 x 47.0 x 33.0	64 / 1899	64	Sold to Bombay & Persia SN Co., 27:05:1914; R/N *Akbar*
77	*Salamis* (2)	Steam	1899	Hall Russell	4617	392.7 x 47.2 x 21.5	54/ 1899	54	Sold to Bank Line 11:01:1912. Sold to Canada Steamship Line, 1919; R/N *Kamarima*. Sold to Cantieri Navale Triestino 1924; broken at Trieste
78	*Sophocles* (2)	Steam	1883	H & W, Belfast	4673	439.9 x 44.2 x 28.9	64 / 1900	64	Built as *Ionic* for White Star. Scrapped at Morecombe 04:1908
79	*Miltiades* (2)	Steam	1903	Alex Stephen	6765	454.9 x 55.1 x 33.1	64 / 1903	64	Lengthened by 50ft, 03:1912. Sold to PSNC, 10:1922; R/N *Orcana*
			1912	Alex Stephen	7827	504.9 x 55.1 x 33.1			Scrapped Holland, 1925

No.	Name	Type of Ship	Built	Builder	Builders' / GRT	Dimensions (ft) Register	GTJ / Co 64ths		Remarks / Disposal
							Initial	Max	
80	*Marathon*	Steam	1903	Alex Stephen	6795	442.0 x 55.1 x 33.1	64 / 1904	64	Lengthened by 50ft, 10:1912. Sold to PSNC, 10:1922; R/N *Oruba*
			1912	Alex Stephen	7848	504.9 x 55.1 x 33.1			Scrapped in Germany, 1925
81	*Pericles* (2)	Steam	1908	H & W, Belfast	10925	500.5 x 62.3 x 31.1	64 / 1908	64	Hit uncharted rock and sank off C. Leeuwin 31:03:1910
82	*Themistocles*	Steam	1911	H & W, Belfast	11231	500.6 x 62.3 x 39.4	64 / 1911	64	Broken at Dalmuir, 24:08:1947
83	*Demosthenes*	Steam	1911	H & W, Belfast	11223	500.6 x 62.3 x 39.4	64 / 1911	64	Broken at Jarrow, 10:1931
84	*Euripides*	Steam	1914	H & W, Belfast	14947	550.7 x 67.4 x 44.1	64 / 1914	64	Sold to Shaw Savill 08:1932; R/N *Akaroa* for NZ trade. Scrapped at Antwerp 06:1954
85	*Sophocles* (3)	Steam	1922	H & W, Belfast	12354	500.4 x 63.2 x 39.6	64 / 1922	64	Chartered to Shaw Savill 1926; R/N *Tamaroa*. Sold to SS&A 08:1932
86	*Diogenes*	Steam	1922	H & W, Belfast	12353	500.4 x 63.2 x 39.6	64 / 1922	64	Chartered to Shaw Savill 1926; R/N *Mataroa*. Sold to SS&A 08:1932
87	*Horatius*	Steam	1919	H & W, Belfast	8010	450.4 x 58.4 x 37.2	64 / 1925	64	Ex-*War Priam* / *Bardic* White Star; purchased 08:1925. Initially named *Hostilius* (?). Sold to SS&A 03:08:1932, R/N *Kumara*

Notes

1. Subsequent to his retirement, George Thompson Jnr held private investments, often in partnership with his old commanders, typically 4/64 or 8/64, in many of the GTJCo vessels.

2. George Thompson Ygst, subsequent to his leaving the main shareholding grouping in 1879, held personal shareholdings in many of the GTJCo. vessels, typically 8/64.

3. In many accounts of George Thompson Jnr's early ship-owning activities, the Nicol Reid-built brig *Arab* is attributed to GTJ. I do not believe this to have been correct, the Thomson involvement in this ship being a different Thomson.

2. Ships in which GTJ and family had private investments other than in Main Line Ships, or in which GTJ appears to have acted as shipbroker only.

No.	Name	Type of Ship	Built	Builder	Builders' / GRT	Dimensions (ft) Register	GTJ / Co 64ths		Remarks / Disposal
							Initial	Max	
201	*Brothers* (1)	Sloop	1807	Fraserburgh	66	53.2 x 17.5 x 9.3	16 / 1827	16	Appears to have been a shipbroking / financing involvement
202	*Morven*	Brigtn	1831	William Duthie	146	72.7 x 21.8 x 13.2	8 / 1831	8	Private investment GTJ with Cattos. Sold 12:09:1836
203	*Brothers* (2)	Brigtn	1814	Leith	93	60.2 x 18.0 x 10.9	12 / 1836	12	

No.	Name	Type of Ship	Built	Builder	Builders' / GRT	Dimensions (ft) Register	GTJ / Co 64ths		Remarks / Disposal
							Initial	Max	
204	*Iris*	Aux. PS	1842	Alex Hall	280	155.3 x 19.2 x 12.0	64 / 1842	64	Aux. paddle steamer. Shipbroking intervention. Sold to Aalborg SS Co. Denmark, Copenhagen – Aalborg service
205	*Ariel*	Brigtn	1837	Nicol Reid	129	69.0 x 19.0 x 12.0	8 / 1846	8	Vessel lost 24:11:1846
206	*Forth*	Ship	1856	Quebec	790	156.6 x 32.8 x 20.8	8 / 1857	8	Vessel lost 18:12:1858
207	*Good Hope*	Brig	?	Garmouth	163	97.3 x 23.0 x 12.3	8 / 1861	8	
204	*Columba*	Barque	1865	Walter Hood	344	146.0 x 25.3 x 15.2	16 / 1865	16	Vessel sold to Shanghai owners, 03:09:1873
205	*Janet*	Brig	1867	Walter Hood	216	111.9 x 23.5 x 13.7	16 / 1867	16	Private investment. Sold to Peterhead 18:04:1881
206	*Ploughman*	Brig	1867	Walter Hood	161	103.0 x 23.0 x 12.8	64 / 1867	64	Private joint investment GTJ. Vessel sold to Aberdeen Commercial Co. 01:03:1869. Lost 11:1893
207	*Lydia*	Barque	1873	Walter Hood	377	148.9 x 25.9 x 15.4	64 / 1873	64	Sold to Scots merchants, Shanghai, 15:02:1875. Lost China Sea 1882
208	*Jan Meyen*	Aux SS	1859	Peterhead	337	119.0 x 29.2 x 17.3	64 / 1867		Private investment, GTYgst + W.H., sold 16:10:1878. Lost in ice off Greenland 27:05:1882

3.   Significant GTJCo. Chartered and Managed Ships

No.	Name	Type of Ship	Built	Builder	Builders' / GRT	Dimensions (ft) Register	Remarks
301	*Atrato*	Aux. SS	1869	Caird, Greenock	3184	335.9 x 42.4 x 31.9	Former RMSP Co. paddle steamer converted to screw. Managed by GTCo for one emigrant run from UK to Australia 1872/73
302	*Norseman*	Steam	1898	H & W, Belfast	10336	516.0 x 62.0	Built as *Brasilia*. R/N *Norseman* 1900, Dominion Line, Liverpool. Chartered by GTJCo. 1910 to 1914 to replace lost *Pericles*. Broken 1920
303	*Gothic*	Steam	1893	H & W, Belfast	7755	490.7 x 53.2 x 33.5	Chartered by GTJCo. from White Star for four voyages 1911–12 to substitute for *Marathon* and *Miltiades* during lengthening
304	*Adolph Woermann*	Steam	1906	Reihersteig, Hamburg	6355	410.1 x 49.2	German East Africa Line. War reparation. Allocated to GTJCo. management for two repatriation voyages to NZ 1919/20. 1921 Sold by UK Govt to Royal Netherlands Mail Line. Scrapped 1938
305	*Bahia Castillo*	Steam	1913	Reihersteig, Hamburg	9949	491.8 x 59.4 x 38.4	Hamburg Süd. War reparation. Allocated to GTJCo. management for two repatriation voyages to Australia 1919/20. Sold to A.G. Stinnes, Hamburg, 10:1922. Broken Hamburg, 12:1932
306	*Chemnitz*	Steam		Vulkan	7542	428.0 x 54.0	Norddeutsche Lloyd. War reparation. Allocated to GTJCo. management for three repatriation voyages to Australia 1919/21. Broken in Holland, 11:1923
307	*Herminius*	Steam	1911	Workman, Belfast	10389	477.6 x 63.1 x 31.3	Shaw Savill's *Waimana*, chartered to GTJCo. 1926 to sustain London berth at time of fleet rationalisation with White Star ex-Liverpool. Returned to SS&A 1932. Destroyed by enemy action, 04:06:1941
308	*Mamilius*	Steam	1911	H&W, Belfast	10898	477.5 x 63.1 x 31.5	Shaw Savill's *Zealandic*, chartered to GTJCo. 06:1926 to sustain London berth at time of rationalisation with White Star ex-Liverpool. Returned to SS&A 1932, R/N *Mamari*, Broken Briton Ferry 05:1950

4.   Aberdeen and Commonwealth Line

No.	Name	Type of Ship	Built	Builder	Builders' / GRT	Dimensions (ft) Register	Remarks
401	*Moreton Bay*	Steam	1921	Vickers Barrow	13855	530.6 x 68.3 x 39.9	Acquired by White Star / Kylsant 05:1928; management George Thompson Sold to Shaw Savill / P&O joint ownership 04:1933; George Thompson managers Scrapped at Barrow 13:04:1957
402	*Largs Bay*	Steam	1922	Beardmore, Dalmuir	13853	530.9 x 68.3 x 39.9	Scrapped Barrow, 04:1957, ending Aberdeen and Commonwealth Line.
403	*Esperance Bay*	Steam	1922	Beardmore, Dalmuir	13856	530.9 x 68.3 x 39.9	Sold to Shaw Savill 1936. R/N *Arawa*; NZ service. Scrapped Newport, 05:1955
404	*Jervis Bay*	Steam	1922	Vickers, Barrow	13839	530.6 x 68.3 x 39.9	Taken over by Admiralty as Armed Merchant Cruiser 09:1939. Lost in action against *Admiral Scheer* 05:11:1940
405	*Hobson's Bay*	Steam	1922	Vickers, Barrow	13840	530.6 x 68.3 x 39.9	As above. R/N *Esperance Bay* 1936. Scrapped Faslane 06:07:1955

Sources

Registrar of British Ships, Aberdeen.
Lloyds Register of Shipping.

Appendix 4
HOOD BUILD LIST

No.	Name	Rig	Built	Tonnage (GRT/NM)	Dimensions (ft)	Owner	Trade	Remarks
1	*Milton*	Brig	08:1839	163	76.7 x 19.0 x 13.5	H. Oswald	St Domingo coffee	Wood construction
2	*Richard Grainger*	Schnr	10:1839	116	67.3 x 18.6 x 12.0	George Cruickshank	Coastal coal	Wood
3	*Janet*	Brig	12:1839	182	82.3 x 20.2 x 14.2	Nicol & Munro	WCSA	Wood, coppered and copper fastened
4	*Alexander Harvey*	Barque	03:1840	292	93.8 x 22.3 x 16.6	**GTJ**	Cuban copper ore	Wood, double wood knees & stringers
5	*Lady Elphinstone*	Schnr.	04:1840	145	72.0 x 19.4 x 12.8	Aberdeen Lime Co.	Coastal coal / lime	Wood
6	*Anemone*	Brig	05:1840	200	85.4 x 20.4 x 14.5	**GTJ**	WCSA	Larch, oak and elm. Wood knees & stringers
7	*Fame*	Brig	07:1840	154	78.8 x 18.8 x 13.5	George Leslie	Baltic & coastal	
		Barq'tn	03:1843	203	85.2 x 19.1 x 13.5	George Leslie	ECSA	Vessel lengthened and strengthened by Hood.
8	*Margaret Hardy*	Barque	08:1840	296	93.9 x 22.4 x 16.6	**GTJ** / William Donald	W/W tramping	
9	*Star*	Schnr	09:1840	156	75.8 x 19.5 x 13.2	Aberdeen Commercial Co.	Coastal coal	
10	*Paragon*	Brig	11:1840	213	86.7 x 21.1 x 14.4	Robert Spring		Built: beech, larch, fir and elm
11	*St Lawrence*	Barque	01:1841	407	105.0 x 24.6 x 18.0	Donaldson Rose	N. Atlantic timber	Built: oak, beech, larch and elm
12	*Ellen Simpson*	Barque	03:1841	376	106.5 x 23.4 x 17.3	Henry Adamson	Cuban copper ore	First known photograph of Hood-built ship
13	*Taurus*	Schnr	05:1841	184	84.6 x 20.5 x 13.5	Nisbet & Robertson	Coastal cattle	Built beech, oak, larch and elm
14	*Michael Williams*	Brig	05:1841	227	89.8 x 20.8 x 15.0	**GTJ**	Cuban copper ore	Hold wood knees & stringers; Deck x2 wood knees; Iron diagonal knees.

No.	Name	Rig	Built	Tonnage (GRT/NM)	Dimensions (ft)	Owner	Trade	Remarks
15	*Agnes Blaikie*	Barque	10:1841	385	116.5 x 23.6 x 17.0	**GTJ**	Cuban copper ore	Built: oak
16	*Seaton*	Barque	01:1842	700		Glasgow owners	India trade	'The largest vessel built in Aberdeen'
17	*Harriet*	Brig	06:1842	165	81.6 x 19.5 x 13.1	Lewis Crombie		
18	*Prince of Wales*	Barque	06:1842	583	133.0 x 25.7 x 18.9	**GTJ**	WCSA	
19	*Chilena*	Barque	08:1842	296		J. & R. Dal	W/W tramping	Built: oak, ash, pitch pine, elm beech & fir
20	*Jane Boyd*	Barque	02:1843	388	109.6 x 23.8 x 18.1	**GTJ**	Cuban copper ore	
21	*Rose*	Barque	05:1843	280	99.5 x 21.0 x 15.5	Donaldson Rose	Quebec	Oak built
22	*Eliza Hall*	Brig	06:1843	200	87.3 x 19.7 x 14.0	George Rennie	Ichebo guano	
23	*Duncan Ritchie*	Barque	07:1843	610		Aikman, Glasgow		Built: Oak, elm, pitch pine, beech and fir
24	*Queen of the Tyne*	Schnr	08:1844	193	106.3 x 21.8 x 13.4	George Leslie	East coast trade	
25	*Neptune*	Barque	08:1844	343	104.5 x 22.8 x 16.4	**GTJ**	W/W tramping	
26	*Consort*	Schnr	04:1845	199	112.6 x 21.3 x 13.6	George Leslie	West Indies trade	
27	*Magnet*	Brig	09:1845	176	77.4 x 20.9 x 13.9	William Connon		
28	*Granite*	Brig	01:1846	187	101.3 x 21.2 x 13.6	Aberdeen Commercial Co.	Coastal coal trade	
29	*Admiral*	Brig	03:1846	187	99.0 x 20.8 x 13.7	William Young	Baltic trade	
30	*Gazelle*	Schnr	04:1846	175	101.2 x 20.5 x 13.2	Aberdeen SN Co. Ltd	Hull coastal liner	
31	*Oliver Cromwell*	Ship	01:1847	478	148.7 x 24.6 x 18.9	**GTJ**	WCSA trade	Wood hanging knees deck and hold; iron diagonal knees and breasthooks. Oak, elm, larch & pine
32	*William Edward*	Brig	01:1847	196	97.8 x 20.7 x 13.6	James Munro	Brazil trade	
33	*Phoenician*	Barque	05:1847	478	146.0 x 24.6 x 19.1	**GTJ**	W/W tramping	As above
34	*Seaton*	Brig	08:1847	185	101.0 x 21.5 x 13.6	Alex Nicol	Baltic trade	
35	*Luna*	Brig	01:1848	187	97.3 x 21.3 x 13.3	Aberdeen Commercial Co.	Coastal coal trade	
36	*John Bunyan*	Ship	03:1848	467	137.3 x 25.0 x 18.3	**GTJ**	China trade	Iron lodging knees in hold; wood lodging knees on deck. Iron knees.
37	*Balgownie*	Barque	08:1848	325	119.2 x 23.4 x 16.6	Alex Nicol	WCSA trade	
38	*Orient*	Brig	10:1848	134	89.0 x 18.3 x 12.0	John Smith	Baltic / coastal	
39	*Victoria*	Schnr	01:1849	180	97.6 x 20.9 x 13.3	Aberdeen Lime Co.	Coastal trade	
40	*Emperor*	Brig	05:1849	200	101.3 x 21.3 x 14.0	John Dinnson	Baltic	
41	*Centurion* (1)	Ship	01:1850	639	157.0 x 26.4 x 19.2	**GTJ**	India / Australia	
42	*Lady Franklin*	Brig	03:1850	201	101.0 x 21.3 x 14.0	British Admiralty	Arctic rescue	Search for John Franklin
43	*Sophia*	Brig	03:1850	113		British Admiralty	Arctic rescue	Search for John Franklin
44	*Gladiator*	Ship	05:1850	534	144.6 x 25.3 x 19.0	Henry Adamson	WCSA / India	Similar to **John Bunyan**
45	*Heather Bell*	Brig	06:1850	191	98.0 x 19.9 x 12.9	David Millar	ECSA/ Australia	

No.	Name	Rig	Built	Tonnage (GRT/NM)	Dimensions (ft)	Owner	Trade	Remarks
46	*Abergeldie*	Ship	02:1851	600	152.3 x 26.2 x 19.2	George Leslie	China trade	
47	*Walter Hood*	Ship	01:1852	918	179.2 x 30.2 x 20.9	**GTJ**	Australia trade	Iron lodging knees and beams in hold. Wood lodging knees and iron beams on deck.
48	*John Knox*	Barque	03:1852	296	128.2 x 21.7 x 14.0	James Munro	China trade	
49	*Wooloomooloo*	Ship	09:1852	627	154.7 x 26.9 x 19.1	**GTJ**	Australia trade	
50	*Granite City*	Ship	01:1853	772	169.0 x 28.8 x 203	Henry Adamson	China / Australia	
51	*Maid of Judah*	Ship	01:1853	665	160.7 x 28.1 x 19.3	Isaac Merchant / **GTJCo.**	Australia	Iron staple lodging knees & oak knees for deck, 10 pairs iron rider beams to floors
52	*Omar Pasha*	Ship	05:1853	1,125	203.0 x 32.7 x 22.3	**GTJCo.**	Australia	Iron hold beam knees. Deck beams, wood lodging knees iron hanging knees, Fels patent knees.
53	*Assyrian*	Ship	12:1854	555	152.7 x 25.9 x 18.6	Alex Nicol	China trade	
54	*Star of Peace*	Ship	09:1855	1,114	215.2 x 35.9 x 22.6	**GTJCo.**	Australia	
55	*Wave of Life*	Ship	05:1856	887	189.6 x 34.2 x 21.0	**GTJCo.**	Australia	
56	*Golden Fleece*	Ship	06:1856	359	145.7 x 24.9 x 15.8	John Dennison	Australia	
57	*Damascus*	Ship	02:1857	964	207.9 x 33.9 x 20.8	**GTJCo.**	Australia	Wood beams, iron knees and breasthooks. Built under cover
58	*Transatlantic*	Ship	05:1857	614	152.8 x 29.5 x 17.9	**GTJCo.**	Quebec / Australia	
59	*Westburn*	Ship	02:1858	593	173.1 x 28.3 x 18.1	Alex Nicol	Australia	
60	*Jason*	Ship	06:1858	878	192.2 x 33.5 x 20.8	Henry Adamson	Australia	
61	*Moravian*	Ship	07:1858	968	199.7 x 33.6 x 21.3	**GTJCo.**	Australia	
62	Cuzco	Barque	04:1859	415	136 x 26 x 16	William Nicol, Liverpool	WCSA guano trade	Wood
63	*Strathdon*	Ship	01:1860	1,011	210.0 x 33.8 x 21.6	**GTJCo.**	Australia	
64	*Marquis of Argyle*	Ship	03:1860	515	152.7 x 27.9 x 17.6	J. Munro, London	Australia	
65	*Nereid*	Brig	07:1860	191	101.9 x 22.9 x 14.3	George Leslie	Baltic / ECSA	
66	*Queen of Nations*	Ship	04:1861	846	190.9 x 32.5 x 20.1	**GTJCo.**	China / Australia	Wood. Iron knees and pillars
67	*Garrawalt*	Ship	01:1862	627	166.4 x 30.4 x 18.8	Alex Nicol	China / Australia	
68	*Kosciusko*	Ship	08:1862	1,192	212.5 x 36.4 x 22.7	**GTJCo.**	Australia	'Carrying capacity upwards of 2,000 tons' A.J.
69	*Fawn*	Brig	11:1862	216	105.3 x 24.2 x 14.1	Dalgety	Australia / Far East	
70	*Glengairn*	Ship	04:1863	895	185.3 x 33.3 x 21.6	Alex Nicol	Australia	
71	*Niniveh*	Ship	03:1864	1,174	210.0 x 36.3 x 22.7	**GTJCo.**	Australia	
72	*Ethiopian*	Ship	08:1864	839	195.8 x 34.1 x 20.3	**GTJCo.**	Australia / China	Deck beams wood, hold beam iron; iron knees

No.	Name	Rig	Built	Tonnage (GRT/NM)	Dimensions (ft)	Owner	Trade	Remarks
73	*George Thompson*	Ship	05:1865	1,128	209.1 x 36.2 x 22.5	Alex Nicol	Australia	
74	*Columba*	Ship	10:1865	344	146.0 x 25.3 x 15.2	Neil Smith	W/W tramping	GTJCo. managers
75	*Harlaw*	Ship	02:1866	894	194.0 x 34.0 x 21.2	**GTJCo.**	Australia / China	
76	*Christiana Thompson*	Ship	08:1866	1,079	203.5 x 35.2 x 21.7	**GTJCo.**	Australia	
77	*Janet*	Brig	03:1867	216	111.9 x 23.7 x 13.9	**GTJCo.** / J.V.	Baltic trades	
78	*Jerusalem*	Ship	04:1867	901	196.5 x 33.8 x 20.7	**GTJCo.**	Australia / China	
79	*Thyatira*	Ship	08:1867	962	201.0 x 33.9 x 21.1	**GTJCo.**	Australia / China	Full composite construction
80	*Ploughman*	Brig	11:1867	177	103.0 x 23.0 x 12.9	**GTJ**	Baltic & coastal	
81	*Ascalon*	Barque	04:1868	998	201.5 x 34.4 x 20.6	**GTJCo.**	Australia	
82	*Thermopylæ*	Ship	08:1868	948	212.0 x 36.1 x 21.0	**GTJCo.**	Australia / China	Full composite construction, under roof
83	*Glenavon*	Ship	10:1868	831	188.2 x 33.3 x 19.9	Alex Nicol	China	Iron construction
84	*Centurion*	Ship	04:1869	965	208.1 x 35.0 x 21.0	**GTJCo.**	Australia / China	Iron beams / knees. Diagonal external plates
85	*Patriarch*	Ship	09:1869	1,405	221.1 x 38.1 x 22.3	**GTJCo.**	Australia passenger	Iron construction
86	*Leucadia*	Ship	03:1870	896	194.2 x 33.8 x 20.4	Alex Nicol	AUS / NZ / China	Iron construction
87	*Aviemore*	Ship	08:1970	1,091	213.9 x 36.7 x 22.2	**GTJCo.**	Australia	Wood construction
88	*Miltiades*	Ship	04:1871	1,452	246.4 x 39.3 x 23.3	**GTJCo.**	Australia passenger	Iron construction
89	*Collingwood*	Ship	06:1872	1,064	211.1 x 34.8 x 21.0	Devitt & Moore	Australia	Iron construction
90	*Samuel Plimsoll*	Ship	09:1873	1,510	241.3 x 39.0 x 23.1	**GTJCo.**	Australia passenger	Iron construction
91	*Lydia*	Barque	11:1873	377	148.9 x 25.9 x 15.4	GTJ private	China trade	Wood construction
92	*Charles Chalmers*	Brig	02:1874	187	102.4 x 23.1 x 12.7	Aberdeen Commercial Co.	Coastal coal	Composite construction
93	*Romanoff*	Ship	08:1874	1,277	222.1 x 36.2 x 22.2	Alex Nicol	Australia	Iron construction
94	*Salamis*	Ship	05:1875	1,130	221.6 x 36.0 x 21.8	**GTJCo.**	Australia / China	Iron construction
95	*Aristides*	Ship	03:1876	1,721	260.0 x 39.5 x 24.5	**GTJCo.**	Australia passenger	Iron construction
96	*Smyrna*	Ship	10:1876	1,372	232.2 x 38.1 x 22.3	**GTJCo.**	Australia	Iron construction
97	*Pericles*	Ship	07:1877	1,671	259.6 x 39.4 x 23.7	**GTJCo.**	Australia passenger	Iron construction
98	*Cimba*	Ship	04:1878	1,174	223.0 x 34.6 x 21.8	Alex Nicol	Australia	Iron construction
99	*Sophocles*	Ship	08:1879	1,176	223.4 x 34.7 x 21.7	**GTJCo.**	Australia	Iron construction
100	*Orontes*	Ship	02:1881	1,383	234.8 x 36.2 x 22.5	**GTJCo.**	Australia	Iron construction; the last ship built by Walter Hood.

Note: Based on original work by Dr Jake Duthie, augmented by information from Lloyds Register of Ships and the Aberdeen Register of Ships.

NOTES

Chapter 1

1   *The Sea Carriers*, L. Cope Cornford 1925.
2   *International Genealogical Index* (IGI), a work of the Church of Jesus Christ of Latter-day Saints, 81.
3   Note by Captain W.R.C. (Peter) Leggatt DSO RN.
4   Letter dated 9 April 1788 to his father, George Thomson, at Hucksterstone.
5   Old Machar Parish Register.
6   Scots Presbyterian Church Register, Woolwich.
7   *Ibid.*/IGI.
8   RA Regimental records.
9   *India Almanac*, India Office Library.
10   Family tree based on the work of Captain Peter Leggatt RN supplemented by information from the *Dictionary of National Biography*.
11   Letter from Captain Peter Leggatt DSO RN.
12   *Recollections of an Old Lawyer*, L. MacKinnon 1935.
13   *Ibid.*
14   Under the Honourable East India Company's trade monopoly, it was to be some years before Aberdeen would be allowed the 'privilege' of direct trade with the Eastern empire.
15   An apparently morbid interest in the Aberdeen gallows by the author derives from the fact that alongside the shipping news in the early nineteenth century *Aberdeen Journal* appeared reports of public executions, cased in the most exquisite Victorian prose. A fatal distraction from the business of nautical research!
16   *The Port of Aberdeen*, V.E. Clark 1921.
17   *Scotland's Northern Gateway*, Captain J.R. Turner, 1986.
18   *Textiles and Toil*, R. Duncan 1984.
19   *Scotland's Northern Gateway*, Captain J.R. Turner, 1986.
20   Testaments of the Aberdeen and Edinburgh Commissary Courts and inventory of the Aberdeen Sheriff Court.
21   Aberdeen Register of Ships *et sequens*.
22   Minute of the General Shipowners Society of 11 December 1823, Lloyd's Register.
23   Alexander Hall archives, Aberdeen Town House.
24   *Aberdeen Journal*, sailing advertisements.
25   *Report of Parliamentary Committee into Aberdeen Harbour Bill*, 1839.
26   *Stowage of Ships*, R.W. Stevens 1869 (*'Stevens on Stowage'*).
27   *British Fishing-boats and Coastal Craft*, Science Museum 1950.
28   *Moray Firth – Ships and Trade,* I. Hustwick 1994.
29   Arrivals and Departures Book, Aberdeen Harbour Board.
30   Banff Collector's Quarter Book, October 1829.
31   *Ibid.*
32   *Aberdeen Journal*, 28 October 1829.

Chapter 2

1　Now an extension of the Aberdeen Maritime Museum.
2　A.M. Williams, as told by Alex Keith, *Eminent Aberdonians.*
3　IGI.
4　*Aberdeen Journal*, 14 January 1835.
5　Aberdeen Journal, 9 May 1832.
6　*Reporting Reminiscences*, W. Carnie 1902.
7　*Aberdeen Journal*, 1 February 1833.
8　*Aberdeen Journal*, 3 July 1833.
9　*Meteorology for Mariners*, HMSO 1967.
10　IGI.
11　*The Sea Carriers*, J. Cope Cornford 1925.
12　*Ships and Sealing Wax*, B.L. Sanderson 1967.
13　*The Villages of Footdee*, D. Morgan 1993.
14　Aberdeen Register of Ships.
15　*Aberdeen Journal*, 25 February 1835.
16　William Donald, a well-known Aberdeen shipowner.
17　Minute books held in the library of the University of Aberdeen, courtesy of Dr Hazel Carnegie.
18　*The Highland Clearances*, J. Prebble 1963.
19　An excellent account of a voyage on an Aberdonian emigrant ship, the **Lord Seaton**, partly owned by GTJ, may be found in *From Aberdeen to Ottawa in 1847*, the diary of Alexander Muir, edited by G.A. MacKenzie 1990.
20　*Le Saint-Laurent et ses îles*, D. Potvin.
21　*Great Britain's Woodyard*, A.R.M. Lower 1973.
22　*Recollections of an Old Lawyer*, L. MacKinnon 1935.
23　*Report of Parliamentary Committee into Aberdeen Harbour Bill*, 1839.
24　*Aberdeen Journal*, 18 July 1843.
25　*Aberdeen Journal*, June 1836.
26　*North of Scotland Bank Ltd 1836–1936*, A. Keith 1936.
27　*Aberdeen Journal*, 1 February 1837.
28　*Recollections of an Old Lawyer,* L. MacKinnon 1935.

Chapter 3

1　*Report of the Proceedings in the Committee of the House of Commons in regard to the Aberdeen Harbour Bill*, 1839.
2　*Stevens on Stowage*, R.W. Stevens 1869.
3　*Aberdeen Journal*, 29 May 1839.
4　*Fast Sailing Ships*, D.R. MacGregor 1988.
5　*The Villages of Aberdeen, Footdee*, D. Morgan 1993.
6　Lloyd's Register Collection, National Maritime Museum.
7　IGI.
8　*Ibid*.
9　Feuing plan 1820.
10　*Aberdeen Weekly Journal*, 5 December 1877.
11　*A Cyclopaedia of Commerce and Navigation*, Homans 1858.
12　*El Cobre: Cuban Ore and the Globilisation of Swansea Copper 1830–1870*, C. Evans.
13　*Travels in the West: Cuba*, David Turnbull, London 1840.
14　Detailed descriptions of the Swansea copper industry may be found in the various Lower Swansea Valley factsheets published by the Swansea Museum under aegis of the Swansea History Project.
15　*The Stowage of Ships and Their Cargoes*, R. White Stevens 1869.
16　*The Photographic Work of Calvert Richard Jones*, R. Buckman 1991.
17　*The Sea Carriers,* L. Cope Cornford 1925.
18　*Aberdeen Journal*, 11 August 1841.
19　*The Stowage of Ships*, R.W. Stevens 1869.
20　*Termo de entrada dos navios mercantes – No. 11, Arquivistico da Dieccao Geral das Alfandegas*, National History Museum, CVI.
21　*From Aberdeen to Ottawa in 1845: The Diary of Alexander Muir*, G. MacKenzie (ed.) 1990.
22　Alexander Hall yardbook, City Archives, Town House, Aberdeen.
23　*The Sea Carriers*, L. Cope Cornford 1925.
24　*New Zealand Examiner*, 7 January 1843.
25　*The Sea Carriers*, L. Cope Cornford 1925.
26　*New Zealand Gazette*, 7 January 1843.
27　*The Sea Carriers*, L. Cope Cornford 1925.
28　*Lloyd's List* etc.

29 *Aberdeen Journal* and *Lloyd's List*, 13 June 1844; Arrival and Departure Book, Aberdeen Harbour Board.

30 *Dundee Courier*, 9 July 1844.

31 Minutes of the Finance Committee of the trustees of the Harbour of Dundee, 20 June 1844. Dundee City Archives GD/DH 4/.

32 *The Sea Carriers*, L. Cope Cornford 1925.

33 A detailed account of the Ichaboe guano trade may be found in the paper 'The African Guano Trade', *Mariner's Mirror*, R. Craig 1964.

34 *Nautical Magazine*, Vol. XIII.

35 *Aberdeen Journal*, March 1845.

36 *Aberdeen Journal*, 3 April 1844.

37 *Aberdeen Journal*, early January 1845.

38 Petition to the Rt Hon. the Lords of the Privy Council of Trade, 27 June 1854.

39 *Slavers in Paradise*, H.E. Maude 1981.

40 *Stevens on Stowage*, R.W. Stevens 1869.

41 'A Primitive Export Sector: Guano Production in mid-19th Century Peru', W.M. Mathews, Institute of Latin American Studies, and various other papers by W.M. Mathews.

42 Guano Registers, Gibbs archives, Guildhall Library, London.

43 *Sydney Morning Herald*, as reflected by the *Southern Cross and New Zealand Guardian*, 17 September 1850, reporting **Oliver Cromwell**'s visit to Auckland (the first visit by a vessel with the Aberdeen bow to that port).

44 *Illustrated London News*, 21 February 1852.

45 Dalgety letter to G. Marshal, 30 November 1846, from an unpublished manuscript on Dalgety by Prof. Max Hartwell.

46 *Sydney Morning Herald*, 17 November 1849.

47 *Sydney Morning Herald*, 6 and 19 January 1850.

Chapter 4

1 By common usage, the title of Lord Provost had been bestowed upon the Provost of Aberdeen since 1833; however, it was not until 1863 that Queen Victoria formally elevated the post of Provost to that of Lord Provost.

2 *North of Scotland Bank Ltd 1836–1936*, A. Keith 1936.

3 *The Tea Clippers*, D.R. MacGregor 1983.

4 *Fast Sailing Ships* (and *The Tea Clippers*), D.R. MacGregor 1988 (and 1972).

5 *The China Clippers*, B. Lubbock 1948.

6 Sources: a) *Lloyd's List* (GTJ) and b) *The Tea Clippers*, D. McGregor 1972.

7 *The Clipper Ship Era*, A.H. Clark 1910.

8 *Black Sea Wreck Club* website.

9 The remains of Franklin's **Erebus** were finally found by a Canadian government-sponsored side scan survey in September, 2014, lying on the seabed in the eastern part of the Queen Maud Gulf, west of O'Reilly Island.

10 *South Australian Register*, 1850.

11 *Sydney Morning Herald*, 3 January 1852.

12 *Sydney Morning Herald*, 27 December 1851.

13 *Fast Sailing Ships*, D.R. MacGregor 1988.

14 *Sydney Morning Herald*, 12 November 1851.

15 *Aberdeen Daily Free Press*, 14 January 1899.

16 *Dalgety*, W. Vaughan-Thomas, H. Melland 1984.

17 *Empire*, 9 August 1853.

18 a) *Lloyd's List*, b) *Shipping Arrivals and Departures, Victoria*, Syme.

19 *Aberdeen Journal*, 21 September 1853.

20 'Cunningham's Self-Reefing Topsails', *Mariner's Mirror*, Col R. St J. Gillespie.

21 *The Cutty Sark and Thermopylæ Era of Sail*, C.L. Hume, M.C. Armstrong 1987.

22 *The Colonial Clippers*, B. Lubbock 1948.

23 Valuation Roll, County of Aberdeen.

24 Unpublished manuscript biography of Dalgety, Prof. Rex Hartwell, Oxford.

25 *A Cyclopaedia of Commerce and Commercial Navigation*, J. Smith Homan 1858.

26 *Dalgety*, W. Vaughan-Thomas 1984.

27 Unpublished manuscript biography of Dalgety, Prof. Max Hartwell, Oxford.

28 *Dalgety*, W. Vaughan-Thomas 1984.

29 *Ibid.*

Chapter 5

1   *Wooden Ships and Iron Men*, F.W. Wallace 1924.
2   *Voyaging*, J.W. Holmes 1966.
3   *Aberdeen Journal*, 31 December 1862.
4   Old parochial registers, St Nicholas, Aberdeen.
5   Register of Ships, Aberdeen.
6   *Illustrated Marine Encyclopedia*, Capt. H. Paasch 1890.
7   *Stevens on Stowage*, R.W. Stevens 1869.
8   *Sail to New Zealand*, D. Savill 1986.
9   *The Colonial Clippers*, B. Lubbock 1948.
10   *Sydney Morning Herald*, 1 September 1864.
11   *Masting and Rigging the Clipper Ship & Ocean Carrier*, H.A. Underhill 1946.
12   *Melbourne Age*, 11 January 1865.
13   Or so I think it translates, having sought advice from historians, judges and classical students, all of whom gave a slightly different innuendo on the meaning!
14   *Fast Sailing Ships*, D.R. MacGregor 1988.
15   *Recollections of an Old Lawyer*, L. MacKinnon 1935, Appendix VIII/3.
16   *Australian Dictionary of Biography*.
17   *Empire*, 15 April 1867.
18   *Sydney Morning Herald*, 30 July 1867.
19   *Sydney Morning Herald*, 7 August 1869.
20   *The Colonial Clippers*, B. Lubbock 1975.
21   *Fast Sailing Ships*, D.R. MacGregor 1988.
22   *Lloyd's Register of Shipping 1760 to 1960*, G. Blake 1960.
23   *Lloyd's Register of Shipping*, Archive Department.
24   *The Log of the Cutty Sark*, B. Lubbock 1924.
25   *Lloyd's Register of Captains*, Guildhall Library.
26   *The Tea Clippers*, D. MacGregor 1983.
27   *Clippers for the Record*, M. Matheson 1984.
28   *China Tea Clippers*, G. Campbell 1974.
29   *The Stowage of Ships and Their Cargoes*, R. White Stevens 1869.
30   *The China Clippers*, B. Lubbock 1984.
31   These figures are based on dates given in *Clippers for the Record*, 1984, by Marny Matheson Miller, who drew her information from her grandfather Charlie Matheson's letters and logs, checked as appropriate against *Lloyd's List*. They have been adjusted to a common basis of departure/arrival port, rather than, for example, passing Lizard.
32   'Thermopylæ v. Cutty Sark: The 1872 Official Logs', J. Crosse, *Mariner's Mirror* Vol. 60.

Chapter 6

1   Lieut. Mathew Fontaine Maury, Superintendent of Charts of the USN, whose published works on ocean winds and currents revolutionised the basis of ocean passage planning.
2   *Harnessing the Wind*: Captain Thomas Mitchell of the Aberdeen White Star Line, Dr H. Carnegie 1991.
3   The rudder vibration would have been caused by vortices shedding alternately to either side creating periodic sideways forces on the rudder. The turbulence generated by the groove (sometimes known as a 'Chatter Groove') prevented rhythmic shedding of vortices from the trailing edge of the rudder (left-right-left-right) hence improving the steerage (with thanks to Frank Scott, the Society for Nautical Research).
4   *Sydney Morning Herald*, 22/23 October 1869.
5   A century later, the author commanded the first Gilbert and Ellice Islands Colony ship, **Moanaraoi**, to bring a cargo of colony copra into Sydney; we discharged at Sydney Cove at the old berth where **Scotsman** probably trans-shipped her cargo to **Centurion**. The prospect of copra heating, leading to spontaneous combustion, especially if the copra had been loaded wet, was always present – a danger exacerbated when co-stowed with wool.
6   Equating to £17.08 per grt; this was the upper limit for iron ships of the time, many of which cost no more than £16 per grt. Composite-built ships cost relatively more at £17 to £19 per grt (David McGregor in a note within *The Official Guide to the FT Clipper Race 1975–76*.)
7   *Sydney Morning Herald*, 12 February 1870.
8   *Sydney Morning Herald*, 18 May 1870; *Lloyd's List*.
9   *Heritage Conservation News*, April 1992.
10   *The Age*, 4 September 1871.
11   *The Colonial Clippers*, B. Lubbock 1975.
12   *The Age*, 4 September 1871.
13   *Ibid.*, 16 December 1872.

14   *Steamship **Atrato***; The House of Commons, 13 March 1873.

15   *Register of Ships,* Aberdeen.

16   Richard Boaden had married in Melbourne two years before. The Melbourne *Age* newspaper (31 December 1873) in a charming reflection on a much more agreeable era of shipping, reported the event:

   Most of the ships in port yesterday donned their holiday attire, and were decked out in all the bravery of their best bunting, as on a gala day. The unwonted eruption of flags was a pleasing compliment, cheerily paid to Captain Richard Boaden, commander of the Aberdeen clipper ship **Star of Peace**, who yesterday entered on the married life, and joined the ranks of the wedded. Captain Boaden is well known and held in high esteem in this port, hence the heartiness of the demonstration.

17   *The Plimsoll Mark,* D. Masters.

18   Lord Shaftesbury, Chairman of the Plimsoll Committee, diary as at 25 March 1873.

19   *The Plimsoll Line*, Rev. G. Peters 1975.

20   *The Annual Dogwatch*, No. 11, Shiplovers' of Society Victoria, Papers of the late Captain William H. Philip Jnr.

21   Basil Lubbock archives, National Maritime Museum.

22   *Voyaging*, Capt. J.W. Holmes 1965.

23   'The Wool Trade in Sail', F.C. Bowen, *Sea Breezes*, February 1946.

24   *Sail*, B. Lubbock & Spurling.

25   *A Maritime History of Australia*, J. Bach.

26   *The Early History of Freight Conferences,* NMM Maritime Monographs and Reports No. 51.

27   *Report on the Royal Commission on Shipping Rings*, HMSO 1909.

28   *Fairplay*, 17 August 1883.

29   *Final Report – Imperial Shipping Committee on the Deferred Rebate system*, 1923.

30   *The North China Herald and Supreme Court and Consular Gazette*, 17 August 1878.

31   *The Colonial Clippers*, B. Lubbock 1948.

32   *The Sydney Mail*, 4 June 1881.

33   *Bulletin of the Australian Institute for Maritime Archaeology*, Vol. 16 No. 2, pp. 9–16.

34   *First Voyage in a Square-rigged Ship*, Cdr F. Worsley 1938. Frank Worsley was Shackleton's sailing master in the **Endurance** Expedition, and was to secure immortality for his navigation of the ship's boat **James Caird** between Elephant Island and South Georgia, a key component in the success of the famous Shackleton Boat Journey.

Chapter 7

1   *On the Triple Expansion Engines of the SS 'ABERDEEN'*, A.C. Kirk, Institution of Naval Architects, 29 March 1882.

2   Letters Patent for Fox's Flue dated 19 March 1877 No. 1097; and 30 June 1877 No. 2530.

3   *Behind the Furnace Doors*, G.A. Newby 1979.

4   *On the Triple Expansion Engines of the SS 'ABERDEEN'*, A.C. Kirk, Institution of Naval Architects, 29 March 1882.

5   *Ibid*.

6   *Sydney Morning Herald*, 24 December 1889.

7   *Recent Practice of Marine Engineering*, W.H. Maws 1883.

8   *Clippers for the Record*, M. Matheson 1984.

9   *The China Bird*, D.R. MacGregor 1961.

10   Unpublished MMS biography of Dalgety, Prof. Rex Hartwell, Oxford.

11   *Ibid*.

12   *A History of the Frozen Meat Trades*, Critchell & Raymond 1912.

13   *Ibid*.

14   *Clippers for the Record*, M. Matheson 1984.

15   *Titanic, a Fresh Look at the Evidence*, J. Lang 2012.

16   *The Log*, D.W. Finch 1997.

17   The Swire archives in the library of the School of Oriental and African Studies, University of London, provide a fascinating insight into John Swire's involvement and leadership in the Far East trades.

18   *Gellatly's 1862–1962*, G. Blake 1962.

19   Memo written by John Swire, Liverpool, 1 January 1888 as a briefing note to Freshfields, solicitors (was this **Aberdeen**?).

20   Memo written by John Swire, Liverpool, 1 January 1888.

21   *Ibid*.

22 Swire to Holt, 11 September 1884.

23 Lord Field – (1892) AC .25.

24 Ibid.

25 Australian National University, Archives of Business and Labour – Ref: N39/45.

26 *Hobart Mercury*, 1 April 1885, 'by submarine telecommunication'.

27 *Royal Commission on Loss of Life at Sea*; *34th day*, 1885.

28 *Steam at Sea*, K.T. Rowland 1970.

29 *Sydney Morning Herald*, 12 March 1888.

31 Company pamphlet dated around 1894.

32 *Ships and Sealing Wax*, Lord Sanderson of Ayot 1967.

33 *Sydney Morning Herald*, 17 January 1887.

34 *Bulletin of the Australian Institute for Maritime Archaeology*, Vol. 14 No. 2, 1990.

35 *Sydney Morning Herald*, 13 January 1892.

36 Hall Russell Archives, Aberdeen City Archives.

37 Hall Russell Cost Book, Aberdeen City Archives.

38 *Sydney Morning Herald*, 1 January 1893.

39 *Argus* (Melbourne), 11 May 1893.

40 *Sydney Morning Herald*, 15 May 1893.

41 P&O archives 3/14 National Maritime Museum.

42 *Sydney Morning Herald*, 25 August 1893.

43 *Australian National Dictionary of Biography*.

44 *Sydney Morning Herald*, 5 May 1893.

45 *P&O Archives Board Report 3/14, 19 July 1894*, National Maritime Museum (NMM).

46 *Sydney Morning Herald*, 2 March 1893.

47 *Argus* (Melbourne), 11 March 1893.

48 *P&O Archives, Sutherland to Withers Letter Book 18/2*, NMM.

49 *Ibid*.

50 *P&O Archives, Letter Book 18/2 1894*, NMM.

51 *The Advertiser* (Adelaide), 14 January 1895.

52 *P&O Archives, Letter Book 18/2 1894*, NMM.

53 *Ibid*.

54 *Tasmanian Mercury*, 23 February 1895.

55 *P&O Archives, Letter Book 18/4, 24 May 1895*, NMM.

56 *P&O Archives, Letter Book 18/4 1895*, NMM.

57 *P&O Archives, Letter Book 18/4 16 August 1895*, NMM.

58 *Melbourne Argus*, 5 March 1896.

59 *North Star to Southern Cross*, J.M. Maber 1967.

60 'In Memoriam', *Daily Free Press* 1895.

61 *Ibid*.

Chapter 8

1 *Daily Commercial News* (Sydney), 19 November 1897.

2 *Sydney Morning Herald*, 4 April 1899.

3 *Ibid*., 21 September 1899.

4 *Sydney Morning Herald*, 6 April 1893.

5 *Sydney Morning Herald*, 16 January 1897.

6 *Sydney Morning Herald*, 28 April 1899.

7 *The Advertiser* (Adelaide), 6 December 1899.

8 The Gulf Line had its origins in Heap's Thames and Mersey Line and the Greenock Steamship Co., managed by Gavin, Birt and Co., latterly Gracie Beazley and Co., who reorganised the Line as the Australian Shipping Co. Gulf went out of business in the Australian steamer trade in the trade depression of the mid-1890s.

9 Australian National University's Archives of Business and Labour, Ref: N8/53 pp. 330–2.

10 *Sydney Morning Herald*, 7 July 1899.

11 *Daily Telegraph*, 14 September 1899.

12 *Sydney Morning Herald*, 21 October 1899.

13 *A Chapter of Accidents*, Western Australia Maritime Museum.

14 *Age*, 28 July 1900.

15 *Sydney Morning Herald*, 4 August 1900.

16 *Sydney Morning Herald*, 2 August 1900.

17 Hixon in the 1850s had served under Captain Denham in HMS **Herald** when Denham undertook extensive surveys of the Coral Sea reefs, the charts from which are still in use to this day.

18 *The Main Line Fleet of Burns Philp*, B.A. Wilkinson & R.K. Wilson 1980.

19 *Daily Telegraph*, 15 December 1903.

20 Australian National University Archives of Business and Labour, Ref: N8/56.

21 *The Brisbane Courier*, 17 September 1903.

22 *The Queenslander*, 9 April 1904, quoting from the London *Dairy World*.

23 *The Western Australian*, 22 October 1904.

24 *Sydney Morning Herald*, 3 April 1913.

25 Australian National University Archives of Business and Labour, Ref: N8/59.

26 *Dalgety,* Prof. R. Hartwell.

27 *Royal Commission into Shipping Rings*, HMSO 1909.

28 *Ships and Sealing Wax*, B.L. Sanderson 1967.

29 *Fyffes and the Banana*, P.N. Davies 1990.

30 *Aberdeen Weekly Journal*, April 1899.

31 *In Memoriam,* 1904.

32 *Kalgoorlie Western Argus*, 3 May 1905.

33 *The Brisbane Courier*, 25 January 1905.

34 *Sydney Morning Herald*, 3 March 1905.

35 *Sydney Morning Herald*, 23 May 1905.

36 *Brisbane Courier*, 29 September 1905.

37 *Brisbane Courier*, 8 September 1905.

38 *Brisbane Courier*, 27 March 1905.

39 *Ships and Sealing Wax*, B.L. Sanderson 1967.

Chapter 9

1 *The Register* (Adelaide), 6 October 1905.

2 *Shaw Savill papers*, NMM.

3 *Fairplay*, 1 February 1906.

4 *Fairplay*, 11 January 1906.

5 *A Business of National Importance*, Green and Moss 1982.

6 *Shaw Savill and Albion papers*, NMM.

7 *Shaw Savill and Albion Annual Report*, *Shaw Savill and Albion papers*, NMM.

8 *The Flag of the Southern Cross*, F.C. Bowen 1939.

9 *Scales (Inspector of Taxes) v. George Thompson & Co. Ltd 1927*, Lloyd's Law Reports.

10 *Fairplay*, 1 February 1906.

11 *The Cook Travel Journal*, T. Cook 1908.

12 *Western Australian*, 10 July 1907.

13 www.trove.nla.gov.au/newspaper VAR 1910.

14 Letter written by Captain Simpson to M.D. of Dalgety, May 1910, *Dalgety Review*, 1 August 1910.

15 There was a degree of artistic licence in Captain Simpson's evidence at this stage. While he had undoubtedly undertaken eighty-one voyages to Australia, a large number of these would have been in sail, which would not have touched by C. Leeuwin.

16 *Northern Star*, 8 December 1910.

17 Western Australian Maritime Museum database.

18 *Western Mail*, 16 April 1910.

19 *Adelaide Advertiser*, 07:X0:10.

20 *Lloyd's Captain's Register.*

21 Shipwrecked Mariners' Society's archives.

22 *The Flag of the Southern Cross 1859–1939*, F.C. Bowen 1939.

23 *Sail to New Zealand*, D. Savill 1986.

24 *Famous Liners of the Past: Belfast Built*, L. Dunn 1964.

25 'Steamers of the Past', *Sea Breezes*, J.H. Isherwood, December 1959.

26 *Sydney Morning Herald*, 22 April 2011.

27 *Shipbuilder*, Vol. VII No. 28, 1912.

28 *The Argus* (Melbourne), 29 July 1913.

Chapter 10

1 *Sea Transport of the AIF,* Australian Naval Transport Board.

2 *Ibid.*

3 *Ibid.*

4 *Ibid.*

5 *AIF Convoy Naval Orders*, 19 October 1914, at Melbourne, on board **Orvieto**.

6 *Albany's ANZAC Convoys*, R. Cunnington 2014.

7 *The Last Corsair*, D. van der Vat 1983.

8 *Sea Transport of the AIF*, Australian Naval Transport Board.

9 For research on the fate of **Halep** and **Scham**, I am indebted to my friend Bernard Langen-siepen, who as an employee of Blohm + Voss engaged on a maintenance contract with the Turkish Navy, was given access to the Turkish naval archives. Also my old friend, the late Gus Britton, deputy curator of the RN Submarine Museum at Gosport, who gave me access to war diaries compiled by crew members in E-11.

10 *Sea Transport of the AIF,* G. Tregarthen.

11 *Service List – Part 1*, Shipping Intelligence Section, Ministry of Shipping 1921.

12 List of Vessels under control of Liner Section, Shipping Intelligence Section, Ministry of Shipping,

13 *Sea Transport of the AIF*, G. Tregarthen.

14 *British Shipping and Australia 1920-1939*, K. Burley 1968.

15 *The Australian Commonwealth Shipping Line*, F. Brennan 1978.

16 *A Tramp Shipping Dynasty: Burrell & Sons of Glasgow 1850 to 1939*, R.A. Cage.

17 *Build a Fleet, Lose a Fleet*, R. McDonell.

18 *Sea Transport of the AIF*, G. Tregarthen.

19 *The Road to France; the Transportation of Troops and Military Supplies*, Crowell & Wilson.

20 *Ibid.*

21 *Ibid.*

22 *Ibid.*

23 *Ibid.*

24 *Annual Dog Watch*, Vol. 30, Victoria Shiplovers' Society and reporting in *Sydney Morning Herald*.

Chapter 11

1   *Scales (Inspector of Taxes) v. George Thompson & Co. Ltd 1927*, Lloyd's Law Reports.

2   *Ships and Sealing Wax*, B.L. Sanderson 1967.

3   Copy of particulars handed to Sir Norman Leslie, 31 January 1924, Savill Shaw & Albion papers, NMM.

4   George Thompson & Co. Report of Proceedings of the Debenture Stock Shareholders 27 January 1932, Sir William McLintock.

5   *Argus* (Melbourne), 24 January 1923.

6   *The Daily News* (Perth WA), 26 March 1919.

7   *British Shipping and Australia 1920-1939*, K. Burly 1968.

8   *Sydney Morning Herald*, 31 July 1919.

9   *The Daily News* (Perth WA), 7 May 1919.

10 *Fairplay*, 16 September 1919.

11 *Brisbane Courier*, 4 September 1919.

12 Lord Kylsant's file as Chairman, British and Commonwealth archives.

13 *Argus* (Melbourne), 2 March 1925.

14 *The Homeboat Strike of 1925*, Baruch Hirson.

15 *Strike Across the Empire*, B. Hirson & L. Vivian 1992.

16 *Argus* (Melbourne), 24 August 1925.

17 *Solidarity Forever, the Life and Times of Percy Laidler*, Bertha Walker.

18 *Sydney Morning Herald*, 23 October 1925.

19 *Argus* (Melbourne), 25 November 1925.

20 *The Advocate* (Brisbane), 19 November 1925.

21 *Sydney Morning Herald*, 12 September 1925.

22 Sir William McLintock, address to 5 per cent mortgage debenture stockholders, 27 January 1932.

23 All accounts of the Aberdeen Line name the vessel initially as **Hostilius**, but this is not reflected in the Register of British Ships. The change of name to **Horatious** was apparently done to appease adverse opinion arising from a war-like name.

24 *Sydney Morning Herald*, 24 April 1926.

25 *The Flag of the Southern Cross*, F.C. Bowen 1939.

26 *Ships and Sealing Wax*, B.L. Sanderson 1967.

27 *Ibid.*

28 *Ibid.*

29 Report to shareholders, Royal Mail AGM 2 May 1927, *Argus* (Melbourne), 16 July 1927.

30 *A Business of National Importance*, Green and Moss 1982.

31 Report to shareholders, Royal Mail AGM 25 May 1927, *Argus* (Melbourne), 16 July 1927.

32 *Straits Times*, 25 March 1927.

33 Memorandum on the 'White Star Group' to the Royal Mail Voting Trustees, Sir William McLintock, 7 April 1930.

34 File ACW/8/6, NMM, and *Ships and Sealing Wax*, B.L. Sanderson 1967.

35 *Ships and Sealing Wax*, B.L. Sanderson 1967.

36 *Build a Fleet, Lose a Fleet*, R. McDonell 1976.

37 *Ships and Sealing Wax*, B.L. Sanderson 1967.

38 *Queensland Times*, 25 April 1928.

39 *Daily Commercial News*, 4 October 1928.

40 *Ships in Focus*, No. 2, Vol. 1, 1997.

41 Memorandum to Sir William McLintock from Shaw Savill about George Thompson & Co., 11 December 1931.

Chapter 12

1   *White Star Line*, paper prepared for McLintock by Duncan McKellar, one his senior assistants, 7 April 1914, PRO/T190/125.

2   *Ibid.*

3   *Ibid.*

4   *Ibid.*

5   George Thompson Liquidation, Shaw Savill papers, NMM.

6   Letter to the Secretary of the Royal Mail Voting Trustees dated 28 August 1931 and George Thompson Liquidation, both Shaw Savill papers, NMM.

7   *Ships and Sealing Wax*, B.L. Sanderson 1967.

8   *RMT 97*, NMM.

9   Memorandum to Voting Trustees dated 11 December 1931 and George Thompson Liquidation, both Shaw Savill papers, NMM.

10 *George Thompson & Co. Ltd, Report of Proceedings of a meeting of Debenture Shareholders 27:01:1932*, Royal Mail Voting Trustees Papers, PRO.

11 Liquidation of George Thompson, Shaw Savill and Albion Papers, NMM.

12 *Journal of Commerce.*

13 By a letter dated 16 March 1933, Dalgety in fact reduced this offer to £75,000 to discount the cost of bringing monies home. Dalgety tied its offer to an undertaking that it would retain agency of the new Line in Australia, always subject to negotiation of the most cost-effective solutions. Dalgety also requested, but would not fall on its sword if refused, a seat on the board of the new company. Dalgety Archives.

14 Both independent subsidiaries of the New Zealand Shipping Company, in turn a subsidiary of the P&OSN Co.

15 *Sydney Morning Herald*, 22 May 1914.

16 *The Argus*, 25 November 1933.

17 *The Chronicle* (Adelaide), 22 June 1933.

18 *Famous Liners of the Past*, L. Dunn 1964.

19 City Editor of the *Daily Mail,* as reported by the *Queensland Courier*, 2 January 1936.

20 *Flag of the Southern Cross*, F.C. Bowen 1939.

21 *The Times*, obituary, 27 July 1937.

22 *Sea Breezes*, October 1947 and December 1959.

23 *Ships in Focus*, No. 2, Vol. 1, 1997.

24 *Advertiser* (Adelaide), 9 January 1952.

25 *Ships in Focus*, No. 2, Vol. 1, 1997.

Bibliography

Published Works

Bach, J., *A Maritime History of Australia* (London: Hamish Hamilton, 1976).

Blake, G., *Gellatly's 1862–1962* (London: Blackie & Son Ltd, 1962).

Blake, G., *Lloyd's Register of Shipping 1760–1960* (London: Lloyd's Register of Shipping, 1960).

Bowen, F.C., *The Flag of the Southern Cross* (London: Shaw Savill & Albion & Co., 1939).

Brennan, F., *The Australian Commonwealth Shipping Line* (Canberra: Roebuck Books, 1978).

Buckman, R. *The Photographic Work of Calvert Richard Jones,* (London: The Science Museum, 1991.

Bull, R. *A Day of My Life on Board the Liner 'Themistocles'* (Unknown).

Burley, K. *British Shipping and Australia 1920–1939* (London: Cambridge University Press, 1968).

Cable, B. *A Hundred Year History of the P&O.* (London: Ivor Nicholson & Watson, 1937).

Campbell, G.F. *China Tea Clippers* (London: Adlard Coles, 1974).

Campey, L.H. *Fast Sailing and Copper-Bottomed* (Toronto: National Heritage Books, 2002).

Carnegie, H. *Harnessing the Wind* (Aberdeen: Centre for Scottish Studies, University of Aberdeen, 1991).

Carnie, W. *Reporting Reminiscences* (Aberdeen: Aberdeen University Press, 1902).

Chapelle, H.I. *The Search for Speed Under Sail* (London: George Allen & Unwin Ltd, 1968).

Clark, A.H. *The Clipper Ship Era* (New York: G.P. Putnam's Sons, 1910).

Clark Wright, E. *Saint John Ships and their Shipbuilders* (Wolfville, NS: Self-published, 1975).

Coleman, T. *Passage to America* (London: Hutchinson, 1972).

Cope Cornford, L. *The Sea Carriers 1825–1925, The Aberdeen Line* (London: The Aberdeen Line, 1925).

Coughlan, N. (Ed.). *Voyaging, Capt. James William Holmes* (London: Hutchinson & Co. Ltd, 1965).

Course, A. *Painted Ports* (London: Hollis & Carter, 1961).

Critchell, J.T. *A History of the Frozen Meat Trade* (London: Constable, 1912).

Crowell, B. *The Road to France I & II* (New Haven: Yale University Press,1921).

Cunnington, R. *Albany's ANZAC Convoys* (Western Australia: Digger Press, 2014).

Davies, P.N. *Fyffes and the Banana* (London: The Athlone Press, 1990).

de Kerbrech, R.P. *Shaw Savill & Albion; Post War Fortunes* (London: Conway Maritime Press, 1986).

Deakin, B.M. *Shipping Conferences* (London: Cambridge University Press, 1973).

Duncan, R. *Textile and Toil* (Aberdeen: Aberdeen City Libraries, 1984).

Dunn, L. *Famous Liners of the Past: Belfast Built* (London: Adlard Coles Ltd, 1963).

Evans, G.L. *Dazzle-painted Ships of World War I* (Bristol: Bernard McCall, 2015).

Fenton. R. *Fleet in Focus – the Aberdeen & Commonwealth Line* (Preston: *Ships in Focus* No. 2 Vol. 1, 1996).

Fitchett, T.K. *The Long Haul* (Adelaide: Rigby Publishers Ltd, 1980).

Froude, J.A., Blainey, G. (Ed.) *Oceana, or England and her Colonies* (North Ryde, NSW: Methuen Haynes, 1886/1985).

Gardiner, R (Ed.) *Conway's History of the Ship – Sail's Last Century* (London: Conway Maritime Press, 1993).

Gardiner, R (Ed.) *Conway's History of the Ship – The Advent of Steam* (London: Conway Maritime Press, 1993).

Gardiner, R. *The History of the White Star Line* (Hersham, Surrey: Ian Allan Publishing, 2001).

Gibbs, C.R.V. *British Passenger Ships of the Five Oceans* (London: Putnam, 1963).

Green, E. & Moss, M. *A Business of National Importance* (London: Methuen, 1982).

Greenlaw, J. *Swansea Copper Barques & Cape Horners* (Swansea: Joanna Greenlaw, 1999).

Griffiths, D. *Steam at Sea.* (London: Conway Maritime Press, 1997).

Hollett, D. *More Precious than Gold* (Cranbury NJ: Fairleigh Dickinson University Press, 2008).

Passage to the New World (Abergavenny: P.M. Heaton Publishing, 1995).

Hook, E. *A Guide to the Papers of John Swire and Sons* (London: School of Oriental and African Studies, 1977).

Hope, R. *A New history of British Shipping* (London: John Murray, 1990).

Hume, C.L. *The Cutty Sark and Thermopylæ Era of Sail* (Glasgow: Brown, Son and Ferguson Ltd, 1987).

Hustwick, I. *Moray Firth, Ships & Trade* (Aberdeen: Scottish Cultural Press, 1994).

Hyde, F.E. *Far Eastern Trade 1860–1914* (London: Adam & Charles Black, 1973).

Ingpen, B. *Horizons; the story Rennies 1849–1999.* (Johannesburg: Rennies Management Services, 2000).

Isherwood, J.H. *Steamers of the Past* (Liverpool: The Journal of Commerce and Shipping Telegraph/Sea Breezes, 1966).

Jennings, E. *Cargoes, the Far East Freight Conference* (Singapore: Meridian Communications, 1980).

Keith, A. *Eminent Aberdonians* (Aberdeen: Aberdeen Chamber of Commerce, 1984).

Keith, A. *The North of Scotland Bank Ltd 1836–1936* (Aberdeen: Aberdeen Journals Limited, 1936).

Keys, R. & Smith, K. *Black Diamonds by Sea* (Newcastle on Tyne: City of Newcastle-upon-Tyne Museums, 1998).

Kludas, A *Great Passenger Ships of the World Vol. 1* (Cambridge: Patrick Stephens. 1975).

Lang, J. *Titanic, a Fresh Look at the Evidence* (Lanham MD, USA: Rowman and Littlefield Publishers Inc., 2012).

Laxon, W.A. *BI: : The British India Steam Navigation Company Limited* (Kendal: World Ship Society, 1994).

Lindsay, W.S. *History of Merchant Shipping …* (New York: AMS Press Inc., 1965).

Louden-Brown, P. *The White Star Line – an Illustrated History* (Coltishall, Norfolk: Ship Pictorial Publications, 1991).

Lubbock, B. *The China Clippers* (Glasgow: Brown, Son and Ferguson Ltd, 1946).

Lubbock, B. *The Colonial Clippers* (Glasgow: Brown, Son and Ferguson Ltd, 1975).

Lubbock, B. *The Log of the Cutty Sark* (Glasgow: Brown, Son and Ferguson Ltd, 1924).

Maber, J.M. *North Star to Southern Cross* (Prescot, Lancs. T. Stephenson & sons. Ltd, 1967).

MacGregor, D.R., *Fast Sailing Ships 1775–1875* (Lymington: Nautical Publishing Co. Ltd, 1973).

MacGregor, D.R., *Merchant Sailing Ships 1815–1850* (London: Conway Maritime Press, 1984).

MacGregor, D.R., *The China Bird* (London: Conway Maritime Press, 1986).

MacGregor, D.R., *The Tea Clippers* (London: Conway Maritime Press, 1983).

MacGregor, D.R., *Merchant Sailing Ships 1850–1875* (London: Conway Maritime Press, 1984).

MacKenzie, G.A. *From Aberdeen to Ottawa in 1845* (Aberdeen: Aberdeen University Press, 1990).

Marriner, S. & Hyde, F. *The Senior – John Samuel Swire 1825–98* (Liverpool: Liverpool University Press, 1967).

Matheson, M. *Clippers for the Record* (Melbourne: Spectrum Publication, 1984).

Maude, H.E. *Slavers in Paradise* (Canberra: Australian National University Press, 1981).

McDonell, R. *Build a Fleet – Loose a Fleet* (Melbourne: The Hawthorn Press, 1976).

Morgan, D. *The Villages of Aberdeen – Footdee* (Aberdeen: Denburn Books, 1993).

Moss, M. *Shipbuilders to the World, Harland and Wolff* (Belfast: The Blackstaff Press, 1986).

Murray, M. *Ships and South Africa* (London: Oxford University Press, 1933).

Newby, G.A. *Behind the Furnace Doors* (Harrowgate: Interprint. 1979).

Nicholls, B. *Bluejackets & Boxers* (Sydney: Allen & Unwin, 1986).

National Maritime Museum The Load Line – a Hallmark of Safety Greenwich: Maritime Monographs and Reports #33; A Trip to the Antipodes #45; The Early History of Freight Conferences #51.

Olson, W. *Lion of the China Sea* (Sydney NSW: P&O Australia Ltd, 1976).

Paasch, H. *Illustrated Marine Encyclopedia* (Antwerp: H. Paasch, 1890).

Plimsoll, S. *Our Seamen – an Appeal* (London: Virtue & Co., 1873).

Sanderson, B. *Ships and Sealing Wax* (London: William Heinemann, 1967).

Savill, D. *Sail to New Zealand* (London: Robert Hall, 1986).

Shewan, A. *The Great Days of Sail* (London: Conway Maritime Press, 1927).

Smith Homans, J. *Cyclopedia of Commerce Vols 1 & 2* (New York: Harper Bros., 1858).

Smith, K. & Watts, C. *Records of Merchant Shipping and Seamen* (Kew: PRO Publications, 1998).

Stammers, M.K. *The Passage Makers* (Brighton: Toredo Books Ltd, 1978).

Stevens, R.W. *The Stowage of Ships and their Cargoes* (London: Longmans, Green, Reader Dyer/Plymouth: R. White Stevens, 1869).

Thearle, S.J.P. *Naval Architecture* (London: William Collins, Sons and Co., 1874).

Tregarthen, G. *Sea Transport of the AIF* (Canberra: Naval Transport Board, 1949).

Turnbull, J. *Travels in the West: Cuba* (London: Longmans, 1840).

Turner, J.R. *Scotland's North Sea Gateway* (Aberdeen: Aberdeen University Press, 1986).

Underhill, H.A. *Deep Water Sail* (Glasgow: Brown, Son and Ferguson Ltd, 1955).

Underhill, H.A. *Masting and Rigging of the Clipper Ship* (Glasgow: Brown, Son and Ferguson Ltd, 1946).

V-Thomas, W. *Dalgety – the Romance of a Business* (London: Henry Melland, 1984).

Watson, N. *Lloyd's Register – 250 Years of Service* (London: Lloyd's Register, 2010).

Wilkinson B.A. *The Main Line Fleet of Burns Philp* (Canberra: The Nautical Association of Australia Inc., 1981).

Worsley, F. *First Voyage in a Square-rigged Ship* (London: Geoffrey Bles, 1938),

Primary Sources

*Alexander Hall yardbook*s. City Archives, Town House, Aberdeen.

Gibbs Guano Registers Guildhall Library, London.

Lloyd's Captains' Register Guildhall Library, London.

Lloyd's Register – Survey Certificates National Maritime Museum/ Lloyd's Register Foundation.

Lloyd's Register of Ships National Maritime Museum/Lloyd's Register/Guildhall Library.

P&O Archives National Maritime Museum.

Register of British Ships Aberdeen Custom House/City Archives/ PRO.

Shaw Savill Archives National Maritime Museum.

Termo de entrada dos navios mercantes – No. 11, Arquivistico da Dieccao Geral das Alfandegas, National History Museum, CVI.

Secondary Sources

'A Primitive Export Sector: Guano Production in mid-nineteenth century Peru' W.M. Mathew, *Journal of Latin American Studies*, Chapt. 9, Vol. 9, 1977.

Aberdeen Press and Journal Shipping movements and reports.

Australian Newspaper Archives TROVE – the National Library of Australia.

'Chilean Coal and British Steamers; the Origin of a S. American Industry' Duncan, R.E. *Mariners Mirror*, Vol. 61:3 271–281.

'Cunningham's Self-reefing topsails' Gillespie, R. St J. *Mariners Mirror*, 31:1 7–12

El Cobre: Cuban Ore and the globalisation of Swansea Copper 1830–1870 Chris Evans, University of South Wales.

Lloyd's List Shipping movements and reports.

Lower Swansea Valley Factsheets 5, 6, 7, 9 and 11. Swansea Museum.

'Peru and the British Guano Market 1840–1870' W.M. Mathew, *Journal of Latin American Studies*.

'Robert Kemball – Master of the *Thermopylæ*' Crosse, J. *Mariners Mirror* 89 – 1 59–70.

Royal Commission on Shipping Rings London: HMSO 1909.

Service List London: HMSO 1921.

Steamship 'ATRATO' – Return to an Order of the Hon. House of Commons London: Board of Trade, 1873.

The Australian Navy Australian Navy Board 1921.

The African Guano Trade Craig, R. *Mariners Mirror* 50:1 25–55.

The House of Gibbs and the Peruvian Guano Monopoly W.M. Mathew; The London Historical Society, 1981.

'*Thermopylæ* v *Cutty Sark* – the Official 1872 logs' Skinner, R. *Mariners Mirror* 60:1 63–72.

'Iron Beam-end fastenings: Fell's Patent No. 8186' Stammers, M.K. *Mariners Mirror*.

'The World's First Clipper' Cable, B. *Mariners Mirror* 29:2 66–91.

Index